Economics and the Left

Economics and the Left

Interviews with Progressive Economists

Edited by C.J. Polychroniou

V
VERSO
London • New York

First published by Verso 2021
© Verso Books 2021

The moral rights of the authors and editors have been asserted

1 3 5 7 9 10 8 6 4 2

Verso
UK: 6 Meard Street, London W1F 0EG
US: 20 Jay Street, Suite 1010, Brooklyn, NY 11201
versobooks.com

Verso is the imprint of New Left Books

ISBN-13: 978-1-83976-379-3
ISBN-13: 978-1-83976-380-9 (UK EBK)
ISBN-13: 978-1-83976-381-7 (US EBK)

British Library Cataloguing in Publication Data
A catalogue record for this book is available from the British Library

Library of Congress Cataloging-in-Publication Data
Library of Congress Control Number: 2021937573

Typeset in Minion by Hewer Text UK Ltd, Edinburgh
Printed and bound by CPI Group (UK) Ltd, Croydon CR0 4YY

Contents

Introduction

This book presents interviews with twenty-four economists whose life-work has been dedicated to both interpreting the world and changing it for the better. These twenty-four people all bring to their work a toolkit of technical skills of the trade. But much more importantly, they are all also people who are committed to the principles of egalitarianism, democracy, and ecological sanity. In various ways, they have all advanced their commitments through both their research work as economists and their engagements in areas of economic policy.

All twenty-four people I interviewed depart dramatically from the tenets of mainstream orthodox economics, even while they have all carved out their own approaches to research and policy interventions. Collectively, they have brought to the forefront issues of class conflict, racial and gender inequality, systemic financial instability, imperialism, the climate crisis, global inequality, poverty, and state-led developmental strategies in original and impactful ways.

These are all fundamental contributions to understanding the functioning, and malfunctioning, of capitalist economies and societies. This is true in general as well as, more specifically, over our current epoch of neoliberal capitalism, which began in the late 1970s and still prevails in all corners of the globe. Neoliberalism is the variant of capitalism in which the priorities and prerogatives of big corporations, Wall Street, and the richest 0.1 percent of the global population dominate all other considerations in the formation of economic and social policies.

It would not be fair to say that all mainstream economists have ignored such considerations altogether. It is, rather, the case that for the most part mainstream economists have either judged these issues to be of secondary importance or to be matters that can best be addressed within the framework of free-market capitalism. They reach this conclusion working from the precept that some close approximation to a free-market capitalist economy has been proven to deliver both higher living standards and more social justice than any alternative.

The twenty-four progressives I have interviewed are well aware of what they are up against in challenging economic orthodoxy. Many of them describe these challenges forcefully in their interviews. Joan Robinson, the renowned Cambridge University economist of the Great Depression and post–World War II eras, beautifully captured both the allure and moral blindness of orthodox economics as follows:

> One of the main effects (I will not say purposes) of orthodox traditional economics was . . . a plan for explaining to the privileged class that their position was morally right and was necessary for the welfare of society. Even the poor were better off under the existing system than they would be under any other.[1]

At the same time, it will quickly become evident to readers that these twenty-four interviewees are not cut from the same cloth—far from it. They come from widely varying backgrounds as well as different generations. It is therefore not surprising that their respective work as progressive economists has proceeded along divergent paths. They have pursued different topics, have utilized different methods in advancing their research, and have aligned themselves with a range of progressive political movements. They also disagree with each other on many issues, large and small. As a result, these interviews are illuminating for their differences as well as their similarities.

The idea for this book emerged from what began as casual conversations I was having with Jerry Epstein and Bob Pollin, the founding co-directors of the Political Economy Research Institute (PERI) at the University of Massachusetts Amherst. Once we concluded that

---

1   Joan Robinson, "An Economist's Sermon: Economics Is the Dope of the Religious People," *Economist's View* blog, July 21, 2007.

producing a book of interviews with progressive economists was a good idea, we then had to decide which economists to include in the project. It should not be surprising that PERI economists are heavily represented, including Jerry and Bob themselves, as well as seven others with formal PERI affiliations of some sort. The other fifteen interviewees are also people with whom Jerry and Bob, and others at PERI, have interacted in various ways over the years. In my view, there is a lot to be gained through hearing from a large number of additional progressive economists in similar interview formats. Indeed, I myself am regularly conducting interviews with many other such people, some with, and others without, PERI connections. Many of these interviews are being posted at the PERI website (www.peri.umass.edu/).

I conducted all the interviews with the same approach. That is, I sent out to everyone a specific set of questions and asked them to respond in writing. I edited their responses to a minimum extent only. The interviews vary in length because I encouraged everyone to answer as briefly or as extensively as they thought appropriate. In assembling the book, I've presented the interviews in alphabetical order, since there did not seem to be any obviously better organizing approach.

In my clearly biased opinion, *Economics and the Left* is loaded with a fascinating mix of personal experiences, reflections on major historical events, and struggles with analytic approaches and research findings. What has emerged from this is a combustible brew of ideas and commitments from twenty-four progressive economists. Now it is up to you, the reader, to decide whether you agree with my assessment of what we have here.

Post-COVID-19 Addendum

I conducted the main body of these interviews over an extended stretch of time, from early 2018 until the spring of 2020. It was exactly when we thought we had finally completed the full set of interviews that the COVID-19 pandemic had begun to spread worldwide. It was clear at that point that we could not simply proceed with publishing the versions of the interviews that we had on hand. We rather needed to offer our contributors an opportunity to reflect, even if provisionally and briefly, on the global COVID pandemic.

With the agreement of our Verso editors, in November 2020 I asked each of the interviewees to respond to the following set of questions in any way they wished:

1. How would you evaluate the ways different countries or regions have responded to the COVID-19 crisis, both in terms of public health interventions and economic policies?
2. Do you draw any general lessons from the COVID crisis about the most viable ways to advance an egalitarian economic project?
3. Does the experience of the COVID crisis shed any light on the way you think about economics as a discipline or, more specifically, the questions you might be pursuing in your own research?

You will now be able to read their responses, along with all the other observations that our interviewees had set down as they saw the world pre-COVID-19.

•••

I owe a great debt in producing this volume to all twenty-four interviewees, who took time to tell their stories and discuss what their life's work has been all about. I also want to thank Judy Fogg for her outstanding copyediting work. Finally, I thank the Political Economy Research Institute for inspiration and financial support for the project from beginning to end.

Michael Ash

Michael Ash is a professor in the Department of Economics and School of Public Policy at the University of Massachusetts Amherst and co-director of the Corporate Toxics Information Project at the Political Economy Research Institute (PERI). He is co-author, with Francisco Louçã, of *Shadow Networks: Financial Disorder and the System that Caused Crisis* (Oxford University Press, 2018) and has written numerous articles on topics including environmental justice, unionization, and public debt. He was selected by *Foreign Policy* magazine as one of the "100 Leading Global Thinkers for 2013."

Tell us about your background, and what drew you into the field of economics.

My father is a math professor (retired), and my mother is a sociologist. Economics, because of its integration of quantitative and math-analytic methods with social science questions, was a natural fit. My family has been politically active in left-wing and working-class politics for four generations. My maternal grandparents fled fascist Europe and got out by the skin of their teeth. My paternal grandparents were dedicated socialists. Economics struck me as a field where one can make a difference in public debate and public policy.

I grew up in the city of Chicago. Reaganomics hit the industrial Midwest very hard and the displacement, hopelessness, and homelessness were clear to me even as a teenager. I also experienced on a day-to-day basis Chicago as a segregated city with its gross inequalities especially split on racial lines. My adolescence was a period of gentrification—my parents were unwitting gentrifiers of the Lincoln Park neighborhood (simply because it was close to their work)—and the birth of the Yuppie. I became aware that my friends' parents worked in something called "commodities trading" and lived rather large.

In graduate school at UC Berkeley, you worked closely with the future Federal Reserve Chair Janet Yellen and future Nobel Prize winner George Akerlof (who are themselves a married couple). How would you describe both of them as economists and mentors to yourself? What would you say Yellen accomplished as Fed chair that was distinctive? How would you describe Akerlof's research contributions relative to both mainstream and heterodox economics?

George and Janet are amazing people—smart and also kind. Watching the two of them work together, operating in what seemed like a shared secret language—hardly any need for nouns ("Hmm, do you think?" "Yes, that could be." "So, let's try it.")—was inspirational. My maternal grandparents, who fled fascist Europe in the 1930s, were both lifelong lovers and academic co-authors (in linguistics at the University of Illinois). I recognized the same love and intellectual communication in George and Janet that I saw in my grandparents. The ancient Greek term for that kind of connection is *homophrosyne*. I'm also in an academic couple—my wife Krista Harper is professor of anthropology at UMass Amherst—and George and Janet's example for me has gone beyond intellectual inspiration to include modeling the way to live life together.

Janet was an extraordinary Fed chair because as Board member and then chair she was able to navigate the politics of the Fed, in particular, the deep-rooted inflation hawkishness, in a way that had proven very difficult for Democratic appointees. Alan Blinder, who was my first economics professor and another great economist, was ultimately boxed out—by Greenspan and the rest—for being a progressive academic because of the suspicion that Alan might prove soft on inflation. Janet, with a similar pedigree and orientation, managed to convince some very difficult parties to accept her judgment and leadership.

George's influence on economics has been enormous. Social psychology and social relationships, the role of identity, and the importance of well-enforced norms and laws against opportunistic behavior are some themes that just begin to scratch the surface of his contributions.

Also while in graduate school, you worked as a staff member of the President's Council of Economic Advisers when Bill Clinton was president and another Nobel Laureate Joseph Stiglitz was chair of the Council. Can you please describe a bit about what that was like? Was Stiglitz a strong progressive voice then on the Council? Were there others?

Joe's mind is exceptionally quick and creative. Although Joe's ideas had already had profound effects on economic thought and policy—in multiple fields of economics—during his years as chair of the Council of Economic Advisers, he was still learning his way around powerful people and policy culture at the highest levels of power and governance. There were many different voices competing for President Clinton's ear—none of them had ideas as good as Joe's ideas, but some of them had a better—or more Machiavellian—understanding of access and power.

The CEA chair has the difficult task of speaking truth to power but doing it privately and in a way that will make power listen. Joe's CEA was on the right side of many issues. For example, the CEA opposed the inhumane welfare reform program that passed Congress in the summer of 1996, but I can't think of any areas in which Joe's CEA importantly changed the administration's position. Perhaps most importantly, CEA failed to slow the march to financial liberalization in the late 1990s, where the consequences were really serious. Joe probably knew more than most people on the planet about the perils of free-market finance, but the CEA was no match for the Fed, the Treasury, or finance-affiliated senators like Phil Gramm.

It was after the CEA that Joe really came into his own as one of the world's most effective public intellectuals. Joe's criticism of IMF interventions was brave and put him in conflict with the neoliberal core of the profession. His work since has been outstanding and politically savvy.

I learned a lot from the other two members of the Council, Martin Neil Baily and Alicia Munnell. Martin has been an influential policy economist and his *Growth with Equity* had a big effect on my thinking. For Alicia, the CEA appointment was a consolation prize. As director of research at the Boston Fed, Alicia had undertaken one of the most thorough and convincing studies of discrimination in home mortgage lending, which was published in the *American Economic Review*. She used the authority of the Fed as banking regulator to get access to closely held data on credit histories that banks typically invoked to deflect criticism of different denial rates between whites and Blacks. Alicia's analysis showed definitively that Black loan applicants are denied more frequently than identical white applicants. The banks were not amused by the exposure, and they have a long memory. So, when President Clinton proposed to appoint her to the Board of Governors of the Federal Reserve, the banks had their senators put the kibosh on the appointment, which would have needed Senate confirmation. Clinton appointed Alicia to the CEA instead, and she brought her strong and principled voice to the Council. Her work on social insurance probably played an important role in saving Social Security from privatizers.

Who, other than perhaps Akerlof, Yellen, and Stiglitz, are the people who have had the most influence on you as an economist, and what has been the nature of their influence?

David Card. By chance David taught me introductory and intermediate microeconomics at Princeton University. I write "by chance" because David's specialty is labor economics, but I think that David may have taught every single course in the Princeton undergraduate catalog during his time there. Then, when I was about halfway through graduate school at UC Berkeley, the Berkeley department recruited David, which was an extraordinary opportunity for the department and for me. David's infinite curiosity, utter and complete commitment to objective analysis of data, and generosity as a mentor make him one of the greatest teachers I have ever known. I would not have finished my dissertation without David, and his advice still echoes through my mind when I try to be a good teacher and advisor.

Michael Reich was a great friend and mentor in grad school. *Segmented Work, Divided Workers* is one of the greatest economics books I have ever read. Its argument is so natural and so deep that it is sometimes overlooked as just a labor history. But if you take the position that history is the history of class relations, then it's clear that this book is a key to understanding society. An update would be an extraordinarily interesting and valuable project.

Bob Pollin has also had a big influence on me. I'll mention two facets: first, he instantly goes to the simple but never too-simple heart of the matter. One of Bob's favorite quotes, a case of maybe-Einstein-said-it-or-maybe-he-didn't, is "everything should be made as simple as possible, but no simpler." For example, on living and minimum wages Bob observed that, complex econometrics notwithstanding, paying a living wage would not make a large dent in revenue for most industries. Second, I've had the good fortune to co-teach with Bob for the past twenty years, since my arrival at UMass Amherst. His engagement with students and his emphasis on persuasive writing about quantitative results have completely shaped the way I teach. Bob also taught me that language matters, that the shorthand used by neoclassical economists reshaped the way that we and the public think about economic problems. Some examples: the casual use of "less skilled" (rather than "less credentialed") to describe workers without a college degree creates a mindset where the sagging fortunes of less credentialed workers seems natural instead of human-made. (As both Bob and I learned from Frank Bardacke, cutting lettuce is highly skilled labor; its pay is institutionally determined.) The failure to distinguish between public and private debt in discussions of private debt bubbles made a hash of understanding the actual imbalances of the early 2000s and created easy pickings for austerity advocates. Bob made me root out every unmodified instance of "debt" in our work from 2013/14. He also taught me to avoid annoying acronyms IYKWIM.

What distinguishes, for you, progressive/left political economy from mainstream economics?

Progressive/left political economy is much more empirically grounded than neoclassical economics. By empirical, I include both quantitative empirical analysis, such as Arin Dube's brilliant econometric work on minimum wages, and historical-institutionalism, such as the work of James Boyce or James Crotty. Much neoclassical economics is based on unrealistic and flimsy assumptions about incentives, common knowledge, actions, interactions, and level playing fields. Another key distinction is that understanding political power—in the broad sense of the political, including, for example, the power of a boss over a worker—is central to progressive/left political economy.

Early on in your career, much of your research focused on issues of health and health care workers. What drew you into this area of study? What were the main findings that distinguished your work in this area?

I came to health care economics by accident. I was looking for a case study on how the changing regulatory and market environment gets passed through to its employees. Colleagues had examined trucking, airlines, telecommunications—areas of substantial deregulation and restructuring in the 1970s and 1980s. Employees in those fields had taken a beating in terms of wages and working conditions. Managed care and its incarnation, the HMO, were in ascendance in the middle 1990s and were receiving a lot of credit—short-lived—for having "bent the cost curve." My thought was that much of the bending was probably on the backs of labor in health care. So I examined pay, hours, and substitution of less-credentialed for more-credentialed labor. The effect on labor was interesting in its own right but it also implied that the cost curve was more likely kinked than bending. And, indeed, after the one-time extraction of value from the reorganization of labor, costs began to rise again.

So I was an accidental arrival in health economics, and I learned quickly that it has its own paradigm (language, methods, modes of thought) that require rites of passage to enter. I had the good fortune to connect with three excellent scholars of health economics: Kevin Grumbach, a physician who has been active in the single-payer health care movement, Joanne Spetz, and Jean Ann Seago. Jean Ann, an RN/PhD, was a particularly patient and effective guide. Jean Ann and I explored how RN unionization affects health outcomes. Using pretty state-of-the-art econometrics, we found that unionized nurses reduce heart-attack mortality by about 6 percent. That study really required cross-disciplinary collaboration and remains one of my most interesting findings.

My background in institutional labor economics, largely imparted by Michael Reich at Berkeley, and Jean Ann's on-the-ground experience of the day-to-day reality for nurses, prepared us to look at health care workers and hospitals in the super-hierarchical setting of the US health care system and to realize the ways that unionization, by empowering workers, can make these organizations more effective at producing healthy outcomes.

Have progressive economists made an impact on public policy with regards to health in the United States, and if so, how?

The ways that health care, almost one-fifth of the US economy, violates the neoclassical economic paradigm in every way imaginable have been manifest from the beginning of health economics. Kenneth Arrow's 1963 article "Uncertainty and the Welfare Economics of Medical Care" and George Akerlof's "Market for Lemons" point to such large holes in the neoclassical fabric, which apply, of course, in health care but also in most other walks of life, that it's hard to imagine how neoclassical economics has survived.

The other dimension of health economics that has had a profound effect are these explorations of how inequality directly affects health—not merely that deprived people have worse health. (It's terrible in itself that people in the United States, one of the richest countries in the world in terms of per capita income, are so deprived that life expectancy is affected.) The key result is that inequality, per se, is bad for health. British researchers such as Michael Marmot, Kate Pickett, and Richard Wilkinson have pioneered this hypothesis. The pathways include the decay of physical infrastructure and social capital permitted by highly unequal societies, but also the direct socio-emotional stresses engendered by extreme inequality. Larry King has developed convincing political economic explanations for stylized facts uncovered by Anne Case and Angus Deaton about rising deaths from despair associated with inequality and deindustrialization.

These studies complement the work of Thomas Piketty and others on growing inequality, and they very much provide answers to the "so what" question about inequality in on-average rich societies.

Finally, progressive economists have maintained public focus on the century-old outrage of widespread exclusion of working people from health insurance and high-quality medical care in the US. Most recently, progressive economists like Bob Pollin and Jerry Friedman have been able to give shape and substance to Medicare for All, which strikes me as the most exciting political movement in the United States for many decades.

The environment, and specifically environmental justice, is also a major theme of study in your research agenda. What do you mean by environmental justice in the age of climate change?

Environmental justice concerns equal access both to process and to high-quality outcomes in the environmental domain regardless of class, income, race or other ascriptive categories. Many national constitutions and many US state constitutions guarantee access to a safe and clean environment. It's a fundamental human right, yet we see frequent violations—for example, in the Flint [Michigan] drinking-water crisis, in exposure to pesticides and industrial toxics, and increasingly in the distribution of the consequences of climate change. There's a significant intersection of knowledge and power in enforcing rights to a clean and safe environment. My colleague Jim Boyce and I developed a peer-reviewed method for assessing corporate environmental justice performance, which complements many existing measurements of corporate environmental performance with respect to the population as a whole. We look at how companies perform in terms of environmental outcomes for communities that are economically or socially vulnerable.

As the climate changes and, I strongly hope, efforts to mitigate climate change grow in importance in the public agenda, it will be very important to keep a fair distribution of the costs and benefits in the public eye (instead of the standard mainstream approach of attempting to aggregate costs and benefits). For example, energy transitions that focus exclusively on carbon reduction with no attention whatsoever to the distribution of the costs and benefits of local pollution associated with carbon might end up worsening the air in poor neighborhoods while reducing global carbon. We need to make sure that global carbon reduction is integrated with local pollution reduction too. It can be—and at a low cost—but someone needs to keep it on the public agenda.

Is there a strong correlation between race, class, and environmental justice and/or environmental inequality?

In a word, yes. The question reminds me of a half-joke from Manuel Pastor, a PhD alum of UMass Economics and now Distinguished Professor of Sociology and American Studies & Ethnicity and Turpanjian Chair in Civil Society and Social Change at the University of Southern California. When Manuel received his first million-dollar grant for the study of environmental justice, an area that he has pioneered and in which he and I have collaborated for many years, Manuel reported the achievement to his aunt (his *tia*). His account of that conversation follows:

Manuel: Tia, I have some great news. I got a big grant—it's for
   $1,000,000.
Aunt: Oh, Manuelito, that's great. I'm very proud of you. What's the
   grant for?
Manuel: The grant is to study environmental justice, Tia.
Aunt: Environmental justice! That's great, Manuelito. Say, what is
   "environmental justice"?
Manuel: Well, Tia, it's the idea that society forces poor people and
   people of color to live with more pollution than rich people.
Aunt: Oh, but Manuelito, everyone already knows that.

So, our projects on environmental justice need to go beyond the
obvious.

*You were co-author, along with graduate student Thomas Herndon and
your UMass colleague Bob Pollin, of the study that overturned the findings
of what had been a highly influential paper by the Harvard economists
Carmen Reinhart and Kenneth Rogoff that purported to show that an
economy's economic growth would necessarily suffer after incurring levels
of public debt beyond a given threshold—90 percent of the economy's GDP.
You and your co-authors found that Reinhart and Rogoff had made coding
errors in their data management, omitted data that would have changed
their results, and used unjustified methods of generating debt-level aver-
ages by country that also changed their results. How do you explain these
failings in the Reinhart/Rogoff paper? Can anything in particular be
learned from this experience insofar as mainstream economic analysis
and public policy is concerned? And, finally, what can we say positively
about the relationship between public debt levels and economic growth?*

In 2010, the world economy was in tatters, with the crisis coming, this
time, from the core of the global economy—a financial crisis followed
by a general crisis in the US and in Western Europe. Unemployment was
high, fraying the social fabric. Expansionary monetary policy and financial system bailouts by the central banks, which had proven effective in
staving off crises over the preceding twenty-five years, were ineffective
or at least insufficient to restart the economy in a robust way. The central
policy debate in the US and in Europe was whether fiscal policy, that is,
deficit spending by governments or through direct transfers, could save

the day. Even before the direct policy intervention, the automatic stabilizers triggered by the Great Recession—the reduction in tax collection
and unemployment insurance and other safety-net expenditures—were
kicking in. Under President Obama, the US had embarked on an ambitious, albeit still undersized, fiscal stimulus program, the American
Reinvestment and Recovery Act (ARRA). Europe was considering similar measures. These policy interventions were controversial. Larry
Summers had already reduced the Obama administration's ask in ARRA
from the $1.6 trillion, which was Summers's best estimate of the needed
stimulus, down to $0.8 trillion, based on Summers's read of the political
prospects of ARRA. (It's worth noting that Summers is an educated
expert in macroeconomics, not in legislative politics; his gut instinct
about what could pass in Congress was worth no more than yours or
mine.) ARRA 2009 passed without a single vote from the opposition
party. Even the undersized ARRA combined with automatic stabilizers
sent the US towards deficits that were large by postwar standards, on the
order of 10 percent of GDP, and public debt, the accumulation of public
deficits, was rising.

Leading academics, deeply steeped in anti-Keynesianism, opened fire
on the deficit-spending approach. Alberto Alesina at Harvard advocated
"expansionary austerity," the proposition that strict maintenance of
balanced budgets, especially by cutting public expenditure, would stimulate business. Into this debate came Carmen Reinhart and Kenneth
Rogoff with their poorly researched but well-written paper "Growth in a
Time of Debt" published in the *American Economic Review*.[1] The article
was not only well-written but also well-illustrated, with an easy-to-read
bar plot showing catastrophic consequences for economic growth if the
public debt-to-GDP ratio crossed the 90 percent threshold. Reinhart
and Rogoff published the paper and then took it on the road with op-eds
and media appearances and even testimony before Congress.

Paul Krugman wrote of this paper, "Indeed, Reinhart/Rogoff may
have had more immediate influence on public debate than any previous
paper in the history of economics. The 90 percent claim was cited as the
decisive argument for austerity by figures ranging from Paul Ryan, the
former vice presidential candidate who chairs the House Budget

---

1   Carmen M. Reinhart and Kenneth Rogoff, "Growth in a Time of Debt," *American Economic Review* 100 no. 2 (2010): 573–78, doi:10.1257/aer.100.2.573.

Committee, to Olli Rehn, the top economic official at the European Commission, to the editorial board of the *Washington Post*.²"

Reinhart and Rogoff were sloppy and wrong in every way. Thomas Herndon, for a term paper in a required graduate course, demonstrated the spreadsheet errors, selection bias, undocumented and ill-considered summary methods, and transcription error that converted an indication of a modest reduction in growth at high levels of public debt into a fiscal cliff that required nothing less than Austerity Now—in the midst of the greatest aggregate demand collapse of the national and global economy since the Great Depression.

It is interesting to note that Reinhart and Rogoff were not alone in 2010 in finding a growth cliff when the ratio of public debt to GDP crosses 90 percent. Papers published in those key years by the *European Economic Review*, the Bank of International Settlements, *Economica*, and the Federal Reserve Bank of Kansas City found and hammered on the same 90 percent threshold for public debt. It was a mass delusion. Rogoff, in academic and media exchanges that followed the publication of Thomas's finding, was fairly graceless, referring to the rebuttal of their study as a "witch hunt," but even he recognized in a kind of backtracking, "Nowhere did we assert that 90 percent was a magic threshold that transforms outcomes."

The finding of a 90 percent threshold for the ratio of public debt to GDP was the kind of sloppy error that comes from received wisdom meeting elite orientation. In the short run, our work launched a re-examination of the flimsy economic underpinnings of the austerity agenda. In the medium run, the advocates of austerity—who were, in many cases, the advocates of the types of financial liberalization that created the conditions for the Great Crash in the first place—have proven disturbingly resilient in their hold on academic and policy power. Their hold continues despite the enormous damage done both by the aggressive deregulation that led to the crash and the insistence on austerity in public budgets that hobbled a more activist response.

The case for austerity pushed by the best economists at the best institutions, which seemed important and damaging at the time, looks in retrospect to be even more momentous and catastrophic. The

---

2   Paul Krugman, "How the Case for Austerity Has Crumbled", *New York Review of Books,* June 6, 2013.

widespread electoral success and extra-electoral power of the anti-liberal right, from Victor Orban to Donald Trump to Jair Bolsonaro to the Alternative for Germany, is the consequence of the failure of their predecessor neoliberal regimes to respond to the crisis of the 2000s. The failure to stimulate, let alone rebuild or restructure the economies towards equitable growth—or even to show sympathy for the victims of the great financial meltdown and the Great Recession—has shaken the foundations of democracy, and I tremble at the thought of what may come.

But I'm also an empiricist and an optimist. I hope that PhD student Thomas Herndon's contribution to pointing out that the emperor has no clothes will inspire rising students to see the world as it is rather than as tired and biased textbooks have told them to see it. And seeing the world is the first step to fixing the world.

Modern Monetary Theory (MMT) argues that public debt levels hardly matter for a country that uses its own sovereign currency. What is your view of the MMT approach?

I am impressed by the success of the economists associated with MMT in renewing public debate over how much we can monetize deficits and public debt. I do not have a strong position on the historical and institutional relevance, precision, or accuracy of the claims made by some MMT economists regarding, for example, the origins of money or the consolidation of the Treasury and Central Bank balance sheets. I would say I am skeptical of those aspects of MMT.

As a practical policy matter, much of the on-the-ground debate over the viability of the MMT policy prescription comes down to views on how much slack there is in the US economy and how much discipline will be exerted by the ruling class against efforts to run the US economy hotter. Will full employment, or—more accurately, since we don't actually have "full employment"—will fuller employment generate inflation? I think we have learned over the past two to four decades that institutional arrangements, the extent to which workers have bargaining power through law, policy, and practice, are more important than one magic number for the unemployment rate.

I suspect that the MMT economists have underestimated the political economic struggle required to reorient priorities. I appreciate the way that MMT has encouraged more expansionary fiscal policy and engendered vigorous debate over feasibility and sustainability.

Your 2018 book with the leading Portuguese economist Francisco Louçã, Shadow Networks: Financial Disorder and the System that Caused Crisis, *poses two big questions at the outset: (1) How did finance become hegemonic in the capitalist system; and (2) What are the social consequences of the rise of finance? A large part of the answer you and Louçã give to these two questions involves the ascendancy of the "shadow banking" system in the US. How has the rise of shadow banking supported the trends in US and global capitalism towards rising income and wealth inequality as well as deepening financial instability?*

My recent book with Francisco Louçã, *Shadow Networks: Financial Disorder and the System that Caused Crisis*, examines the shocking resiliency of the intellectual, policy, and corporate networks that led the way to the crisis and then deflected criticism and derailed badly needed reform efforts afterwards. Finance is at or near the center of these networks, both historically and functionally.

Finance had led the way into the previous disaster of the Great Depression, and it was tamed but never fully defeated by the New Deal legislation that emerged from the wreckage of the Great Crash. Jennifer Taub documents how financial interests went to work on undermining financial regulation and finding and inserting loopholes pretty much the instant the ink was dry on the Glass-Steagall Act (the core New Deal legislation regulating finance after the Great Crash).

Finance can mobilize a lot of cash and a lot of people—experts in econ departments and law faculties, lobbyists, central bankers and their staffs, legislators, and industrialists who are invited to wear a second hat as financiers—and these experts become the policy-makers and the regulators.

Meanwhile finance spends a lot of time cultivating the art of avoiding regulations. "If you ain't cheating, you ain't trying" was the watchword of a Barclay's Bank vice president in the LIBOR scandal. The main danger from banking comes from the lure of leverage. It's tempting to take big risks with other people's money. So one of the main points of banking regulation is to limit these risks. But bankers are persistent. Bankers formed an entire shadow world of unregulated banking both in parallel with and in implicit and explicit communication with the world of regulated banks. And that parallel, interconnected system has accumulated a lot of wealth, a lot of risk, and a lot of power.

If it took until the ink dried on Glass-Steagall, the war on Dodd-Frank 2010 (the complex, inadequate yet at least partially effective financial reform legislation after the Great Crash in 2008) began before the ink even got put on paper. Controlling private finance—or banishing it altogether if it refuses to play by the rules—is probably the single most important political economic intervention for building an egalitarian democracy in the rest of the twenty-first century.

You served for six years as chair of the UMass Amherst Economics Department. UMass is widely recognized as the most distinguished left research-level economics department in the country, if not the world. How would you describe the trajectory of UMass Economics over time? What do you think its major accomplishments have been? What are things that you think could be done better at UMass? And finally, do you think that the UMass program in some semblance of its historical orientation can continue and even grow stronger over time?

The department is very collaborative, and we made some great hires during the years that I was chair, but these were the outcome of group effort and departmental consensus and would have happened with or without me. My biggest contribution was in developing the undergraduate program.

It became clear through the experience of liberalization, privatization, marketization, and deregulation of the 1970s through the Great Crash that regardless of intellectual merit, progressive economists had lost touch with a public for whom neoclassical economics and its neoliberal policy prescriptions had become "common sense" (in the worst sense of that term). People with one or two undergraduate economics courses or with an undergraduate economics major were effectively primed to accept neoliberal propositions, such as that the minimum wage causes job loss.

This loss of connection between outstanding critical research in economics and the broader public became all the more critical during the debates on austerity after the Great Crash. The austerians' case was flimsy, but it could carry the day with a public that had been primed to accept unfounded propositions without critical examination. ("The national economy is like a family budget; we have to tighten our belts during recessions.")

The department doubled the enrollment of Jerry Friedman's popular Introductory Microeconomics lecture (taught from Jerry's book, *Microeconomics: Individual Choice in Communities*, which questions and contextualizes the hyper-individualism of conventional microeconomics, and taught entirely with Jerry's standard poodle by his side). I also commissioned Bob Pollin to develop and teach a new, engaging Introductory Macroeconomics course, with a particular focus on the challenges of unemployment and ecological crisis. One goal here, in addition to preparing majors for more advanced courses in economics, was to reach students who might take only one or two undergraduate economics courses and to make sure that they can come at problems as citizens with critical open minds and a better understanding of historical and social context. These educated citizens are more likely to ask probing questions when a politician promises that financial deregulation or tax cuts will help the economy grow or argues that inequality creates useful incentives. I encouraged Sam Bowles and Daniele Girardi to rebuild our upper-level undergraduate microeconomics course around thought-provoking real-world problems. We reduced the size of our upper-level courses to emphasize writing and data analysis for majors.

I know that much of this sounds more like an administrative CV than provocative economic analysis, but I assure you that I am not running for dean. It's at the level of translating decades of accurate critical analysis into undergraduate classroom experience that a progressive program can contribute to public education and public debate. Obviously, we need the analysis to keep coming, but communication and pedagogy are critical as well.

In which direction do you see your research agenda unfolding in the years ahead? In this context, are there specific issues of particular concern to you that you haven't yet investigated but hope to in the future?

Climate change and energy transition are my current focus. For a long time, I thought that climate change and energy transition could, for better or worse, be managed within the framework of contemporary capitalism and the inadequate US welfare state—that is, climate change and energy transition would neither necessitate nor entail a social revolution. After years of stalemate and inaction on climate, I am less sure. The French "yellow jackets" [*gilet jaunes*], in reacting to a carbon-reduction tax plan that was biased towards the rich, declared that their president was talking about the end of the world, but their problem was making ends meet until the end of the month. It's clear that equality and justice will need to be tightly integrated with climate change policy and energy transition, and I hope that economists can help.

Responses on the COVID-19 Pandemic

How would you evaluate the ways different countries or regions have responded to the COVID-19 crisis, both in terms of public health interventions and economic policies?

I'm deeply troubled by the entire COVID period in the US. The failure to mobilize mass testing and contact tracing, the failure to keep essential workers working safely and to keep almost everyone else supported at home, and the failure to set priorities to get kids back to school safely make me feel as if we are living in a failed state. While I usually prefer structural explanations, it's hard not to pin at least some of the US debacle on Trump himself—his lack of interest, his lack of curiosity, his lack of attention span, his lack of scientific commitment, his lack of empathy, and his inability to listen to anything other than sycophantic happy talk. Of course, there are deeper structures underlying the US nightmare, and I comment on some of these below. I'll summarize here: the US response is a world historical disgrace. The richest, most powerful country in the world may never in history have worse bungled a crisis that it would have been straightforward to surmount.

I have a couple of other thoughts on comparative responses. We can learn from some of the really successful cases, especially South Korea and Vietnam.

I'm baffled by the Swedish response—I wish I knew the micropolitics that let a Social Democratic government approach the crisis with the type of insouciance and incompetence that looks more like Trump or Bolsonaro.

There was apparently substantial variation in the quality of the response across the new personalistic semi-authoritarian (I won't yield the term "populist" to them) regimes, meaning Orban, Bolsonaro, Trump, Netanyahu, Putin, Modi, Erdoğan, and others—in their COVID-19 responses and effectiveness. ("Apparently" is relevant because the wheel is still in spin, and we'll see where the year ends up.) I have not seen a good explanation of the variation across these regimes. I'm disinclined to attribute the variation to variation in the individual smarts of the "great man"; so it will be interesting to learn more about why and how each of these regimes responded.

Do you draw any general lessons from the COVID crisis about the most viable ways to advance an egalitarian economic project?

In retrospect, this crisis has radically exposed existing fault lines in our society. The types of social problems that we're seeing in the context of COVID—many of these were problems that we had that were maybe not completely self-evident, but a lot of them involve the unfinished business of building a social democracy. Those problems include deficiencies in the health insurance and unemployment insurance systems; inadequate sick-leave policies that force many people to go to work sick, potentially infecting others, because they can't afford to lose income; and a nutrition crisis that made many school systems reluctant to close because so many families rely on the free meals their children receive at school. The COVID crisis also exacerbated other social problems: the "digital divide" that leaves some people unable to work or learn from home, homelessness, domestic violence, and a lack of affordable high-quality childcare.

Does the experience of the COVID crisis shed any light on the way you think about economics as a discipline or, more specifically, the questions you might be pursuing in your own research?

When I teach the class Economics of Health and Health Care, I emphasize to students five reasons why health is different from other domains of economic activity: (1) the inability to pay; (2) monitoring and information problems; (3) third-party payment; (4) externalities; and (5) endogenous preferences in caring for others and the risk of becoming a

Prisoner of Love. The COVID crisis provides a case study of all of these, but I'll focus on the fourth, externalities. The first three are pretty standard in health economics courses. The fifth delves into the world of care work, building on my research on nursing and Nancy Folbre's major contributions to the economics of care work. Regarding the fourth, externalities, I've always sort of mumbled in passing, "Well, you know, with contagious diseases and vaccination, one person's self-interested behavior may bear on the health and well-being of others," but it really took the COVID crisis to drive home to me just how interdependent our health and health care are. From factory farming to working sick to mask resistance to overflowing emergency rooms to vaccine skepticism, the spillovers and the consequences for others of self-serving actions—whether those actions are desperate, in the case of working sick, or simply capricious, in the case of mask resistance—are simply overwhelming. Talking about contagion had a "last century" feel to it, but that's no longer the case.

The school of economics that has been most thoroughly proven right by this crisis is Feminist Economics. The care crisis is manifest in every dimension of the crisis and the public nonresponse, from the abandonment of frontline workers with inadequate access to personal protective equipment [PPE], to the schools disaster, to women withdrawing from the labor force in droves to cover all of the loose ends left dangling when COVID smashed into our inadequate social democracy. Colleagues like Nancy Folbre and Katherine Moos had identified the neglected investment in social reproduction—the pay-no-attention-to-that-woman-behind-the-curtain dirty secret of capitalism—years in advance of the COVID crisis. Anyone who can't see it now is just not looking.

The other school of thought that has been radically vindicated is the Public Health approach to health and health care. The investment in public health in this country is virtually nil; it's a rounding error on the health care bill. The public health approach—focusing on prevention, on social causes and social pathways of disease, on agriculture and food systems in relation to health—could have prevented an enormous amount of suffering. We do not have a health care system that is well equipped to interface with the public health approach. Few want to pay for public health because its benefits, while enormous, are diffuse and not very easy to patent or monopolize. Few want to cede to public health the kind of authority that could quickly make a difference—for example, to regulate agriculture; to order lockdowns, quarantines, distancing, mask wearing, and vaccination; to convert business-as-usual enterprises to PPE manufacture; to prioritize schools ahead of bars and country clubs.

Finally, I'm deeply impressed by the scientific brilliance and hard work that developed viable COVID vaccines in less than twelve months after the outbreak began. It's important to tally the gigantic public investment in this scientific development program. There's likely to be a fight over interpreting the development of the vaccine: triumph of the private pharmaceutical companies; or a triumph of public-funded scientific research and development. The evidence is pretty strong for the latter, but I predict we will hear a lot about the beneficence of Big Pharma and its need for patent protection for its profits.

Representative Publications and Influences

Publications

Michael Ash and Robert T. Fetter T. R. (2004). Who Lives on the Wrong Side of the Environmental Tracks? Evidence from the EPA's Risk-Screening Environmental Indicators Model. *Social Science Quarterly*, *85*(2), 441–462.

Michael Ash and Jean A. Seago (2004). The effect of registered nurses' unions on heart-attack mortality. *ILR Review*, *57*(3), 422–442.

Thomas Herndon, Michael Ash, and Robert Pollin (2014). Does high public debt consistently stifle economic growth? A critique of Reinhart and Rogoff. *Cambridge Journal of Economics*, *38*(2), 257–279.

People who have been influential: David Card, George Akerlof, Janet Yellen, Joe Stiglitz

Literature that has been influential:

Stephen A. Marglin (1974). What do bosses do? The origins and functions of hierarchy in capitalist production. *Review of Radical Political Economics*, *6*(2), 60–112.

George Akerlof and Janet Yellen (1990). The fair wage-effort hypothesis and unemployment. *The Quarterly Journal of Economics*, *105*(2), 255–283.

David Card and Alan Krueger (1993). *Minimum Wages and Employment: A Case Study of the Fast-Food Industry in New Jersey and Pennsylvania* (No. w4509; p. w4509). National Bureau of Economic Research.

Nelson Barbosa

Nelson Henrique Barbosa Filho is Full Professor at the São Paulo School of Economics in Brazil. Barbosa has served in various top-level macroeconomic positions in the Brazilian government, including serving as Brazil's minister of finance from December 2015 to May 2016. He is the author of numerous articles on open economy macroeconomics in both developed and developing countries.

Can you tell us a bit about your personal background? In particular, what was the path that led you to decide to study economics?

I was born in 1969, in Rio de Janeiro. My father was a civil engineer and had a small construction firm. My mother was a schoolteacher and I have two older sisters. I grew up in Rio de Janeiro and was drawn to economics because I liked math and history. When I was in high school, in the mid 1980s, Brazil was still dealing with the effects of its foreign debt crisis and facing chronic high inflation. During that time, there were a series of failed stabilization attempts to control inflation and that brought my attention to economic issues, which were the talk of the day.

I did my undergraduate and master's course at the Federal University of Rio de Janeiro (Universidade Federal do Rio de Janeiro or UFRJ) in the late 1980s and early 1990s. After that, I worked at the Central Bank of Brazil for three years. I left the Central Bank in 1997 to do my PhD in economics at the New School for Social Research (NSSR). I defended my dissertation and returned to Brazil in 2002, when I became an Adjunct Professor at UFRJ.

In 2003, with the beginning of the Lula administration, I moved to Brasília to work for the government, first as deputy chief economist at the Ministry of Planning. I moved in and out of many government positions during Lula's and Rousseff's administrations, in 2003–16.

I am now a Full Professor at the Getulio Vargas Foundation, in Brasília, and I also teach economics at the University of Brasília (UnB).

Why did you choose the New School for Social Research for your doctorate degree? What did you think about the intellectual environment there during your graduate school years?

The mainstream one-theory/one-model approach to economics never seemed correct to me. Also, in my undergraduate course at UFRJ, we were exposed to a pluralistic approach to economics, which compared alternative interpretations for all economic problems.

With this background, the NSSR seemed and was the best choice for my PhD in economics. I wanted to improve my quantitative skills and learn more about the classical and Marxist approaches to economics, to complement the post-Keynesian formation I had at UFRJ. I arrived at the NSSR in the fall of 1997, after working for three years at the Brazilian Central Bank. The environment was great, with many foreign students and Lance Taylor, Edward Nell, and Anwar Shaikh as the leading professors in the department back then.

Who are the economists that have influenced you significantly? What have been the ways that they influenced your thinking and work?

I had the luck of having very good teachers, both in Brazil and in the US. At UFRJ, four economists influenced me most. The first was Mario Possas, who taught us a comprehensive course in economic theory that emphasized the importance of effective demand and imperfect competition for understanding capitalism.

The second was Fernando Cardim de Carvalho, who was an expert in Keynesian macroeconomics and taught us the foundations and many strands of post-Keynesian theory. He was also a model scholar who led by example, through his professionalism and courtesy, in debating academic issues and economic policy.

The third was Antonio Maria da Silveira, who was in charge of the courses on Philosophy of Science and Economic Methodology at UFRJ. Through him I learned about competitive paradigms of science, complexity, the limits of any economic model, and the need to incorporate history into our analyses.

The fourth was Maria da Conceição Tavares, who supervised my MA dissertation at UFRJ and always challenged any explanation, theoretical or otherwise, down to its very foundations. With her, I learned to be prepared to debate anything.

In the US, at the NSSR, my main influence came from Lance Taylor and his courses in structuralist macroeconomics. With Lance, I learned how to model problems in terms of alternative theoretical closures and how to look for the appropriate solution for the problem at hand through empirical or econometric investigations. I still do what could be called Lance Taylor's macroeconomics today.

And Duncan Foley was also a leading figure at the NSSR during my time, even though when he arrived there I had already finished my coursework. I audited his courses anyway and have been trying to develop and apply some of his ideas since then.

You have given a lot of attention in your research to issues around demand-led growth, both in abstract terms and with respect to real-world economies. What are the main features of a demand-led growth strategy?

Capitalist economies are demand-constrained—even "Austrian" economists recognize that—but, for ideological and methodological reasons, most of mainstream macro theory works under the assumption that demand fluctuations do not have any long-lasting consequences and that output always converges to its exogenous supply-driven path in the long run.

Demand-led growth inverts the logic of this vision. It is expected demand that drives production in a monetary economy, as pointed out by Keynes and Kalecki more than eighty years ago. Since at least one of the factors of production can be produced—capital—it is potential output that adapts to effective demand in the long run, not the other way around.

The main feature of demand-led growth is that productivity and capital accumulation can be driven by demand rather than by exogenous supply factors in capitalist economies.

This does not mean that exogenous changes in technology and other supply factors are unimportant, but only that there may be alternative equilibrium points in terms of the level of economic activity and income distribution in any capitalist economy.

To understand this perspective, we have to combine effective demand with social conflict. In general terms, the vision is that the growth of effective demand determines the rate of unemployment at the steady state, which, in its turn, is given by the level of economic activity necessary to discipline the workers' wage claims in a way that is consistent with the desired rate of profit.

To close the logical sequence in a Marxian or Sraffian way, the target rate of profit depends on technological and institutional issues, with market and political power being their most important determinants, but this issue is usually ignored in most mainstream economic models.

What are the primary strengths of this approach for countries at varying levels of development?

The demand-led approach also helps one understand the dynamics of developed and developing economies, since changes in demand stemming from financial constraints drive most income and employment fluctuations and have long-term effects through their impact on productivity. The 2008 financial crisis was an example of that—that is, a collapse of effective demand due to excessive financial leverage à la Minsky.

For developing economies, balance-of-payments and fiscal constraints are also basically demand-led and can explain most business cycles and trend growth of output, through hysteresis. Because of this, demand-led growth can explain the recent failure of austerity to quickly revive economic growth in many countries after the 2008 crisis.

Again, demand-led growth does not mean that any level of growth is feasible since, at the end of the day, there are physical constraints on output. The main idea is another, that income and employment can be stable at low levels of economic activity for a long time because of financial and distributive constraints, not necessarily technological ones.

How would you describe the development experience over the past thirty years in Brazil? To what extent, and in what ways, would you say that Brazil has been on a viable growth path? Have the benefits of growth been shared equitably, in your view?

I have to go back forty years. Brazil was hit hard by the 1980s debt crisis, given its fragile foreign financial position and the widespread indexation of prices that happened during the 1970s to cope with domestic inflation. When the debt crisis hit, there was a maxi-devaluation of the currency, with both major recessive and inflationary impacts on the country. As a result, economic growth stalled in the 1980s and 1990s while the country tried to reduce its high inflation.

The solution came only in the mid 1990s, when a favorable international situation allowed a stabilization plan based on an exchange-rate peg, the Real Plan, named after the currency introduced at the time and valid since then. The exchange-rate peg was devised to bring inflation down quickly and was successful in doing that. The cost was a very high real interest rate, of 25 percent per year in the late 1990s, to sustain the peg. The system was not financially sustainable, though, and it did not last very long.

After the East Asian and Russian crises of 1997–99, Brazil had its own currency crisis in 1999 and we moved to floating exchange rates, inflation targeting and fiscal rules to control the government primary balance. This is the system we have had since then, and, so far, it has been robust, enabling Brazil to withstand domestic and international shocks.

Economic growth was slow throughout the 1995–2002 stabilization period. The main priority at that time was to control inflation and manage the balance-of-payments constraints, with the government resorting to the IMF twice to avoid a sharp depreciation of its currency. The next wave of change came in the early 2000s, from the combination of an extremely favorable scenario abroad and a major change in political power domestically.

Commodity prices and demand soared in the early 2000s, and this allowed Brazil to grow without any major balance-of-payments constraint. The economy also adapted itself to the floating exchange rate, which diminished the costs of adjustments to external shocks. More important, starting in 2005 and following the example of other emerging economies, Brazil accumulated a sizable stock of foreign reserves, which in turn reduced the country's vulnerability to external shocks.

On the political side, the victory of the Workers' Party (Partido dos Trabalhadores or PT) in the 2002 elections was also important for what came next. The PT administrations made poverty reduction and social inclusion its main priority from the start. In practical terms this meant that part of the macroeconomic gains from commodity prices were channeled to low-income families, through income transfers and a substantial increase in the real minimum wage.

The gross tax burden grew with the profits from high commodity prices and demand, but the net tax burden remained practically the same, since most of the extra fiscal revenue went back to society through income transfers. This pushed consumption and investment up, but benefited mostly the nontradable sector, because high commodity prices came together with the appreciation of the domestic currency. It was a period of boom and deindustrialization for Brazil.

To try to sustain growth from the supply side, the government also launched a massive investment plan in 2007, based on high public investment and concessions in infrastructure. The initiative was successful until 2011. The situation started to change in 2012, when commodity prices and demand decelerated, and this hit the government budget hard. The successes of the previous period also demanded some change in policy, since reducing poverty through income transfers had created an important but temporary boost to demand and production.

As the rates of unemployment and inequality fell, the expansionary effects of distribution tended to diminish and something else had to take its place for growth to be sustainable. The ideal candidate was high direct or indirect public investment in infrastructure, which would require fiscal reforms to open space in the budget without raising the tax burden excessively.

However, because of the deceleration of growth in 2012 and the reduction in the competitiveness of the Brazilian tradable sector since 2007, the government decided to change its priority to stimulate private investment through tax cuts and financial subsidies in 2012–14.

The new expansionary strategy did not work out because of different initial conditions and the adverse international situation. When Brazil first adopted a fiscal stimulus, in 2007, the primary surplus was still high and public debt was falling. When it tried the same thing in 2012, the primary surplus was already low and public debt was growing. This difference, coupled with falling commodity prices and exchange-rate depreciation, increased economic uncertainty about the sustainability of fiscal policy.

If everyone expects a fiscal adjustment in the near future, consumption and investment plans tend to be postponed until it becomes clear who will pay most of the cost. This happened in Brazil in 2012–14. The inevitable adjustment came in 2015, but it was initially too drastic in face of the new adverse shocks to the country's terms of trade and the evolution of the domestic political situation. The increasing polarization of the Brazilian political debate blocked most government attempts to correct its course after the initially drastic adjustment of 2015.

The political crisis escalated in 2016, with the impeachment of President Rousseff, and in 2018, with the imprisonment of former President Lula. Both events were based on questionable judicial rulings and should be interpreted as political actions against the left rather than impartial legal decisions.

Brazil has been living a political stalemate since 2016, and this has prevented the government from solving its domestic fiscal problems. The left-wing government tried to distribute the costs of the adjustment more evenly while in power, but since 2016 the right-wing administration has favored a more drastic approach based on the failed hypothesis of expansionary austerity.

Looking back at the PT period in the government, economic growth mostly benefited the poor, and there was a reduction in poverty and inequality, measured by household surveys. However, in such an unequal society as Brazil, one can never say that the benefits of growth have been shared equitably. It is always possible to do more. I can only say that the benefits of growth were shared less unequally under the PT administrations than before or after in Brazil.

To what extent was the strong growth trajectory of Brazil building on the demand-led approach that you have developed in your research?

Both the income redistribution and investment plans of 2006–10 were based on the demand-led approach to macroeconomics, on the idea that productivity would accelerate given the structure and initial condition of the Brazilian economy. This proved to be right for 2007–10, when there was idle capacity and high unemployment in the economy, and the initial fiscal situation was sound enough.

The other demand-led strategy, based on tax cuts and financial subsidies, did not work so well in 2011–14 for three main reasons. First, the economy was already close to full employment by 2011. Second, the multiplier of tax cuts and financial subsidies is smaller than the one of transfers to the poor and investment in infrastructure. And third, the more fragile fiscal situation of the government and the more adverse international situation increased the economic uncertainty about the sustainability of economic policy.

How have your views of Brazil's long-term performance been affected by the most recent years of severe recession?

The Brazilian 2014–16 recession was the second biggest recession in our history, measured in terms of GDP per capita, and was the result of multiple factors. There were adverse exogenous shocks, from low commodity prices and a severe drought, which raised power prices in Brazil. There were errors in economic policy too, mostly in 2012–14, when the government tried to boost demand through another round of fiscal expansion while controlling some key prices to avoid a rise in inflation.

There were also errors in 2015–16, when the government changed its strategy abruptly to make a severe recessive adjustment, both on fiscal and monetary policy. When the government finally tried to correct this error, in 2016, the political situation did not allow any further adjustments.

All three factors combined would be enough to cause a recession, but their impact was amplified for institutional reasons: the initially recessive impacts of the fight against corruption, which resulted in a sudden halt to many investment projects that became the object of investigation.

Fighting corruption is a duty of any public official and, in the long run, the gains from it outweigh any short-run cost. With less corruption the economy tends to function more efficiently on a permanent basis— that is, it tends to waste fewer resources in inefficient rents to corrupt politicians. Having said that, I have no doubt that, in 2014–16, the initial impact of fighting corruption in Brazil clearly contributed to the fall in investment and income. Hopefully, this was the price we had to pay to have a more efficient economy and more just society in the near future.

When we put all factors together, Brazil's long-term performance has not been good during the last thirty years. On the one hand, the country was able to reduce inflation, move to floating exchange rates and become less exposed to international shocks than in the past. On the other hand, the country was not able to sustain growth and continue to reduce inequality without generating an unsustainable fiscal situation when hit by adverse international or domestic shocks.

The root of the problem has been more political than economic—that is, the inability of the Brazilian political system to manage the social conflict over income—which manifests itself mostly in the government's budget during periods of hardship.

How would you compare the development trajectory of Brazil over the past thirty years relative to two of the three other BRIC countries—that is, Russia, India, and China?

The BRIC group is a basket of very different continental countries, each one with its own idiosyncrasies. I am not an expert on India and China and so am unable to draw comparisons, but Brazil surely had the worst macroeconomic performance of the three in the last thirty years.

From a political and social view, I can only say that the Brazilian experience reflects the attempt of a Western society to combine economic development and full democracy, starting from a very unequal distribution of income and wealth, and subject to high macroeconomic volatility due to the economy's historic dependence on commodity exports to finance its balance of payments.

Progress has been slow in Brazil, but there has been progress when we compare Brazil with itself, thirty years ago. Whether or not this will eventually match the recent economic progress in China and India is too early to tell.

Can developing economies experience rising productivity as well as an expansion of decent job opportunities? Or should we expect that an inevitable feature of improving productivity is that people are thrown out of low-productivity work in agriculture without an obvious prospect for decent employment in other economic sectors, including, perhaps, high-productivity agriculture?

In theory, we can combine growth, employment, and lower inequality through appropriate policies. The golden age of Western economies in the 1950s and 1960s is one example of that, but the specific conditions that allowed such a performance no longer exist.

We now live in a world of high capital mobility that tends to promote a race to the bottom between capitalist economies, each one trying to become more competitive against another through deregulation, wage repression, and other liberalizing initiatives. At the end of the day, this increases the bargaining power of capital and raises income inequality.

In the specific case of developing economies, we still have a clear dual structure, in which a small modern sector pays high wages and interacts with a large backward sector that pays low wages. In the past, the backward sector was rural, based on subsistence agriculture. Nowadays it is urban, based on informal services, the care or "servant" economy.

In both cases, the endogenous development of the modern sector alone has been insufficient to bring enough people to the formal economy and high-productivity jobs. It is necessary to accelerate the process through higher investment and innovation, and some developing countries have been successful in doing that.

And for economic growth to benefit all, it is also necessary to combine productive diversification and development with social inclusion. This means social programs to reduce poverty, provide universal education and health care, and raise the bargaining power of workers in a way that promotes cooperation within firms.

Unlike most academic economists, you have also been very active and have held high-level positions in the realm of policymaking, including as chair of the Bank of Brazil (2009–2013), executive secretary at the Ministry of Finance (2011–2013), and, briefly as Brazil's minister of finance (December 2015—May 2016). What were your main responsibilities in each of these positions? To what extent was your direct policy work guided by your research work and your overall perspective as an economist?

I worked for the government during most of the PT administrations, from 2003 through early 2016. I was initially deputy chief economist at the Ministry of Planning, Budget and Administration and later moved to the Brazilian National Development Bank (BNDES), as an economic advisor.

I got more involved in economic policy only in 2006, when I moved to the Ministry of Finance. I was first deputy secretary of economic policy there, then secretary of economic monitoring and later secretary of economic policy. This was in 2006–10, during the Lula administration, when I worked mostly with macroeconomic and regulatory policy.

My main duties during the 2006–10 period were to coordinate the government investment programs and macroeconomic initiatives. This included formulating new policies to deal with the 2008 crisis, when I also worked on financial and exchange-rate issues, together with the Brazilian Central Bank.

I became deputy finance minister in 2011, in the beginning of the first Rousseff administration, and remained in that position until early 2013. During this period my main activities were to coordinate government tax policy, manage the financial relationship between the federal government and subnational administrations, and interact with Congress to get approval of the government's main legislative initiatives.

I left the Ministry of Finance in May 2013 because I did not agree with the direction of economic policy at that time. More specifically, I proposed that the government should absorb the macro shocks through a temporary reduction in its primary balance and compensate this with structural but gradual reforms in its spending. This was not the decision of the government, which opted for fiscal expansion, price controls, and no structural reforms to deal with its immediate problems.

I returned to the government in 2015, this time as minister of planning, budget, and management, to help President Rousseff change the course of her economic policy. My job was to coordinate the government's budget and spending reforms.

I remained at the Ministry of Planning until the end of 2015, when I moved to the Ministry of Finance. At that time, the government had just gotten congressional approval to relax its fiscal policy in order to stabilize the economy, with the implicit compromise of adopting structural reforms to stabilize the public debt in relation to GDP in the medium run. I worked on these issues until the impeachment of President Rousseff, in May 2016.

Can you describe some of the major policy achievements that you have been involved in? What was the basis for the success of these efforts? What about policy mistakes or outright failures? What led to these failures?

I was involved in many policy initiatives during my period in the government. The most successful ones were the Growth Acceleration Program (Programa de Aceleração do Crescimento or PAC) in 2007–10, which contributed to increased government and private investment. During that same period, I also worked on a new housing program for low-income families (Minha Casa Minha Vida or MCMV), which boosted residential investment in 2009–10.

In the aftermath of the 2008 crisis, I also worked on the special loans of the Treasury to the Brazilian National Development Bank, which in its turn was an important mechanism for injecting liquidity into the economy and avoiding a credit crunch in 2009–10.

In 2011–13, I worked mostly with tax, pension, and financial reforms. During that period, the government successfully approved a change in state taxation to eliminate a loophole that benefited imports over domestic production, created a new pension system for its civil employees, and eliminated the floor interest rate paid on savings deposits, which opened the way for lower interest rates later on.

In 2015–16, I also worked mostly on reforms, this time on spending, and contributed to the change in the government's system of unemployment insurance and financial transfers to low-wage workers.

As finance minister, in 2016, I proposed an increase in the government budget deficit to stabilize the economy, together with a ceiling for government expenditure and social security reform to control public debt in the medium run. The first two initiatives were adopted shortly after President Rousseff's impeachment, while social security reform has been on the government's agenda ever since.

As for mistakes, the excessive reliance on tax cuts and financial subsidies to boost economic activity in 2012–14 proved to be an error. The reduction in firms' payroll taxes in exchange for an increase in their sales taxes, adopted in 2011, was also problematic, not exactly because of the idea itself, but because the political situation at the time distorted the government's initial intentions and ended up creating a huge tax cut. And, finally, the cuts in spending in 2015 proved too large in the face of the other contractionary shocks that hit the economy at the same time.

In most of the cases of success, the political environment was favorable, the change in policy was gradual or the issue at hand was straightforward enough to draw political support from Congress. In the cases of failure, either the change in policy was too drastic or the political environment too volatile to allow even small changes.

Brazil has undergone wrenching political upheaval since you were active in policy when the Workers' Party was in power. Can you envision one or more scenarios through which Brazil returns to some variant of an egalitarian growth path, as advanced by the Workers' Party?

The left was in power for a little more than thirteen years in Brazil, and it could have remained so, provided it was able to adapt its economic policy to the changing domestic and international situation of the country. Its inability to do so compromised the continuance of growth and social inclusion before the political attack from the extreme right, which became more violent only in 2013.

Brazil now lives under a censored democracy, in which the judicial system clearly uses a double standard when it has to analyze similar issues regarding left- or right-wing politicians. Because of this asymmetry, it may take a long time for Brazil to return to full democratic status, where everybody is equal before the law.

If and when Brazil has a free and fair election, the left may return to power. This may be expedited by the economic policy of the Bolsonaro administration, which advocates tax cuts for the rich and benefit cuts to the poor as a way to increase incentives to work and invest in an already highly unequal society.

Despite support from financial markets and the conservative media, trickle-down economics did not work in the advanced world, and the same will probably happen in Brazil. Whether or not this will open the way for the return of more egalitarian social democratic initiatives will depend on the state of democracy in the country by then.

Were there things that you learned in your policy work that you could not have learned as an academic economist? How, if at all, has your experience as a policy-maker changed your overall thinking as a macro economist?

Working in the government changes and improves one's perspective as an economist. First, in contrast to the complexity of economic research, successful economic policy is usually based on intuitive narratives that translate economic principles into common sense. For example, the government is not a household, but it still faces budget constraints. One should be able to explain the difference while retaining the importance of trade-offs and social choices in a democracy.

Second and related to the first point, in economic policy it is not sufficient to be right on a technical level. It is also necessary to be right politically, that is, to be able to convince noneconomists of the benefits of any initiative, as well as to be clear about its costs and risks.

Third, economists and politicians tend to concentrate only on the benefit side of their proposals, for obvious reasons, but this tends to limit the political debate, since when the costs finally become clear, voters feel betrayed since they did not know about it in advance.

Fourth, no matter how better a new steady state is in relation to the current economic situation, the transition period is very important in politics. As Keynes said, in the long run we are all dead. Voters understand this well. Long-run objectives are important for economic policy, but they cannot build large coalitions by themselves. There must be some clear checkpoints and returns during the transition period for any policy to be feasible in a democratic society.

Fifth, in the academy, we emphasize differences. Even if I agree with you on 99 percent of an issue, we will debate the 1 percent we disagree on. In politics, the reverse is true: even if I disagree with you on most of the issues, we can still work together on the little we agree on. This is a major difficulty for orthodox economists, who usually bring their academic/technocratic vision to government.

Sixth, monopolistic power is much more important than is usually emphasized in macroeconomics. Improvements in competition and transparency can usually bring huge welfare gains, and the same holds for incremental institutional changes that reduce transaction costs and eliminate rents. Macroeconomics should include a greater role for competition and regulatory policies.

Seventh, economic policy is about solving problems, not proving academic hypotheses. Theory and hypotheses are important for the advancement of economic knowledge and help with real-world issues down the road, but the main task of any policy-maker is to solve concrete problems rather than offer an interpretation of them. This is what is expected from us when in office.

What are your ongoing research projects and future research plans?

I am now back at the academia, at the University of Brasília and the Getulio Vargas Foundation. I still participate in political debate, both within the PT and in the media, where I write a bi-weekly column for Brazil's largest newspaper (*Folha de São Paulo*).

I am currently working on applied macroeconomics, mostly on fiscal rules and their implications, and on a Keynesian version of the three-equation structure of most DSGE models for policy analysis and simulation.

I also resumed my previous work on stock-flow models and have been trying to develop a simple way to introduce financial leverage in the usual structuralist or post-Keynesian toolkit of effective demand and social conflict to model and estimate credit cycles.

Would you be open to returning to government in a senior policy-making role of some kind?

I worked in and out of the government for thirteen years and currently do not have any intention to return to policy-making. As the saying goes, one should never say never, but I feel that I have already done my civil duty as an economist and now can contribute more from outside the government.

Responses on the COVID-19 Pandemic

How would you evaluate the ways different countries or regions have responded to the COVID-19 crisis, both in terms of public health interventions and economic policies?

The COVID-19 pandemic led to similar responses around the world, but with different intensities. There were lockdowns and social isolation to slow down the spread of the disease, and fiscal and financial initiatives to attenuate the economic impact of a sudden stop in many sectors.

I am not a specialist in health interventions, so I cannot judge each country's response in that area. On the economic front, countries that adopted a large fiscal stimulus or disaster-relief programs have been able to attenuate the impact of the crisis on income and employment, which was nevertheless substantial and negative.

The best combination of disaster-relief policies seem to have included at least seven items: (1) reduced work hours with part of the wage bill footed by government; (2) additional cash transfers to the unemployed; (3) emergency cash transfers to informal workers and the poor in a temporary, universal basic income framework; (4) liquidity injections and regulatory flexibilization by central banks; (5) tax deferrals; (6) extraordinary budget transfers from the national treasury to regional governments, in large federations; and (7) emergency credit lines to busi-nesses, partially backed by the national treasury and/or the central bank.

Most disaster relief initiatives worked well, but as the world gets out of the depth of the COVID recession, reconstruction policies may also be needed, though this is far from certain. By the end of 2020, there were already grow-ing concerns about public debt and fiscal solvency in both advanced and emerging economies. Even though it has already been shown by Keynes that "the boom, not the slump, is the right time for austerity in the Treasury," the world risks embarking on another premature fiscal consolidation after the pandemic, similar to what happened in many Western democracies just a few years after the Global Financial Crisis of 2008.

Do you draw any general lessons from the COVID crisis about the most viable ways to advance an egalitarian economic project, focusing on this question in any way that you wish?

The main lesson is that a large part of the population is outside the social safety net, especially in developing countries, where a large part of the labor force works in informal activities.

In developed nations, the increase in the "gig economy" and the fragility of some jobs in the service sector also showed that we need to improve and adapt social protection to the economic and technological realities of the twenty-first century.

In the age of information and big data, nobody should be invisible to the government. COVID showed that we need a better and comprehen-sive record of income and wealth, for tax and transfer policies. The tax information from income and wealth taxation is the place to start, but the construction of a national income security system should be expanded to include people in poverty and/or informal and precarious jobs.

The final objective should be to expand unemployment insurance to income insurance, reaching informal workers and people outside the labor force. With this kind of system, governments would be able to do both regu-lar and emergency transfers to those who need it, which can later be devel-oped into a basic income network and help full-employment policies.

Does the experience of the COVID crisis shed any light on the way you think about economics as a discipline or, more specifically, the questions you might be pursuing in your own research?

The COVID crisis shed light on the dual nature of both advanced and emerging economies. This was already important before the crisis, but the pandemic made it clear that capitalism functions in at least two velocities, with part of the population employed in dynamic, high-wage or high-income activities, and the rest crowded in stagnant, low-wage or low-income jobs, which are a form of disguised unemployment.

Contrary to some economists' usual view, there is no endogenous economic mechanism to avoid income and wealth inequality from increasing in a dual economy. Government action is needed, with more tax and transfer programs, but the transfers should include more than cash. Social inclusion also requires an adequate supply of universal public services, especially in public health, as shown by the pandemic.

Representative Publications and Influences

Publications:
Nelson H. Barbosa-Filho (2001). The balance-of-payments constraint: From balanced trade to sustainable debt. *PSL Quarterly Review*, 54(219).

Nelson H. Barbosa-Filho (2004). A Simple Model of Demand-Led Growth and Income Distribution, *Revista Economia*, Brasilia (DF), 5(3), p.117–154.

Nelson H. Barbosa-Filho and Lance Taylor (2006). Distributive and Demand Cycles in the US Economy? A Structuralist Goodwin Model. *Metroeconomica*, 57(3), 389–411.

People who have been influential: Lance Taylor, Mario Possas, Fernando Cardim de Carvalho, Antonio Maria da Silveira, Duncan Foley

Literature that has been influential:
Mario Possas (1987). *A Dinâmica da Economia Capitalista: Uma Abordagem Teórica*, Editora Brasiliense.

Fernando Cardim de Carvalho (1991). *Mr. Keynes and the Post Keynesians: Principles of Macroeconomics for a Monetary Production Economy*, Edward Elgar.

Lance Taylor (1991). *Income Distribution, Inflation, and Growth: Lectures on Structuralist Macroeconomics*, MIT Press.

James K. Boyce

James K. Boyce is Emeritus Professor of Economics at the University of Massachusetts Amherst, where he is also a senior fellow at the Political Economy Research Institute (PERI). His areas of research include ecological economics, inequality, and economic development. His books include *Economics for People and the Planet* (2019), *The Case for Carbon Dividends* (2019) and *Agrarian Impasse in Bengal* (1987). He has written for *Harper's*, *Scientific American*, *Politico*, the *New York Times*, the *Los Angeles Times*, and numerous scholarly journals, including *Proceedings of the National Academy of Sciences*, *Ecological Economics*, *Environmental Research Letters*, and *Climatic Change*. He is the recipient, among other honors, of the 2017 Leontief Prize for Advancing the Frontiers of Economic Thought.

Can you please tell us something about your personal background?

I grew up in the Detroit suburbs. As a kid my great loves were reading books and exploring the great outdoors. I came of age in the 1960s, a time when the civil rights movement and the war in Vietnam made it clear to anyone paying attention that we do not live in the best of all possible worlds. Like many of my generation I felt impelled to do what I could to make things better. I still feel that way.

In 1968, when I graduated from high school, I worked as a volunteer for antiwar candidate Eugene McCarthy at the Democratic Party convention in Chicago. The contrast between the partying of good-old-boy delegates and the violence against protesters on the streets made a deep impression on me.

That fall I started at Yale University on a scholarship. In my sophomore year, I heard about an experimental program called the Yale-Carnegie Five-Year BA that would pay transportation and specialized training costs and maintain your student draft deferment while working for a year in a non-Western country. The prospect of leaving school and the country without a gun in my hands appealed to me, and I applied.

I ended up working in India on a Gandhian land reform and rural development project. First, I studied the Hindi language and green revolution agriculture with a group of Peace Corps trainees in central India. Then I lived and worked in Bihar, one of the poorest states in the country, with some of its poorest people. I came to see how the world works and doesn't work through their eyes. It was a life-changing experience.

Before you went to graduate school in economics, you co-authored with Betsy Hartmann the book A Quiet Violence: View from a Bangladesh Village. *How did that project come about? What were the main themes you explored in this book? How did this experience influence your decision to study economics at the graduate school level?*

Betsy and I met in 1972 when we both returned to Yale after working in India. The Bangladesh Liberation War had taken place in 1971, while we were there, and Betsy visited the newly independent nation on her way home. We designed our own majors at Yale—Betsy's was South Asian history, mine was agricultural development—that built on our experiences in India. Upon graduation, she won a fellowship and I received a peace prize, and, funded by these, we decided to return to South Asia, learn the Bengali language, and live for a year or so in a village in Bangladesh with the aim of writing a book about it. We wanted to address some of the basic questions that readers in the West had about developing countries: What are the causes of poverty and hunger? What is the position of women? What is the role of religion? What are the impacts of foreign aid? We tackled these through stories of real people—we saw our book as an oral history of the present.

While working on the book, we published magazine and newspaper articles about Bangladesh. Several pieces described how foreign aid often served to bolster the power of the country's ruling elites, from politically connected individuals in the capital to the biggest landlord in the village, and these got a lot of attention. We published an abbreviated version of the book, *Needless Hunger*, in 1979. The full book, called *A Quiet Violence: View from a Bangladesh Village*, was published in 1983.

Along the way, we received many rejections from publishers—more than thirty, as I recall—and, as a result, we realized that writing books about unpopular topics (like Bangladesh) from an unpopular point of view (we were critical of many foreign interventions there) was going to be a difficult way to make a living. We needed to pay the rent. I saw the choice before me as going either into journalism or academia. All my academic friends told me to go into journalism, and all my journalist friends told me to go into academia. In the end, I took the academic route.

I was attracted to Oxford for my graduate studies by the presence of Keith Griffin, a development economist whose book *The Political Economy of Agrarian Change* addressed many of the problems that I had encountered in India and Bangladesh. In fact, that's really the main reason I became an economist. If Keith instead had been an anthropologist or geographer, I would have wound up in a different discipline.

Who were the main economists who influenced your own work while you were a graduate student?

Keith Griffin was a wonderful mentor. It is not an exaggeration to say that I read just about everything he had written. His work spanned Latin America, Africa, and Asia, an example that helped me to decide not to confine my work to South Asia, even though the Indian subcontinent and its people will always have a special place in my heart. When I finished my doctorate, Keith asked me to write a book in a series on development strategies that he was commissioning for the OECD Development Centre in Paris. I decided to write about the Philippines, partly because the country had been the birthplace of the green revolution in rice, and partly because at the time (this was 1985, when the Marcos dictatorship was nearing collapse) I thought the country might become the scene of another disastrous US military intervention like that in Vietnam.

The other great influence on my thinking at Oxford was Amartya Sen. In my first term there, I faithfully attended three different lecture series that he was delivering. Once when he saw me sitting in the front row, he asked me, "Don't you get tired of listening to me?" I said no, and it was true. Sen addressed what I think are the deepest questions in economics: Why do individuals behave as they do? What is individual welfare? How can we aggregate individuals' views to arrive at a robust notion of social welfare? These questions, lying at the intersection between ethics and economics, captivated me. Listening to Sen and reading his work, I understood that neoclassical economics is only one chapter in the long history of human efforts to grapple with these questions, and not necessarily the most insightful one.

There was a third person from whom I learned much during my graduate studies. In 1982 I lived in Kolkata (at the time, it was still spelled Calcutta) to conduct the research for my dissertation, which was about agricultural growth in Bangladesh and the neighboring Indian state of West Bengal. There I was fortunate to have the economist Nripen Bandyopadhyay as my mentor and friend. Nripen worked at the Centre for Studies in Social Sciences, Calcutta, where I was a visiting scholar. Nripen knew rural West Bengal intimately, and my dissertation, ultimately published as the book *Agrarian Impasse in Bengal*, benefited greatly from his insights and guidance.

Who were some of your major influences in terms of the broader literature and schools of thought? For example, to what extent were you influenced by dependency theory as advanced by scholars such as Andre Gunder Frank and Samir Amin? To what extent have you seen your work as connecting with the Marxian and other traditions in heterodox economics?

My experiences in South Asia made me acutely conscious of the human costs of inequality and oppression. Let me give you an example. Near the school for "untouchable" children where I worked in Bihar was a village with a big house, the home of a landlord who controlled vast properties in the area. He oversaw his domain in the manner of a feudal fiefdom—in the worst sense of feudalism. One of the tasks of the men who supervised his tenants and farm laborers was to let him know when the daughters of the poor families who lived in the miserable huts of the village reached puberty. They were brought to the landlord and he would rape them. If their families objected, he had their huts burned to the ground—with them inside.

When I returned to college, I tried to make sense of what I had seen and learned. I read Paul Baran's *Political Economy of Growth*. I read others in the *Monthly Review* school, including dependency theorists like Frank, who maintained that underdevelopment in the Global South was the flip side of the coin of capitalist development in the Global North. They found support for this understanding of imperialism in the writings of Marx, but others who also called themselves Marxists took a very different view, maintaining that capitalism was a necessary stage on the trajectory to socialism and that imperialism was in this sense a progressive force. These divergent understandings reflected the fact that Marx's own views changed over time. Marx never visited India or other colonized countries, but that didn't stop him from writing about them. Maybe it's not surprising that his writings on this topic were less than consistent. For me, the realities I'd come to understand in India were more important to my education than the writings of any theorists, past or present.

Of course, I see a connection between my own work and that of heterodox traditions in economics, including Marxism. Above all, I share the concern for human well-being and how it can be undermined by deep inequalities of wealth and power. But I have not been a partisan or follower of any particular school of thought. I consider myself to be a political economist, and I define political economy as being about the allocation of scarce resources not only among competing ends (the contemporary textbook definition of economics) but also among competing people—competing individuals, competing groups, and competing classes.

From the time you finished graduate school in 1985 to the present, one could argue that the biggest change with respect to developing countries has been the major gains in average per capita income of the East Asian countries, starting with China, but certainly not only China. How would you characterize the East Asian export-led model? How would you respond to the idea that this model has accomplished more than any other economic policy approach over the last century for lifting people out of extreme poverty?

China's post-1985 experience came after similarly rapid growth since the Second World War in per capita incomes in Japan, Taiwan, and South Korea. Despite their very different political circumstances, all four countries shared one thing in common: all implemented thorough land-to-tiller agrarian reforms after the war. In Japan this happened under the US military occupation commanded by General Douglas MacArthur. In China it happened in the course of the Communist revolution led by Mao Zedong. In Taiwan and South Korea, it happened under US-backed regimes that were seeking to build a popular base.

The impacts of land reform extended well beyond agriculture itself. Land reform broke the chokehold on political power previously exercised by the landed oligarchy. By democratizing the distribution of wealth, it democratized the distribution of power, too. Freed from rack-renting landlords, rural families for the first time could save and invest not only in their farms but also in educating their children, and this helped prime the pump for industrialization.

In all four East Asian countries, the state played a pro-active role. Credit allocation, capital controls, limits on imports, incentives for exports—measures broadly known as "industrial policy"—all were important. These policies were a far cry from the free-market fundamentalism embraced by the Bretton Woods Institutions during the "Washington Consensus" of the late twentieth century. In 1993, the World Bank published a study called *The East Asian Miracle* that explored how East Asia's experience had managed to be so at odds with the predictions and prescriptions of the reigning orthodoxy. The study concluded that the distinctive attribute that allowed the state to play a positive role in these countries has been "technocratic insulation," meaning that policy-makers had been shielded from the capture and corruption by political elites, maladies that free marketeers assumed would normally—or even inevitably—infect the state.

If so, how can we explain this insulation? I think that land reform was key. It served to inoculate the body politic with antibodies against oligarchy. I remember hearing the late Alice Amsden deliver a talk based on her pathbreaking book on the South Korean experience, *Asia's Next Giant*. A key feature of that experience, she said, was that "the state disciplined the capitalists." Someone in the audience asked, who disciplined the state? Her reply stuck in my mind: the students. Students? Really? The answer made little sense to me until I visited Korea en route home from the Philippines. The taxi driver who picked me up at the airport was wearing a black armband. When I asked why, he explained that a student had been killed by the government—then still a military dictatorship—at a demonstration. I saw more black armbands as we drove into town. And I realized that abuses of power that were routine in the Philippines and many other countries were considered beyond the pale in Korea. Soon afterward the dictatorship fell.

China's most rapid economic growth came in the wake of the market reforms introduced after Mao's death. Some commentators have interpreted this as a vindication of the market, but, again, the state played a central role. Marx may have seen capitalism as paving the way for socialism, but the Chinese experience suggests that socialism can pave the way for capitalism as well.

The rapid growth in per capita income in China has been accompanied by sharply widening inequalities in the distribution of income and wealth. This is not entirely surprising, given the concentration of power in the hands of a single political party and the resulting opportunities for self-serving actions. These disparities could diminish the country's prospects for sustainable and stable growth in the years ahead.

You have been a member of the UMass Economics faculty for thirty-five years, and a leading contributor to the Political Economy Research Institute at UMass since its inception in 1998. In your view, what have been the main contributions of UMass Economics and PERI?

UMass Economics has been an oasis of intellectual diversity in a discipline characterized by a high degree of intellectual monoculture. This is why I came to UMass after finishing my doctorate.

The UMass faculty employ a variety of methodological approaches in their work, ranging from the use of econometric and mathematical models to institutional, historical, and qualitative analysis. I see this mix as healthy. Sadly, it is also rather unusual. For example, UMass is among the small minority of PhD economics programs in the US that require students to study economic history. When you think about it, that tells us a lot about the state of the profession.

Even more important, I think, is the department's openness to diverse ideas as to the proper criteria for evaluating economic outcomes. Neoclassical orthodoxy upholds a single overriding criterion for making value judgments. It's called "efficiency," but with a special meaning that differs from everyday usage of the term. In everyday parlance, efficiency means cost-effectiveness, the most efficient way to accomplish a goal. A student deciding how to get to class from off campus, for example, may choose between walking, biking, driving a car, or taking the bus. Neoclassical economics uses the term to mean something more: the choice of the ends as well as the means. Is it "efficient" for the student to go to class at all? Do the benefits of attendance outweigh the costs?

Formally, neoclassical efficiency is defined in theory as Pareto optimality, a situation where no one can be made better off without making someone else worse off. In the real world, there aren't many opportunities for making such Pareto improvements. Most economic policies bring benefits to some people but costs to others. Via the trick of the "compensation test"—could those who benefit compensate (in theory, seldom in practice) those who are harmed and still be better off?—neoclassical efficiency morphs into being equated with the biggest possible dollar pie ("maximizing net present value" in the language of cost-benefit analysis), period.

In UMass Economics, a number of other normative criteria are in the mix. These include distributional equity, human rights, environmental sustainability, liberty, and justice. Different faculty members may vary in the relative weights they place on different criteria, but what we generally share, I believe, is a willingness not to put neoclassical efficiency above all else in arriving at value judgments and policy recommendations.

PERI has enriched the life of the department in many ways, above all by encouraging and facilitating engagement with pragmatic issues of public policy. Again, the range of questions addressed by PERI researchers is wide and diverse, including such topics as living wages, macroeconomic stability, economic development, financial regulation, gender and care work, health policy, climate change, and environmental justice. Our work builds on the vision of economics expressed by the late Robert Heilbroner, "as the means by which we strive to make a workable science out of morality."

A major area of your research work in recent years has been on capital flight out of Africa. How severe is this problem in your view? How would you respond to a critic who might say, "If capitalists saw good investment opportunities in Africa, they would be investing there. They aren't because government policies in Africa have deterred investment rather than attracted it."

My colleague Léonce Ndikumana and I have calculated that cumulative unrecorded outflows of capital from Africa (this is the standard measure of capital flight) since 1970 have exceeded $1.4 trillion. This compares to Africa's total external debt outstanding of about $0.5 trillion. In this sense, Africa is a net creditor to the rest of the world. The difference is that the external assets accumulated through capital flight are in private hands, largely held by Africa's economic and political elites, whereas the continent's external debts are public, owed by African governments on behalf of their people.

Africa today is the home of many of the poorest people in the world. Children die of malnutrition and preventable diseases. Women die in childbirth owing to inadequate medical care. Millions survive in extreme poverty with incomes below two dollars a day.

Is the hemorrhage of capital from Africa a severe problem? I'd say so.

There is no single explanation for capital flight from Africa. Flawed governments and government policies—including kleptocratic regimes, political instability, and inadequate infrastructure investment—are part of the reason, but not the whole story. In our writings, including our 2011 book, *Africa's Odious Debts: How Foreign Loans and Capital Flight Bled a Continent*, Léonce and I have sought to paint the bigger picture, analyzing the international financial architecture through which money flows in and out of Africa. We see capital flight from Africa as an outcome of the unaccountable power that is wielded today by an international plunder network that is comprised of not only African elites but also their foreign partners and bankers. Those who are harmed by capital flight include not only ordinary Africans, but also ordinary folks in the countries that have become destinations for capital flight, including Europe and the US, where inflows of hidden wealth drive up rents and property values in international cities and corrode the integrity of financial institutions and the political process.

You also have been a major contributor to research on environmental justice in the US and globally. What, in your view, are the major elements of the environmental justice research agenda?

As a normative or prescriptive claim, environmental justice is based on the proposition that access to a clean and safe environment is a human right, not a commodity that ought to be allocated on the basis of purchasing power nor a privilege to be allocated on the basis of political power. No one should suffer disproportionate harm from pollution or natural resource depletion by virtue of belonging to a social group defined on the basis of race, ethnicity, class, or gender.

Within the US, there is a large body of evidence showing that people of color and low-income communities often bear disproportional environmental burdens. The extent of disparities varies, however, across locations and different types of environmental hazards. Analyzing these variations, the reasons for them, and their consequences are important tasks for researchers. There is mounting evidence of similar disparities in other countries, too, including in China, India, and Europe; more needs to be done to document these and their effects.

At the international level, we see environmental injustice most blatantly in the toxic waste trade when the hazardous by-products of production and consumption in high-income countries are dumped in low-income countries, and within these countries typically in or near low-income communities. This is a good example of why "efficiency" is defective as the sole basis for value judgments and policy prescriptions. An internal World Bank document in the 1990s known as the Summers memorandum posed the question, "Just between you and me, shouldn't the Bank be encouraging more migration of dirty industries to the LDCs [less developed countries]?" It argued that "a given amount of health-impairing pollution should be done in the country with the lowest cost, which will be the country with the lowest wages," and concluded that "the economic logic behind dumping a load of toxic waste in the lowest-wage country is impeccable and we should face up to that." This memo provoked an outcry when it came to light in the press, but I think it served a very useful purpose: it laid bare the logic of neoclassical efficiency in language that anyone can understand. Environmental justice advocates start instead from the premise that a clean and safe environment is a human right held in common by all. This is a profoundly different basis for policy-making.

How do policies to advance environmental justice both connect with, and differ from, policies to fight climate change and support climate stabilization? For example, is it accurate to characterize environmental justice policies as consistent with, and maybe even identical to, a Green New Deal framework?

Consistent, yes; identical, no. There's certainly an overlap between climate stabilization and environmental justice, but its extent will depend on what specific policies enter into the Green New Deal or other frameworks.

In one important sense, any effective climate policy helps advance environmental justice, since the pain from climate change will be felt disproportionately by low-income countries. And, within the richer countries, the pain will be felt disproportionately by low-income people, as illustrated by what happened in New Orleans during Hurricane Katrina. Climate change is like a new kind of toxic waste.

But environmental justice does not only mean fighting climate change, important as that is. It also means fighting against the burdens all too often imposed on people of color and low-income communities by other sorts of pollution and environmental degradation. The burning of fossil fuels itself emits many hazardous air pollutants, apart from carbon dioxide, and these "co-pollutants" are concentrated in specific locations. In the US, these are often places with above-average percent-ages of Blacks, Latinos, and households below the poverty line. Just cutting carbon emissions does not guarantee that these disparate burdens will be remedied. Indeed, it is possible that emissions of co-pollutants could increase in vulnerable communities, even as they decline overall. There is evidence that this has occurred in California. Explicitly incorporating air quality benefits and environmental justice into the design of climate policies can expand the overlap between them.

A centerpiece of the Green New Deal is large-scale investment in clean energy and energy efficiency. Ensuring that disadvantaged communities receive their fair share of this investment, and that disad-vantaged workers receive a fair share of the jobs it creates, again can expand the complementarities between the fight against climate change and the fight for environmental justice.

What do you think is the most workable approach for achieving climate stabilization over roughly the next thirty years? What do you think the chances are that any such policies will be successful—that is, that we can successfully stabilize the climate and avoid the major negative effects from ongoing climate change? What are the main barriers to overcome for achieving a successful climate stabilization path—both the technical and political? Do you think there is a nontrivial possibility that we are facing a true ecological disaster with respect to climate change?

Let me take these questions in turn. First, the most workable approach. I do not believe that any single approach will be a panacea. What we need is a smart mix of policies, including public investment and incentives for private investment in the clean energy transition; smart regulations to spur technological innovation and ensure a just distribution of air quality co-benefits; and crucially, in my view, absolute ceilings on the amount of fossil fuels we allow to enter the economy, set to guarantee emissions reductions on a trajectory based on climate stabilization targets.

What are the chances of success? Each item in the policy mix is important, but only strict ceilings on the use of fossil fuels—embodying the commitment to "keep fossils in the ground"—can guarantee success. Without ceilings, all we can do is hope for the best, since we cannot know with certainty how much emissions reduction will result from investments, regulations, or carbon prices not anchored to a fixed emission trajectory. If other policies in the mix prove to be sufficient, the ceilings will be redundant. They will have no effect, and do no harm. But if other policies prove to be insufficient to do the job on their own, the ceiling will constrain use of fossil fuels and cause their prices to rise. The higher prices will not only limit short-run demand but also strengthen long-run incentives for energy efficiency and clean energy investments. But if the price increases are substantial—if they add, for example, a dollar or two or five to the price of a gallon of gasoline—the impact on consumers could trigger a political backlash. There is a straightforward way to deal with this problem: take the extra money that is paid for fossil fuels (via a cap-and-auction system or a carbon tax indexed to emission quantities) and return a substantial fraction of it to the public in the form of universal, equal dividends. I make the case for such a policy in my 2019 book, *The Case for Carbon Dividends*.

What are the barriers? The most important barriers to climate stabilization are political, not technical. To be sure, we have yet to solve all the technological challenges involved in the transition from fossil fuels to clean energy. Smart grid and low-cost battery storage technologies for electricity are examples. We are also likely to need to develop negative emission technologies, for example, ways to sequester more carbon in soils. But I believe that, if we can send a man to the moon, we can meet these challenges, too. The main political barrier is the power of vested interests, particularly in the fossil fuel industry. There is only one way to surmount this barrier: wide and deep popular mobilization to demand climate action.

Are we facing a true ecological disaster if we do not act? I suppose it depends on what you consider to be a "true disaster." The planet will survive. After all, all the carbon stored in fossil fuels was once in the Earth's atmosphere. Life on Earth will survive. Humankind will probably survive, too. So failure to act will not mean the end of the world in the literal sense. But the scale of deaths and destruction that would result—the toll inflicted on humans and other living things—would be truly horrendous, and truly disastrous. We have a moral responsibility to our children and grandchildren to act now to prevent this. And we can do it in ways that benefit most people today thanks to cleaner air, green growth, and the boost to household incomes from carbon dividends.

At this juncture, it looks like we will not be able to avoid the adverse impacts of climate destabilization entirely. For too long, world leaders have dithered and succumbed to the power of fossil fuel corporations and petrostates as well as to political inertia. Every delay only increases the urgency of action to curb emissions, since their climate damages increase exponentially: each additional ton of carbon does more harm than the one before. But it also means that we now must pay serious attention to adaptation—measures to protect people and ecosystems from the effects of climate destabilization that no longer can be avoided. Here, too, the ethical criteria by which we make decisions will be crucial. Will adaptation investments be guided by "efficiency," prioritizing the protection of high-value property and high-income people? Or will they be guided by the principle that everyone, rich and poor alike, has an equal right to a safe environment? The adaptation choices we make as a society will have life-and-death consequences.

What do you think about socialism as a viable goal for the global left in our current historical period? Do you think we can achieve climate stabilization within the existing capitalist economic framework? Do you think that the overarching goal of the global left should be to create socialist societies?

The terms "socialism" and "capitalism" carry a lot of baggage, meaning different things to different people. If by socialism you mean something like the former Soviet Union, I would say it's neither viable nor desirable. If you mean a society in which wealth and power are distrib-uted more equitably than they are today, I would say that this is a viable and highly desirable goal. The latter meaning seems to be reflected in the opinion polls that today show more support for socialism than for capitalism in the United States.

Similarly, if by capitalism you mean the present order, in which fossil fuel firms and other mega-corporations wield enormous power, and are able to buy politicians and manipulate public opinion, then no, I do not think we can solve the problem of climate change within it. If you mean a society with markets, in which private property, common property, and public property co-exist, then yes, I think we can do so.

The task of the global left, I think, should be to fight for the more equitable and democratic distribution of wealth and power, and build an economy that works for everyone, including future generations. I discuss this in my 2019 book, *Economics for People and the Planet*. In the nine-teenth and twentieth centuries, the left–right axis usually was defined in terms of the relative scope of the market and the state. But history shows that a more fundamental distinction is the difference between democ-racy and oligarchy. When wealth and power are concentrated in the hands of a few, we see unhappy results for the great majority of people, no matter whether it's a laissez-faire or state-controlled economy.

What research questions are you aiming to pursue in your own work over the next several years?

I'll keep working on and for effective and equitable climate policy as long as it takes. But I also want to think more about the interface between humans and nature, and about the ethical criteria by which we value environmental changes, defining them as good or bad.

For a long time, many people believed in something called the "balance of Nature." Humans, at least once we stopped living as hunters and gatherers, were regarded as disturbing this balance, and the goals of conservation and environmental protection were framed as limiting the human footprint to stay within nature's self-healing capacities. The ideal state of nature, especially in America, was thought to be "wilderness" untouched by human hands. The management objective at Yellowstone National Park, for instance, was to return its ecosystems to their condi-tion before Europeans had any impact on them.

In recent decades, ecologists have left behind this static view of nature in favor of a more dynamic one in which change and disturbance are the rule, not the exception, and there is no timeless baseline that defines the ideal state of nature. In so doing, they are starting to reframe the goals of conservation and environmental protection in terms of sustaining ecosystem functions rather than preserving a snapshot of a landscape at some more or less arbitrary point in time.

If we abandon the notion that wilderness or some other baseline is a satisfactory basis for defining better and worse environmental outcomes, what new criteria should we use in making these value judgments?

I've begun working on a new book that explores this question through the particular lens of our interactions, both good and bad, with birds. The first installment was a piece on the demise of the passenger pigeon in *Harper's* magazine. Once the most numerous bird species on Earth, the passenger pigeon was driven to extinction a century ago by habitat loss and large-scale slaughter for urban meat markets. But the birds-and-people story does not end there, and it has some happier chapters, too.

Responses on the COVID-19 Pandemic

Since we conducted our original interview, the world has been wracked by the COVID-19 pandemic. Do you draw any general lessons from the COVID crisis about the most viable ways to advance an egalitarian economic project?

COVID's menace is worldwide but its impacts are highly unequal within and between countries. Within countries, low-income people and politically disenfranchised minorities have often experienced disproportionate harm, mirroring other dimensions of environmental injustice. Across countries, it is no coincidence that the death toll has been exceptionally high in nations with extreme inequality, like the United States and Brazil. This is not simply because those at the bottom of the wealth-and-power pyramids in these highly unequal societies are at greater risk. It also reflects the reality that their entire population is at greater risk due to extreme inequality's deadly effects on the society as a whole.

Among the ways that inequality puts whole societies at risk, three stand out. First, extreme inequality shreds social safety nets in general, and eviscerates public health services in particular, as the rich and powerful opt to cut taxes (on themselves) and slash government expenditures (on behalf of others). Compare, for instance, the public health system's very effective infrastructure for COVID contact tracing in places like South Korea to the abysmal situation here in the US. By the time this pandemic ends, it seems likely that the COVID death rate in the US will surpass Korea's by a factor of 100, if not more. In other words, 99 out of every 100 American lives lost could have been saved had comparable public health measures been in place.

Second, closely related to this debacle, is the indifference with which the wealthiest stratum in extremely unequal societies views the suffering experienced by others. In fact, in many cases they don't "view" it at all—they remain quite oblivious to it. Just as in normal times, when the rich can afford to live in less polluted neighborhoods in metropolitan areas, during the pandemic they have escaped to safer havens. In New York City, the population in the wealthiest neighborhoods went down more than 40 percent when COVID hit. Meanwhile, the city's low-income workers, many of whom were suddenly found to be "essential" (though not paid accordingly) had to keep riding the bus to work. At a time when "social distancing" has become a watchword for social responsibility, it is worth pausing to consider its darker side—when distance takes the form of a yawning gulf between social classes and not just six feet between individuals.

Third, extreme inequality stirs a toxic brew of fear, disinformation, and hate. In such an environment, we can see favorable conditions for the rise to power of demagogues whose desire for self-aggrandizement overrides any concern for the public good. We see this with Trump in the US and Bolsonaro in Brazil.

Inequality in a society is much like blood pressure in an individual: it's OK when in a normal range, but it can be deadly when elevated. Once the pandemic ends, the US and similarly unequal societies will remain at great risk of further health disasters unless they cure this pre-existing condition. This, I believe, is the most important lesson we should draw from the COVID crisis.

To advance the egalitarian project, there is much that can and should be done. Here in the US, implementing universal health care and providing free quality education for all children, supported by more robust taxes on the wealthy, would be important steps. But one thing the pandemic has revealed starkly is the deep mistrust with which many Americans regard their own government. The widespread aversion to wearing face masks and resistance to government "mandates" are not simply outgrowths of a hyper-individualistic culture. They also are a legacy of government by self-centered elites who all too often have turned a blind eye to the needs and struggles of working people.

This mistrust represents a formidable obstacle to public policies that would redress inequality. Whenever egalitarian policies are perceived as coming at the expense of individual liberty, they inevitably encounter determined resistance not only from the rich but from broad swaths of the American public as well. To escape this impasse, we must build on the strong complementarities that can be forged between egalitarian distributions of wealth and of power. The first is the foundation of a just economy. The second is the foundation of liberty. They can and must go together. It is vital to design and frame these egalitarian projects.

Representative Publications and Influences

Publications:
Elizabeth Hartman and James K. Boyce (1983). *A quiet violence: View from a Bangladesh village*. Zed Books.
James K. Boyce (2002). *The political economy of the environment*. Edward Elgar Publishing.
James K. Boyce (2019). *Economics for People and the Planet*. Anthem.

People who have been influential: Amartya Sen, Keith Griffin, Nripen Bandyopadhyay

Literature that has been influential:
Keith B. Griffin (1979). *The Political Economy of Agrarian Change*. Macmillan.
Amartya Sen (2000). *Development as Freedom*. Oxford University Press.
Frank Ackerman (2009). *Can We Afford the Future?* Zed Books.

Ha-Joon Chang

Ha-Joon Chang is University Reader in the Political Economy of Development at the University of Cambridge. He is the author of numerous works, including *Kicking Away the Ladder: Development Strategy in Historical Perspective* (2002) which won the European Association for Evolutionary Political Economy's 2003 Gunnar Myrdal Prize, *23 Things They Don't Tell You About Capitalism* (2010), and *Economics: The User's Guide* (2014). He was awarded the 2005 Wassily Leontief Prize for Advancing the Frontiers of Economic Thought from the Global Development and Environment Institute.

You were born in South Korea and attended Seoul National University. How did you come to study economics?

When I was a primary school kid in the 1970s, like most other Korean kids at the time, I wanted to become some kind of scientist—building spaceships, making robots, going around the world observing and protecting animals, you name it. After all, this was the time when most people believed that we were going to soon conquer the universe with the help of science.

As I grew up, I realized that I wasn't really cut out to be a scientist and found out that I loved history and politics. So, until I was fifteen or sixteen, I toyed with the idea of becoming a historian or studying international relations to become a diplomat (a very "exotic" job at the time, because foreign travel without government permission was banned in Korea until the late 1980s, in an attempt to conserve scarce foreign exchange).

When I was in the second year of high school, however, I learned this thing called comparative advantage. I was taught the Ricardian version of it in a subject we had that was called "Politics and Economics," which was a strange mixture of ideological propaganda justifying the military dictatorship of the time (euphemistically called "Korean-style democracy") and some basic economics. The idea of comparative advantage was so counter-intuitive—even if you are less efficient than everyone else in the world, you can still increase your income by specializing in activities in which you are the least bad at and trading with other countries—that got me interested in the subject of economics, which at the time was a rather esoteric subject in Korea, especially if you are a sixteen-year-old kid.

This is rather ironic, because I have spent a good chunk of my professional life showing the limitations of trade and industrial policies based on the theory of comparative advantage. However, I still think the idea of comparative advantage is one of the most original ideas in economics—it is absolutely correct in the short run, where everything (your technological capabilities, institutions, culture, and what not) can be taken as given; the problem begins when you try to use it to guide your long-term economic development, where everything can be, and often should be, changed.

There was also the encouragement from my father, who was then working in the Ministry of Finance, in charge of the Inland Revenue Bureau—he was only the deputy director of the bureau, but the director was an ex-army general who didn't know anything about taxes but was honest enough to admit that he didn't know anything (and left it to my father to run the place, while providing him with political protection). Like most other high-ranking officials in Korean economic ministries at the time, my father had studied law in university, but he taught himself quite a lot of economics for his work and even did a part-time PhD in it in his late thirties. He didn't push me in any particular direction in terms of my career choice, but he did tell me that this exotic subject called economics is quite useful.

However, he was very clear about the limits of the subject. If I translate what he told me in modern theoretical terms, he told me that the world is too complex and uncertain to be understood by abstract models with very simplistic assumptions and that tacit knowledge, which people accumulate through experiences, is often much more powerful than what you learn from abstract theories.

Once I got interested in economics, thanks to the idea of comparative advantage and to my father's encouragement, it was very easy to see how exciting and relevant economics is, given that the country I was living in was then going through one of the fastest economic transformations in human history (although I didn't realize its true significance until later, when I started doing my PhD at Cambridge).

Did politics have anything to do with your decision to pursue economics as a field of study?

I decided to study economics when I was in the second year of my (three-year) high school back in 1980, when I was sixteen. I wasn't precocious enough to have a "political view" at that age.

However, I was broadly to the left of center, although the very term "left" was considered seditious by the Korean military at the time, so I did not think in those terms. While I came from a privileged background (my father was a high-ranking civil servant, which meant financial security, although not necessarily affluence), my extended family was very anti-military and pro-democracy. I was also exposed to stories of labor repression, crushing poverty in rural areas, and the violent eviction of slum dwellers, which made me realize that all was not well in the "miracle" economy that we were supposed to be living in.

Also, my father's family came from a region (Cholla-do or Cholla Province), which was heavily discriminated against by the rest of the country at the time (it still is to an extent), so I was exposed to so many stories of people from the region, including my father and relatives, being unfairly rejected for a job application, denied marriage by their prospective partner's parents, passed over in promotion exercises, and so on. This sensitized me to the issues of discrimination and oppression, although, at that age, it was impossible for me to understand the socioeconomic roots of these things.

When I was in my first year in high school in 1979, a political earthquake shook the country, politically awakening me and my contemporaries. In October of that year, we were told that our president, General Park Chung Hee, had been assassinated by the chief of his secret police in the midst of waves of protests by students, workers, and the urban poor that had rocked the country for the previous few months. Park, having come to power in a military coup in 1961, had been the president of the country all my life (I was born in 1963), so for me and my friends, this was like being told that there will be no typhoons—something feared and disliked but that you accept as part of life—anymore. He had been, of course, the motor force behind the Korean economic "miracle," raising living standards to unprecedented levels, but his increasingly brutal rule and abuse of power, as well as the conditions of the greatly disadvantaged, were rapidly coming to be resented.

Park's assassination brought about a brief period of pro-democracy movements and social activism (the so-called Seoul Spring). However, it was dramatically ended in May 1980 when martial law was imposed by a military junta led by General Chun Do Hwan. When citizens of Gwangju (then the opposition stronghold and my father's home town) refused to accept martial law and went on demonstrations, the junta sent in paratroopers and massacred hundreds (some say thousands) of civilians. The new military junta told people that only dozens had died and that more or less all of them were North Korean spies or their sympathizers, but more and more people knew that this wasn't the case, thanks to rumor mills and underground pamphlets.

This massacre was, in the long run, the turning point in Korean history. General Park assassinated his political enemies, imprisoned political activists on the slightest excuses, and tortured many of them (sometimes to death), but his regime had never sent the army to kill civilians. Chun's junta did. This was simply unforgivable to everyone who knew about it.

By late 1981, students started agitating against the new military dicta-torship with renewed vigor, and the campuses were on fire when I entered the university as an economics undergraduate student in March 1982 (the Korean academic year starts on March 1). Some students hunkered down and studied for the High Civil Service Examination or to get the high GPAs that would get them into top American graduate schools. But for most of us, it was very difficult to pretend that things were all right. All our lectures were monitored by plainclothes police-men, in case the lecturer said anything seditious (that is, anything criti-cal of capitalism or military dictatorship). Throughout the campus, there were numerous clumps of plainclothes policemen hanging around, ready to spring into action to break up spontaneous student demonstrations and beat up and arrest those students that they could get their hands on. When the plainclothes cops were not enough to stop a demonstration, riot police in full gear would move onto campuses shooting tear gas and wielding their truncheons.

In that kind of environment, it was not possible for any student with a critical mind to take our professors seriously. Most of them were teaching us neoclassical economics, which postulates that the economy is always in equilibrium and, should any external shock knock it off equilibrium, it will return to equilibrium sooner or later, with no accompanying social conflicts, through the workings of the "invisible hand" of the market mechanism. They also taught us that (neoclassical) economics is a science, one in which politics has no role to play. You just couldn't reconcile these views with what was going on around us—huge economic transformations upending everything good and bad about our traditional economy and society, workers striking in protest against the world's longest working hours and appalling working conditions, police beating up slum-dwellers so that they could be evicted for property developers, the army massacring people in the name of defending capitalism and "free" society, and the very visible police presence on campus and especially in the lecture rooms.

Many of my friends joined underground student movements in the hope of changing the country's economic and political systems, many of them with explicit socialist goals. However, even many of those who did not join those movements, like myself, taught ourselves "heterodox" economics, especially, although not exclusively, Marxist economics and dependency theory. These theories are very conscious of the inseparability of economics and politics, so we naturally got to develop a view of "economics as a political subject," which is actually the title of a lecture series that I am teaching for the first-year undergraduate students at Cambridge these days.

How did you end up going to Cambridge University for your graduate studies? What was your experience like at Cambridge in comparison to that at Seoul National University?

My choice to come to Cambridge to study was considered very unusual in Korea at the time (I joined Cambridge as a post-graduate student in

1986). As Korea had (and still has) very strong ties with the US, most people went to the US to study.

Many people have asked me, then and later, "Why England?", but I didn't choose to go to England. I wanted to go and study at Cambridge, because it was the best place at the time where I could study what I wanted.

I've said that I was totally disillusioned with neoclassical economics during my undergraduate days, although I got good marks in my courses. So I wanted to study non-neoclassical economics. In addition to Cambridge, I actually applied to several graduate schools in the US where they had some (usually one or two) non-neoclassical economists. I got admitted into some of them, but when I was accepted at Cambridge I jumped at it, because it was the place with the strongest and the largest line-up of teachers who specialized in what I wanted to study—development economics. There were Ajit Singh, John Sender, Peter Nolan, and Gabriel Palma. In contrast, very few non-neoclassical economists in the US schools I was admitted to were development economists. There was no contest.

Going to Cambridge was a huge adventure for me in every sense of the word, in every way. First of all, back in 1986, getting to England from South Korea was a major expedition. It was during the Cold War, so a South Korean plane could not fly over China or the USSR. This meant that you had to go over the North Pole, via Anchorage in Alaska. So, nine hours from Seoul to Anchorage, a couple of hours' stop for refueling, and then another nine hours to Paris, where I had to wait for three hours for my flight to London. So, it took me twenty-four hours to get from Gimpo Airport in Seoul (this was years before the larger Incheon airport) to London Heathrow. Door-to-door, we are talking thirty hours. This would have been hard for a seasoned traveler, but it was my first long-haul flight.

Second, my trip to England was the first time ever that I was outside Korea. These days, by the age of twenty-two (as I was then), many Koreans will have traveled easily to a dozen countries and some of them will have lived in one or two of them. Until the late 1980s, it was impossible for Koreans to travel abroad (they wouldn't be issued a passport) unless you had government permission, which was given only when you had "big" reasons, like studying abroad or going on a business trip for a government-approved company. Having to live in a foreign country without having ever been to one was, to put it mildly, challenging.

Third, I had done well enough in English language tests like TOEFL (for the US) and ELTS (for the UK) to get admissions from top universities, but my English was still dodgy, which, as you can imagine, is a bit of a problem in England. My reading was good, but for some complicated texts I could spend half an hour to go through a page. My writing was decent, but it took me a long time to write. My spoken English was still rather poor and, moreover, most of the spoken English I had been exposed to had been the American version, not the British one. I attended a language school for four weeks before the start of my graduate program, which helped, but one can expect only so much from a four-week program.

Fourth, the way things were taught in Cambridge was very different from what we had in Korea then. In Cambridge, we were constantly made to write essays and, more importantly, express our opinions, often against "authorities." In Korea, we had the idea that for every question there is one correct answer. It was difficult to get used to this new way of thinking. The Korean way of teaching was not due to its "hierarchical" culture, as many people (including Koreans) assume—after all, the country is famous for dissident politics. However, our teaching culture— teaching by rote—had been shaped by the country's drive to expand education with meager resources. (Is there another way to teach than by rote when you have 100, even 120, kids in one classroom?) Even at the university level, where at least some professors wanted to encourage independent thinking, the lack of resources meant that they simply could not put their educational philosophy into practice. My macroeconomics course had 700 students. I was one of the more eager ones, but I got to ask one or two questions in the fifty or so hours of lectures we had. Few courses, except the more specialized ones, say, with thirty or forty students, offered by smaller departments, like sociology, involved any essay writing. In the whole of my four years at Seoul National University, I had written two or three essays. In Cambridge, I was made to write one almost every week.

I had a new country to get used to. I had to learn and think in a different way, and my dodgy English meant that I had to spend a lot of time simply absorbing the necessary information and presenting what I knew. I guess I survived basically by working twice as hard as the other students.

At Cambridge, you worked with the well-known leftist economist Bob Rowthorn. Can you tell me a bit about that collaboration and what influence it had on your overall thinking about economics?

Bob was my PhD supervisor and I owe him a huge debt. Bob has a very interesting background. He was a mathematics major as an undergraduate at Oxford and did graduate study in math and philosophy at UC Berkeley. There he got interested in economics and came back to the UK to do some graduate work in economics (but he never got a PhD—professors not having a PhD were quite common in the UK until the 1980s). He was originally trained in neoclassical economics by John Hicks, but a few years after he started teaching in Cambridge he became a Marxist. Between the late 1960s and the early 1980s, he was one of the world's leading Marxist economists. By the time I arrived at Cambridge in 1986, he had moved away from Marxism and was beginning to pursue other theories—institutional economics and evolutionary economics, in particular.

What I really appreciate about Bob's teaching is that he never pushed me in any direction. He had a strong Marxist background, but he never made me do Marxist economics. He introduced me to a wide range of economic theories—neoclassical, Marxist, institutionalist, Austrian, behavioralist, and developmentalist theories. And he let me combine these theories as I saw fit, because he believed that my PhD topic—the political economy of industrial policy—needed a combination of different theories. He never made me do any mathematical modeling despite himself being a first-rate mathematician—legend has it that he once quipped to Frank Hahn, the famous general equilibrium economist who co-authored with Kenneth Arrow, "Shut up, Frank, I have forgotten more math than what you know," when Hahn tried to pick faults with Bob's math in a seminar. His view was that my PhD required analyses of history, politics, and institutions, rather than abstract mathematical modeling. Of course, while he was letting me do this, he was supervising other students using all sorts of different approaches—one of my contemporaries was doing a dissertation on the most esoteric Marxist labor theory of value, another was doing a neoclassical modeling of wage bargaining, while yet another was doing an institutionalist analysis of macroeconomic policy and economic development in Scandinavia.

Bob's view was (and still is) that the nature of the theories and the analytical tools (for example, mathematical modeling, historical analysis, political economy) that you should use should be determined by the questions you ask. This was markedly different from the approach of most other economists, across the political spectrum, who try to apply the theoretical framework and analytical tools that they think are best to all problems.

I don't have any set idea about what is the best theory. What is the best theory depends on what problem you are analyzing—for an analysis of the electricity market, neoclassical economics would be the best, but that theory is not very good for, say, the analysis of long-term structural transformation of developing countries. The best analytical tool will be also determined by the questions you are asking. For example, I didn't need to use mathematical modeling or econometrics in writing the book *Kicking Away the Ladder*, which exposed the historical hypocrisy of the rich countries in preaching free-trade and free-market policies to developing countries, despite the fact that they themselves used protectionism, subsidies, regulation of foreign direct investments, and state-owned enterprises. However, recently I have co-authored a paper trying to identify ideological biases among economists that use randomized controlled experiments (done through an online survey), mathematical modeling, and econometrics (I must admit that most of the technical work has been done by my co-author).

This methodological pluralism is Bob's greatest lesson for me, although he has taught me so much in terms of substantive issues—theories of the state, theories of institution, the role of power and conflict in the economy, industrialization and de-industrialization, you name it.

To what extent has your work been influenced by Marxian and Keynesian perspectives, among Cambridge economists and beyond?

As I mentioned earlier, I have been heavily influenced by Marxist economics. I read various types of it as an undergraduate student in Korea. Bob taught me not only the more intricate aspects of Marxist theories but also how Marxist theories relate to other schools of economics—the Austrian, the Schumpterian, and the institutionalist schools. I also read a lot of Marxist literature on my own.

This is obviously a massive simplification, but I think Marx is arguably the economist who understood capitalism in the most sophisticated way. He was the first one who systematically introduced innovation and technological progress (although he did not use those terms) into economic analysis. He understood that different factions of capital (industrial, merchant, finance) are often in conflict with each other and that the balance of power between them determines the path of economic development as well as income distribution. He was the first economist who understood the importance of the role of the state in the economy, not simply as an entity that fills the gaps left by the market (the "market failure" approach of neoclassical economics) but as an entity that creates and shapes markets by influencing property rights, capital–labor relations, and the conflicts between different factions of capital. He was one of the few economists who first pointed out the importance of the firm as an institution (in contrast to many other schools of economics, including the neoclassical one, which focus on markets). He is the first one who understood the power of limited liability companies (or joint stock companies, as they were called in his days), which until then the free-market economists, including Adam Smith, denounced for their ability to create "moral hazard" (in modern terms) by allowing professional managers to take risks with "other people's money" (Smith's expression). Marx also put emphasis on labor issues, which get almost totally ignored by other schools—working hours, working conditions, trade unions, and most importantly the key role of work in shaping human beings.

Of course, Marx had this teleological view that capitalism will collapse under its own weight, hastened by the increasingly class-conscious working-class movement, so some of his analyses—and those of his followers—were often seeing things that are not there—the imminent collapse of the world capitalist system, the inevitable advent of workers' revolution, and the scientific inevitability of all these, proven by Marxist economics.

Also, Marx's view of socialism was, at best, sketchy, and the subsequent developments of the theory and the practice of socialism were too much influenced by the difficulties of developing a sophisticated planned economy in the Soviet Union, which was economically very backward at the time, on the one hand, and influenced by the political dogmatism of the Stalinist era, on the other hand.

The most regrettable thing about Marxist economics is that, despite some notable exceptions (such as Bob Rowthorn, Andrew Glyn, Geoff Hodgson, and Harry Braverman, to name a few), it did not develop very much the most original elements in Marxist theory that I mentioned above (regarding institutions, the firm, technology, labor) and got stuck in the more esoteric aspects of the labor theory of value and crisis theory, making it far less relevant for the analysis of real-world problems than it could have been.

As for Keynesian economics, Cambridge is of course where it originated and where it was dominant until the early 1980s, but I am afraid I have not been very much influenced by it. It is not that I disagree with it, but I work on topics in which Keynesian economics has little to say (such as long-term economic development, industrialization, and technological changes), so I haven't really used it very much. The only exception is the work I have done on the 1997 Asian financial crisis and the 2008 global financial crisis, where I extensively draw on Keynesian economics, but this is a relatively small part of my work, so it is not significant in the bigger scheme of things.

What other economists have influenced you significantly?

I often say that three economists have influenced me the most—Karl Marx on the left, Friedrich von Hayek on the right, and Herbert Simon in the middle (or perhaps to the left of the middle). This is not idle chatter. I refer to them in my work all the time and make sure that all my PhD students read all three of them.

People find it difficult to understand that a left-leaning person like myself can take Hayek seriously. However, he is a very profound economist, although in the end I violently disagree with him.

These days, Hayek is considered an eccentric European version of Milton Friedman, but Hayek's theory—that is, Austrian economics—is very different from Friedman's neoclassical theory. Indeed, Hayek is very abusive about certain aspects of neoclassical economics, especially its theories of competition and information, as you can see in his 1944 *American Economic Review* article.

Unlike the neoclassicals, the Austrians see the world as very complex and uncertain and individuals as highly limited in their rationality—in that sense, their world view is closer to the Keynesian, the behavioralist, and the institutionalist ones than to the neoclassical one. The Austrian defense of the free market is therefore based on the limits to rational planning—by any individual, and not just by the state—whereas the neoclassical one is based on the very possibility of rational planning, albeit only by individuals (with the individual firm being treated as a monolith). I find the Austrian justification of the free market far more convincing than the neoclassical one.

I have learned a lot from reading Hayek, but in the end I totally disagree with him.

Ethically and politically, I cannot accept his priorities. For him, the "liberty" to use one's property freely is the most important thing and therefore everything else—democracy and freedom from repression included—can be sacrificed for it, which is why he openly supported Pinochet's military dictatorship in Chile.

Also, theoretically, his vision is more fit for the nineteenth century, rather than the twenty-first. Hayek's biggest point is that, given the complexity of the world and the limited rationality of human beings, the only way to run a complex economy is through the "spontaneous order" of the market. However, he does not realize that today's economy is full of "constructed orders" and, more importantly, will collapse without them. The most obvious of these constructed orders is the government, Hayek's bugbear. In some countries, 55 to 60 percent of GDP goes through the government—whether in the form of consumption, investment, or transfers (through the welfare state). In almost all countries, the government is the biggest employer—in some countries, it could employ up to 25 percent of the labor force, whereas even the biggest private-sector employer (such as Walmart or Tesco) employs only around 1 to 1.5 percent of the labor force. Moreover, today's economy is dominated by huge firms spanning the globe that use planning rather than voluntary exchanges to run themselves. It is estimated that, these days, at least a third and possibly one-half of "international" trade is transferred within the same firm; a Toyota factory in Thailand "exporting" car engines to an assembly plant in, say, Mexico in quantities and at "prices" fixed by the Toyota headquarters in Japan. Given these realities, Hayek's view that we should run things through the spontaneous order of the market is a couple of centuries out of date.

Another big influence on me is Herbert Simon, the father of the behavioralist school (although what passes for behavioral economics these days is often "neoclassified"—and shallower—versions of Simon's theory). His theory of "bounded rationality" is arguably the most underrated theory in the history of economics. He may not be the only one who said that the world is complex and uncertain and that the rationality of individuals is limited, or "bounded" in his terms (Veblen, Hayek, and Keynes, just to name a few, said the same), but he built the most systematic theory showing why our bounded rationality in a complex and uncertain world makes it necessary for us to build personal habits, organizational routines, socio-economic institutions, and economic systems.

Simon's influence on me may not be as obvious as the influences of Marx or Hayek in my work, but it is no less important. It has really shaped the way I see the world. If I hadn't read Simon, I may have gone only so far as acknowledging the complexity and the uncertainty of the world, as described by, say Keynes or Hayek. However, because I have read him, I also understand that despite—or, rather, because of—this complexity and uncertainty, we do things to shape the world we live in—building new institutions, creating new organizations, and improving our economic systems. Of course, by definition due to our bounded rationality, the results of these actions are imperfect, but it is a fantasy to think, like the Austrians do, that we can do away with these things. Also, Simon's theory lets me appreciate human agency. If we are perfectly rational, as in neoclassical or Marxist theories, there isn't any agency in our action—either we are carriers of some inevitable historical forces (as in Marxism) or translators of structural constraints, only mediated by differences in our taste—orange over apples, Samsung over Apple (as in neoclassical economics). It is only because Simon's theory lets me see how "imperfect" we are that I can appreciate the choices people make—in apparent contradiction to their "objective" material interests that any rational human being should be able to calculate.

A lot of your work has been on developing ideas around industrial policy. How did you come to focus on industrial policy as a research topic? What have been the major questions you have examined in this area?

My initial research started with a rather naïve desire to understand how South Korea, my own country, could achieve an economic "miracle" despite not following either of the two dominant economic models of the time—American-style free-market capitalism or Soviet-style central planning.

Until the mid-1980s, the dominant view was that Korea (and other East Asian "miracle" economies, such as Taiwan and Singapore) had achieved its "miracle" thanks to (almost) free-trade and free-market policies. The interesting thing is that this interpretation was accepted across the political spectrum, from the free-market economists associated with the World Bank peddling Korea and Taiwan as models for other developing countries, on the right, to the dependency theorists who condemned those countries for being the worst cases of untrammeled capitalism built on serving transnational corporations with hyper-exploited labor, on the left.

From my personal experience and from what I knew about other East Asian countries, I knew that this was total nonsense. Their governments practiced planning, although of the "indicative" rather than the "directive" (Soviet-style) ones. These governments decided which industries got credits on what terms, based on their long-term plans for the national economy and individual industrial sectors, using state-owned banks and strict regulations over private-sector banks. They protected their "infant" industries with high tariffs, quotas, import bans, prohibitive inland taxes (for luxury consumption items), and most importantly total government control over foreign exchange. They had draconian capital controls—you could be hanged for shipping out large sums of money without government permission in Korea, and financial investments by foreigners were virtually banned, while all the East Asian countries had strict controls and conditionalities for foreign direct investors. The "free market" interpretations were fantasies created by economists, both from the right and from the left, who wanted to point to real countries that "prove" their theories.

So I decided to look at the aspect of East Asian economic policy that was most different from those practiced in other countries—that is, industrial policy, which I define as government intervention at the level of industrial sectors but with a view to changing the overall structure and efficiency of the economy in the long run.

During my PhD and my early career as a researcher-cum-teacher in the late 1980s and the early 1990s, there was an upsurge of interest in industrial policy, especially in the context of the increasingly heated debate on the East Asian "miracle." Chalmers Johnson, Alice Amsden, Robert Wade, and Sanjaya Lall were the main names on "my" side, providing evidence that discredited the then dominant interpretation of the East Asian "miracle" as a result of "free market, free trade" policies. Their works were more empirical than theoretical, so I devoted most of my early research on developing a theoretical understanding of East Asian industrial policies.

Subsequently, my research on industrial policy was generalized in many directions. One important strand was to examine the history of economic development in today's rich countries in Europe and North America, which showed that actually these countries used East Asian–style industrial policies in their days as catch-up economies. This result was published in *Kicking Away the Ladder* in 2002. The work countered the then dominant message from the mainstream economists that "all countries, with possible exceptions of a few East Asian countries, with unique cultural and historical conditions, have developed on the basis of free-market, free-trade policies," thereby helping developing country policy-makers overcome their fear that, in contemplating unorthodox interventionist policies, they may be running against the tide of human history. My work, I am told, also helped them stand their ground in the WTO negotiations by exposing the double standards of the rich countries in imposing on developing countries economic policies that they themselves had never practiced.

Another important extension of my work on industrial policy has been to broaden and deepen the theoretical horizons of industrial policy. I have broadened it by using more varieties of economic theories than I had initially used, in order to understand industrial policy better. I have deepened my work by, first, exploring the nature and the evolution of productive capabilities, the building of which is central to success in industrial policy; second, by exploring the relationships between policy goals, policy tools, and the policy environment (especially in relation to national politics and international policy regimes).

The third extension has been to further explore the political, institutional, and organizational requirements of successful industrial policy. These requirements were of course discussed by many people in the debate on the East Asian miracle, but most people have taken them as given (usually to argue that the East Asian policies cannot be replicated in other countries with different political, institutional, and organizational conditions). I have tried to explore exactly why certain political, institutional, and organizational conditions contribute (or not) to the success of industrial policy and, more importantly, how policy-makers can actively change those conditions so that they can use certain types of policy. Of course, I fully recognize that these conditions are not always subject to change, especially in the short run, but I show how they can be—and have been—changed significantly, with sufficient political will, resource investments, and organizational reforms.

In 2010, you published a popular book called 23 Things They Don't Tell You About Capitalism. *Who is the "they" of the title? And why don't "they" want to tell us those "23 things"?*

"They" are of course necessarily vague, but by that I mean what is often called the "establishment"—most, although not all, of the moneyed class, the political elite, the top economists, and the leading financial journalists.

These are people who have an interest in preserving the socio-economic order that has enriched them and given them more power since the 1980s—that is, the neoliberal economic order, based on deregulation, privatization of state-owned enterprises, trade liberalization, and the liberalization of international capital flows (both financial investment and foreign direct investment). This socio-economic order is based on (and is justified in terms of) a strong belief in the power of the market to generate efficiency and innovation, and in the negative consequences of any "collectivist" interventions (by the government, by communities, or by nonprofit organizations) in the workings of the "natural" order of the market.

It is well known that, compared to the regime of the "mixed economy" between the end of World War II and the 1970s (which had higher taxes, stricter regulations, and greater restrictions on internal flows of goods and capital), this regime has increased inequality, increased the rate of unemployment, made jobs more insecure, and lowered the quality of jobs. However, it is less well known that it has actually slowed down economic growth significantly. The world economy, in per capita terms, used to grow at around 2.6 to 2.8 percent during the era of the "mixed economy" (or what some people call the "Golden Age" of capitalism), but, at 1.4 to 1.5 percent, it has grown at half that rate during the neoliberal era. This is quite an embarrassing record for a regime that has prided itself for its "growth machismo"—it may be weak on "soft" things like inequality and unemployment, as its supporters have argued, but the regime certainly does not deliver on growth—but it is not very well known, partly because neoliberal propaganda has been so successful.

Despite this poor record, many people accept the neoliberal order because they think that the economic system that we have today is, even though they don't like it, the best we can get. This "fatalism" exists at least partly because people have been led to believe that things are the way they are because they have to be (information technology, the increasing importance of services, Chinese competition, and what have you) and that there really are no credible alternatives.

I believe that breaking this pessimism among the opponents of neoliberalism is vital in challenging the neoliberal world order, so I wrote the book (and my 2014 book, *Economics: The User's Guide*) in order to encourage ordinary citizens to reject the myths propagated by the neoliberals and to challenge the dominant socio-economic order. You, as a democratic citizen, have to learn some economics if you are to challenge the political and corporate elite (and those economists who act as cheerleaders for them) when they say that there is nothing negative about rising inequality, that the CEOs earn $50 million because they have high productivity, that austerity is the right policy for the UK or Greece, or that the smaller the government is the better it is for the economy. If we are going to have a world in which ordinary citizens can have influence on how things are done through democratic processes, we need a citizenry that can speak (perhaps not with equal fluency) the language of the rulers, that is, economics.

Much of your recent work revolves around an effort to oppose austerity policies that became dominant in most of the Eurozone following the 2007–09 global financial crisis. What exactly are the main problems with austerity economics, generally and within the Eurozone in particular? Why, in your view, have policy-makers embraced austerity as a dominant policy framework?

Those who have supported austerity—more recently in the Eurozone and in the UK, but also in developing countries under IMF-World Bank Structural Adjustment Programs (SAPs)—base their argument on a simple but intuitively powerful idea—that is, you should not spend money that you do not have, or in other words, you should not live beyond your means. So, if a government runs a deficit, it should naturally cut its spending.

The idea that you should not live beyond your means may seem like such an obvious dictum that makes perfect economic and moral sense, but it is a very backward idea. It may make more sense for individuals, as spending beyond your means can lead to personal bankruptcy, but even for them, it is not true. When we are young, we typically borrow money to invest in education, acquire skills through training, or buy a house to have a more stable everyday life that will increase our productivity at work. When we make these investments, we can actually increase our earning power, so actually spending the money that you don't have today can mean that you actually have as much (or even more) money later, as your earning power will have increased. The same goes for companies. A company that "lives beyond its means" by borrowing to invest in the short run, only to generate more revenue and more profit in the future, may be taking a more productive course of action than another that refuses to borrow and invests only with money that it already has.

So, even for individuals and companies, "living within one's means" is a very passive, unproductive idea. However, if it is applied to the government, the idea that one should always live within one's means can become positively toxic.

First of all, it goes without saying that what I have just said about investments by individuals applies to the government, too. Governments running deficits to invest in things that will increase the economy's productivity in the long run (for example, transport infrastructure, "green" energy generation, R&D, and education) is a sensible thing to do, even if it means a larger budget deficit today.

But, second, and more specifically in regard to the case of government income and spending, we cannot treat the government in the same way we treat individuals. The problem is that one person's expenditure is another's income, so if, in an economic downturn, some individuals— say, workers who have lost their jobs—cut their spending, the income of the bakeries and the drugstores that they used to buy from will fall. This may prompt those bakers and drugstore owners to cut their expenditures, forcing the flour mills, which used to sell flour to the bakers, and the pharmaceutical companies, which used to supply the drugstores, to cut their expenditures. Then it will hit the farmers who used to sell wheat to the flour mill and the chemical companies that used to sell ingredients for medicines to the pharmaceutical company. And the process continues, creating a downward spiral in the economy. In this situation, the only one who can halt the downward spiral is the government, which, unlike individuals or companies, can spend more than its income without having to worry about going bankrupt (of course, countries without hard currencies that have borrowed too much from abroad may more easily go "bankrupt," but that is another story). If the government halts and reverses the economic downturn by deficit spending, it may actually be better for the government to "live beyond its means." If the deficit spending is invested in raising productivity in the future, it may be even better.

The austerity policies that we have seen first in the IMF Structural Adjustment Programs forced upon the developing countries in the 1980s and the 1990s, and then in the weaker Eurozone economies after the 2008 global financial crisis, have done the exact opposite of what should be done in an economic downturn. In the Eurozone crisis, the austerity policy forced the governments of Greece, Spain, and Portugal to spend drastically less in the middle of a massive economic downturn, during which private-sector agents—firms and individuals—were cutting their spending. These cuts made the economy shrink. This, in turn, meant that even while the government was cutting spending, their budget deficits as a proportion of GDP hardly fell—or even rose. This was because the numerator (the budget deficit) was not shrinking or even rising (because, even while government spending was falling, government tax revenue was also falling due to the fall in GDP) while the denominator (GDP) was getting smaller, due to the negative effect of austerity on GDP.

The broader point is that government should generate revenues (through taxes, through dividends from state-owned enterprises or by borrowing) and spend them for the benefit of the society, not for itself. Its actions should be judged in terms of their impacts on the whole economy, not its own finances. There is no inherent virtue in a government running a budget surplus (or deficit). Unfortunately, in the neoliberal age (as in the pre-Keynesian age), "sound finance" has become a virtue—or even "the" virtue—that a government should pursue, with devastating consequences, as we have seen in the SAPs and the Eurozone crisis.

What do you perceive your role to be as an economist?

I see my role at a number of levels. First of all, I am a researcher. Like all other research-active economists, I try to give answers to questions that I think are interesting and, moreover, useful in promoting new knowledge. However, I take it as my task, as a pluralist economist, to do my research in a way that respects different traditions in economics and, when possible, combines and synthesizes their insights.

Second, I am a teacher. These days in the economics profession—and in much of academia—teaching is extremely undervalued. Your worth as an economist is valued almost exclusively by your research output—more specifically how many articles you publish in the "top" (four or five) journals (all of neoclassical persuasion). If you invest time in teaching, people think there is something wrong with you. They think that you do so because you cannot do serious research and therefore have a lot of spare time on your hands. In the last several years, I have intensified my teaching at the PhD level. At any given point of time, I have around ten PhD students. It is hard work but most rewarding, because they are the ones who are likely to carry my ideas and improve on them in the future. Also, in the last several years, I have worked with the international student movement, Rethinking Economics, to campaign for the reform in the teaching of economics in a more pluralistic, interdisciplinary, and real-world-oriented direction.

Third, I see it as my duty to engage with those who "run" real-world economies. I am not saying that every economist should be engaged with the real world. Some economics research simply isn't directly relevant for real-world actors and organizations. However, insofar as you are doing work that has direct relevance for the real world, I think it is your duty as an economist to engage with people making decisions and taking actions in governments, international organizations, NGOs, corporations (both private sector and public sector), and trade unions. Through my engagements with these "real-world" people, I have learned how deficient the academic economist's knowledge is of how the economy works. I have done my best to incorporate the knowledge possessed by real-world people, which many academic economists regard as somehow inferior, but which I regard as simply different forms of knowledge. In engaging with real-world people, I have also improved my skills in distilling knowledge to its essence (since they don't have years to think about particular problems) and in communicating with them better (they haven't got the luxury to listen to and think about one thing for a long time).

Fourth, I have seen it as my duty to engage with the general public. In the last couple of decades, I have written for and been interviewed by over a hundred news media in dozens of countries. I have written three mass market books, *Bad Samaritans*, *23 Things They Don't Tell You About Capitalism*, and *Economics: The User's Guide*, which collectively have been translated into forty-one languages in forty-four countries (and counting) and sold nearly 2 million copies. I do this because I believe, as I have pointed out earlier, that it is vital that the general public understands economic issues (and some of the theories behind them) if we are going to have a meaningful democracy.

What direction do you foresee for your research agenda in the years ahead?

There are a couple of broad research areas I have been working on for the last few decades. And I plan to deepen my research in these areas.

The first such area is what I call the ITT policies—industrial, trade, and technology policies. I have done a lot of work on this topic, publishing several books and dozens of articles, over a wide range of topics, ranging from infant industry protection and government support for R&D to intellectual property rights and the World Trade Organization. Even so, I will keep working in this area, as things are changing and evolving all the time, with new technologies, trade patterns, national policies, and international agreements on trade and investment.

There are mainly two new directions that I am taking in this area. One is digging deeper to understand the nature of productive capabilities, whose enhancement is after all the key goal of ITT policies. By better understanding how production is organized in the real world, and how different types of production and different types of government policies shape the development of productive capabilities differently, we can understand ITT policies better. Another new direction is to incorporate more recent changes in the real-world economy in the analysis of ITT policies—the spread of the so-called global value chain, the so-called Fourth Industrial Revolution (whose very existence I doubt, but there are certainly new technological trends that deserve closer attention), the (alleged) rise of the so-called post-industrial knowledge economy, and the changes in the global regime for international trade and investments.

The second area of my usual research is that of the role of institutions and politics in economics. I have developed what I call the Institutional Political Economy framework (most clearly set out in my 2002 *Cambridge Journal of Economics* article, "Breaking the Mould") and applied it (without usually blowing my own trumpet about the IPE framework) to a range of issues—from the institutional foundations of the market to the political economy of industrial policy in particular countries (Korea, Taiwan, South Africa, and Ethiopia, to name a few). I also intend to develop further my theory of power in economics and the theory of the political nature of economics (despite the insistence by mainstream neoclassical economics that it is a "value-free" science).

There is one area of research that I haven't done much work on so far but am slowly moving into. It is the issue of inequality. With younger colleagues who have stronger backgrounds in this area, I am incubating a couple of projects that try to understand inequality dynamics better by looking at changing patterns of economic activities (for example, industrialization, de-industrialization, outsourcing), by building better theories of politics and institutional changes surrounding different patterns of inequality across countries, and by engaging in more systematic international comparisons of different politico-economic regimes of inequality.

Responses on the COVID-19 Pandemic

How would you evaluate the ways different countries or regions have responded to the COVID-19 crisis, both in terms of public health interventions and economic policies?

The management of the pandemic has been quite different across countries. The contrast between the "West" and East Asia has been remarkable. According to the Johns Hopkins database as of December 26, 2020, deaths due to COVID-19 per 100,000 people were 167 in Belgium, 118 in Italy, 105 in the UK, 101 in the US, and 93 in France, but only 2 in

Japan, 1.5 in South Korea, 0.5 in Singapore, 0.3 in China, and 0.03 in Taiwan.

Some people have tried to attribute these differences to the culture of "obedience" in East Asia and/or political repression in the case of China. However, this is a false argument. First of all, many East Asian countries have a very disobedient citizenry—in particular, South Korea has forced four presidents out of power (through abdication, assassination, and impeachment) through citizen protest and put no fewer than four presidents in jail in its seventy-plus years of existence. Second, there are "Western" countries that have had very low COVID-19 deaths—deaths per 100,000 are 10 in Finland, 8 in Norway, 4 in Australia, and 0.5 in New Zealand.

In my view, the difference between these countries has been mainly created by hubris (or the absence of it). Countries that have "ruled the world" at one point and had a false sense of superiority and invulnerability did not take the pandemic seriously and failed to take early action against it. Once you lose your grip on the pandemic, you end up with a "trade-off" between health and the economy, which is totally avoidable if you take an early action and repress the disease early on.

Another important thing to note is that a lot of developing countries have performed much better than many of the rich countries in terms of pandemic management. Deaths per 100,000 are 8.5 in the Philippines, 7.5 in Egypt, 6.5 in Nepal, 4 in Uruguay, 3 in Kenya, 0.09 in Thailand, and 0.04 in Vietnam.

Part of this must be due to the relative youth of the population in the developing countries and in some (but not all) cases climate (making outdoor activities easier). Some people have tried to dismiss this difference by saying that most, if not all, developing countries have poor statistical services and nondemocratic regimes. I have insufficient basis to assess this claim regarding individual countries, but it is totally implausible to argue that death statistics in Vietnam are deliberately under-reported by a magnitude of 2,500 times, which would be necessary for Vietnam to have the same death rate as the US. This is totally implausible. Unfortunately, countries like the UK and the US are very reluctant to face these stark facts.

Of course, given the limited fiscal space they have and especially given the weakness (or even absence) of welfare states, citizens of the poorer countries suffered more from the same degree of restrictions on economic activities. But by taking early action and being innovative about the management of the test, trace, and isolate system, many developing countries have come out of this pandemic much better than the rich countries.

This experience is going to change the way different countries perceive themselves and each other in subtle but important ways in the coming years.

Do you draw any general lessons from the COVID crisis about the most viable ways to advance an egalitarian economic project?

The COVID-19 crisis has reminded us that no one is truly safe unless everyone is safe. In countries where there is no provision for a minimum standard of living and/or job security, a lot of people had to go out and work even when they knew they were infected. In countries that have failed to control the disease early on, the clamp-down on economic activities had much more negative impacts on the poor and the precariously employed if the welfare state was smaller and labor rights weaker. As a result, there is a growing recognition that the welfare state and labor rights need to be strengthened.

On top of that, the crisis has reminded us of the importance of the care economy, or the reproductive economy. In many countries, those who work in the care economy—health care workers, those who work in the education sector, workers in care homes, those who work in shops selling the essentials (especially food), and delivery workers—were given recognition as "key workers" (the UK) or "essential employees" (the US). The crisis has also made a lot of people realize the importance of the household work and care work that women perform at home. However, all these workers in the care economy, except for medical doctors, are poorly paid (unpaid in the case of household work), and they work under difficult and precarious conditions.

Despite the recognition of the "essentialness" of the work performed by these workers, there have so far been few steps taken to improve their wages and working conditions. However, there are moves, both by the people and by some governments, to improve them and I think these moves are going to form a very important part in our attempt to build a more egalitarian society.

Does the experience of the COVID crisis shed any light on the way you think about economics as a discipline or, more specifically, the questions you might be pursuing in your own research?

I have come to take the care economy more seriously, but my thoughts are still evolving on this.

Representative Publications and Influences

Publications:

Ha-Joon Chang (1994). *The political economy of industrial policy*. St. Martin's Press.

Ha-Joon Chang (2002). *Kicking away the ladder: Development strategy in historical perspective*. Anthem.

Ha-Joon Chang (2008). *Bad samaritans: The myth of free trade and the secret history of capitalism*. Bloomsbury Press.

People who have been influential: Bob Rowthorn, Karl Marx, Friedrich Hayek, Herbert Simon

Literature that has been influential:

Robert Rowthorn (1975). What Remains of Kaldor's Law? *The Economic Journal*, 85(337), 10.

Robert Rowthorn (1977). Conflict, inflation and money. *Cambridge Journal of Economics*, 1(3), 215–239.

Robert Rothorn (1980). *Capitalism, conflict and inflation*. Lawrence & Wishart London.

Jane D'Arista

Jane D'Arista is a research associate at the Political Economy Research Institute at the University of Massachusetts Amherst. She is an expert on monetary policy, financial regulation, and issues of international finance. Previously, D'Arista served as a staff economist for the Banking and Commerce Committees of the US House of Representatives and as a principal analyst in the international division of the Congressional Budget Office, and has lectured in graduate programs at Boston University School of Law, the University of Massachusetts Amherst, the University of Utah, and the New School for Social Research. Her economics publications include *The Evolution of US Finance* (two volumes) (2009), *All Fall Down* (2019), and numerous articles. She published a book of her poems, *The Overgrown Copse*, in 2014, and a book of her poems with drawings by Sigrid Miller Pollin, *Erratic Boundaries*, in 2020.

Can you please tell me something about your personal background?

I was born in Jacksonville, Florida, to parents whose families came from Georgia and the Carolinas. I left home to attend Barnard College in New York, met and married Robert D'Arista, and traveled with him the following year to Florence, Italy, on his Fulbright Fellowship. On our return, we lived in New York until, after another residence in Italy, we moved to Washington, DC, where he began teaching painting at the American University, I began working for the US Congress, and we raised our four children. In 1986 we both took teaching positions at Boston University and, after his death in 1987, I moved to Connecticut, accepted short-term teaching assignments in the economics departments at the University of Massachusetts Amherst, the New School, and the University of Utah, and wrote analyses of flow of funds data and international capital flows for the Financial Markets Center.

You got into the world of economic research and publishing as a policy analyst in the US Congress in Washington, DC. Can you describe how that happened? What were the main issues you worked on as a policy staffer in Congress?

When my children were young, I worked as a part-time editor for various organizations in DC and, through one of those contacts, was offered a job organizing and cataloging the papers of House Banking Committee Chairman Wright Patman for the then-proposed Lyndon B. Johnson Library in Austin, Texas. The need to ask questions about some of the material brought me into frequent contact with this remarkable public servant and led to conversations that sparked what became my life-long interest in monetary policy and financial regulation. At the end of the cataloging assignment, Chairman Patman invited me to join the committee staff to provide research for a proposal to revive elements of the Reconstruction Finance Corporation and work on a project analyzing the early years of the Federal Reserve System. Over the following twenty years, monetary policy, domestic and international financial regulation, the expansion of international financial markets, and the build up in the debt of developing countries were the primary issues I worked on as a staff member for the House Banking Committee, the Congressional Budget Office, and the Subcommittee on Telecommunications and Finance of the Energy and Commerce Committee.

Who were some of the major authors who influenced your approach to economics?

The major authors who influenced my approach to economics were J.M. Keynes, H. Minsky, C. Kindleberger, R. Triffin, and N. Kaldor. I have relied heavily on Keynes and Minsky to gain an understanding of systemic interactions in the economy as a whole; Keynes, Triffin,

Kindleberger, and Kaldor provided the foundation for understanding international monetary structures and policy, and Kindleberger engendered an ongoing interest in economic history and in the role of institutional structure and regulation in the development of financial crises. I have profited enormously from the work of colleagues and numerous other authors, but the authors I've named above were foundational in shaping my approach to economics.

As a person with left political convictions, did you think that the environment for congressional staff research was supportive of the types of issues you thought were important to pursue? Alternatively, did you feel isolated in your work as a congressional staffer?

The congressional committee setting proved to be a very favorable environment for research on the issues I thought important to pursue. Because of its specific role and mandate, I found the Congressional Budget Office less accommodative to the research I proposed. My work for the Banking Committee and the Energy and Commerce Subcommittee was very satisfying, and I feel very fortunate to have served under the chairmen and staff directors of those committees and in the overall congressional environment during the years from 1966 to 1986.

In 1994, you published the classic two-volume monograph, The Evolution of US Finance. *How would you describe the main features of this book? How did your book differ from mainstream perspectives in terms of understanding the US financial system? As one specific example, how did your own history of US finance differ from the highly influential 1963 book by Milton Friedman and Anna Schwartz,* A Monetary History of the United States?

The main features of these two volumes are their focus on the interactions between public and private financial institutions and the economy, the tensions inherent in maintaining the necessary balance between the fiduciary and entrepreneurial responsibilities of the private financial sector, and how well finance meets the needs of nonfinancial participants. The focus of the first volume of *The Evolution of US Finance* is on the development of countercyclical monetary policy, its implementation in the early years of the Federal Reserve System by Benjamin Strong, governor of the Federal Reserve Bank of New York, and the monetary crisis that emerged at the end of the 1920s when the Fed renewed its adherence to the procyclical "real bills" doctrine and returned to reliance on the discount window rather than open market operations as the tool for policy implementation.

The second volume of this work provides a historical overview of the development of the structure and regulation of the US financial system and perceptions of the missions of particular financial sectors and their regulators over time. Written in the period when the long-standing segmented system was being dismantled, it offered an analysis of some of the effects of the breakdown on the missions and regulation of financial sectors and some of the economic outcomes of those changes in structure and regulation.

The emphasis in these two volumes on the role of financial structure and regulation in shaping the economy differs from mainstream perspectives on the US financial system in that it provides support for arguments against assumptions about and pressures for deregulation at that time. It argues in favor of an active role for government in defining and using structural and regulatory change to achieve desirable economic outcomes. In that respect, it differs markedly from the Friedman and Schwartz history. The depth of the research and analysis in their history supported its emphasis on the importance of monetary issues and, while it renewed and widened interest in these issues, its free market bias tended to short-change the importance of the institutional framework in which finance functions as a conduit for monetary policy through its interactions with the real economy. The ascendency of the free market ideology so forcefully promoted by Milton Friedman contributed to the erosion of acceptance of the fiduciary responsibilities of private financial institutions in favor of their pursuit of entrepreneurial opportunities.

In addition to your books, in this same period you also published an important 1993 paper with Tom Schlesinger, which described what you then termed the "parallel banking system." We now use the term "shadow banking system" to characterize the same institutional development on which you focused back in 1993. How would you define the "parallel" and "shadow" banking systems? Are they the same thing? Why was the development of this institutional form important back in 1993? Why is it still important today?

The "parallel banking system" developed in the 1960s involved a symbiotic relationship between mutual funds (the gatherers of savings) and finance companies (the lenders). It created institutions that effectively assumed the role of banks without the regulatory or monetary constraints imposed on depository institutions, and without a safety net comparable to deposit insurance for savings. The growth of this sector at the expense of banks' role in lending to businesses and households significantly reduced banks' balance sheets as a share of financial activity and encouraged the larger and medium-sized banks to expand investment and contingency lending activities that generated fees such as guaranties of loans to commercial paper issuers. The growth of promises to lend in the event of one or another contingency led to the expansion of banks' off-balance-sheet accounts, since a contingency contract could not be held as an asset or liability until exercised.

The shift to contingency lending through guaranties, derivatives, and other channels economized on banks' required capital backing and, in time, as these accounts became larger and more complex than on-balance-sheet activity, were recognized as a "shadow banking system." The "parallel" and "shadow" banking systems are not the same in terms of institutional structure, but both were critical developments that reduced traditional banking activity by moving the bulk of saving and borrowing by households and businesses from banks to the capital markets and outside the regulatory guidance and safeguards of a bank-based system. In addition, the off-balance-sheet structure of the "shadow" system provided a framework for developing accounts that inaugurated the enormous volume of proprietary trading by large financial institutions that led to systemic collapse in 2008.

Following the publication of your 1994 book, you became increasingly connected with the community of heterodox political economists, having taught at UMass Amherst, the New School, and the University of Utah. You have also had a long formal association with the Political Economy Research Institute at UMass. How would you say your work is engaged with the broader project of political economy research and advocacy coming out of this community? What do you see as some of the strongest aspects of this line of political economy work? Where do you think there are weaknesses and gaps in this political economy framework?

My good fortune in being able to interact with other heterodox economists in academic settings has allowed me to bring the issues I have
followed into the broader project of political economy research and
advocacy in the progressive community. One of the strongest aspects of
the political economy work of members of that community is their
commitment to teaching and handing down progressive values to their
students. In addition, progressives have worked effectively on behalf of
public policy in interactions with labor unions, a wide variety of
consumer groups, nonprofits, and other groups representing the public
interest. No less important has been their efforts to promote their ideas
through the formation of the Union of Radical Political Economics
(URPE) and in conferences and other gatherings that expand their
knowledge of the work of other members of their community.

There is, of course, always the need to do more, and more funding for
research and advocacy would help. But if there is a weakness, it is
perhaps the lack of access of progressives to institutions of power such
as the Federal Reserve, Congress, the World Bank, and the International
Monetary Fund. Finding appropriate channels to bring progressive
ideas to these institutions—petitioning them for opportunities for
discussion rather than waiting to be invited—would be a useful counterbalance to the influence of mainstream views.

*The late Professor Hyman Minsky described his analytic framework as a
"Wall Street paradigm." Within that framework, Minsky argued that capitalist economies were inherently unstable systems, due to the inherent
drive of financial markets to become dominated by speculative practices
over time. Do you agree with this basic framework developed by Minsky?
In what ways, if any, do you see the operations of financial markets under
capitalism differently from Minsky?*

I agree with Minsky's analytical framework and have clearly profited
from his arguments and insights. In addition to his analysis of systemic
instability, he was also deeply interested in the particular manifestations
of ways in which financial institutions developed innovative speculative
activities that resulted in increased instability. One of the topics discussed
in his summer workshops in the early 1990s focused on the emergence
of particular speculative activities in individual institutions. His commitment to examining the real world provided the solid foundation for his

analytic framework and, while my own interest in speculative activity differs from his in terms of its focus on sectoral and international markets, I have continued to follow his example in giving priority to the need to describe institutional developments.

In your 2018 book All Fall Down *you provide original perspectives on two fundamental questions: first, what caused the 2007–2009 global financial crisis; and second, what needs to be done to prevent another such calamity. Can you give us a short summary of the main findings of the book along both of these lines—both on causes and on policies to prevent a recurrence?*

All Fall Down provides an overview of the more important structural, regulatory, and product changes in the US and international financial systems over the past fifty years and the ways they contributed to the financial crisis of 2007–2008. It argues that the distortions in structure and regulation created by these changes have not been addressed and will continue to create financial instability and ongoing threats of financial crises. The critical systemic change that occurred was the shift from a bank-based to a market-based system without recognition that this shift undermined the effectiveness and safeguards of the existing regulatory framework, reaffirmed under Dodd-Frank, that assumes a primary status in the system for a shrinking level of traditional banking activity. Among the major developments contributing to this shift were the expansion of contingency borrowing and lending that initiated the "shadow banking" paradigm, the rising volume of trading activity by banks and other large financial institutions in both external ("euro") and national markets, the interconnectedness that resulted from increased reliance by financial institutions on other financial institutions as sources and uses of funds, the unintended consequence of the Employee Retirement Income Security Act (ERISA) in moving household savings from banks into securities markets, and banks' own transformative actions in moving housing loans to the capital markets through securitization.

One critical outcome of this shift from a bank-based to a market-based system was that it undermined the implementation of monetary policy. The central bank's ability to influence the supply of credit through changes in reserve requirements on depository institutions was lost, and it had to rely primarily on influencing the demand for credit through the influence of open market operations on interest rates. The assumption that increased capital requirements for banks would succeed in monitoring the soundness of the system and constrain credit expansion was widely embraced in the 1980s, and the run-off in reserve requirements, a target of proponents of deregulation, succeeded in reducing this critical monetary cushion for the financial system. The result was the introduction of a powerful pro-cyclical tool that, because capital is plentiful in a boom and scarce in a downturn, ensured that the Fed would have to deal with insolvency in the event of a financial crisis. Moreover, the lack of constraint on banks was compounded by the shrinkage in traditional banking activity subject to capital requirements, and the growing dominance of other sectors not subject to capital requirements and outside the regulatory influence of the Fed. The fact that capital requirements were reaffirmed as the central regulatory tool for moderating credit expansion and providing systemic soundness ensures that containing a future crisis will likely be more difficult than it was in 2007–2008, as the Fed's only effective response will be, once again, to shift nonperforming bank and nonbank assets from the holdings of private institutions onto its own balance sheet.

A related issue in *All Fall Down* is its emphasis on the way financial structure determines economic outcomes. One major example analyzes the way in which the dollar-dominated key currency system required all countries whose currencies are not accepted for cross-border payments to adopt an export-led growth model that relies on trade surpluses to acquire the means of payment needed to engage in international trade and investment. From the 1980s through the mid 2000s, this model was an underlying cause of crises in developing countries, but it also posed a growing threat to the key currency country itself. The dollars earned from trade surpluses of other countries were invested in US financial assets that provided the credit Americans needed to buy the imports that generated those savings. The effect of ongoing US trade deficits was a build up in debt at home and rising foreign debt. While this pattern of debt-fueled growth allowed the nation as a whole to live beyond its means, the rise in the debt of households and businesses, and in the debt to the rest of the world relative to GDP, indicated that the growing share of income needed to repay debt was a threat to economic growth and to creditors at home and abroad—a threat that was realized as the financial crisis emerged in 2007.

The US continues to rely on debt-fueled growth, but the ongoing rise in household, business, and foreign debt has once again reached a point that suggests another crisis may be on the way. Moreover, since the backing for confidence in the dollar-based international monetary system depends on the ongoing growth of the US economy, the pressure on US growth resulting from the rise in the share of US output needed to repay debt poses a serious threat to the international monetary system. Another crisis affecting the US could lead to a loss of confidence in the dollar and other fiat currencies and create chaos in the global economy.

All Fall Down proposes a number of specific regulatory changes needed to restore systemic stability but the main focus is on monetary reform. It argues that to regain central bank influence over the supply of credit in the US financial market and restore its countercyclical capacity, the Fed must create interest-free liabilities as reserves for all financial institutions that can be contracted in a boom and augmented in a downturn. At the international level, it argues that the monetary framework must inaugurate a new system based on Keynes's proposal for a public authority that would hold the reserves of member countries. The new system proposed in this book would obviate the need for a key currency and allow all countries to use their own currencies for international payments. It would also reduce the role of private-sector banks as the sole intermediaries in the international payments system and create an effective lender-of-last-resort for member countries.

In the aftermath of the 2007–09 crisis, you organized SAFER along with Jerry Epstein—a Committee of Economists for Stable, Accountable, Fair and Efficient Financial Reform. What were the main objectives you were trying to accomplish with SAFER? How well did you think you succeeded?

The main objective of SAFER was to ensure that the regulatory ideas and perspectives of progressive economists were included in legislative decisions on the Dodd-Frank Act. We joined with Americans for Financial Reform (AFR), a newly formed group of consumer advocates and labor unions, in visiting members of Congress and their staff, participating in conference calls and writing position papers to be distributed to Congress and to academics. I think we did well in disseminating our ideas and supporting the commitment of AFR and other groups to the cause of financial reform. Given the influence of private financial institutions and their interest in preserving a bias towards deregulation, it is no surprise that reform remains a work in progress—indeed, one that has experienced more steps backward than forward in the years since the passage of Dodd-Frank. Nevertheless, the expertise of staff and members of AFR and other financial reform groups has grown; they have become important voices in the ongoing debate.

In 2010, the US Congress passed the Dodd-Frank financial regulatory bill. The bill was then signed into law by President Obama. In your view, how much does Dodd-Frank accomplish in terms of promoting financial stabilization in the US and globally?

The main accomplishment of Dodd-Frank was to revive and reassert awareness of the need for financial regulation and the role of government oversight of the financial system. Sections of the legislation—especially those dealing with proprietary trading, derivatives, and interconnectedness—were effective in promoting financial stabilization in the US and globally but, as noted above, lobbyists' assaults on these and other provisions have weakened the act in the years since its passage. Nevertheless, awareness of its goals has survived and is sure to resurface when the political balance shifts or the next crisis hits.

What are the ways, if any, through which financial regulations can be designed to promote greater equality as well as financial stability?

A recurrent focus of debate throughout the history of the US financial system has been the issue of access—the belief that the availability of financial services is a right, not a privilege. Existing regulations such as the Community Reinvestment Act and restrictions on red-lining in lending were put in place to address that issue, but without forceful oversight and implementation the results have been less than robust. Widespread dependence on payday loans with exorbitant interest rates is an indication that equality of access is lacking. The growing ascendency of free market ideology over the past five decades has effectively stymied proposals for public-sector solutions tailored for poor and middle-class borrowers and savers. It is time to revive both the ideas and solutions that addressed access in the New Deal era—the Reconstruction Finance Corporation, for example, which made a loan to the city of Chicago to pay its school teachers, extended the term of small business loans from ninety days to one or two years, and created the self-amortizing mortgage—and the farm financing facilities and development banks that flourished in the US and around the world in even earlier decades. There is need for public institutions that receive social security and disability payments as direct deposits for the homeless to make short-term loans in anticipation of those payments. One could go on since it is not a lack of ideas that is the problem, but a lack of will to challenge the financial sector and explore ways finance could promote greater equality.

In addition to your writings on economics and finance, you are a published poet. Do you see any connection between your work, respectively, in economics and poetry?

That is a hard question to answer, though I think I bring the same sense of the importance of words and their meaning to both areas of my work. There is also a reliance on the concrete and acceptance of uncertainty in both areas. Using historical methodology in economics, I rely on evidence from research to build hypotheses, recognizing that changing circumstances over time may make hypotheses appropriate for one period of time inapplicable in the future. My skepticism about the value of theory in economics is reflected in what in poetry John Keats called "negative capability"—the ability to accept what is not known and entertain doubt and uncertainty about efforts to reach the absolute. My work in both areas reflects doubt in the ability to know the future and the need to accept uncertainty to create space for openness, curiosity, and anticipation.

Responses on the COVID-19 Pandemic

How would you evaluate the ways different countries or regions have responded to the COVID-19 crisis, both in terms of public health interventions and economic policies?

Critical flaws in economic systems surface during crises as they become impediments to recovery. Unless addressed, they create problems that will set the stage for subsequent crises from which it may be even more difficult to recover. One problem that has become evident in the economic crisis produced by the pandemic is the existing high level of household and business debt, which has led to a significantly over-leveraged private sector. Another is gaps in the public safety net.

Inauguration of the PPP program and the additional payments added to unemployment insurance began new and innovative efforts to address these problems that can be improved for current and future use. Nevertheless, the focus on maintaining employment that made these programs very effective in getting relief out quickly left out many individuals and businesses most in need and led many families to increase their level of debt by using credit cards to pay for housing and food, adding more high interest rate payments to existing credit card balances.

A reminder of the scale and level of innovation that may be needed to create programs that can address these problems, as the pandemic continues to ravage the economy, can be found in the innovations that targeted problems of debt and created new public safety nets during the Great Depression—innovations that contributed to economic growth and stability in the post–World War II era. The most important of these included the inauguration of the Social Security Administration to provide retirement, disability, and unemployment benefits.

A more immediately effective safety net for individuals and businesses was deposit insurance, which guaranteed that, in a time of cascading bank failures, demand deposits and personal savings accounts would not be lost in banks insured and regulated by the government even if those banks failed.

Another critical innovation was a major reform of the home mortgage finance system. Under the old system in place in the 1930s, a home buyer only paid interest on a loan taken out for a given number of years, and rolled it over by taking out a new loan at the prevailing rate when the old contract expired. As the rate of foreclosures rose, a new agency was created within the Reconstruction Finance Corporation authorized to insure mortgages and inaugurate the self-amortizing mortgage—a borrowing contract that promoted home ownership and helped reduce the rate of foreclosures until the proliferation of abuses by lenders that led to the financial crisis of 2007–2009.

The Reconstruction Finance Corporation also introduced critical changes in business lending. An agency backed by the government and authorized to issue its own debt securities, the RFC made loans to state and local governments as well as private enterprises and subsequently became the principal channel for financing the war. The change it made in financing business was transformative. At that time, the standard ninety-day loan made by banks conformed to the belief held by adherents to the "real bills doctrine": that the purpose of bank lending was to finance goods in transit. When the RFC began making loans for terms as long as three years, that belief gave way to recognition that companies needed working capital to finance current and future operations, and that longer term funding was necessary for recovery and growth.

These brief descriptions of some of the innovative programs and reforms that were part of the response to crisis under the New Deal are intended to make the point that they were, in fact, highly innovative and targeted to specific problems that had contributed to the crisis and were impeding recovery. It is equally important to recognize their scale both in terms of cost and macroeconomic impact. They are a needed reminder that dealing with the impact of COVID-19 on the US economy will require efforts no less powerful than those made by the generation that confronted the crippling effects of the Great Depression.

Representative Publications and Influences

Publications:
Jane D'Arista (1994). *The evolution of U.S. finance.* M.E. Sharpe.
Jane D'Arista (2009). The evolving international monetary system. *Cambridge Journal of Economics, 33*(4), 633–652.
Jane D'Arista (2018). *All Fall Down; Debt, Deregulation and Financial Crises.* E. Elgar Press.

People who have been influential: John Maynard Keynes, Hyman Minsky, Charles P. Kindleberger, Robert Triffin, Nicholas Kaldor

Literature that has been influential:
Charles P. Kindleberger (1981). Dominance and leadership in the international economy: Exploitation, public goods, and free rides. *International Studies Quarterly, 25*(2), 242–254.
Charles P. Kindleberger and Robert Z. Aliber (2011). *Manias, panics and crashes: A history of financial crises.* Palgrave Macmillan.
Charles P. Kindleberger (2015). *A financial history of Western Europe.* Routledge.

Diane Elson

Diane Elson is Professor Emerita of Sociology at the University of Essex and a former Professor of Development Studies at the University of Manchester. She is noted for her work on issues of development and human rights. A theme in her more recent work is gender inequality and economic and social rights. She is the author of the books *Male Bias in the Development Process* and *Rethinking Economic Policy for Social Justice: The Radical Potential of Human Rights* (with Radhika Balakrishnan and James Heintz, 2016), as well as many other publications. Elson has also worked with many nongovernmental organizations, including as a special advisor for the United Nations Development Fund for Women (UNIFEM) and the UK's Women's Budget Group. She was a winner of the Leontief Prize for Advancing the Frontiers of Economic Thought in 2016.

Tell me about your educational background and why you chose to pursue economics as an academic career?

I grew up in a working-class family in the industrial Midlands of England. My father worked in a factory in Coventry and was an active trade unionist. My mother was a shop worker and active in local women's organizations. They were very keen that their children should have the education that they had been denied, and they supported me and my younger brother to pass exams to attend the selective state secondary schools in the nearby town of Nuneaton. I was the first member of my family to go to university and went to Oxford University in 1965 on a generous scholarship to read Philosophy, Politics and Economics. I chose this degree because I was interested in securing social justice. I was taught development economics by Keith Griffin, and this persuaded me to pursue economics as an academic career. My first job was as research assistant to another development economist, Paul Streeten. Both were heterodox economists.

Who have been the people who have most influenced your thinking as an economist?

Keith Griffin and Paul Streeten introduced me to the structuralist school of development economics and taught me the importance of institutions and context specificity. I was also influenced by the Marxist and heterodox economists who I worked with as a research officer at the Institute of Development Studies, Brighton, in the mid 1970s, especially Robin Murray and Hans Singer. My formation as a feminist economist was also at IDS, through membership in a multidisciplinary collective working on the subordination of women in the process of development. My thinking was particularly influenced by my interaction with Ruth Pearson and Maureen Mackintosh (both development economists), Ann Whitehead (an anthropologist), and Maxine Molyneux (a sociologist). This experience taught me the value of collaborative work, and throughout my career I have worked closely with other feminist economists, co-authoring and coediting.

In your early work you were concerned with putting into proper historical and theoretical context Marx's labor theory of value. Why was the labor theory of value considered to be of critical importance to the development research agenda in the 1970s and 1980s? And in what ways did Marx's ideas and views on colonialism influence development studies and development researchers?

My work on Marx's labor theory of value did not arise directly from my work as a development economist, and I did not study Marx's views on colonialism. Rather, this work stemmed from my participation in debates in a UK organization called the Conference of Socialist

Economists. I was particularly interested in how to understand the dynamic transformation of economies, through commercialization and industrialization, and what commodification meant for different kinds of labor. I was reacting to a static and mathematizing reading of Marx's labor theory of value, which elided the difference between Marx and Ricardo. I argued that Marx was not concerned to set up a model in which prices are determined by embodied labor in a way that can be depicted through a set of equations. Instead, I argued for a dialectical reading, one that understood "value," as used by Marx, as the concept of equivalence of different products which presupposed, and was underpinned by, the equivalence of different kinds of labor. This equivalence was produced by the treatment of all types of labor by owners of capital as merely ingredients in the production of profits (and thus labor became, in a real sense, abstract labor). This equivalence is never absolute and is in contradiction with the specificity of different kinds of products (use values) and labor (concrete labor). I did not engage any further in debates on Marx's value theory, but my subsequent work was influenced in terms of the methods I used, and did not use. I remained very aware of the limitations of mathematical models in understanding dynamic historical processes, and always interested in the hidden presuppositions of economic theories and the invisible underpinnings of the monetized economy. I adopted a dialectical approach in my work with Ruth Pearson on the implications of the creation of a new female waged workforce in export-oriented industrialization in Asia and Latin America. We argued that this employment could not be seen as simply empowering or exploitative. We discussed ways in which, although many preindustrial forms of gender inequality, constructed around the power of fathers, are decomposed in the course of development, new forms of gender inequality are recomposed, and persist, in the capitalist workplace, including unequal pay, occupational sex segregation, and sexual harassment.

You wrote a classic paper in 1988, "Market Socialism or Socialization of the Market?" Can you explain what were the main issues at play in this paper? To what extent do you regard these issues as continuing to be significant today? In other words, how, in your view, should we think about the prospects today either for market socialism or socialization of the market?

This paper, published in 1988, was an intervention in debates about how to organize a socialist economy, in which capitalist ownership of the means of production has been abolished. Does socialism also require the abolition of markets, money, and prices, with the economy coordinated entirely through central planning? Or is this both impossible and undesirable, leading to a concentration of too much power in the hands of the planning apparatus, and stifling innovation and initiative? Is the answer a market socialism in which, though some key sectors may be centrally planned, the rest of the economy is coordinated through money, prices, and markets, leaving room for decentralized decision-making and local initiative? These were not just theoretical questions, but real considerations in discussions of reforms of communist economies in Eastern Europe.

I argued against both these approaches, suggesting that money, prices, and markets are not inherently capitalist and could be transformed into socialist forms of money, prices, and markets—a process I called "Socialization of the Market." My arguments presupposed that there are no longer capitalist enterprises, only publicly owned enterprises, cooperatives, and self-employed producers. The foundation for socialization of the market was that the production and reproduction of labor power should be freed from dependence on selling labor power, through a combination of free access to public services like health, education, water and sanitation, urban transport, etc.; and provision of a guaranteed basic money income, a universal grant made to everyone. Since basic income is now at the forefront of discussions in many countries, let me quote from my article: "advocacy of universal grants as an essential feature of a socialist economy does not in my view entail support for replacing welfare-state capitalism, including legislation to protect employees' rights, with universal grant capitalism. The universal grant has to be taken as part of a package of social arrangements . . ." I acknowledged the potential free-rider problem, and suggested that in return for the basic income grant, all able-bodied adults would be required to undertake some kind of unpaid care work, either in their own families or through community organizations. A socialist economy would not only reduce unpaid care work through public provision but redistribute it by sharing it equally between women and men.

The foundation for socialization of markets would be real-time sharing of information about technologies, costs and needs between enterprises, households, public regulators, commissions and consumer unions, using newly available information technologies. In 1988 these were only in their infancy, but now are much more developed. However, their progressive potential cannot be realized while they are owned by capitalist enterprises, and while information is privatized. As I noted in my article: "The barrier is not technical: it is social and political." Using shared information, public regulators and commissions would be able to operate marketplaces, both real and virtual, and issue price guidelines. There would be no involuntary unemployment because a public regulator would act as a holding company for anyone whose job had been scrapped due to changes in needs and technologies. Their wages would continue to be paid and they would be given training to acquire new skills and assistance in finding new jobs.

Money would serve only as a means of payment and would be unable to take on the life of its own that allows it to dominate the lives of people in a capitalist economy. People would use money rather than being used by money.

Today, there is no immediate prospect of creating socialist economies, but I think it is important to have a positive vision of what one would look like. An economy of public ownership that is not centralized and bureaucratic; that fosters decentralization and local initiatives; in which enjoying a basic decent standard of living does not depend on selling your labor power; in which everyone shares in the provision of care; in which information about all aspects of the economy is a public good; and economic decisions can be taken democratically.

Another area where you have been a pioneer is in integrating feminist considerations into development economics. What have been the basic deficiencies of development economics resulting from neglecting gender considerations? In what ways have feminist perspectives created new ways of thinking about development?

Development economics (both mainstream and heterodox) ignored the ways in which economies are structured by gender, and the implications this has both for gender equality and for economic development. It ignored the sphere of social reproduction in which unpaid work, largely done by women and girls, plays a key role in the way that people are reproduced on a daily and intergenerational basis. It ignored the way in which gender as a structure of power leads to pervasive and persistent occupational sex segregation in paid work, with most women being confined to a narrow range of low-paid jobs. The lack of engagement with gender meant that analysis and policy was faulty.

Mainstream development economics argued for dealing with debt crises in developing countries by neoliberal policies, such as cutbacks in public spending, privatization, and currency devaluation. I argued that this would not result in the supply side response that mainstream development economists expected, because the structure of gendered power was a barrier to smooth reallocation of labor to new opportunities. Implicit in mainstream development policies was the presupposition that women would provide the ultimate safety net and through their unpaid work would cushion their families and communities in times of crisis and restructuring. It was presumed that although living standards might deteriorate in the short run, in the longer run they would recover and improve in response to neoliberal policies. I argued that women's unpaid work was not infinitely elastic and women would be unable to prevent the depletion of the human capacities of themselves and their families through lack of food and access to health services, and overwork in unhealthy conditions.

Heterodox development economics, of course, rejected mainstream analysis and neoliberal policies, but it ignored the inequalities within households and only looked at inequalities between households. Class was recognized as a structure of social and economic power, but gender was not. The way that women and men experience class in different ways was not recognized. Public investment in physical infrastructure directed to increasing productivity of paid work was emphasized. Public investment in social infrastructure to reduce unpaid care work, and in social protection measures, such as parental leave to redistribute unpaid care work from women to men, was largely ignored.

All varieties of development economics presupposed that the organization of social reproduction could safely be ignored, and analysis and policy should focus only on the paid economy. Feminist economics has challenged this and called for statistics, such as on time-use, that make unpaid care work visible, public investment in social reproduction, and attention to inequalities within households as well as between households.

Have concerns about gender in development materialized in any concrete way so far into actual policies? If so, can you give some examples?

Some of these concerns have to a certain extent been taken on board in policies in a range of countries, but not always in ways that feminist development economists have advocated. There is concern in many countries to increase women's participation in paid work, as a route to higher economic growth. Much attention has focused on eliminating legal barriers to women setting up their own businesses and improving women's access to financial services (not problems that I had highlighted). Not so much attention has been paid to improving conditions and earnings of women employees or own-account subcontracted home-based workers (issues that I had highlighted). Women's unpaid work is now widely seen as an economic policy issue, but only as a barrier to women participating in paid employment, and hence as a barrier to higher economic growth. There has been investment in the provision of water and sanitation services, which reduces the amount of time and effort that women and girls have to spend fetching water. But millions of low-income women and girls in low-income countries still lack these services. In higher-income developing countries, such as South Korea, China, Chile, and Mexico, there has been investment in early childhood education and care services. But the quality of employment in these services is low in some countries.

Many of the same problems are present in so-called developed countries, where economic policy has also focused on increasing women's participation in paid work as a way of increasing economic growth. All over the world, policy has not paid much attention to the issue of the distribution of the benefits of women's increased participation in paid work. How much goes to the women themselves, and how much is appropriated by employers and subcontractors?

It has been argued that Western liberal feminism is at odds with the real issues facing women in the Global South. In fact, such criticisms go even further by charging Western liberal feminism with having a paternalistic attitude or mindset in the way it deals with women's issues and concerns in the Global South. What is your view of such criticisms?

There has always been criticism that feminism is at odds with the real issues facing women, back to the very first attempts to fight for women's rights in the nineteenth century. Some of this criticism is justified; some of it stems from the view that women's rights are a distraction from supposedly more important issues of class struggle and national self-determination; some of it stems from a desire to disarm feminism and preserve an unequal structure of gendered power.

It is important to recognize both the heterogeneity of feminism and the heterogeneity of women. Western feminism is not monolithic. Not all Western feminists are liberals—and many others would count ourselves socialists. Not all feminists are in the Global North. There is home-grown feminism in many countries in the Global South. Advocates for women's rights played a vital role in anti-imperialist struggles in many countries, though they were too often sidelined in postcolonial nation-building. Not all women in the Global South are materially worse off than women in the Global North: some are very wealthy and employ lots of paid domestic workers. So it is important to be specific about which Western feminists, which particular attitudes and practices, and which women in the Global South, when making such criticisms: the best critics have been specific in these ways. I think there is a particular danger when Western feminists engage with so-called "traditional practices" in marriage and sexuality in the Global South. For instance, I have seen examples of work by Western feminists in relation to female genital cutting I would characterize as "missionary." But that does not mean that I think Western feminists should endorse female genital cutting, out of respect for the culture of others. No culture is without its internal contestations, some overt, some more tacit. All cultures are in process, never completely fixed and static. "Tradition" is an invention, and it is important to be alert to the contributions of colonialism in the creation of traditions. There is a substantial body of work by scholars from the Global South that show this.

It is vital for Western feminists to engage in dialogue with feminists in the Global South and take a lead from feminists in the Global South. It is also vital to ensure that feminists from the Global South have a strong presence on international platforms. It is a particular responsibility of Western feminists to engage critically with the impact on women in the Global South of Western governments and multinational companies and Western-dominated international financial institutions; and to support the scholarship and activism of feminists in the Global South. In the 1990s I was a member of an organization that helped to build bridges between organizations of women garment workers in Europe and in Asia, and to alert European consumers to the conditions of "the labor behind the label." I have collaborated with several feminist economists from the Global South, including pioneer Indian feminist economist Devaki Jain. I have learned a lot from working with women from the Global South.

But these are not just issues for feminists. All progressive social scientists should honestly recognize the dilemmas in researching lives that are not theirs and arguing for policies that they think will improve the lives of people who are deprived in various ways, whether within their own countries or in other countries. Inevitably, there is a gulf between middle-class researchers and less well-off people. It is important to be respectful, to be aware of intersecting structures of disadvantage—the lived experience of class is not separate from lived experiences of race and gender and sexuality—and to be imaginative in understanding the lived contradictions of late capitalism, without surrendering one's critical faculties. It is important to point out that identifying oppression and exploitation does not entail denying agency to people who are oppressed and exploited. Rather, it involves criticizing the structures that constrain their agency and thinking of ways that, through collective action, their agency can be enlarged. It also means being willing to look critically at one's own ideas of what a better life would look like. Male heterodox economists need to recognize that the belief that economic growth is the most important thing in improving people's lives is not shared by all; just as feminist economists need to recognize that their belief that decent jobs are key to a better life for women is not shared by all. We all need to have a dialogical approach to analysis and policy.

Do you feel that international organizations like the United Nations have done much so far to advance the cause of gender equality and sustainable development in the Global South?

The cause of gender equality was on the UN agenda right from its formation, with the setting up of the Commission on the Status of Women, on which women from the Global South have always played a leading role. But UN efforts to advance the cause of gender equality have always been fragmented and underfunded. Women's organizations from around the world have challenged this and campaigned for setting up a more powerful women's agency within the UN to bring together some of these fragmented efforts and to secure resources much more in line with those provided to UNICEF, the United Nations Children's Fund. UN Women was indeed set up in 2010, but the required funding did not follow. This illustrates the important point that the UN is in the end a creation of member states. If they are not willing to allocate adequate resources to UN Women, then efforts to support gender equality will be hampered. Gender equality is high on the agenda of some other UN organizations. The International Labour Organisation (ILO), for instance, has played a leading role in developing an international agenda on women's rights to paid work and rights while performing that work, as part of its decent work agenda.

What the UN has been good at is securing agreement of member countries on international norms and standards, such as human rights treaties; ILO conventions; climate change conventions; and development goals, such as the Sustainable Development Goals. Gender equality has had an increasing salience in these international norms and standards over the last twenty-five years, not least because of the efforts of international coalitions of women's rights organizations. But implementation depends in the end on the actions of member governments, and their commitment to implementation is very variable, as people living in the US are now experiencing firsthand.

UN organizations have supported real improvements in the education and health of women and girls, and in the access of low-income women to basic services like water and sanitation. Though as UN reports themselves demonstrate, much remains to be done. The UN human rights system has provided a platform for women's rights organizations across the world to publicize violations of women's rights and has played an important role in the last twenty-five years in focusing international attention on gender-based violence, in the home, in the workplace, and in public spaces. But there is undoubtedly a backlash against women's rights in many countries, including the US, so gains can never be taken for granted.

Some UN organizations, such as ILO and UNCTAD, have been very critical of the impact of neoliberal economic policies and multinational companies on gender equality. But at the same time other UN organizations have made agreements with multinational companies, not least because this is an avenue to secure more resources, since funding from member governments has fallen. These issues are hotly contested within UN organizations themselves and are subject to ongoing struggles.

The two most important international financial institutions, the IMF and World Bank, have now fully embraced the cause of gender equality in their public pronouncements, flagship reports, and research outputs.

But they embrace gender equality in terms of greater gender equality being more efficient and leading to greater economic growth. They do recognize women's unpaid work, but primarily as a barrier to women undertaking more paid work. Many economists and the IMF and the World Bank do now take gender seriously in their analyses, but they incorporate gender in ways that do not call into question their basic paradigm. Moreover, the operational divisions of the IMF and the World Bank still attach conditions to loans that jeopardize efforts to secure greater gender equality (through, for instance, cutting public expenditure and privatizing public services). In all this, they treat gender equality in the same way that they have treated poverty reduction and reduction of income inequality between households, as issues that can be addressed without questioning the fundamentals of the neoliberal paradigm.

Despite the limitations of the UN system, it is important for progressive economists to engage with it, as it still does provide some spaces in which more progressive economic thinking can be articulated and the IMF and World Bank can be challenged. An example is the Committee for Development Policy, of which I am a member, and the flagship UN Women report, *Progress of the World's Women,* on whose advisory board I sit.

Most recently, much of your work has been focused on the economics of human rights. In what ways does this current work connect with your earlier research on the economics of socialism and feminist economics? Would your conception of an economics that explicitly takes account of human rights also be an economics that advances variants of both socialism and feminism?

My recent work on economics and human rights, in collaboration with Radhika Balakrishnan and James Heintz, is concerned with introducing human rights activists to heterodox and feminist economics to assist them in challenging economic policies that violate human rights. It also aims to introduce heterodox and feminist economists to the potential of human rights as an ethical framework for development of economic policy and as a site of struggle against unjust economic policies. When I was young it seemed possible to engage in successful struggles for socialism in many parts of the world (I graduated in 1968). But those hopes were disappointed, and it became clear that we had to engage in a long march through the institutions. And we needed to find a way of engaging with people who were convinced that the collapse of communism in Russia and Eastern Europe demonstrated that socialism was impossible. I think one of the reasons for the collapse of communism is that it was state-centered, bureaucratic and denied individual rights. Any new progressive form of organizing economic and social life has to be built on a new synthesis of individual rights and collective action and public provision. Ingredients for such a synthesis can be found in the international human rights system, which includes economic, social, and cultural rights, as well as civil and political rights; and which puts obligations on states to promote, protect, and fulfill all these rights. The rights are held by individuals, but they include rights to engage in collective action to claim, defend, and advance rights, including rights to common property and cultural resources.

I first learned about the international human rights system in the late 1990s, as a feminist scholar and activist engaging with many women from around the world. We had fought for the introduction of the International Convention on the Elimination of All Discrimination Against Women (CEDAW), which calls not just for the abolition of discriminatory laws and equal opportunities, but also for the achievement of substantive equality in outcomes. These women had also fought successfully to transform the international human rights system so that it recognized domestic violence as a human rights issue. Women's organizations were using the international human rights system as a resource in their national struggles to secure women's rights, not just to end discriminatory laws, but to secure the provision of key public services. Even in the US, which is one of the very small number of countries that has failed to ratify CEDAW, activists used CEDAW as a standard against which to judge policies and achievements. They were successful in persuading mayors of several large American cities to commit their administrations to aim at compliance with CEDAW at the city level.

I subsequently learned, in the early 2000s, about the ways in which many social justice organizations all over the world were attempting to hold their governments to account for their obligations, under the International Covenant on Economic, Social, and Cultural Rights. These organizations included a wide range of groups campaigning for specific rights, including labor rights, but also rights to goods and services, such as housing, food, and health. They have brought cases to court over the failure of governments to comply with obligations in relation to the right to housing, the right to food, and the right to health. They have

submitted independent shadow reports to the UN Committee on
Economic, Social, and Cultural Rights when their governments were
reviewed for compliance with the covenant, and used these to try to
influence public opinion and to provide a resource for progressive politicians. They have argued that economic policies should be evaluated in
terms of human rights. But they were not quite sure what arguments
they could make against, for instance, austerity policies, and how exactly
to link economic policies to the provisions of the covenant. Radhika,
James, and I began to work on these issues in cooperation with human
rights activists. We quickly saw that heterodox economists also had a lot
to gain from engagement with the human rights framework, as an alternative ethical framework to the utilitarian framework that dominates
formulation of economic policy; and as a framework that can connect
macroeconomic policy to the concerns of activists. For instance, we
were able to show how taxation of the rich is a human rights issue and
we shared these insights with the international Tax Justice Network.

The economics that advances realization of human rights is indeed an
economics that advances the core concerns of both socialism and feminism in terms of addressing at the same time public provisioning, collective action, and individual rights. We have found that some heterodox
economists in the US find this difficult to understand because they see
the international human rights system through the lens of the one-sided
misappropriation of human rights arguments by successive US governments on behalf of imperialist foreign policies. They do not understand
how progressive forces in many parts of the world are making counter-
use of the human rights system. Heterodox economics needs an ethical
framework and a way of connecting with a wide variety of grassroots
struggles for economic, social, and cultural rights. We think engagement with the human rights system provides both. It enables us to
mount a moral challenge to neoliberal capitalism, to put forward
progressive policies that do promote, protect, and fulfill human rights,
and to work with activists engaged in a variety of rights struggles, not
only in trade unions but in many other types of organizations.

*As we continue to live through the fourth decade of neoliberal capitalism
as a dominant social structure, what do you see as the prospects for
advancing social structures that embrace your concerns for socialism,
feminism, and human rights?*

We live in times that demand pessimism of the intelligence but optimism of the will. The political situation in many parts of the world presents a profound challenge to prospects for socialism, feminism, and human rights. The rich have been able to buy political power. Globalization has disrupted lives and increased insecurity around the world. In Europe, the forces of fascism are once more gathering strength. In the UK, the narrow majority vote for Brexit has given new life to racism, xenophobia, and Islamophobia. Neoliberal capitalism has its internal contradictions and is fractured by trade wars and financial fragility. The realities of climate change are beginning to make themselves felt. But economic crises and climate-related disasters may strengthen, rather than weaken, the forces arrayed against socialism, feminism, and human rights. There are some resources of hope in the many grassroots initiatives, working to organize provisioning of daily life in new, more sustainable, more collective ways. There are some resources for hope in the links being made in many places between women campaigning on violence against women and sexual harassment and those campaigning for better public services and an end to cuts in public spending; and in the mass mobilization of women to defend and extend their reproductive rights. There are some resources of hope in the movements of students of economics to challenge mainstream economics and to demand a pluralist curriculum with much more room for heterodox and feminist economics. We all have to fight where we stand.

Do you have new areas of research that you are exploring now? If so, can you please describe them briefly?

I am involved in some collaborative research on so-called "inclusive growth." Every international development agency and many governments have responded to the evidence of growth in inequalities in income and wealth by adopting "inclusive growth" as their slogan and policies for inclusive growth that are supposed to lead to shared prosperity. Gender equality is supposed to be addressed by getting more women into paid employment by reducing supply-side barriers. The research will unpack the many ways in which "inclusion" and "growth" can actually be harmful to people; identify criteria for gender-equitable inclusive growth that is beneficial (in terms of types of employment and types of goods and services produced) and reduces inequalities between households, between women and men, and between labor and capital; and identify the kinds of policy frameworks and specific policies that are needed to secure this.

Responses on the COVID-19 Pandemic

How would you evaluate the ways different countries or regions have responded to the COVID-19 crisis, both in terms of public health interventions and economic policies?

Internationally there is big gap between the kind of support packages (for health services, wage earners, and businesses) that high-income countries have been able to provide and those that middle- and low-income countries have been able to provide. The rich countries are currently able to borrow as much as they want at very low rates of interest and have been encouraged to do so by the IMF and the OECD. Indeed, the managing director of the IMF has warned high-income countries against policies to reduce debt and deficits at this time. But the middle- and low-income countries do not have the same fiscal space, and for many of them, the IMF is already requiring "fiscal consolidation"—the polite term for austerity policies that, going by experience, will make inequalities and poverty worse. Internationally there is also a big gap in access to the vaccines that are now becoming available. There has been a campaign for a Peoples' Vaccine that will override patents and make new vaccine technologies freely available for manufacture across the world. But this has not been heeded. The best offers (from some providers) are to make vaccines available to middle- and low-income countries at cost, but this cost will be beyond the reach of many. And in the queue to get vaccines the poorest people in the poorest countries are likely to be last. There has been international talk of the need to "build back better" but there is no sign of this happening in international financial and health policies.

In the UK, the Conservative government tore up the constraining fiscal rules that had been in operation since 2010 and has borrowed at a level unprecedented since World War II to fund increases in expenditure of the National Health Service (which delivers free care to everyone living in the UK—with the exception of some categories of migrants—but which has been starved of necessary funds as a result of austerity policies during the last decade); to support a furlough scheme; to temporarily increase the value of the main welfare benefit for unemployed and low-income people (Universal Credit); and to provide grants, loans, and tax exemptions for some self-employed people and businesses. This has been complemented by a large new program of quantitative easing from the Bank of England.

However, these support measures have been implemented in ways that reinforce existing inequalities of gender, race, class, disability, and location—and that reinforce the power of the private sector. Much of the additional public expenditure for health has been spent on outsourcing procurement of personal protective equipment, testing for COVID-19 and contact tracing of those testing positive, and to private-sector companies with no previous experience in such activities, but with close contacts to Conservative Party MPs and ministers. Many of these companies have failed to meet the targets that were set. The normal rules for public procurement were suspended, on grounds that there was an emergency, which opened the door to cronyism. Support for businesses affected by lockdowns was provided with little scrutiny and no conditions (though, for example, not paying any dividends could have been made a condition). Tax exemptions were made available to businesses regardless of how the lockdowns are likely to affect them—public opinion has now pressured some of the large supermarket chains, whose profits have increased and which have been able to operate throughout the lockdowns and enhance their online home delivery services, to repay the tax exemptions they received. Requirements for businesses to report their gender pay gap and their plans for reducing it were suspended, again on grounds that they can't be expected to do this in an emergency.

The most egregious failure has been in providing support to people asked to quarantine themselves by the Test and Trace system. Many people have not been able to afford to quarantine because they either have no entitlement to "sick pay" from the social security system, or because their entitlement is so low that it does not cover their living costs. The UK has one of the worst "sick pay" systems in Europe, sharply contrasting with, for example, the much better system in Germany. Not surprisingly, rates of infection have again risen sharply, especially in areas of greatest deprivation, including large parts of the north of England. Public finance is highly centralized in the UK, and there has not been much leeway for the devolved governments of Scotland, Wales, and Northern Ireland to introduce better support measures. Hardest hit cities and regions in England have been denied sufficient extra resources to cope with the added costs of COVID-19 and associated lockdowns.

In November, the chancellor of the exchequer introduced a one-year expenditure plan that did nothing to rectify these failures, and he included a freeze in the pay of public-sector workers like teachers, police, fire and rescue, and staff of local government services. He said that the national debt and budget deficit could not go on rising and implied there would be austerity measures in 2021.

What we have had in the UK is short-run Keynesianism for the better-off, making very clear that it matters not only how much the government spends, but how the money is used; not just how many bonds the central bank buys, but from whom they are bought. Quantitative easing may save jobs by preventing bankruptcies, but it pushes up share prices and increases wealth inequalities.

Do you draw any general lessons from the COVID crisis about the most viable ways to advance an egalitarian economic project?

In the UK, in lockdown again in December 2020, it is hard to be optimistic. We have a Conservative government, with a large majority in parliament, that is opposed to any egalitarian economic project. From this government, we might get some tinkering with the tax system next year, for instance to tax capital gains at the same rate as earnings, but we will not get a wealth tax. The government was forced to consider how to improve provision of free meals to low-income children after a major campaign on social media, led by a young Black British footballer, who is now well-off and famous, but who grew up in poverty, relying on free lunches provided to him at school. The growing numbers of hungry children in a rich country is considered appalling by large numbers of people, who can be mobilized by a charismatic figure to put pressure on the government for a specific change. It is harder to mobilize in the same way for a transformation of the whole social security system to provide real security in times of stress, in a way that cares for people and respects their dignity and autonomy. However, many more people have become personally aware of the way in which the social security system has been utterly degraded by a decade of austerity, and know from their own experience of illness, unemployment, and income loss, that people who get social security benefits are not idle scroungers, and that these benefits are far too low to meet the cost of living. This may make it possible to rebuild support for an egalitarian social security system.

Also, there are underlying fragilities in the current configuration of political power. As I write, the outcome of the negotiations on a post-Brexit trade deal between the UK and EU is still unknown. If it is a deal, the Conservative Party may split; if it is no deal, the UK may split, as this would drive up support for independence in Scotland above the unprecedently high levels it has already reached. The Scottish government is supportive of more egalitarian measures, as is the Welsh government, but their powers to implement such measures are limited.

Moreover, in 2021, if the vaccines lead to a fall in the rate of infection and large public gatherings are again possible, we may see a resurgence in two big street mobilizations of young people: Black Lives Matter, mobilizing to end racism; and Extinction Rebellion, mobilizing to end the climate and ecological emergencies. Many young people are eager for transformation of the economy.

So we have to be ready with ideas for advancing an egalitarian economic project if the political context becomes more propitious. With this in mind, I chaired an independent Commission on a Gender Equal Economy, set up by the UK Women's Budget Group. We published a report in October 2021: *Creating a Caring Economy*, arguing for a transformation of the economies of the UK, to support equality, well-being, and sustainability, and to roll back the domination of pursuit of short-term financial gains (see www.wbg.org.uk/commission). We wanted to tap into the concern with caring for one another that became prominent in the few months after the arrival of COVID-19, not only arguing for more public investment in publicly provided care services as a strategy for economic recovery, but also for dethroning the pursuit of profit and economic growth and focusing on the creation of good jobs throughout the economy that are open to everyone on an equal basis, and that are designed to enable everyone, men as well as women, to combine paid work with unpaid care for family and friends. An equal economy requires us *all* to have time free from care, and time free to care, on an equal basis.

We have been sharing these ideas in a number of virtual international working groups and learning of the ideas of other groups in different countries and organizations. One of the unexpected by-products of

COVID-19 lockdowns has been the flourishing of progressive international webinars, which we must sustain even if COVID-19 subsides.
Less international travel is an important contribution to environmental
sustainability.

*Does the experience of the COVID crisis shed any light on the way you
think about economics as a discipline, or, more specifically, the questions
you might be pursuing in your own research?*

Progressive economists must challenge widely held concepts of "efficiency"
and "productivity." Feminist economists have been arguing for years that
conventional concepts of "efficiency" as minimization of financial costs
ignores the transfer of real costs from the paid economy to the unpaid
economy. This became very clear in the COVID crisis in the UK, which
revealed the rundown of capacity of the National Health Service and the
public sector in general in pursuit of so-called "efficiency gains." Some gaps
were filled by unpaid volunteers, on furlough from their usual jobs, but too
many gaps resulted in falls in well-being through stress and exhaustion.

Feminist economists have also been arguing that conventional
concepts of "productivity" are based on mechanical models of economies, not on organic concepts of economies. They are particularly
unsuited for services in which the quality of the interaction between
provider and user and the time spent in the interaction matters, such as
health, education, and care. The "productivity" of care homes for frail
elderly people in the UK has been increased by driving down labor
costs, but this has meant high staff turnover and staff moving at short
notice between different care homes, which proved a disaster when
trying to contain the spread of COVID-19.

COVID-19 revealed that many low-paid workers are essential if the
economy is to function—for instance, bus drivers, delivery drivers,
cashiers at supermarkets, cleaners and porters in hospitals—while many
higher-paid workers (in jobs in finance and accounting, for instance)
are not essential. This provides an opportunity to challenge conventional wisdom about how wages are determined and decisively reject the
idea that wages can only be raised by raising productivity.

Progressive economists must also pay more attention to changing the
ways in which macroeconomic issues are understood outside of universities, research institutes, and think-tanks. One example is the way in

which government debt is understood and presented though analogies with household debt. A group of progressive economists in the UK wrote in late November 2020 to the BBC challenging the misleading way in which BBC correspondents present the rise in government debt in terms of "maxing out the national credit card."

In my own future research, I will be looking further at how the COVID crisis has intensified inequalities (of gender, race, class, disability, and location), but also what opportunities it might have opened up for challenging and reversing these inequalities. Maybe the contrast between the extraordinary profits some businesses are making as a result of the COVID crisis, and the needless suffering of so many people as a result of the lack of preparedness and mismanagement of the COVID crisis, will provide a basis for putting together the wide and deep mobilizations that will be needed to transform our economies. But I am taking nothing for granted.

Representative Publications and Influences

Publications:
Diane Elson (1988). Market Socialism or the Socialisation of the Market?, *New Left Review, 172,* 3–44.
Diane Elson (1995). *Male bias in the development process.* Manchester University Press.
Radhika Balakrishnan, James Heintz, and Diane Elson (2016). *Rethinking Economic Policy for Social Justice: The Radical Potential of Human Rights.* Routledge.

People who have been influential: Keith Griffin, Paul Streeten, Robin Murray, Hans Singer, Ruth Pearson, Maureen Mackintosh

Literature that has been influential:
Keith Griffin and John Enos (1970). *Planning Development.* Addison-Wesley.
Robin Murray (1971). Internationalization of capital and the nation state. *New Left Review, 67,* 84–109.
Keith Griffin (1974). *The Political Economy of Agrarian Change: An Essay on the Green Revolution.* Macmillan and Harvard University Press.

Gerald Epstein

Gerald Epstein is Professor of Economics and Co-Director of the Political Economy Research Institute, University of Massachusetts Amherst. He was a co-founder with Jane D'Arista and Jennifer Taub of SAFER (*Economists' Committee for Safe, Accountable, Fair and Efficient Financial Reform*), and a staff economist with the Center for Popular Economics. He is the author, most recently, of *The Political Economy of Central Banking: Contested Control and the Power of Finance* (2019), *What's Wrong with Modern Money Theory? A Policy Critique* (2019), and *Breaking the Bankers' Club: Finance for the Rest of Us* (2021).

Can you tell us a bit about your personal background?

I grew up in Albuquerque, New Mexico. My father was the co-owner of a small potato chip company called Zip Potato Chips (the motto was: "Zip is a pip of a chip!") and my mother was a "homemaker," as they called women in those days who stayed home and did all the care work from there. Growing up I was a bit of "jock" (though not a very skilled one). But as the civil rights and antiwar movement got going, and some of my high school teachers started talking about these things, I got more and more interested in politics. By the time I went to college in 1969, I was really looking for a more critical and activist community and set of ideas. But I really didn't know much about these things at the time. Fortunately, the college I went to—Swarthmore College outside of

Philadelphia—like many other colleges at that time, was a hotbed of activity, though in its own small college, hyper-intellectual kind of way. Within my first year of being there I was hooked on left-wing politics and critical analyses stemming mostly from Marx.

You left political science for economics. Why?

Though I was hooked on Marx and anti-capitalist politics, very few of the professors at Swarthmore at the time were knowledgeable or even particularly sympathetic towards these approaches. So there was not an obvious major to take based on the professors. I first picked political science because I thought changing the world was about understanding politics. But the more I got into Marx and Marxist ideas, the more I realized that understanding economics is key, and I decided to focus on that as well. Of course, I was young and I didn't really know what I was doing, but that was my thinking at the time. It worked out OK, I guess.

After I graduated from college I wanted to focus on economics. And by a series of lucky breaks, I got into graduate school, first in public policy and then in the PhD program in economics, both at Princeton.

What was it like to study economics at Princeton in the 1970s and early 1980s, at a time when neoliberalism was on the ascent?

The professors (and most of the students) in economics at Princeton, like those at most graduate schools at the time, were mostly interested in learning mathematical approaches to modeling, and to answering pretty narrow questions about whether markets do or don't allocate resources efficiently. Questions about inequality, power, imperialism, discrimination, exploitation, economic crises, epochs in economic history and their evolution, key differences in modes of production, the profound importance of institutions—none of this was of interest to people in the Economics Department at the time. One mild example of this: W. Arthur Lewis, a towering figure in development economics from St. Lucia, and the only Black person to win the Nobel Prize in Economics, was at Princeton (as an emeritus) when I was there. He had a deep understanding of development from a poor-country perspective. And even though he would spend a lot of time in the library doing research, the Economics Department *never* mentioned him the whole time I was there. They just were not interested in broader understandings of economics. (And Lewis was no Marxist, to be sure).

When I was at Princeton, it was still primarily a neo-Keynesian ("bastard Keynesian" as Joan Robinson called it) department. These were in the days when the neo-Keynesians of Yale, MIT, Harvard, etc., led by Samuelson, Solow, and Tobin, were fighting the "monetarists" of Chicago, led by Milton Friedman. But the terrain was fairly narrow—over the effectiveness of monetary versus fiscal policy, for example, and not over the bigger issues I mentioned earlier. Meanwhile, as Nancy MacLean has shown in her brilliant book, *Democracy in Chains*, the Chicago School, including Milton Friedman and James Buchanan, was playing a deeper game: undermining democracy and spreading neoliberalism in economics, politics, and law, using Pinochet's Chile as a testing and proving ground. The neo-Keynesians were clueless about this. Radical economists, like those at UMass, who thought deeply about the intersection between politics and economics, understood to some extent what was going on, especially when the crimes in Chile were exposed.[1] Radical economists Tom Weisskopf, Arthur MacEwan, and others also exposed this bigger game in Latin America at the time. In fact, when I was a student in public policy at Princeton in the early 1970s, just as the Chicago Boys were advising Pinochet, Arnold Harberger, one of the architects of the Chicago-Pinochet advice machine, taught a special course in cost-benefit analysis (filled, of course, with "Harberger Triangles"), and not a word was mentioned by anyone about his role in Chile.

There were two exceptions to the general pattern of obliviousness in the Economics Department at the time: William Baumol, who had an interest in the history of economic thought, and Peter Kenen, an international economist, who actually knew and cared about institutions, politics, and power, though his economics classes didn't have much about those subjects in them.

So intellectual influences in the Economics Department for me were pretty slim pickings, to put it mildly. (I should add: my advisors, Stephen Goldfeld and Alan Blinder, were helpful and tolerant of my "odd" approach, even if they could not be helpful apart from technical issues.)

---

1   See, for example, Sam Bowles and Herb Gintis, "The Invisible Fist: Have Capitalism and Democracy Reached a Parting of the Ways?" *American Economic Review* 68:2 (May 1978): 358–63.

Fortunately, there were a lot of great graduate students in the Political Science Department and I became friends with them. It was these people who most influenced me as a graduate student, especially two of them: Joel Rogers and Tom Ferguson. Tom and I have remained good friends to this day, and I continue to learn a great deal from him about the interface of politics and economics. In the end, I did end up trying to integrate economics and politics—and especially issues of class and power and how they shape and are shaped by capitalist dynamics. That's where I started out in college and I guess I have been continuing to try to do that throughout my career.

How did you end up at UMass Amherst?

I ended up at UMass Amherst through a combination of political/ professional desires, personal situations, and a lot of good luck.

First, I should say, that from the very beginning of being in grad school, UMass Amherst was always my idea of the ideal teaching job. I thought that it, along with the New School, was where the most interesting colleagues and students were and where there was a commitment to doing both rigorous research and activist political work, though, wonderfully, at the time, other places had good heterodox programs: Riverside, Notre Dame, and Utah. When I thought about wanting to go into teaching, I always wanted to go to UMass. I am very lucky that I eventually got there.

How I got to UMass Amherst is a bit of a long story but I won't bore you with the details. Here is the outline: My first teaching job after graduate school was at Williams College in the northwest corner of Massachusetts. There I had the good fortune to meet Joan Robinson, who was visiting, and the very good fortune to meet Julie Schor, another of the people who has had a big influence on me and who I am fortunate enough to still have as a very good friend. David Gordon recruited Julie to direct the research wing of a new progressive institute he was creating in New York, an extension of the Labor Institute, which he had been very involved with for a number of years. Julie asked me if I wanted to co-direct the research department with her and I jumped at the opportunity. The deal was that I would be half-time at the institute and half-time teaching at the New School. This was a dream come true, and of course I said yes. Unfortunately, soon after I quit my job at Williams and moved to New York, funding for David's project fell through, so I ended up with only a half-time job at the New School. But it was a great education for me. For the first time, I was surrounded by colleagues and students who were experts in Marx and Keynes and radical economics—the whole package. I learned a lot more in my three years at the New School than I did during my whole time in graduate school at Princeton.

In the meantime, I met my now wife of more than thirty-five years, Francine Deutsch, who was teaching in Western Massachusetts at Mt. Holyoke College. We got married and soon had a baby; so the commute was becoming intolerable. Luckily, I was able to get a job at UMass in 1986 and here I am.

Tell me about the Political Economy Research Institute, which you helped establish in 1998 and have been co-director of ever since. How did PERI come about, and what is its primary mission?

Bob Pollin and I met at a conference when we were graduate students, but the idea for PERI began much later. Bob and I had both been invited to an EPI conference on progressive economic policy, and we discovered that we were on the same page about a lot of issues—in particular, both the necessity and feasibility for strongly progressive macroeconomic policies for full employment and a vastly restructured financial system. Most of the others at the conference said that these kinds of macro and financial policies were no longer feasible in a globalized world and that we should forget about them. Within a few weeks after the conference, Bob called me up to ask if I wanted to co-organize a project, conference, and book with him (and Gary Dymski), fleshing out these issues in a number of areas. I said, "Yes! Of course." The project brought together many economists who have remained top progressive economists in these areas to this day. Our coedited book, *Transforming the US Financial System: An Equitable and Efficient Structure for the 21st Century,* was published by EPI, and some of the chapters in that book were, in fact, really quite prescient.

In any case, not only did we get a good book and solid relationships with a large number of progressive economists out of the project, but it also formed the foundation of Bob's and my professional relationship. So, when an opportunity arose to start an institute, it was natural that the two of us would try to pursue it together.

That opportunity came a few years later when Bob was asked if he wanted to direct a new policy institute at the New School. I am very thankful that Bob contacted me and asked if I would like to do this with him. What a fabulous opportunity! I checked with my wife, Fran, and though in principle she would have loved to move back to New York, she didn't think it was financially feasible. Also, she would have had to give up her job at Mt. Holyoke. So I suggested to Bob that we create an institute at UMass instead.

It took some work for us for a year or a bit more, but it all came together. In the fall of 1998, Bob and Sigrid and their kids moved to Amherst and PERI began.

The idea that Bob and I had in establishing PERI was pretty simple: we wanted to create an institute that was rooted in rigorous progressive economic research but had a focus on policy-relevant topics, like macro policies for full employment, financial regulation, tackling low wages, etc. At the time, Bob was very involved with work on "living wages" initiated by activist groups in Los Angeles and elsewhere. So, by "policy relevant" we meant work that could link up with activists organizing on these issues.

We sometimes referred to wanting to build a Brookings Institute of the left. But we also had a key objective to train graduate students who were also interested in policy-relevant research topics. In addition, we wanted to help build and sustain former heterodox students who were now teaching in dispersed liberal arts colleges to help give them research support, build networks of engagement, etc., so that it would be easier for them to remain engaged in this kind of work. Hence, unlike Brookings, we wanted to be closely associated with (but not formally part of) a graduate department focusing on heterodox economics. UMass was perfect for this.

Who are some of your strongest intellectual influences?

At the grand level, Karl Marx and John Maynard Keynes are, of course, my major intellectual influences: Marx for his focus on class processes and his overall macroeconomic vision; and Keynes for his focus on aggregate demand and his brilliant insights into the finance/investment nexus. But I have had strong intellectual influences much closer to home, as well. Two strong ones are, first, Jim Crotty, who has taught me most of what I know about the deep insights of Keynes and how they are interconnected with the analysis of Marx; and my old graduate school friend Tom Ferguson, who taught me a great deal about politics and the political economy of finance. I have learned a great deal from Jane D'Arista and Robert McCauley about the workings of the international financial system. And last, but far from least, I have learned a great deal from Bob Pollin, including the importance of connecting academic work with progressive political movements.

Your research in the early stages of your academic career concentrated primarily on Federal Reserve politics, monetary policy, and central banking in general. Was this because of the phenomenon of stagflation that plagued the US economy in the 1970s?

The stagflation of the 1970s certainly was an important factor. But the main related factor was the central role played at that time by the Fed in trying to fight stagflation, and especially the powerful role played by Federal Reserve Chair Paul Volcker. At the time, Volcker was called the second most powerful person in Washington, right after the president. Yet leftist economists had no analysis of the Federal Reserve, or central banking more generally. None. It was just folded into the undifferentiated "theory of the state." Yet, under Volcker at least, it was completely running the show.

I was inspired by the work of Jim Crotty, Ray Boddy, and Leonard Rapping, who wrote seminal pieces on the political economy of macro-economic policy from a radical political economy perspective. Building on that, I wanted to focus on what I saw as a key component of macro-economic policy: the central bank.

Focusing on the Fed immediately forced me to develop an analysis of the financial system and the political economy of finance, since that is such an important component of monetary policy, and the institutional structure and politics of the central bank. And given the massive growth of US finance into the international arena, that ensured that I would have to study international finance as well. So that pretty much settled my research agenda for the rest of my career until this point.

What caused stagflation, and can it happen again?

Yes, of course, it can happen again. The most convincing theories of stagflation emphasized class and intra-class conflicts over income shares, exacerbated by supply shortages, and accommodated by the financial system, including the central bank. These theories were developed by Bob Rowthorn, Tom Weiskopf, and others in the 1970s and had a lot of explanatory power for the stagflation of the 1970s. Such stagflations not only could happen again, but do happen right now in various countries these days: Argentina, Zimbabwe, and elsewhere.

Could it happen in the rich countries again? There are various plausible scenarios one could spin out for future stagflation. To me, the most likely ones involve climate change. Climate change is likely to lead to droughts, famines, water shortages—classic supply shortages that will lead to national and global struggles over real income shares. Our current financial system is highly liquid, and central banks will be under pressure by some to accommodate these shocks (and others not to accommodate them), so the level of conflict-driven inflation will once again become a major political struggle, as it was in the 1970s and 1980s. I know it might seem hard to believe in this day of mostly low inflation and steady economic growth, but such climate related problems are, at best, just around the corner.

The last financial crisis raised once again critical questions about central banking and its legitimacy, given that central bankers remain unelected policy-makers. However, in an era in which the public does not trust politicians and has no faith in experts, who should run central banks, and what's the best way to conduct monetary policy?

These are important and difficult problems. For most of my career, I have advocated for "democratically controlled" central banks, and have criticized the popular notion of the "independent" central bank. I have argued and continue to believe that "central bank independence" is a misnomer; there is no such thing as an "independent" central bank. Central banks are political creatures, as are all important and powerful economic institutions. In the United States, the Federal Reserve is, in principle, controlled by Congress, and administratively, is formally influenced by the president through the power of appointment. Yet the Fed currently retains a great deal of autonomy and tries to maintain that autonomy by cultivating a strong constituency that will protect its independence from Congress and the president. Typically, in the US and elsewhere, that constituency is made up mostly by bankers and financiers—Wall Street. As Milton Friedman, of all people, put it years ago (and I am paraphrasing here): "When central banks are independent of government they will be too dependent on the commercial bankers." So the question is not how "independent" the central bank is; the question is who will the central bank be dependent on: Wall Street, some other faction of capital, or the society more generally.

Given the choice between Wall Street and "the people," I have always chosen "the people."

But, as in most things, the devil is in the details. How do you make the central bank democratic? How do you do that when the political system is corrupt, or controlled by autocrats, or by oligarchs? In the United States, Trump tried to gain more control over the Fed in order to promote his re-election. Trump's opponents, even some of those on the left, were crying out for the sanctity of "central bank independence"!

What are we to make of all this? In my view, democratizing the central bank is still the right principle. But if the political institutions are corrupt, then that might mean more community or decentralized control; it might even mean more control by technocrats who must answer to community and labor institutions, rather than just to the banks. In the US, for example, as Bob Pollin wrote, it might mean more control by the regional reserve banks of the Fed, which, in turn, have been democratized through more community and labor control.

In thinking these ideas through, it is important to remember, as we say in critique of neoliberal policy, one size does not fit all. The best institutional structure will vary from place to place and circumstance to circumstance. The institutions and facts on the ground matter a lot.

The study of financialization has been an important component of your research agenda in recent years. Does financialization represent a new stage in the evolution of capitalism? Is it directly related to neoliberalism and globalization? And to what extent has the unprecedented expansion of information technology contributed to the expansion of financial markets and financial liberalization programs?

I think the idea of "financialization" has provided a useful umbrella through which we can conceptualize and study some important dynamics of capitalism in recent years. The concept has connected with a lot of good research in the areas of sociology, political economy, economics, history, and other fields. There are many definitions of "financialization," largely because this is such a multifaceted phenomenon. It seems to me that a key idea is the idea that financial thinking, financial goals, financial groups, and financial institutions increasingly dominate economic and political activity and decisions.

As with other academic concepts and buzzwords, however, it can be over-used and over-academicized (if that is a word). So, as with other such ideas, we have to be careful not to act as if this is the only lens through which we can usefully analyze the dynamics of capitalism and social and political life.

It seems to me that the best way to think about "financialization" is that it is very closely connected to neoliberalism and globalization. These forces reinforce and propel each other in powerful ways, so that it is impossible to clearly disentangle them. Analytically, of course, it can be useful to analyze the components and forces operating in an overall dynamic, but one should not lose sight of the integral whole that they make up.

In doing this, of course one needs to include the key role of information technology—and digitalization. Thus, the development of Marxian "forces of production" are crucial here, as they are in many aspects of the development of capitalism.

Does financialization represent a new stage of capitalism? I have trouble answering such questions because I know that, in Marxist and other theoretical literature, concepts such as "stage" are highly contested and fraught. I have tried to keep my sanity by not getting involved in such debates, as important as they might be.

One of the most controversial questions surrounding financialization is its relationship to the real economy, with much of progressive political economic analysis suggesting that the former's impact on the latter is one of a mainly parasitic nature. Do you subscribe to this completely negative view of financialization?

This is an extremely important issue. I would like to say that the jury is still out on this one; but the fact of the matter is, much to my great disappointment, there is no jury on this one. This is one of those topics on which everyone seems to have an opinion, but no one has done the

serious research to figure out what "the truth" is. I really wish graduate
students and other researchers would develop some research strategies
to seriously study this question and then we could have an informed,
rather than an ideological, debate about it.

This would be a great series of research projects. The researchers
could utilize many of the tools used to study other important phenomena: identifying the channels through which financialization can affect
the economy; estimate the impacts of these channels and their interactions, using econometrics, comparative case studies, etc. It would be a
great set of projects.

There is already good theoretical work on some of these issues. But
we need the hard-core empirical evidence to make progress.

*There is also growing concern that financialization may impede climate
change mitigation. What's your own take on this matter?*

Unfortunately, I am not an expert on this topic, but, as you can see from
my answer to your question below, this is a topic I hope to turn my
attention to soon.

But I can make a few points in response now. There appear to be
forces moving in both directions. On the one hand, it is well known that
financialization is associated with short-termism. This would tend to
discourage longer-term investments of the type needed in some areas of
climate change mitigation and avoidance.

On the other hand, financialization is associated with the creation of
huge pools of liquidity looking for financial returns. To the extent that
climate change investments can mobilize these resources, it might actually contribute to mitigation.

As I said, I am not (yet) an expert on this topic but hope to learn more
in the future.

*Neoliberalism is now well into its fortieth year, and is widely regarded by
progressive and radical political economists as the root of all our problems.
How do you explain the rise and spread of neoliberalism, and are you
surprised by its durability?*

It would take a library to answer this question. In fact, libraries of books
and articles have been written on this. I do wonder about how durable

it has been. I think we might be entering a new era that, like all era transitions, contains elements of the new, old, and even older . . . there are many layers of economic and social relations contained in society at any given time. So, of course, elements of neoliberalism will remain as forces that benefit from it and fight like hell to preserve it. But, in my view, neoliberalism is not well suited to the emerging era dominated by global climate change. As I suggested above, there will be increased conflicts over resources, borders, profits, and the basics of life. Governments will have to get much more involved in resource alloca-tion decisions, income and wealth distribution processes, national security and border issues. These processes will either become much more authoritarian or more progressive, but markets, liberalization, and liberalism are likely to play a smaller role in this than they have in the period of neoliberal ascent.

Given the current state of research and scholarship in the dismal science, do you think economists are trying on the whole to solve the right prob-lems? Or, to put the question differently, is economics a real science, couched in terms of standards of scientific objectivity?

Economics as a discipline has gotten more diverse, in my view. It is not as subsumed under an overarching vision of the invisible hand and the overall, obvious desirability of capitalism and markets as it once was. Its lack of an overarching vision is both an improvement, but in some ways a shortcoming, in comparison to many heterodox economists. And to be sure, the hardcore neoliberals with a retrograde vision of the singular virtue of the invisible hand are not only still present in many depart-ments, but they still dominate much graduate training in economics and editorial control over journals. This is a serious problem for the pros-pects of economics as a discipline really breaking free of the chains of neoliberalism that are still so strong.

Any discipline that is guided by an ideology is not "a real science," fraught as that concept is on its own terms. On the other hand, hetero-dox economics, in my view, has gotten much stronger in the last several decades: it has a smaller component of pure ideological posturing, and more serious research devoted to understanding the world and learning how to change it. It has gotten broader, incorporating truly important work on gender, race, ethnicity, and the environment, among other factors. So, if we can just preserve and preferably grow the institutional bases of heterodox economics, then we can continue to make progress.

This, in fact, was the main objective Bob Pollin and I had in establishing PERI.

What about your own research agenda? In which direction do you see it going next, and what new topics do you think progressive political economy should focus on in the third decade of the twentieth-first century?

As for my research agenda: I hope to engage more with and eventually contribute to research on climate change. Since my area is finance and political economy, I suspect that these will be my entry points into my research on climate change and its mitigation.

As for what progressive political economy should do? I do hope more political economists address issues of climate change. I am still surprised at how few graduate students are interested in these topics, given the seriousness of the problem. I hope this changes.

But, of course, there is no shortage of important issues. I am gratified to see that more heterodox economists are engaged in empirical, historical, and institutional research and are engaging in policy relevant work. Theoretical work will always be important to any discipline, heterodox political economy included. I would just like to see the balance shift a bit to more applied work so that, among other things, we can more easily help progressive political struggles.

Responses on the COVID-19 Pandemic

Do you draw any general lessons from the COVID crisis about the most viable ways to advance an egalitarian economic project?

It has become almost a cliché now to remark that COVID-19 has shed a spotlight on and greatly exacerbated long-standing, pre-existing inequalities in our economic and social system. While true, there are nonetheless some odd aspects to putting the issue this way. These inequalities and their devastating impacts have been apparent for decades. They are certainly massive with respect to their global aspects. But they are also critical within the United States. Focusing here on the US, for years, these inequalities in working conditions, health care provision, and failures of the social safety net have dramatically worsened the lives of racial and ethnic minorities, many women, and working-class people. Yet the capitalist and political elites not only have ignored these inequalities, but they have actually thrived while worsening them.

What has been made clear, especially in the United States, is the iron grip that capitalist practices and structures have on our society and economy. This means, to my way of thinking, that the key to advance egalitarian projects is to directly confront this political reality as part and parcel of our engagement with the political economy of progressive policy reform and transformation.

Of course, successfully confronting this has to be done on multiple fronts simultaneously: the continued mobilization of progressive political forces, such as Black Lives Matter, the Sunrise Movement, and the revitalization of progressive forces in the union movement; the continued emphasis on voting for progressive candidates to build the electoral strength of progressives at all levels; building the programs for training progressive cadres of economists and other social scientists and experts both within and outside the academy; and the mobilization and effective action of elected officials to effect policy.

And, though there are many, many problems facing our society and economy, we will necessarily need to focus on a few areas, such as fighting climate change; generating full employment in good, well-paying jobs; creation of a universal, fair, and efficient health care system; providing adequate support for education and the care sector; and eliminating systemic racism and gender discrimination.

Thus, to me, a key lesson of the COVID crisis is that progressives at all levels must keep up a relentless political mobilization to gain political power wherever possible to create the space for implementation of the many excellent, well-conceived, and well-developed policy proposals developed by progressive economists and others: these include, for example, a Green New Deal, Medicare for All, criminal justice reform, care work provision, living wages, and publicly oriented credit creation and allocation (for example, using public banks).

In short, the development of progressive policy and the cultivation of political power must go hand in hand if we are to slow down, stop, and then reverse the powerful forces of capitalist reaction that are on the march across the globe.

Does the experience of the COVID crisis shed any light on the way you think about economics as a discipline, or, more specifically, the questions you might be pursuing in your own research?

Yes, as I suggested in my previous answer, the COVID crisis and the policy response to it has reinforced the need for a political economy power analysis to accompany important policy analyses for reform and transformation.

The COVID experience has also brought to the fore for me the increased need for economists to study the processes of planning and administration in conjunction with capitalist and market forces. We have been witnessing the mostly failed attempts of governments to deal with the fallout from the COVID crisis, and then the more successful processes of developing vaccines. The massive logistical need to administer these vaccines to the bulk of the world's population is next on the agenda and the ability of state planning and administration processes will be critical to the outcome. These factors will also weigh heavily on our ability to carry out a Green transition, and our ability to solve other major national and global problems.

The rise of neoliberalism and the fall of the Soviet Union led to a marginalization of state planning and administration as an important topic of study. But it is once again clear how important these issues are. For those doing political economy, the same issues of capitalist incentives, political power, property rights and class, gender and racial prejudice and inequality will rear their heads in this planning context as well.

As the coronavirus has reminded us of the need for the state, planning, and administration, we economists will have to incorporate these issues more fully and rigorously back into our field of study.

Representative Publications and Influences

Publications:

Gerald Epstein and Thomas Ferguson (1984). Monetary Policy, Loan Liquidation, and Industrial Conflict: The Federal Reserve and the Open Market Operations of 1932. *The Journal of Economic History*, 44(4), 957–983.

Gerald Epstein (2019). *What's Wrong with Modern Money Theory? A Policy Critique*. Palgrave/Macmillan.

Gerald Epstein (2019). *The political economy of central banking: Contested control and the power of finance, selected essays of Gerald Epstein*. Edward Elgar Publishing.

People who have been influential: Jim Crotty, Karl Marx, John Maynard Keynes, Grant Trippel, Tom Ferguson, Jane D'Arista, Bob Pollin

Literature that has been influential:

Raford Boddy and James Crotty, "Class Conflict and Macropolicy: The Political Business Cycle", *Review of Radical Political Economics*, April 1975.

James Crotty (2009). "Structural causes of the global financial crisis: A critical assessment of the "new financial architecture." *Cambridge Journal of Economics*, 33(4), 563–580.

James Crotty (2019). *Keynes against capitalism: His economic case for liberal socialism*. Routledge.

Nancy Folbre

Nancy Folbre is Professor Emerita of Economics at the University of Massachusetts Amherst and Senior Research Fellow at the Political Economy Research Institute. Folbre's research focuses on the economics of care. Folbre is the author of numerous books, including *Who Pays for the Kids* (1994), *The Invisible Heart* (2001), *Greed, Lust and Gender: A History of Economic Ideas* (2009), and *The Rise and Decline of Patriarchal Systems* (2021). She has served as president of the International Association for Feminist Economics (IAFFE), as an associate editor of the journal *Feminist Economics* since 1995, and as a member of the editorial board of the *Journal of Women, Politics & Policy*. Nancy Folbre has been the recipient of a MacArthur Foundation Fellowship Award, the MacArthur "genius" prize, among other honors.

Economics has always been a male-dominated field, and remains so down to this day. This is true, even though high-powered positions in institutions such as the Federal Reserve and international organizations such as the International Monetary Fund have been recently occupied by women. What inspired you to pursue economics as a field to study and work in?

I grew up in a household where the disconnect between productive contribution and personal compensation was particularly conspicuous. My father was a fixer for a family of somewhat dysfunctional Texas millionaires. He managed their investments, minimized their taxes, arranged their hunting trips, discouraged their self-destructive habits, and rescued them from various embarrassments and discomforts. He often patiently explained to me that money does not buy happiness. On the other hand, when I suggested that it could possibly buy happiness for other people who really needed some, he simply said that I would understand this problem when I grew up.

Who were some major influences on you as you began working in political economy? How did you make the connection between political economy more generally and what we now call feminist economics? Who were the major early contributors to feminist economics that influenced your own intellectual development?

Here, "who" is less relevant than "what." I was involved in the antiwar movement, then in larger anti-imperialist and environmental efforts that made economics politically relevant. I got to know some women activists that made me aware of feminist concerns, and then had the experience of being purged from the Venceremos Brigade partly as a result of being tagged a counterrevolutionary women's liberationist. The others in my group who were tagged the same way agreed to undergo self-criticism. I did not.

I did not really connect with feminist theory until I left Texas to go to graduate school at the University of Massachusetts Amherst. One of my mentors there, Sam Bowles, was good friends with a faculty member in the philosophy department, Ann Ferguson, who introduced me to socialist feminist ideas.

You have made a significant contribution to feminist economics. Did you start out being consciously aware of the fact that many economic principles are gendered-shaped, or was it something that evolved through time?

My personal experiences with issues of sexual and reproductive rights offered some pretty important lessons. The parallels between capitalist and patriarchal hierarchies became apparent to me at a pretty early stage, but it took me a while to figure out how to articulate these.

What would you say are the central principles of feminist economics?

I think the most important political principle is that women have some collective interests as women that are sometimes at odds with the collective interests of men. The process of articulating these interests requires attention to processes of reproduction and family care as well as production and family income. And attention to processes of reproduction and family care challenges simplistic definitions of individual self-interest. I have always emphasized this threesome of feminist theoretical issues: collective interests based on gender, the importance of nonmarket work, and the economic impact of commitments to the well-being of dependents.

Do you think feminist perspectives help illuminate all or most areas of economic reality, or are feminist concerns limited to a relatively narrow set of concerns?

Feminist perspectives grew out of concern for gender inequality, but they have often been inflected by concerns about parallel dimensions of inequality based on class, race, and citizenship. The desire to develop a more cooperative and egalitarian society requires a broad explanation of how and why hierarchical systems evolve. Feminist economics, like environmental economics, points beyond market exchange to institutional frameworks that affect collective bargaining power. Indeed, there is good reason to believe that patriarchal institutions emerged at a very early stage of human history and provided a template for other exploitative institutions such as slavery, violent appropriation of assets, and inheritance of private property.

To what extent do you think that feminist economics draws usefully from the more traditional Marxian view of capitalism?

I think feminist economics can learn a great deal from the Marxian theory of historical materialism, an early effort to understand and explain institutional change. But the most important feature of Marxian theory, in my opinion, is its emphasis on collective conflict. Traditional Marxian theory, however, often features a single-minded focus on class conflict and a tendency to blame some abstract "capitalism" for everything that is wrong with the world.

You have argued that "capitalism doesn't care that much about care." Can you elaborate a bit on how this critical realization helps to enhance the traditional left critique of capitalism as an essentially unjust and inhumane socio-economic system?

Capitalist systems aren't the only unjust and inhuman systems around, and they cannot take all the blame for inequalities based on gender, race, and citizenship, which often shape the incidence of class inequalities. Traditional Marxists tend to cling to an idealized view of precapitalist societies, as well as an unrealistically romantic view of postcapitalist societies. Many so-called socialist revolutions have led to extremely undemocratic outcomes that cannot be explained away by the claim that they were really just disguised forms of capitalism.

It is not easy to design cooperative and egalitarian institutions that are politically and economically sustainable, and this task cannot be accomplished simply by "ending" capitalism.

In The Invisible Heart, *you argued that society must establish a new set of rules for mutual responsibilities. What might those rules be in the age of a global neoliberal economic order?*

I am not a schoolmarm telling the children what rules they need to follow. I am an economist pointing out that short-term economic interests often come into conflict with long-term economic interests. Care of our natural and social environment imposes costs on those who take responsibility for it. These costs should be equitably shared. If they are not, we will all be caught up in a race to bottom in which nice gals (and guys) finish last, and the not-nice will eventually run each other into the ground.

Participation of women in the labor force has increased substantially virtually throughout the world. How does the level of women's labor force participation enhance economic well-being?

Why would you think that women's labor force participation has different effects than men's labor force participation? Are you defining "labor force" as participation in wage labor? Has it occurred to you that this definition is fundamentally misleading?

If increases in women's employment enable us to raise living standards and improve human capabilities in sustainable ways, it potentially increases economic well-being. Obviously, much depends on how economic well-being is distributed. Much also depends on whether men become more willing to contribute to nonmarket work.

Why should unpaid work be treated as work, and what are the primary concerns you have about unpaid work?

I think you have phrased this question in a peculiar way. Why shouldn't unpaid work be treated as work? How do you think work should be defined—as any activity that is paid for? Work is, more generally, any activity that someone else could perform on your behalf. Women perform a great deal of unpaid work on behalf of children, the sick, individuals with disabilities, and adult men who devote a larger percentage of their time to paid work. The economic rewards that women receive for this work are often meager and generally unreliable.

You were a graduate student at UMass Amherst and then spent most of your professional career as a UMass Amherst faculty member. What are the ways in which UMass has been conducive to the development of feminist economics?

The Economics Department here has always been open to heterodox and unconventional views. The diversity of both faculty and students has contributed to a fertile intellectual environment. While the Marxian tradition has often been unsympathetic to feminist theory, it has generally supported the cause of "women's liberation."

Can you share with us what you see as your main research concerns over the next five years?

I am trying to develop a more coherent explanation of the rise and decline of patriarchal systems, and, more specifically, the complex and contradictory interaction between patriarchal and capitalist dynamics.

I am also trying to provide empirical evidence of the undervaluation of care work in families, communities, and in paid employment. I believe that this undervaluation is now a major determinant of gender inequality.

Responses on the COVID-19 Pandemic

How would you evaluate the ways different countries or regions have responded to the COVID-19 crisis, both in terms of public health interventions and economic policies?

I believe the US is the clear winner of the Worst in the World Public Health Pandemic Response Prize, awarded on the basis of what I would call the effectiveness ratio—actual response divided by potential ability to respond.

Our residents are more affluent and better educated than those of most other countries in the world. We also have a relatively low population density. We have some of the best research scientists, physicians, and public health experts in the world.

This all mattered little in the face of perverse leadership, social division, and partisan politics.

I haven't done any detailed analysis of economic policies, but co-authors and I have looked at the relative pay of essential occupations in the "paid care sector" (those employed in health, education, and social services) in the US.[1] They clearly earn less than other essential occupations—and not just because they are dominated by women.

I have also collaborated with Leila Gautham, Franziska Dorn, and Martha McDonald on a comparison of hazard pay policies for essential workers in the US, Germany, and Canada, all countries with a federal governance structure in which policies vary considerably by state or province.[2] The US government has done virtually nothing on this front.

It has been reported that mortality rates from COVID are especially high among Blacks and Latinos in the US, largely because they tend to be in jobs that involve a higher risk of infection, with less opportunity to work from home.[3]

Yet the US does not collect occupational data on death certificates, so

1   Nancy Folbre, Leila Gautham, and Kristin Smith, "Essential Workers and Care Penalties in the US," forthcoming in *Feminist Economics*.

2   Franziska Dorn, Nancy Folbre, Leila Gautham, and Martha MacDonald, "Cheap Praise: Supplemental Pay for Essential Workers in the COVID-19 Pandemic," manuscript, Department of Economics, University of Massachusetts Amherst.

3   Gina Kolata, "Social Inequities Explain Racial Gaps in Pandemic, Studies Find," *New York Times*, December 9, 2020.

there is virtually no systematic information on occupational risk from COVID-19 exposure. This seems like a serious violation of Occupational Safety and Health Administration principles, and one that will hamper effective planning for vaccination triage.

Do you draw any general lessons from the COVID crisis about the most viable ways to advance an egalitarian economic project? Does the experience of the COVID crisis shed any light on the way you think about economics as a discipline or, more specifically, the questions you might be pursuing in your own research?

My answer to both these questions is about the same: The general lesson, I think, is that almost half the electorate in the US is unable to focus on anything like an egalitarian economic project, for reasons that may—ironically—be related to the weakening of this project.

A sense of decreased economic security and downward mobility has contributed to a xenophobic and racist paranoia, a toxic surge of misinformation, and a vicious attack on democratic institutions. I thought that the pandemic would, like any "external" attack, elicit patriotic solidarity and commitment to mutual aid. So far, it has not—just the opposite.

Intersectional dynamics can take some of the blame: somehow divisions based on race/ethnicity, gender, sexuality, and age have come to trump class. Also, class differences have developed new dimensions—breaking along lines of education (a kind of proxy for annual income) rather than wealth ownership.

Class seems to have morphed into new forms. The Republicans, once dubbed the party of financial capital, now seem to represent the interests of real estate speculators and fossil fuel companies. The Democrats, once dubbed the party of the people, now seem to be the party of human capital—people with enough credentials and/or marketable skills to gain at least minimal economic security in a new economic environment characterized by increased global competition and headlong technological change.

Most of my work focuses on the care economy, and I continue to believe that this focus can help build progressive coalitions in the US and elsewhere. I also continue to believe that the pandemic will, in the long run, heighten public awareness of the advantages of single-payer health care, childcare, and elder care services alongside greater public support for family care.

On Biden versus Trump, the gender gap in choices was not as great as I thought it might be, but it remained at the historic high it reached in 2016. The even bigger racial/ethnic gap is essentially holding steady. Intersectional political economy emphasizes the potential to build successful coalitions by showing how much the vast majority of Americans have to gain from equitable and environmentally sustainable forms of growth.

It seems pretty clear that old political and religious dogmas have combined with new social media to change the ecology of information in the US. The delegitimization of scientific knowledge hurts social science as well as public health. We need a better understanding of what's driving it.

Representative Publications and Influences

Publications:

Nancy Folbre (2001). *The Invisible Heart: Economics and Family Values*. The New Press.

Nancy Folbre (2009). *Greed, Lust and Gender: A History of Economic Ideas*. Oxford University Press.

Nancy Folbre (2021). *The Rise and the Decline of Patriarchal Systems*. Verso.

People who have been influential: August Bebel, Heidi Hartmann, Susan Moller Okin

Literature that has been influential:

August Bebel (1910). *Woman and Socialism*. Socialist Literature Co.

Heidi I. Hartmann (1979). The unhappy marriage of Marxism and feminism: Towards a more progressive union. *Capital & Class*, 3(2), 1–33.

Susan M. Okin (1989). *Justice, gender, and the family* (Vol. 171). New York: Basic Books.

James K. Galbraith

James Galbraith holds the Lloyd M. Bentsen Jr. Chair in Government/ Business Relations and is a Professor of Government at the University of Texas at Austin. Galbraith is a Senior Scholar of the Levy Economics Institute, and chair of Economists for Peace and Security. He is the author of dozens of articles and numerous books, including *Welcome to the Poisoned Chalice: The Destruction of Greece and the Future of Europe* (2016); *Inequality: What Everyone Needs to Know* (2016); *The Predator State: How Conservatives Abandoned the Free Market and Why Liberals Should Too* (2008); and *Created Unequal: The Crisis in American Pay* (1998).

Can you share with me some things about your education as an economist?

My education as an economist began when I arrived on the staff of the Committee on Banking, Finance, and Urban Affairs of the US House of Representatives, in June 1975, at the start of the fiscal crisis of New York City, and just as the committee was launching the first serious exercise in congressional oversight of monetary policy. It developed strongly in the early 1980s when I became executive director of the Joint Economic Committee and had responsibility to develop and direct a full-scale opposition to the so-called "Economic Recovery Program" of the Reagan administration. It continued through the debt crisis of the 1980s, a moment of hot debates and interesting interventions into financial policy around the world. In the period before and at various times during those years, I attended Harvard and graduate schools at Cambridge and at Yale, but most of that was intellectual tourism. My real education was on the ground. Later on, in China in the 1990s as chief technical advisor to the State Planning Commission on Macroeconomic Reform, and in Greece in 2015, as well as advising the US congressional leadership on the financial crisis in 2008, I learned a bit more. I also participated in presidential campaigns, beginning seriously with McGovern in 1972—I wrote the "McGovern on the Issues" book in 1971—Udall in 1976, Jackson and Mondale in 1984, and Hart in 1987, as well as a bit for Tom Harkin in 1992. Writing policy papers and speeches for presidential candidates is a useful exercise in economic education.

Since 1985, here in Texas, my education has flowed largely upward from my students, particularly on a large project now ongoing for over twenty years, concerned with effective measurement of economic inequalities and the analysis of common patterns in that data. This work, of the University of Texas Inequality Project, has led to about six books and about seventy working papers, many of them published in journals, so it forms the major portion of my academic contributions. I've also done a bit of historical research, notably into Kennedy's 1963 decision to begin the full withdrawal of all US forces from Vietnam. Somewhat related, I worked for twenty years with fellow members of Economists for Peace and Security, and they have kept me engaged in larger problems of war and peace.

Was the decision to pursue economics influenced by the fact that your father happened to have been one of the most renowned economists of the twentieth century?

Not really. What I got from my father was a body of ideas, an appreciation of certain skills, notably clear expression, some values and useful habits—rather than any particular ambitions. The fact that his generation of economists were all known to me personally as a young person probably made a difference, as well. They were much more interesting and accomplished than the later generations, including mine.

Aside from the influence that your father has had on you, what other economists would you single out as having played a central role in your intellectual development and the shaping of your economic views?

Wassily Leontief was my first economics professor, deeply immersed in the investigation of empirical facts. Nicholas Kaldor I got to know in Cambridge, mostly over Sunday dinners at his home; he impressed on me that the job of an economist is to engage in the policy questions of the day. Joan Robinson, I knew a bit. Robert Eisner was a friend, a rigorous mind, and deeply engaged in the debates of the early 1980s. Luigi Pasinetti is a model theorist and still a close friend. Adrian Wood was my Cambridge tutor in 1974–75. Peter Albin, an early builder of complex system models, helped persuade me to follow my own path when I was beginning to develop my ideas on inequality and numerical taxonomy. There were smart faculty at Yale; I did not, however, work closely with anyone and was only loosely supervised by my congenial and permissive thesis chair, Sidney Winter.

Among larger influences and mentors, I would cite Henry Reuss, chair of the Banking Committee in the 1970s and later of the Joint Economic Committee; I worked for Reuss on and off for eight years and learned thinking, writing, politics, and economics from him. In terms of more remote writerly influences, I would cite the usual suspects: Marx, Veblen, Schumpeter, Keynes. Maybe Georgescu-Roegen. And the econometrician Henri Theil, who provided the analytical framework that I use in my work on inequality. Among friends and colleagues, I'd mention Phil Mirowski, Lance Taylor, Sandy Darity, Anwar Shaikh, Duncan Foley, Ping Chen, Grzegorz Kolodko, Kunibert Raffer, Bruno Amoroso, and Yanis Varoufakis. There are not that many who have survived, prospered, and done important work in the climate of economics departments in recent years. Physicists, biologists, sociologists, anthropologists, historians, and even political scientists are often more interesting.

Your work seems to be broadly within the post-Keynesian analytic framework. Can you explain what, in your view, are the central attributes of that framework? What distinguishes it from mainstream neoclassical economics? Why do you consider this framework to be a superior foundation relative to mainstream neoclassical economics, both in general and in your primary areas of research in macroeconomics and inequality?

I consider myself to be a policy economist with a pragmatic, institution-alist, and Keynesian background, but mainly concerned with applied research into quantitative aspects of economic inequality and public policy. In recent years, I have tried with Jing Chen to develop the idea of a biophysical framework for economic thinking, but the topic is too far from the comfort zones even of heterodox economists to have much influence yet. Monetary policy has been an important topic for me in the past, since I developed the Humphrey-Hawkins framework for congressional hearings on monetary policy (under the dual mandate, full employment and price stability, which I helped draft) back in the 1970s. I read my Keynes at Kings, so I'm Old School. I am of course sympathetic to the post-Keynesians and to the new movement known as Modern Monetary Theory, but I make no claim to be central to either one. Out of hundreds of papers, I have published just three in the *Journal of Post Keynesian Economics*, and one in the *Oxford Handbook of Post-Keynesian Economics*, but that was on income distribution.

As for mainstream neoclassical economics, an assistant professor I knew well at Harvard once said to me, around 1973, "It's a joke!" I have not wasted my time on it since then, except to the very minimal extent absolutely required. One of the interesting features of working on "macroeconomics and inequality" is that there is no classification code in the *Journal of Economic Literature* for work on the "macroeconomics of inequality." Inequality is defined by neoclassical economics as a microeconomic phenomenon. This is annoying, for it means that an article on the macroeconomic determinants of inequalities is guaran-teed to be directed towards a hostile, or at least indifferent, referee.

In 2008, you used the 25th Annual Milton Friedman Distinguished Lecture to launch a devastating critique against "free markets" and monetarism. Yet, in spite of historically unprecedented levels of inequality and the erup-tion of a global financial crisis that, at least according to Ben Bernanke, was the worst in modern history, surpassing even the Great Depression, the economics of neoliberalism continue to reign supreme. How do you explain this economic (and political) anomaly?

"Wealth is power, as Mr. Hobbes says." Adam Smith wrote that. It's in the *Wealth of Nations*. What else do you need to know?

A few years ago, Piketty's Capital in the Twenty-First Century *took both the political and economics world by storm. But you have been critical of Piketty's economic analysis regarding capital in the age of globalization. Can you elaborate a bit on this?*

I've written a number of things on Mr. Piketty's book and have no wish to restate them. I recommend an article by my former student Noah Wright, published in the *World Economic and Social Review*, entitled "Data Visualization in *Capital in the Twenty-First Century*." Wright shows that the key evidence printed in Piketty's own book does not support the claims he makes for it.

In early 2015, you served as an advisor to former Greek Finance Minister Yanis Varoufakis and, among other things, you were part of a team assigned with the task to produce a secret Plan B in the event the European Central Bank sought to stop providing liquidity to Greek banks. What was Plan B really all about?

The Greek government needed to prepare for the possibility that the ECB would collapse the banks. I assisted those preparations as best I could. I deal with this matter very thoroughly in my book *Welcome to the Poisoned Chalice: The Destruction of Greece and the Future of Europe*, published by Yale University Press in 2016.

What's your sense about the direction of economics in the years ahead? Specifically, will neoclassical thinking continue to dominate economics?

Economics needs two things: *glasnost* and *perestroika*. Glasnost is opening up, and it means that research contributions should be judged on their merit and not by a fixed hierarchy of journals, themselves controlled by tribal cliques, which is the current situation. I am trying to contribute to that by serving as managing editor of a journal, *Structural Change and Economic Dynamics*. Perestroika is restructuring, and that means establishing new academic units that are smaller, more flexible, more diverse, creating a range of career paths for economists not controlled by the so-called mainstream. The decision to do that must rest with academic administrators. Given that mainstream economists often become deans, I'm not optimistic. So I believe that intellectual development in economics will continue to happen only on the far fringes of professional hierarchies, in fits and starts, fed by the discontent of agitated students and by the manifest failures of economic performance.

And what's in store for your own research agenda in the years ahead?

I'm not sure. I'm working with Yanis Varoufakis on the Democracy in Europe Movement and specifically on the program for a European New Deal, with Benoît Hamon on the 1717 project, and with several groups in Italy. I've got a connection to the team around Bernie Sanders, but it's quite loose, and US politics generally at the moment appear to be intractable. The Inequality Project will continue but on a fairly slow track, compared to the previous pace of work. At the moment there is a Galbraith revival going on in Russia, and I'm planning to give some lectures there, later in 2018, on my father's work. I've no desire to keep writing the same book, a fate sometimes visited on economists. So I may just wait for the next collapse and try to be useful at that time. An old ambulance chaser of financial crises, such as myself, can usually find something to do.

Responses on the COVID-19 Pandemic

How would you evaluate the ways different countries or regions have responded to the COVID-19 crisis, both in terms of public health interventions and economic policies?

There is in the world a plethora of actual success in containing and suppressing the coronavirus. Apart from the mega-case of China, successful actions were taken and maintained in Vietnam, Korea, Singapore, Hong Kong, Taiwan, New Zealand, Iceland, Cuba, and for significant periods of time in Slovakia, Greece, and also Italy, notwithstanding the terrible toll of the pandemic in Italy in the first months and the recent resurgence. In Latin America, also, Argentina and Uruguay did relatively well.

What these countries and regions had in common, without exception, is that they took the pandemic seriously from the start—from the very first WHO and Chinese warnings on January 3, 2020. In many cases, they had epidemic task forces, steering committees, and plans ready to go, having learned from SARS in 2003. They closed their borders and implemented testing and quarantine for anyone coming across as well as mandated distancing at home. This kept the spread of the virus down to levels that could be tested and traced. Isolation was intense for those exposed. In many cases people were not left at home, but taken to special facilities, locked in, and taken care of for two weeks, whether they showed symptoms or not. In Vietnam, with 97 million people, social distancing was enforced by cadres at the block level. In Cuba, once the first case arrived in February, doctors and medical students visited every household, to check for symptoms, almost every day. In Korea, case levels remained so low that specific spikes in the timeline for the whole country can be identified and linked to this church or that Starbucks—and the virus could therefore be not merely contained, but suppressed. In all successful countries, popular mobilization against the virus was total, cooperation nearly universal, and (as a result) the success became a matter of intense national pride.

The contrast is with countries and regions that did not react quickly, uniformly, and with social solidarity. The United States is the most notorious example, but there are others, notably Brazil, India, and Russia, where vast distances, decentralized administration, and distrust of the government led to disaster. One can also point to Spain, France, Belgium, the United Kingdom, and, in large, to Europe generally. A slow start, a vacillating leader, administrative decentralization, and political polarization combined to give the virus openings, which it took, and continues to take. And there is the problem that internal lockdowns, and draconian isolation from the outside world, cannot continue forever. European countries that were successful in the spring, or that locked down effectively in the summer, were overwhelmed by new waves in the fall—as also happened in the United States.

Generally, in economic terms, those countries that suppressed the virus effectively without regard to economic consequences in the short run were able to recoup most of their economic losses. Those that traded off public health against economic interests in the short run found their economies overwhelmed by the exponential spread of the disease.

Do you draw any general lessons from the COVID crisis about the most viable ways to advance an egalitarian economic project?

The crisis underscores the fragility of our post-industrial economic system, of financialized globalization, of an economy largely sustained for most people by interdependent services, and supported by a vast tissue of private debts. At the same time, it points towards the inadequacy of neoliberal redistributionism, of the idea that the deficiencies of the system can be remedied by measures that change the post-tax, post-transfer distribution relative to the market outcome.

The problem is in the structure of the market institutions themselves. The solution—if there is one—lies along three lines. First, the advanced technological capacities of the system—in energy, information, aerospace, construction, and other areas—will need to be mobilized and repurposed towards public ends. Second, the structures of the services world will need to be reconfigured along largely cooperative lines, with some public support, and with a federal job guarantee as a backstop. Third, the panoply of private debts that cannot be paid because of the pandemic will need to be restructured, written down, and often written off, along with a concomitant reorganization of the financial sector. These measures go far beyond merely raising low-end wages and taxing the rich. They will bring about a more egalitarian society, but more importantly, a less fragile and precarious one.

Does the experience of the COVID crisis shed any light on the way you think about economics as a discipline or, more specifically, the questions you might be pursuing in your own research?

I would judge that two reactions dominated the profession. There was a "freshwater" view, which was the underpinning of a lot of silly talk about the "V-shaped recovery" in the spring of 2020—everything back to normal as soon as the virus is taken care of. It was obvious in May that the collapse of March/April would be followed by a partial rebound, and when that occurred it was taken by the same voices as evidence of their early claim. But it was equally obvious that a partial rebound and a complete return to the prior world are two very different things, and this reality is now being felt.

And there was a "saltwater" view, for which the policy of writing checks to people and to companies was essentially the end-point of discussions and decisions. That view is still dominant, and the palliative of cash assistance is, of course, necessary. But the notion that it is sufficient is (characteristically) thoughtless. We will discover over time that the world is not heading back to the *status quo ante*, and by the time we do understand that, a vast price will have been paid and many opportunities will have been lost.

In short, the crisis has done nothing to improve my view of the way the mainstream of the economics profession operates.

Representative Publications and Influences

Publications:

James K. Galbraith (1984). Galbraith and the Theory of the Corporation. *Journal of Post Keynesian Economics, 7*(1), 43–60.

James K. Galbraith (1997). Time to Ditch the NAIRU. *Journal of Economic Perspectives, 11*(1), 93–108.

James K. Galbraith (2012). *Inequality and instability a study of the world economy just before the great crisis.* Oxford University Press.

People who have been influential: Wassily Leontief, Nicholas Kaldor, Luigi Pasinetti, Philip Mirowski, Henry Reuss, Karl Marx, Thorstein Veblen, Joseph Schumpeter, John Maynard Keynes, Henri Theil

Literature that has been influential:

Luigi Pasinetti (1975). *Growth and Income Distribution,* Cambridge University Press.

Nicholas Kaldor (1985). *Economics Without Equilibrium,* Routledge.

Philip Mirowski (1989). *More Heat Than Light: Economics as Social Physics, Physics as Nature's Economics.* Cambridge University Press.

Teresa Ghilarducci

Teresa Ghilarducci is the Bernard L. and Irene Schwartz Professor of Economics at the New School for Social Research, and the Director of the Schwartz Center for Economic Policy Analysis (SCEPA) and of the New School's Retirement Equity Lab (ReLab). Ghilarducci is a labor economist and nationally recognized expert in retirement security. Her most recent book, *Rescuing Retirement* (co-authored by Hamilton "Tony" James, 2016), outlines their proposal to create Guaranteed Retirement Accounts (GRAs) for all American workers. Ghilarducci has authored several other books on retirement security, including *Labor's Capital: The Economics and Politics of Employer Pensions* (winner of an Association of American Publishers award in 1992).

Can you tell me something about your educational background and why you chose to study economics?

I went to public schools in a California valley town—and if you think the two Californians are NorCal and SoCal, that's wrong. California is split between the paradise communities on the coast and the poorer interior cities in the Central Valley. I grew up in Roseville, a small rail-road town near Sacramento. My father was also born in Roseville (though he did not speak English until about third grade).

My high school was not accredited by the state of California because not enough students could read or write at the eighth-grade level.

Fortunately, the year I was born Sputnik boosted education spending and later the LA poor neighborhood—Watts—"burned" and augured the Great Society programs. The space race and urban uprising meant money poured into public junior colleges, state universities, and the University of California (UC) system, and the Great Society programs meant that poor kids, like me, were targeted for aid. I pretended I was a senior when I was a junior. I applied to UC San Diego—where I went as a freshman—and the next year to UC Berkeley.

They didn't ask, and I didn't tell. I left high school at sixteen and don't have a high school diploma.

I turned sixteen when *Roe v. Wade* was promulgated, and Judge Thurgood Marshall declared that the abortion rights decision gave every sixteen-year-old girl that day the right to determine her own destiny. The Great Society and further female emancipation and my biography helps explain why I chose economics. When I was eleven my parents divorced and my father lost his job—I always worried about money (and food, if the full truth be known). Also, the pressing issues of the day were the environment and welfare reform—was my single-parent family deserving of AFDC and Medicaid? That economics was the "fix it" profession appealed to me. When I got fifteen bucks for my birthday I bought three books: *The Communist Manifesto*, *Free to Choose*, and *There Ain't No Such Thing as a Free Lunch*. And some saint left copies of the *Worldly Philosophers* in my high school home room. I went to night economics classes at a local junior college when I got my driver's license. So those were the four books that I read before I was fifteen. Heilbroner topped them all, and Milton Friedman's book was one of the best written—Friedman was a good stylist.

Who are the economists that have influenced you the most?

There isn't much of a distinction between me as an economist and me as a person because I have been reading economists since I was fifteen. In our teenage years, we lay down facts and frameworks for long-term memory. I've already mentioned the dead male economists from my high school days. My undergraduate teacher, Professor Steve Goldman, taught a Keynes and Axel Leijonhufvud seminar at Berkeley; Bill Tabb and Michael Reich taught Marx, a great influence; Professor Lloyd Ulman made me read Sidney and Beatrice Webb, and the Harvard labor economist bible, by Slichter, Healy, and Livernash. *The Economics of Collective Bargaining* is a book full of stories of struggle and sophistication of workers and employers and industries coming together in a growing economy to accommodate each other. Ed Lazear's book, *Economics of Personnel Management*, is the neoclassical functional explanation of management norms. Clair Brown's books on time use and living standards were an important source of imagination. Gary Becker and Nancy Folbre could describe how women and men try to live with each other and how employers use the stratification between men and women to their advantage.

Michael Piore, Paul Osterman, and Tom Kochan provide stable and fundamental connections between firm and industry structure and labor relations. I have come to view employers as leveraging work intensity and compensation to increase surplus.

George Akerlof, Joseph Stiglitz, and Bill Dickens formalize the daily interactions between people when one is capital and the other is labor. My account of my early struggle with framing explanations about unemployment, pay, and discrimination and respecting the complexity of the labor market cannot go on without mentioning Chuck Craypo, who was by my side for years at the University of Notre Dame. For over ten years we ran an annual conference on segmented labor markets and Chuck was strategic; he brought in Frank Wilkinson and Ajit Singh from Cambridge University, using endowed chair money for rotating chairs rather than a super star permanent faculty.

We really had something going on in institutional labor economics that was very different from the seminars at NBER and those organized by IZA and the *Journal of Labor Economics*. How different? Labor economics has always been empirical and the segmented labor market analysis is no exception. Conventional labor economics often explains employment and pay as outcomes of individual labor leisure choices. Our seminar and framework kept a close eye on employers as drivers and active agents.

What drove you to concentrate on labor economics and the study of pension policies as the primary areas of your research?

Economics seemed the most important subject to study since I was thirteen and my life depended upon my mother's job. But thirteen-year-olds are idealists—probably a selective factor for the human species—and Earth Day created a vision for the future that even I could see at a young age depended on changing relative prices of fossil fuels.

On the home front, I felt the importance of economics every time my mother changed jobs because we were on and off food stamps and Medicaid; my adolescent classmate's mom worked at the telephone company—she and thus he knew when our phone lines were cut. He teased me; but his mother turned our line back on for free. Go, Richard's mom!

Social policy was a lived teenage experience. The focus on Social Security and pensions came up later in two ways: I won a United Auto Workers "scholarship" for graduate students who wanted to learn more about labor. The prize was attending a union members' retreat at Black Lake in Upper Michigan, where I took classes from the union economist who negotiated pensions in collective-bargaining agreements for UAW Chrysler. Those details linked national policy to Social Security and Medicare with the complex and political arrangements of saving money with your employer—imagine the trust in the union, employers, and financial system to give up money now for money later. The other source is that when I was in graduate school—I entered early at twenty—I was a research assistant at Berkeley's labor center. My job was to arrange and provide curriculum for unions in their negotiations—pension plans were a complex area. One of those contracts was for my mother when she worked at the *Sacramento Bee* selling classified ads—one of the few Newspaper Guild locals that organized the "girls" in advertising. I help negotiate contracts for the Stanford University employees as well.

What school of thought of economics does your work fall in?

I am an institutional labor economist, and some of my colleagues at the New School would say that that means I use a neoclassical framework. In approaching situations, I follow the money and incentives and usually find that a struggle and contestation over rents explains the outcome I'm trying to model.

My models are riddled with concepts of rents and employment and wage indeterminacy. I often use a neoclassical concept—"rents"—because it gives a narrative that explains falling labor shares. While the neoclassical model helps us understand that a relative constraint on supply creates rents, the idealization leaves too much out to be of practical use. The empirical observation that rules are constructed through the political process by interests made influential by their corporate or family wealth is left out. And that bit is too important to leave out even when simplicity could enlighten us.

So what does my practice make me? An institutionalist. As J.E. King wrote in 1980, "Labour economics has always been disputed territory, a battlefield normally occupied by the massed ranks of neoclassical armies, though never securely and always subject to attack."

I describe institutionalism in economics as an emphasis on the economic actors' self-interested rent-seeking behavior and how the welfare state shapes those actions. One should also take into account how entitlements and expectations are formed and how the welfare state could affect those expectations. From time to time, dominant interpretations of the functioning of capitalism changed, which leads to changes in welfare policies. The shift from Keynesianism to monetarism is an example of a paradigmatic shift in how the political economy of the welfare state was shaped.

Daniel Hamermesh has an especially glib quote where he brings out a special feature of labor economics, and that highlights its necessary interdisciplinary aspects. The labor market is not like any other input market. It is different. Why? "It can walk away." As Marxists and non-Marxists—David Gordon, Sam Bowles, Herb Gintis, George Akerlof, Joe Stiglitz, Armen Alchian, and Harold Demsetz—would point out, labor can withhold effort. In other words, labor economics is unique because labor is a human input.

The distinctions are not large, but institutionalism differs from political economy because much of institutionalist thought focuses on the oddities of contracts made in markets that may or may not be made with equal power, honesty, and intent. Clark Kerr and Oliver Williamson wrote about the "new institutionalists" who care about market distortions and expect them to happen—quirks of information or interventions are not the exception, they are the rule. The political economist also challenges the idealization that contracts made with little interference are fair expressions of mutually beneficial compromises—political economists understandably conclude that since labor is a perishable good, labor needs the deal more urgently, vitally needs the exchange and therefore has less ability to walk away. Every buyer and seller has opposite interests except the trade; the good or service is valuable to the buyer and costly to provide for the seller. Sam Bowles and Herb Gintis call markets a system of claims and agreements that give rise to "contested exchange." Claims and agreements in the labor market are no different: it's a market characterized by contest and struggle. Sandy Darity's surplus population idea, a clever use of—not Marx's—"reserve army of labor," explains that having a population that will substitute for workers who demand higher wages and jobs that don't kill or maim helps employers intensify labor and keep compensation down, is consistent with a reserve army framework. Darity takes his use of "surplus populations" from Charles Dicken's 1843 *A Christmas Carol*:

> "Are there no prisons?"
> "Plenty of prisons . . ."
> "And the Union workhouses," demanded Scrooge. "Are they still in operation?" . . .
> "Both very busy, sir . . ."
> "Those who are badly off must go there."
> "Many can't go there; and many would rather die."
> "If they would rather die," said Scrooge, "they had better do it, and decrease the surplus population."

Has the study of labor economics changed from the time you started out? If so, how?

When I entered the academic labor market in the 1980s with my dissertation from UC Berkeley, universities were seeking economists specializing in housing demand and labor supply when homeless and joblessness were at all-time highs. "Job Openings for Economists" could have been meat for John Oliver's satirical comedy show if it had existed. The Reagan administration had just deeply cut Section 8 housing and public housing subsidies (the Trump administration has threatened to do the same), spurring a sharp rise of homelessness—22 percent annual rate increase in the mid 1980s. Also, the peak of the recession occurred in late 1982, and the nationwide unemployment rate was almost 11 percent, the highest since the Great Depression.

The University of Notre Dame's Economics Department was hiring and its chair—Chuck Wilber—had just advised the Catholic Conference of Bishops on inequality and economic growth. Professor Wilber sought economists specializing in labor, poverty, public policy, and development. I was hired as an assistant professor in 1984—and I stayed for twenty-five years teaching ten different graduate and undergraduate courses including intermediate macro and graduate labor economics—with wonderful colleagues committed to academic rigor and social justice.

Let me get back on track here. You asked how labor economics has changed since the 1980s or so.

Back in the early 1980s, two papers represented the field. One by Martin Feldstein, who claimed that unemployment insurance causes more unemployment; and the second by Richard Burkhauser, who proffered that the existence of Medicare contributed to bad health habits of young Americans because they knew at age sixty-five that medical insurance would be free. The constructs were cartoonish and derived from a primitive kind of neoclassical economics. The formalism of *The Market for Lemons*, of course; *Unemployment as a Discipline Device* helped frame my work as a labor economist in terms of the microfoundations of the contested exchange between managers and workers.

Further, labor economists have made great strides by insisting on better data, which leads to better models. Labor economists are increasingly using data sets that link employers to employees in the United States; this data was a "holy grail" and a project of visionaries, including those in the US Department of Labor. The new labor economics will be using these data; key economists doing this work include John Abowd, Clair Brown, David Autor, and Till Von Wachter. Careful work from data from employers is also an advance.

Henry Phelps Brown compared US and UK labor economics not so much on ideology as much as on how data and methodology shape ideology. In the United Kingdom, the research data is oriented towards firms, firms as the agent, and firms as the mover and shaker. Therefore, outcomes in the labor market could be explained by the incentives and practice of that actor, the employer. In similar fashion, unions are studied: Jill Rubery's article on how workers' organizations influence the structure of labor markets is found on many syllabi for graduate labor economics.[1]

---

1   Jill Rubery, "Structured Labour Markets, Worker Organisation and Low Pay," *Cambridge Journal of Economics* 2:1 (1978): 17–36.

The United States collects comprehensive data on individual workers and, together with the ideology of individual choice and utility maximization, outcomes are explained based on individual wants, needs, and preferences. American economists explain that women work in low-paying, dead-end jobs because they wanted them, to have time to raise families. Preferences don't explain the sexist outcome. Sociologist Paula England found that never-married women and women without children had similar outcomes to married mothers.

How important is the distinction between normative and positive economics for you? Or, to put it differently, do you believe that economics should strive as much as possible to be value free?

Economists, as well as all social scientists, could be accused of using theories or paradigms as vending machines. Ethicist Nancy Cartwright's characterization: "You feed certain prescribed forms for the desired output; it regurgitates for a while; then drops out the sought-for representations, plonk on the tray, fully formed, as Athena from the brain of Zeus."[2]

And, since economics is about the formation of markets, which in turn, are created by and manifest from rules and regulations that come from a vision and political maneuvering about the way society should be, there doesn't seem to be much difference between normative and positive.

Let me provide an example. Richard Thaler won a Nobel Prize in economics for generating the field of behavioral economics; he is eager to influence public policy, writing the best seller *Nudge*. He and Cass Sunstein, his co-author, argue that people should have choice and the nation should create an architecture of incentives to do many socially beneficial acts—for instance, save for retirement. They call "mandating" savings for retirement not feasible and their complex system of rules and tax breaks "libertarian paternalism."

Thaler and Sunstein's policy recommendations come from a normative position. They do not recommend mandatory enrollment in a supplemental retirement plan even though most people need to be in a

---

2   As quoted in Kwame Anthony Appiah, *As If: Idealization and Ideals,* Cambridge, MA: Harvard University Press, 2017, 13.

supplemental retirement plan to Social Security to be insured against superannuation and poverty in old age. They argue it is ethical to provide a "choice architecture" that will have people automatically enrolled in their employer's retirement account plan rather than the worker having to actively declare they want to save. Their contributions will be automatically invested, and increases in saving will come from auto escalation. The proposal for auto enrollment, auto investment, and auto escalation is all normative: there isn't even a claim that their enhanced 401(k) plans are efficient, effective, equitable, or enhance productivity. That some American social policies should not be mandated because they are "paternalistic" is entirely a normative statement. The Nobel Prize in Economics was awarded to one of the most normative policy economists alive!

Circling back to the question of what responsibility academic economists have, academe is a job and a position in society of trust and privilege. A 2012 Gallup poll asked respondents to rate occupations by their levels of honesty and ethical standards. College professors rank seventh: nurses are at the top, followed by pharmacists, medical doctors, engineers, dentists, and police officers. Clergy ranks eighth. Car salespersons were last. Only 10 percent of individuals thought college professors had very low ethical standards. With trust comes responsibility.

Journalists talk about their faith to the public and we should, too. I am pleased that the American Economics Association has adopted rules requiring disclosing monetary conflicts, and that require academic papers to state the source of the authors' money. I have been quite intrigued by a prominent economist a while ago who stated that he does not take positions on issues he researches, like the minimum wage. I think he is trying to achieve the authority of a neutral who approaches data analysis with wide-eyed curiosity.

Since the rise of behavioral economics and economic philosophy we economists are more aware how our beliefs frame our judgments and models. The best thing economists can do is not strive to be value-free, but to be mindful and explicit about the values they hold.

Bottom line: we will retain trust if we (humbly) admit our values in full-throated disclosure. Economists should understand their own philosophies and state very clearly how much normative judgment is in what seems to be a positive outcome.

Pensions have a long history, although the modern retirement system did not start until the late 1800s with German Chancellor Otto von Bismarck. How and why did pensions come about?

One view is that state pensions, a system of paying for "superannuated" people who spent a lifetime selling their labor, developed because in complex, industrial, advanced capitalist economies families can't save for retirement alone. Superannuated is a very cool and poignant concept. I want that old-fashioned word to come back to the US. "Superannuation" means that you may be needing and willing to work, but no employer will hire you because of some aspect of old age.

Another view of why pensions exist comes from a neoclassical notion of individual preferences and income and wealth elasticity as a source of entitlement. As we get richer, we demand the eight-hour day and five-day week. How many hours, days, weeks, months, and years a person has to sell is contested terrain. "The worker must have bread, but she must have roses, too."

The third view is what is called the "labor contracting" view, which argues that firms in complex manufacturing and services (note the actor at center stage—the firm) require implicit contracts and incentives for workers who are trained to stay with the firm and deliver for the employer their "marginal product" as they acquire special and specific skills. One incentive to stay longer with a firm is "tenure-weighted" benefits. Within this view pensions are a device to secure internal labor markets, which in turn are devices to elicit the most productivity in the most peaceful way from workers and firm coming together.

Let's take a historical view. Pensions have been around since armies. Soldiers are among our first pensioners. The Romans knew disgruntled former military men were dangerous; pensions mollified their rebellion. Cicero is credited with first mentioning pensions as *cum dignitate otium*, which might mean that pensions were a political category and that retirement meant "peaceful leisure full of studies in absence of danger."

The other reality revealed in Roman times is an early Roman reference to retirement as "peaceful leisure"—and such leisure was reserved for the upper classes. One of the happy consequences of market-based democracies is that the rich and the workers alike have claimed entitlement to de-commodified labor, including retirement!

Father Paul Harbrecht in the 1950s referred to the differences between the AFL and the CIO to explain pensions. The American Federation of Labor (a more conservative federation of mostly native-born skilled workers) conceived of pensions in their bargaining situations as deferred payments, something earned but a deferred regular employee benefit. The Congress of Industrial Organizations (a newer federation of unions of industrial workers, many of them more recent immigrants) had a different conception of pensions. Workers' entitlement to pensions was derived from the nature of work, which depreciates the human body. This depreciation meant that pensions should be paid by capital—not by labor—as a form of "capital" depreciation allowance. The entitlement of a pension, argued the more militant and radical labor organization, the CIO, springs from capitalist extraction and depreciation of human talent and mental and physical ability. In short, since "work kills," employers should pay for the depreciation.

My view? American workers are denied secure pensions because of political economic reasons, not instrumental ones. Pensions stem from workers' ability to make employers pay and from employers' ability to pay. Weaker unions weaken workers' ability to de-commodify their labor time in old age.

In recent years, there have been numerous calls for overhaul of pension systems virtually throughout the advanced industrialized world. Let us start with the United States, where calls to revise Social Security and overhaul public employee pensions at state levels have been gaining ground since the Reagan revolution. You yourself have written about a "plot against pensions." What are the main arguments in favor of pension-overhaul bills and how valid or invalid are they?

My phrase "plot against pensions" is a quote and allusion to Philip Roth's *Plot Against America*, a dystopian novel imagining America if proto-fascist Charles Lindbergh had won the election for president instead of FDR in 1940. A "plot" implies a plan by people to benefit from a plan. Cutting pensions and forcing elders to seek work benefits some employers and parties that want lower taxes, since many pensions (and medical benefits) are government financed.

Putting off paying full compensation promised in the future can be sensible if the return to the labor of the private or public worker to whom the future benefit is promised is higher. Not paying a police officer or teacher on an upfront, cash basis, means you give them an incentive to stay on the job, improve, and exhibit loyalty and connectedness. These traits are important for workers who have the public trust and whose quality of work is not well-measured. A trusted promise to pay pensions in old age immediately helps improve quality. Pensions solve all sorts of monitoring processes when humans are involved.

Turning to more concrete issues in the US system, recall that the United States cut Social Security benefits for mid to late Baby Boomers (those born 1945–1962) in 1983, during the Reagan administration, by changing the formula that calculates Social Security benefits. The reforms "increased the retirement age"—the "so-called" full retirement age (FRA), which only means that benefits were cut about 13 percent.[3] Malcom Lovell, Reagan's deputy labor secretary, anticipating the unfolding hardship on elders' incomes, told Congress that older people should work more.

The current system of 401(k) plans and individual retirement plans generates lower and riskier than necessary returns for most people for three reasons. The tax benefit is regressive—the rich get a higher after tax return; fees are higher for lower-income workers—the rich get a higher after-fee return; and risk adjustments have to be made for undiversified liquid portfolios—the rich get a higher return from less liquid accounts. Because individuals in the bottom 60 percent or so of households (by income) get little tax relief as a result of their low marginal tax rate, the retirement accounts for these households can easily earn negative real returns after deductions for fees are taken into account. This is unfair and inefficient.

Earners who do best in a 401(k)/IRA system are people who have more income and have stable jobs.

The different economic lives of the bottom 90 percent of earners, compared with the top 10 percent, are interacting with the system's design to cause downward mobility for middle-class workers as they

---

3   The formula for all Social Security benefits pivots around what age is deemed the "full retirement age," the age at which full benefits are collected. In 1983, the FRA was increased from 65 to 67 over a period of twenty-five years, starting in 1984. For all workers born after 1960, the normal retirement age is 67. Every year the FRA increases, benefits fall by about 13 percent.

age. Forty percent or 8.5 million older middle-class workers and their spouses will be downwardly mobile in retirement, falling into poverty or near poverty in their old age because of inadequate retirement account balances.

I have an active research team at the New School in a dry lab called "The Retirement Equity Lab," and we document that most elders have inadequate pensions. This stark fact means elders have a low reservation wage and will work out of desperation.

Low-income households are more likely than rich to withdraw money before retirement age and so are more likely to pay a tax penalty for early withdrawal. In addition, low-income savers get little tax relief. And for some, withdrawing money is too easy. Some IRAs are linked to checking accounts for easy access. This means that, for many Americans, a mattress is a better vehicle for their retirement money than an IRA because a mattress doesn't charge excessive fees; it is heavy and hard to withdraw from; and, if you do withdraw, you don't pay a penalty. The erosion in secure retirements cannot be fixed with minor tweaks.

People born between 1966 and 1975 (Gen Xers) are predicted to get 40 percent of their old age income from guaranteed, reliable, insurance-based sources—Social Security and defined benefit (DB) plans—and the rest from work. The poverty rate and near poverty rate is expected to grow, along with measured income inequality among the retired population.

As Social Security retirement age rises, benefits are cut and Medicare premiums increase, which reduces the Social Security replacement rate. The financialization or liberalization or individualization of the welfare state means that more households are expected to bear more financial risks effecting the distribution of wealth, income, and security in old age.

Put simply, the thirty-seven-year financialization of American retirement has failed most Americans. The 401(k) and IRA system works to create inequality in retirement wealth, retirement income, and retirement time. The top 10 percent of workers with stable lives, consistent employment, and the highest incomes get the most tax subsidies, pay the lowest investment fees, and have the best investment advice. The top 10 percent win under a financialized system.

Pension retrenchment and pension "financializing" arrangements are spreading to Europe, but the forms differ quite a bit across different European governments. Many nations in the OECD have taken on some of the characteristics of US workers' retirement; that is, more elders will be obtaining their income in retirement from individually saved or invested assets. The privatization of risk—and the provision against risk—has been the most dramatic change in the form of pension provision in the OECD countries.

Bottom line: Income security wrongly and inappropriately is beginning to depend on a financial system that sideswipes insurance against the contingency of old age and welfare. But most people want insurance that won't outlast their money. Insurance is called for when we all face similar risks and we all risk being too old to work and too young to die.

Why is it that the advanced capitalist societies could support rather generous pension plans at a time when, according to standard measures of national income, they were less rich than they are today?

Great question, but it is what they call in courtrooms a leading question—the kind that has the answer embedded in the very way the query is posed. Let me examine the paradox you are trying to expose when you wonder why welfare states were more generous when nations were less wealthy. You might be implying that wealth and affordability determine how a nation takes care of its elderly.

T'was that it were true. Affordability for a welfare state explains a part of why some nations' social insurance system helps middle-class workers stay middle-class retirees, or why a nation's safety net helps reduce poverty. Let me show you some crude data and analysis, with hope it will lead to more economists studying the welfare state—an area that has been left to sociologists and political scientists. If I measure "affordability" of social insurance and safety nets in Western capitalist economies with the indicator GDP per capita, one finds only a slight positive correlation.

Generosity for pensions does not depend on the wealth of nations, and it is not clear how much economists have helped understand the varieties of capitalism and the varieties of the welfare state. Certainly, a political economist would be struck by the weak relationship between the wealth of a nation and the institutions that maintain the population above a poverty level—measured by the OECD as the share of people with incomes less than 50 percent of median household disposable income. Norway is both rich and experiences low rates of poverty, but the US has a high GDP per capita and high rates of poverty among the elderly (and the whole population). (Though most nations have lower poverty rates for elders than the whole population, the US, the UK, Japan, Australia, and Switzerland have higher rates for the elderly.) Generosity is only slightly related to affordability. And the United States is certainly retrenching its retirement income security system, not modernizing it.

I want to spend some time arguing the equity case for an equal distribution of dignity and the security of income in older age and superannuation. Social scientists and gerontologists have contemplated old age as a period of withdrawal and renewal in the life course. In economics, especially in the liberal conception, economists view retirement as a period of time people can buy their leisure with accumulated assets and credits. (The self-employed and self-identified homemakers [up to age sixty-five] are not considered retired because, though they may not have a direct supervisor, they sell or exchange their labor directly or indirectly to a market: the self-employed sell labor to clients, homemakers reproduce the labor capacity of the main earner.)

And, since people in lower socio-economic (SES) classes likely have jobs that impose relatively more mental and physical stress, including being in a subordinate position at work, we expect those with low SES to experience forms of cumulative disadvantage that make their health worse in old age. It is too bad traditional defined benefit plans have disappeared for the people whose working environments are injurious to their health, so they could retire earlier to compensate for their shorter lifespan, which helped equalize the distribution of retirement time in the past.

When pension formulas allowed disadvantaged groups to retire earlier than others to accommodate their shorter life expectancy and higher morbidity (often the effect of union contracts in manufacturing, metal, and extractive industries), we slouched towards more progressive pension design.

The United States stands apart with its weak retirement system. In other advanced market economies, government policy, trade union demands, and employer human resource management practices all play a role in permitting most workers to retire. This dynamic has weakened considerably in the US. I have spent the last five years researching the distribution of retirement and healthy retirement time with my colleagues. We found the obvious. Americans with lower socio-economic status have higher mortality and morbidity, and Blacks, independent of SES, become sick and die sooner than whites. In addition, minorities and lower-income individuals are less likely to have adequate retirement resources.

Risk shifting also erodes security. In many countries, especially in the US, financial responsibilities for retirement security have been transferred to individuals in the do-it-yourself pension experiment since the 1980s, when the 401(k) plan was hatched. The state has limited its role, and citizens have more responsibility for their own welfare.

Bottom line, your question is on to something. The US, richer than it ever was, is reducing Social Security benefits and has overseen a system where the voluntary, employer-based system is less effective for most of the population.

It is notable that pensions in the broad form are not more austere in less-rich countries. In other words, the welfare state is retrenching in some Western capitalist economies, like the United States, and modernizing in others, like Norway and other nations that don't penalize long spells of unemployment, an approach that hurts women. But the United States stands out. The US has among the lowest replacement rates from Social Security compared to the replacement rates of other nation's pay-as-you-go systems. The United States replacement rate from Social Security for a middle earner who retires at sixty-six (and most retire by age sixty-four) is 49 percent; the OECD average is 63 percent; and in France, one of the largest and most generous nations in the OECD, the replacement rate is 75 percent. Generosity in replacement rates is linked to poverty: elder poverty rates in the US is a whopping 21 percent, in the OECD, 12 percent; and in France, 4 percent.

Some years ago, you wrote an article in which you argued that the solution to the pension crisis is more pensions. Can you elaborate a bit on this?

We have a retirement income and security crisis, not a pension funding crisis. Foundations and journalists confuse the two when reporting the high costs of pensions for state and local government. Over half of Americans approaching retirement will not be able to sustain their living standards, and almost 40 percent of older middle-class workers will be poor or near-poor elders. The solution is more pensions. And the

United States can afford pensions for all. The United States spends over $100 billion a year on tax breaks for pensions that benefit households who need help the least. That $100 billion can be redistributed to cover 65 million people without pensions, improve retirement security for everyone, and do so with no extra taxpayer costs.

Congress, year after year, has helped create the retirement income security crisis. It has permissively regulated individual directed retirement accounts and has enabled the system's expansion by continually raising the contribution limits for 401(k)s while imposing stringent regulations on defined benefit plans. In 2017, total annual contributions made by an employee and their employer can be up to $61,000—which is far higher than the median annual earnings for full-time American workers ($44,000). Because they get larger tax benefits, higher-income people contribute more and more often to 401(k)-type plans (defined contribution plans). Also, higher-income households are more equipped to handle the social and technical aspects of hiring and managing a financial advisor. Only the very highest earners can take full advantage of the full benefits of the tax break, or even the system.

Only 7 percent of this forgone revenue went to the bottom 40 percent of earners, while 66 percent accrued to the top 20 percent of earners. Of this 66 percent, close to three-quarters of the tax incentive went to the top 10 percent of earners. For example: a lawyer earning $200,000 makes a $1,000 contribution to their income tax and saves $350—assuming a 35 percent marginal tax rate. Their receptionist, earning $20,000, makes the same $1,000 contribution (which is much less likely) and saves only $150 in taxes—at a 15 percent marginal tax rate.

In the United States, we have a hidden welfare state: provisions in the tax code that favor certain kinds of activities. Taxes not collected on pension contributions and earnings equal a fourth of annual Social Security contributions and, at over $114 billion, are perversely larger than household savings, totaling just over $151 billion.

There may be some momentum for mandatory pensions on top of Social Security. In the early part of 2018 four experts from different political perspectives called for the creation of mandatory retirement savings accounts to replace the failed "do-it-yourself" voluntary system. This includes myself and my *Rescuing Retirement* co-author, Tony James, who is former president of the private equity firm Blackstone; Jason Fichtner, a former Bush administration economist and a member of the

Koch brothers' Mercatus Center at George Mason University; and Third Way, a centrist Democratic think-tank. I call for a public option and there is a shared call for mandatory retirement accounts. I do not share the others' solution, because they ignore or want to reduce Social Security. A complete solution to the retirement crises cannot neglect protecting and expanding Social Security.

Now, don't think I am delusional. There is political support for universal retirement security. The American public persistently tells pollsters that Social Security is highly popular and they want a national solution. It is economically feasible to fund Social Security fully (about .9 percent of GDP), to expand it to prevent elderly poverty (less than .5 percent of GDP), and to mandate individual retirement accounts on top of Social Security (which does not cost the government anything).

Affording pensions for all is not that expensive.

First, 2.78 percent of payroll to secure Social Security (one way among many to provide needed revenue). This would ensure that workers receive their full and promised Social Security benefits and provide retirees with an average of 36 percent of their pre-retirement income.

Second, an additional 0.02 percent would raise the special minimum benefit to bring almost every elder above the poverty line. The special minimum benefit places a floor under the benefits of lifetime low earners but has eroded over time and now almost no new claimants qualify.

Third, 3 percent to fund mandatory individual savings accounts for retirement. Alone, this contribution is unlikely to permit all workers to maintain their living standards in retirement. However, it is designed to add on to retirees' monthly Social Security benefit to ensure that they can live well clear of poverty or near poverty. We could follow the lead of Australia's mandatory retirement savings program, which started with a 3 percent required contribution and is now up to 12 percent. The program will also allow for those who want to contribute more to do so.

Bottom line: to ensure all workers a secure retirement and the end of elderly poverty would require an additional $500 billion in retirement contributions from workers, employers, and the government. While less than 3 percent of GDP, $500 billion is not trivial. Rather, it is similar in magnitude to the ten-year cost of $5.5 trillion to fund the recent GOP tax cut.

You have also argued that pension policies can help to minimize economic crises. How so, and what are the actual macroeconomic stabilization effects of a system like that of Social Security?

Social Security functions as an automatic stabilizer, while 401(k) and IRAs function as automatic destabilizers. Automatic stabilizers adjust aggregate demand over the business cycle by injecting or absorbing spending. They are called "automatic" because no legislative body needs to authorize a fiscal injection of income to households or businesses, or spend on a government program, during, say, a recession. Automatic stabilizers are designed to work fast, even before statistical agencies, much less the Fed or Congress, are made aware of a downturn or expansion.

The most effective automatic stabilizer is the federal personal income tax because of its progressivity. In upturns, when incomes increase, households may cash out unexpected robust capital gains, and taxpayers with more income move into higher tax brackets and pay more taxes. The effect is to reduce the consumption multiplier in an expansion. The opposite happens to personal income and the multiplier in a downturn.

In the Great Recession, 2007–09, consumers and businesses spent dramatically less suddenly in the last quarter of 2008 and in the first quarter of 2009. In January and December 2009, the US federal government injected $700 billion in one-time stimulus programs. Meanwhile, built-in automatic stabilizers "did their thing" by injecting billions into the spending stream of the economy. Traditional automatic stabilizers such as unemployment insurance (UI), the Temporary Assistance for Needy Families (TANF) program, the Supplemental Nutritional Assistance Program (SNAP), and the program with the largest effect—the progressive tax system (the average marginal tax rate shrinks as more people fall into the lower brackets)— helped avoid the Great Recession becoming a colossal depression.

Though unemployment and welfare are appealing automatic stabilizers, my co-authors, Eloy Fisher and Joelle Saad-Lessler, found that Social Security had a much bigger effect in stabilizing aggregate demand than previously appreciated by early Keynesian economists and current macro textbooks. Disability insurance was a more important stimulus than a shrinking unemployment insurance system.

We found what everyone, especially in the 401(k) industry—employers, participants, and brokers—knew, that 401(k) plans were destabilizing. Here is the pathway. Old age social insurance programs and 401(k) plans—financialized retirement plans—affect the macro economy through three channels: income, wealth, and labor market channels.

Social Security works as an automatic stabilizer partly because it is big: 93 percent of public and private sector workers participate in Social Security, as well as 15 million state and local public employees who have similarly structured plans. The design of these plans—benefits are paid out as an annuity and do not fluctuate with the value of the financial assets—allows older workers to collect benefits and withdraw from the labor market when times are tough. Thus, Social Security and other defined benefit systems are counter-cyclical.

In contrast, individual financial retirement accounts—like 401(k) and IRA (most of the assets in Individual Retirement Accounts [IRAs] come from 401(k) plans)—depend on total contributions, investment performance, and fees. A household plans to retire partly based on the size of the account. Also, because households are attuned to "numbers," especially big numbers, the wealth value of their financialized retirement accounts, their 401(k) or IRA balances, affects perception and behavior. In other words, the wealth effect (where having a valuable portfolio causes investors to feel more confident and spend more) is real and, because of it, household spending is related to the 401(k) and IRA balances. Financialized accounts make household labor supply and durable good spending sensitive to market fluctuations. That's not good.

Financialized accounts create pro-cyclical, not counter-cyclical, work and spending behavior. Households with financialized retirement accounts increase labor supply and decrease pension at precisely the wrong time—when the economy is contracting. I am calling for more scholarship on effective and ineffective automatic stabilizers!

In your latest book, co-authored with Tony James, Rescuing Retirement: A Plan to Guarantee Retirement for All Americans, *you offer a comprehensive plan to help workers live life after work with dignity. What are the main ideas behind your plan to rescue retirement in the US? How likely, in your view, is it that a plan such as yours will be adopted in the US or elsewhere?*

The good news is that fixing the coming retirement crisis is possible; but the bad news is that the fix won't be quick and easy. The good news is that the fix is not a radical separation from the decent, often union-negotiated plans many workers had in the past. The bad news is there will be resistance from the retail money management industry because our plan is a low-cost, not-for-profit, and effective alternative to the existing 401(k) and IRA plans.

We don't propose going back to the past system of voluntary, company-based defined benefits, so called "traditional" pensions. Competitive norms among firms have changed; firms are more likely to bid down in wages and benefits, so if one company provides pensions it could suffer. Even if an individual company provides a good retirement plan, they suffer if the added cost is not shared by their competitors. And no pension insurance scheme—like the Pension Benefit Guaranty Corporation—can protect workers if an entire industry fails at the same time, like integrated steel.

We propose a new, universal public option so that all Americans can supplement their Social Security with a plan as close to a company-defined benefit as possible, with all the positive aspects and not the negative aspects.

The comprehensive plan—Guaranteed Retirement Account—is described in our book, *Rescuing Retirement*. The plan meets all of the twelve principles of a stakeholder organization formed right before the Great Recession, Retirement USA, which can be summarized into four major principles: (1) universality—covers all workers; (2) pooled investments—no more individual accounts; (3) annuity payments—people get a lifetime benefit, not a lump sum, which is difficult to manage; and (4) the tax breaks are redistributed so that the lowest income savers get the highest proportional benefit, not the other way around. Of lesser practical importance, but important to some political constituencies and the practical issue of being taken seriously in a policy environment, the proposed Guaranteed Retirement Account plan requires no new taxes, does not increase the deficit, and actually reduces the administrative burden on companies that sponsor plans.

In sum, our proposed plan achieves universality, giving everyone a Social Security supplement. The plan achieves higher returns with lower risk; savings in the GRAs are pooled and invested. It is a hybrid between a capitalized system and social insurance and it complements, not substitutes, Social Security.

How do you see your research agenda shaping up in the years ahead?

I am working hard with my research team at the Schwartz Center for Economic Policy Analysis to work with legislators and advocacy groups to show the harm done when the US does not shore up its retirement income security programs.

I worry about the growing majority of elders who cannot afford to retire and will work or seek work to make up for eroding pensions. Or worse, these workers without adequate retirement income will have to retire anyway and they will live in low-income, isolated misery.

My new book project—I am wondering what you think of the proposed title: *Let Us Now Praise Retirement: Second Thoughts about Older Workers*—will hone in on this one point: work in old age is not the answer to the challenges posed by an aging population. I aim to describe elders in new ways, and explore the age discrimination against older workers; the monopsony exploitation among older workers; the persistence of low wages and contingency among older workers; and the way that job requirements outpace the capacities of older people.

The United States is in a unique position among rich nations to afford universal adequate pensions; but the US is the only rich nation that leans so heavily and clings so strongly to work as the answer to inadequate retirement income security.

I want to do for retirement poverty and overwork what was done to health insurance and obesity. It is not flawed humans that is causing inadequate retirement savings, it is flawed design.

Writing a book praising retirement is tricky because of the highly charged and deeply conflicting feelings about retirement in America. Some people can't even say the word "retirement." Ask a worker in their sixties if they are going to retire and the answer, especially if they are white collar, is something like, "No, no, no, I'll do something!" It is as if you asked them to throw themselves away. But ask a blue- and pink-collar worker and you get a different answer, perhaps an answer in months and days. Increasingly, there is no class difference in who might answer, "Uh, you kidding? I don't have a retirement account worth anything and Social Security won't be enough."

The last word: my new book project praises work *and* retirement. Let us act as if a good society makes retirement possible without shame or deprivation, and every civilized functioning market economy provides jobs to every adult who wants one. And, here as a labor economist, I conclude knowing the value of guaranteed income in raising the reservation wage of us all: good pensions help older workers get good jobs.

Responses on the COVID-19 Crisis

How would you evaluate the ways different countries or regions have responded to the COVID-19 crisis, both in terms of public health interventions and economic policies?

I'm writing this in November, when the EU nations—who overall had more coordinated and enriched responses to the novel virus compared to the US—are experiencing a second wave of COVID-19 cases along with the United States. So it may seem that the virus takes its own course and that policies don't matter. But most Western democracies, while flattening their disease curves, also flattened inequity by keeping their schools open. Because the US will not engage in enough nonpharmaceutical interventions—such as mandating masks—nor provide funds for more space between students and school-based personal protective equipment (PPE)—many children who don't have private pods, internet, adult supervision, and private schools will be left behind. At the same time, others are merely inconvenienced. Not continuing the extra stimulus checks and generous unemployment benefits reduced income replacement for the most economically vulnerable families.

Do you draw any general lessons from the COVID crisis about the most viable ways to advance an egalitarian economic project?

The complicated models economists produced in response to COVID-19 attempt to maximize two objectives—health and wealth. These models strived to show how to get as much economic activity with as little illness as possible. But we economists need a third objective: equity. We need models that solve for maximizing health, wealth, and equity subject to constraints. Those models would be pro-poor growth models, and if we used such models we would keep most business open, replace working families' incomes due to the recession, maintain high-quality care by extending in-person school days and years and mandate masks, discourage gatherings, and provide schools with resources to stay open, provide PPE, close indoor dining, bars, sports events, and hire bartenders, etc. to be contact tracers.

Does the experience of the COVID crisis shed any light on the way you think about economics as a discipline or, more specifically, the questions you might be pursuing in your own research?

I was stunned at the rapid response of economists to the crises. The profession seemed eager to help policy-makers see the wisdom of standard economic and monetary policy —justify the stimulus, create protective work practices, utilize automatic stabilizers, etc. They were quick to use techniques—difference in difference—to evaluate policies. Many economists were brought up short by the increase in inequality caused by the lockdown and the health inequality caused by the repression, with almost all the unemployment concentrated in the bottom half of the economic distribution. Most economists found their inner policy-economist self, and that is a good thing.

Representative Publications and Influences

Publications:
Teresa Ghilarducci, Joelle Saad-Lessler, and Eloy Fisher (2012). The macroeconomic stabilisation effects of Social Security and 401(k) plans. *Cambridge Journal of Economics*, 36(1), 237–251.
Teresa Ghilarducci (1992). *Labor's capital: The economics and politics of private pensions*. MIT Press.
Teresa Ghilarducci (2008). *When I'm sixty-four: The plot against pensions and the plan to save them*. Princeton University Press.

People who have been influential: Robert Shiller, Karl Marx, Sidney Webb, Beatrice Webb

Literature that has been influential:
Sidney Webb and Beatrice Webb (1975). *Methods of social study*. London School of Economics and Political Science.
Beatrice Webb (1979). *My apprenticeship*. Cambridge University Press.
Sidney Webb, Beatrice Webb, and Robert A. (1896). *The History of Trade Unionism*. Longmans, Green and Company.

Jayati Ghosh

Jayati Ghosh is Professor of Economics at the University of Massachusetts Amherst, Professor Emerita of Economics at Jawaharlal Nehru University, New Delhi, a Senior Research Associate at the Political Economy Research Institute, and Executive Secretary of International Development Economics Associates (IDEAs). Her core areas of study include international economics, employment patterns in developing countries, macroeconomic policy, and issues related to gender and development. She is the author of dozens of articles and of many books, including *Crisis as Conquest: Learning from East Asia* (with C.P. Chandrasekhar 2001); *The Market that Failed: Neoliberal Economic Reforms in India* (with C.P. Chandrasekhar 2004); *Never Done and Poorly Paid: Women's Work in Globalising India* (2009); and *The Making of a Catastrophe: The Economic Fallout of the COVID-19 Pandemic in India*. She is a recipient of the International Labour Organisation's 2010 Decent Work Research Prize, among many other awards and honors.

Tell us a bit about how you came to embrace economics as your academic field of study, and what made you turn to development economics as your primary area of research.

As an undergraduate, I began with sociology as my major subject (or honours, as we call it in India), essentially because I was and remain greatly interested in how societies and social relations are formed, evolve, and transform over time. But after some time, I began to feel that I was still scratching at the surface, that social processes were reflecting deeper economic forces that I did not understand, and that I could not understand society without understanding the economy.

This is why I switched to studying economics for my MA degree, and then went on to research in that discipline as well. As for the focus on development economics—this was to some extent inevitable for me, given the nature of my interests: not just that I come from India, which is still very much a developing country, but because, to me, all meaningful economics is very much development economics—that is, it analyzes how economies evolve and change. In fact, the early political economists in Europe and across the world (about which the mainstream economics profession knows too little) were all development economists. It is actually quite unfortunate that the ahistorical approach that began with the marginalist revolution sought to confine the discipline of economics into a much narrower and ultimately less useful frame. As this neoclassical approach ultimately became dominant, it pushed development economics to the fringes of the subject and made it less "fashionable." Even worse, this approach began to permeate development economics as well, bringing in its own rigid and unrealistic assumptions, lack of attention to history, and inability to incorporate various different perspectives into the study of development.

This is truly a concern, because to my mind economic development (which is something that happens in all societies, and is not a process that has been "transcended" by the so-called advanced economies) can only really be understood through a more holistic approach that incorporates different disciplinary perspectives. So, in a way, I have come full circle in my intellectual understanding, for I now believe quite strongly that you cannot understand the economy without understanding society and politics.

Do you associate yourself with any particular methodological and epistemological approach in the field of political economy? I ask this question because left political economy developed after the Second World War into different branches and schools of thought (for example, dependency theory and world systems) and the anti-colonial struggles in the Third World played a significant role in the reshaping of the political economy research agenda both in the developed and developing world.

I would broadly classify myself as a Marxian/post-Keynesian political economist, but not in a very rigid sense—and I also definitely consider myself to be a feminist and a socialist, so those predilections also inform both my choice of subjects of study and my approach to them. However, over the years, I have become increasingly wary of pigeonholes in terms of epistemological approaches. It may reflect my underlying laziness or lack of rigor, but perhaps too much of my youth was wasted in wading through what I now see as relatively pointless debates about the "correct" understanding of Marx or other writers, and being caught in the midst of esoteric arguments about fine conceptual distinctions and purity of theoretical positions. Therefore, while I recognize the importance of particular schools of thought (including dependency and world systems approaches, inter alia), I am increasingly more relaxed about picking insights from different schools to combine in my own understanding, as long as they help to understand economic processes.

It is true that the anti-colonial struggles played a big role in providing some underpinnings to the theoretical frameworks and research concerns of many economists in the developing world. But I am not sure how significant those are even among progressive economists today because of the more complex international economic arrangements, which make imperialism appear in new and different forms, and which therefore require correspondingly nuanced analyses.

What's the best way to understand the dynamics and contradictions of contemporary capitalism?

It is fairly obvious that global capitalism is in dire straits, notwithstanding the brave talking up of output recovery that is now more widespread. But at the same time, it is also true that those hoping and mobilizing for bringing in an alternative system are everywhere scattered, weak, and demoralized. In effect, contemporary globalized capitalism has been too successful for its own good, and so has to confront the contradictions generated by its success. It has managed to extend over the entire globe, leaving no geographical area or sphere of human activity untouched. It has also managed to overrun and conquer its opponents, such as associations of workers that could reduce capital's bargaining power, democratic accountability that might give rise to regulatory structures that limit or constrain its activities and its profits, and collectivities that voice the requirements of the larger social good, to the point where it is now almost completely untrammeled. As a result, there are no checks and balances of the kind that in various periods in the past have generated both less economic volatility and more social stability. In an almost textbook extension of the biological argument of the prey–predator relationship, capitalism has killed off most or all of its prey, to the point that its own very existence is now threatened.

In economic terms, this "success" means less expansion of demand for products that the system must keep coming up with in terms of its own logic. It also means less ability to create new sources of demand, as financialization and credit bubbles also appear to have run their course, despite very loose monetary policy. Increased inequality, volatility in financial markets, and slow growth or stagnation are thus inextricably linked. In socio-political terms, this has generated more widespread despair, alienation, and individualized responses that create more unpleasant and unstable political tendencies, and even threaten the very basis of functioning societies. This is not a problem confined to advanced capitalist economies—it is also pervasive in the developing world, and could even be more extreme in many poor countries.

What do you consider to be the most pressing issues facing developing countries like India?

The problems facing the Indian economy are somewhat unusual in Asia, although similar concerns are evident in other developing regions. One of the major failures of the development project in India has been the inability to ensure structural transformation, in terms of moving labor from low productivity activities to higher productivity (and better remunerated) activities. This persistent significance of low productivity agriculture and services in employing the bulk of workers is in some sense the "original sin" that has then affected many other evident failures: the uneven development that has left most of the country and the population relatively poor despite pockets of sometimes vast enrichment; the low employment generation and terrible human development indicators despite decades of relatively rapid aggregate income growth; the pervasive reliance on unpaid and underpaid work of women; and so on. These economic concerns in India have been compounded by the introduction of neoliberal market-based policies in a socio-economic context characterized by the unique forms of socio-economic discrimination that persist in India, such as the caste system.

In your view, what are the most fundamental problems with neoliberal economics, both as a theoretical and a policy framework?

Neoliberal economics is based on a simplistic theoretical framework that relies on completely unrealistic assumptions that are pretty much universally recognized to be completely inapplicable in real economies: perfect competition, full employment, symmetric information in all markets, and so on. Even though most of the policy prescriptions of such a framework simply collapse when these assumptions are violated, this has not deterred its proponents from using these arguments to push for greater and greater liberalization and deregulation of all markets, including product, labor, and financial markets. Increasingly, it is being used to push for privatization and deregulation of activities that were earlier seen as the domain of the state, such as infrastructure and amenities, health, and education. This is often seen as "the withdrawal of the state" from economic activity, but that is really not the case: it is rather that the state shifts the nature of its engagement, and chooses to privilege the requirements of capital over the rights of citizens. The state remains significant and even crucial in terms of enforcing private property rights, preventing workers from being able to exercise their democratic rights, ensuring the legal and institutional conditions that facilitate maximal extraction of surplus, and so on. The rush to protect finance from the consequences of its own actions after the 2008 crisis, by drawing on fiscal resources taken from taxpayers who were subsequently denied their rightful entitlements, was just one more reminder of this.

Effectively, therefore, neoliberal economics is the ideology of large capital in its various manifestations, and even as it claims to be pro-market, it does not hesitate to use government intervention when it serves the interests of large capital. Simultaneously, however, because state policies become so clearly skewed in this manner, there is increasing distrust and alienation among the mass of people. Neoliberalism also posits the most extreme and regressive forms of individualism and competitive tendencies in quotidian life, seeking to commercialize everything and push all human endeavor and interaction into a straitjacket of self-seeking calculations of profit and loss.

In seeking to come to terms with the political economy of contemporary capitalism, what are the most important ways that a gender-based frame of reference contributes to an overall critique of neoliberal capitalism?

One of the major failings of classical Marxian political economy was the way that it overlooked the significance of social and relational inequalities in shaping economic processes. Thankfully, a lot of perceptive work over the past century has sought to rectify this. I believe that a gender perspective is essential to understanding capitalism, not only because of the significance of gendered division of labor, the ways in which that affects labor markets and social reproduction, but because most of the important features of contemporary globalization rely in some way on the gender construction of societies. These affect food supply and distribution, patterns of production across global value chains, migration patterns and their economic significance, for example in the internationalization of the care economy, and a host of other features. Furthermore, contemporary capitalism simply cannot be understood without taking into account the role of unpaid labor in various forms, which is also crucially determined by gender relations.

Imperialism as a concept has lost some of its resonance in development studies, even among left political economists. In your view, has imperialism lost its value as an analytical construct in twenty-first century economic reality?

I think it's a serious mistake to ignore the continuing significance of imperialism. If we define imperialism broadly, as the complex intermingling of economic and political interests that are part of the efforts of large capital to control economic territory, it's clear that imperialism has not really declined at all. Rather, it has changed in form over the past half-century, especially when we embrace a more expansive notion of what constitutes "economic territory." To my mind, this includes not only the more obvious forms such as land and natural resources, as well as labor (which are all still fiercely fought over), but also new markets— defined by both physical location and type of economic process. These are closely linked to neoliberalism.

For example, the commercialization of basic amenities and social services that were earlier seen as the sole preserve of public provision creates and provides new markets in different parts of the world. The institutions of the global economic order (the IMF, the WTO, the World Bank, even the World Economic Forum) all actively encourage private investment in formerly public sectors, in a more complicated but still consequential expression of the drive for control over economic territory. Similarly, the commercialization and privatization of knowledge and its dissemination, through "intellectual property rights," disproportionately reward multinational companies, allowing them to monopolize production, set high prices, or demand high royalties, and contribute to further enhancing their bargaining power and tendencies to concentration of industries. This is then reflected in the distribution of profits across global value chains, whereby workers and small producers (mostly in developing countries) get next to nothing compared to the multinational companies that generate profits and rents out of pre-production (through patents and design) and post-production (marketing and branding) processes.

So, imperialism has not become less important, but it has changed its form. In the nineteenth century and the first half of the twentieth century, it was explicitly related to colonial control; in the second half of the twentieth century it relied on a combination of geopolitical and economic control deriving also from the clear dominance of the United States as the global hegemon and leader of the capitalist world dealing with the potential threat from the Communist world. It now relies more and more on an international legal and regulatory architecture—fortified by various multilateral and bilateral agreements—to establish the power of capital over labor.

In contrast to prevailing economic views, your analyses of the economic situation in India suggest a greater role for the state with regard to employment, investment, and banking. Is a return to social Keynesianism possible in a globalized economic environment, in India and more generally?

Clearly, corporate-driven financial globalization has made it much more difficult for countries across the world to engage in autonomous policies, particularly of the Keynesian variety. The threat of capital flight is an ever-present constraint upon governments wishing to engage in expansionary fiscal policy, while financial liberalization has not only meant the loss of directed credit (without which no country in the world has successfully industrialized), but has also exposed individual national economies to domestic volatility driven by cross-border capital flows. So greater limits on private financial flows are definitely necessary to promote neo-Keynesian macroeconomic policies or even longer-term policies that promote structural change for development.

In that regard, it is worth remembering that the most successful economies even during the recent globalization have been those that retained a significant degree of policy autonomy, most of all with respect to controls over financial flows and financial markets. For example, China's control over most of the banking system and the continued ability of the state to direct finance to desired areas played a critical role in its rapid industrialization and export success until 2008, while the gradual liberalization of finance since then has also brought with it greater fragility and dependence on debt-driven growth.

For the Indian economy, the problem is that while our development project is still in its infancy in terms of structural transformation, with the bulk of our workers stuck in low productivity informal jobs in agriculture and traditional services, recent rapid growth has been accompanied by low or nonexistent expansion of formal employment. The state also does not have the levers that would allow it to control the level of aggregate demand and change the composition of output towards more employment-intensive activities. So greater public intervention (by a more democratically accountable state) is essential: through macroeconomic policies as well as trade and industrial policies. These will require some management of both capital and trade accounts. But this does not seem as extreme or impossible as it might have appeared even a few years ago, because of changing political currents. As the discontents of globalization increasingly express their unhappiness in countries across the world, including in advanced countries, at least some of the (false) received wisdom fed by votaries of neoliberal globalization is coming into question.

The idea of the "universal basic income" is receiving increased interest, primarily in certain Western countries. There seems to even be something of a convergence of left and right economic thinking on the matter. How do you explain this paradox?

The Universal Basic Income (or UBI) is perceived in the advanced world as one way of coping with technology-induced unemployment that is projected to grow significantly in the near future, as well as reducing inequalities and increasing consumption demand in stagnant economies. The right-wing case for this can be traced (inter alia) to Milton Friedman, who saw this as a substitute for the "ragbag" of other government social assistance and welfare programs, which would remove the need for a legislated minimum wage and increase the availability of cheap labor, thereby benefiting businesses. The left-wing perspective is that guaranteed minimum income that would be more general and generous, and at the same time less dependency-creating, than existing social assistance programs, would also counter the problem that rapid automation would lead to displacement of labor with strongly negative social impacts.

Certainly, there is much to be said for the idea, especially if it is to be achieved by taxing the rich and particularly those activities that are either socially less desirable or are generating larger surpluses because of technological changes. But this type of intervention effectively ignores distributional effects even while ostensibly purporting to deal with unequal income distribution, and so may fail in terms of its intended outcome of reducing or doing away with poverty because of the inflationary implications of such transfers. By contrast, "job-based strategies" like employment programs affirm the dignity of labor in various forms and can move towards making full employment a permanent feature of the economy.

In countries like India, there are other concerns. Unlike successful examples of cash transfer programs in some countries that have delivered such transfers in addition to expanding the quality and coverage of essential public services in health, education, nutrition, and so on, the Indian attempt has been to use them to replace such essential public spending, which is already far too low. Proponents argue that the government can cut not just subsidies but also a significant amount of spending that such analysts find to be unproductive, and simply replace it with direct transfers into bank accounts. Paradoxically, therefore, this shift to providing direct cash transfers in the guise of "basic income" would actually reduce public spending, not increase it! This is the opposite of what progressive advocates of the UBI would generally suggest. In general, achieving all or any of the elements of a universal social protection floor, which is something all societies must take seriously, cannot be seen as a substitute for public provision of basic goods and services; rather it must be an addition to it.

You have argued recently, with regard to the current state of the global neoliberal economy, that "we may be living through one of those moments in history that future historians will look back on as a watershed, a period of flux that marked a transition to quite different economic and social arrangements." What's the alternative?

Obviously, history moves in complex and convoluted ways, and it does not follow that new socio-economic arrangements will necessarily be more desirable. But progressive alternatives do remain distinct possibilities. As a socialist feminist living in what is described as the developing world, I naturally hope that the progressive alternatives will prevail. This, in turn, means some variety of socialism, which requires greater public involvement in the economy, but with much greater democratic control over that public or governmental sphere. I would argue that these must differ from previous experiences of "socialist" regimes in some crucial ways. First, there must be an emphasis on democracy, both electoral and in other ways. Second, a rejection of over-centralization and of glorification of the "large" is required, so a socially appropriate balance between "large" and "small" is achieved. Third, the recognition of rights is crucial, for individuals and communities—and while human rights must be given precedence over property rights, some forms of property rights cannot be entirely dispensed with, as was earlier attempted. Fourth, class divisions are of obvious significance, but other forms of social discrimination and exclusion must be recognized and addressed, such as those of gender, social category (like caste), ethnic or racial group, and so on. Finally, the issue of ecological sustainability is paramount, which implies a much deeper interrogation of the relationship of human societies with nature.

If I had to dream of my ideal society, I would say it is one in which someone's basic conditions and opportunities would not depend so critically on the accidents of birth, determined by location, class, social group, and gender: everyone's life chances would be broadly similar, but at the same time other cultural differences would be respected and even cherished.

In September 2017, we celebrated the 150th anniversary of Das Kapital. *What are the most important ways that Marx's magnum opus remains vitally relevant in the twenty-first century?*

Many of the concepts elaborated in *Capital* remain hugely relevant and significant today. Consider the central point about capital: for Marx, it is not just a resource in itself, a simple factor of production analogous to land and labor, but an expression of very specific social relations of production, which requires workers to be "free" in a double sense: "free" to sell their own labor power (not bound by other socio-economic ties and constraints) and "free" of any ownership of the means of production, so that they have no choice but to sell their labor power for their own material survival. Even when matters appear to be more complex because of the emergence of subcontracting and the "gig economy," this underlying social relation is still critical.

Another central concept is that of "commodity fetishism": the situation in which relations between people become mediated by relations between things: commodities and money. Commodities (goods and services produced for exchange) are not simply things or objects, because they possess both use value (they meet human needs or wants) and exchange value (as a thing that can be traded in return for something else). But value then gets seen as intrinsic to commodities rather than being the result of labor, and the exchange of commodities and market-based interaction are seen as the "natural" way of dealing with all objects, rather than as a historically specific set of social relations. This is the illusion emerging from the centrality of private property in capitalism, which then determines not only how people work and interact, but even how they perceive reality and understand social change. The urge to acquisition, the obsession with material gratification of wants and the ordering of human well-being in terms of their ability to command different commodities, could all be described as forms of commodity fetishism. The obsession with GDP growth per se among policy-makers and the general public is an extreme but widespread example of commodity fetishism today.

The concentration of ownership of the means of production in a few hands is effectively what enables capital to play its role in production. But this concentration was necessarily based on expropriation from those who previously possessed it, such as peasants and small artisans who could have produced on their own. This "primitive accumulation" has often been a violent process, but it can also occur—and still continues to occur—in other more complex ways, because of the uneven development of capitalism in different regions and in different sectors, which in turn is not confined to a single arena, but characterizes all social and economic relations.

Thus, there is an inherent tension between the expansion of the productive forces and the ability of the economic system to generate sufficient demand for the goods that are produced. There is disproportionality between the expansion of fixed and variable capital, which makes it more difficult to generate profits. There is disproportionality between sectors that emerges in the process of accumulation. This geographical uneven development simultaneously creates both "developed" and "underdeveloped" areas. This can be extended to understand imperialism, which can be understood as the struggle for control over economic territories of different kinds. And the imbalance between money as a medium of exchange and money as a measure of value gets amplified by the development of credit and finance, creating more tendencies to crisis.

The system generates many conflicts and contradictions, only some of which culminate in periodic crises. Since the basic dynamic of capital is simultaneously to aggrandize itself and impoverish other classes such as workers and peasants, within and across nations, it obviously generates class conflicts. But the system also generates intra-class conflict, pitting individual capital against other capitals and the individual worker against other workers. There is a Darwinian struggle for survival constantly at work, so individualism, conflict, and competition become the driving forces of the system. These also create "the anarchy of the market" and the inevitable tendency towards crises, resulting from over-accumulation and under-consumption, which are driven by the inequality that capitalism creates.

A fundamental feature of the capitalist system as Marx described it is alienation. This does not refer to an isolated experience of an individual person's feeling of estrangement from society or community, but to a generalized state of the broad mass of wage workers, because of the loss of control by workers over their own work. Workers can never become autonomous and self-realized human and social beings under capitalism. This alienation, combined with commodity fetishism, creates a peculiar kind of unfreedom—which is often not even widely noticed, because individual emancipation appears to result from "universal salability." Every living creature is thus effectively transformed into property and all social relations become transactional.

Clearly, there is strong contemporary resonance of many of these ideas, so even when there are important issues that were not captured in *Capital* (such as the role of unpaid labor, especially in social reproduction and care work within families; the relationship of the economic system with the natural environment) it remains essential reading even today.

Responses on the COVID-19 Pandemic

How would you evaluate the ways different countries or regions have responded to the COVID-19 crisis, both in terms of public health interventions and economic policies?

The COVID-19 pandemic has acted like an X-ray machine exposing the major inequalities and failures of the global capitalist system that I have already noted. It has wrought an unprecedented economic crisis, deeper and wider than any since the Great Depression, with still no certainty about how prolonged, severe, and widespread the damage will be. What we already know is terrifying: globally, extreme poverty is rapidly increasing; hunger is more widespread; health conditions are worsening even beyond the spread of the coronavirus infection; livelihoods and incomes have been destroyed, many never to be fully or even partly regained; income and asset inequalities have reached unimaginable levels in many countries; relational inequalities like those of gender are worsening; and power imbalances are increasing as various governments seize the opportunity for greater centralization, control, and suppression of dissent.

The sharp increases in global inequality resulting from the pandemic could have been expected, but even so they have been startling in their speed and intensity. Developing countries have been massively and disproportionately affected (other than China, where the infection originated and which went through some grueling months, but which has since recovered significantly). In most cases, the impact has not only been because of the spread of the disease, but also the policy responses, in particular aggressive lockdowns. These affected livelihoods, especially in countries with large informal sectors, but were not adequately compensated for by social protection measures, and therefore led to both economic collapse and humanitarian tragedy. Most of all, the variation in fiscal responses is worth noting: while governments in advanced countries have generally gone in for significantly increased public spending as well as substantial central bank intervention, developing country governments have been much more muted, with less fiscal stimuli than they provided after the Global Financial Crisis, even though this is a much bigger disaster.

This highlights the importance of a global response, since the crisis is global in scope (in both health and economic terms) and will not be contained by nationalist measures within a single country. The fact that this is combined with the looming climate crisis that is also already unfolding, makes the need for combined and coordinated responses even more urgent, as these could really be a tipping point for human survival. It is therefore clear that we need a Global New Deal—but it must go beyond being green, to becoming multicolored. It will be a New Deal, because as in the storied US experience of the 1930s, recovery would have to be based on very significantly increased public expenditure, along with more systematic regulation of capital and other markets and redistribution, as the main elements.

Of course, it must be Green, because significant amounts of public spending and a major part of the regulatory changes will have to be oriented towards recognizing, respecting, and preserving the environment; reducing carbon and greenhouse gas emissions; addressing climate challenges and enabling better adaptation and resilience; and changing patterns of production and consumption accordingly. It must also be Blue, recognizing the enormous and growing concerns about water and human mistreatment of our common water sources, and working towards preserving oceans, rivers, and water bodies and ensuring equitable access to clean water.

But there are other pressing challenges that the pandemic has brought to the surface. It has exposed the horrifying effects of decades of public underfunding of health and societal undermining of care work. So, the New Deal must also be Purple, with an emphasis on the care economy and massive investment to fund enhanced and improved care activities. This requires recognizing the different forms of (paid, underpaid, and unpaid) care work; rewarding and ensuring better conditions for care workers; reducing and redistributing unpaid care work between households, public and private provision, and within households across gender; and representing care workers and giving them greater voice. The decades of neoliberal policy hegemony have led to drastic decline in per capita public health spending in rich and poor countries alike. It is now more than obvious that this was not just an unequal and unjust strategy but a stupid one: it has taken an infectious disease to drive home the point that the health of the elite ultimately depends on the health of the poorest members of society, and therefore those who advocated reduced public health spending and privatization of health services did so at their own peril. What has also emerged is that this is true at a global scale as well, so the current pathetically nationalist squabbles over access to protective equipment and drugs betray a complete lack of awareness of the nature of the beast. This disease will not be brought under control unless it is done so everywhere, so once again international cooperation is not just desirable but absolutely essential.

The New Deal must be Red, with a critical focus on addressing and reducing inequalities: in assets, income, access to food, essential public services, and employment opportunities. These have to be reduced across different dimensions: gender, race, ethnicity, caste, location, age. This requires more careful regulation of markets, including of financial markets, labor and land markets, and of interactions with the natural environment. It also requires more active redistribution, such that new public spending is financed by taxing the rich (through a small wealth tax that could still bring in much-needed public revenues because of extreme asset inequality) and by taxing multinational companies that have managed to evade taxes by exploiting legal loopholes, with a system of unitary taxation and a common minimum tax rate across countries.

All of this requires international cooperation, which is why this Multicolored New Deal must necessarily be global in scope, with appropriate international architecture, with controlled finance and capital flows, more equitable and just rules for managing external debt, revised rules for trade, cross-border investment, and intellectual property rights that prevent concentration and monopoly rent-seeking and encourage good quality employment generation. Immediately, this requires a significant increase in access to liquidity for developing countries, including through a major issue of Special Drawing Rights by the IMF; debt standstills and effective debt relief for economies in distress; enabling and assisting capital controls to curtail surges in inflows and outflows and to arrest sharp changes in currency and asset prices (if only regional at this point) would be essential.

This may seem like an impossible agenda, but the constraints are mainly political, reflecting the massive lobbying power of big business and the nexus between states and corporate leaders. Finally, these constraints are binding only because citizens of the world do not put sufficient pressure on their leaders to force them to change course. The pandemic and other ongoing crises may still serve to generate the necessary public pressure.

Representative Publications and Influences

Publications:

Jayati Ghosh (2010). The Unnatural Coupling: Food and Global Finance. *Journal of Agrarian Change*, *10*(1), 72–86.

Jayati Ghosh (2012). Women, labour and capital accumulation in Asia. *Monthly Review*. 63(8), 1–14.

Jayati Ghosh (2013). Microfinance and the challenge of financial inclusion for development. *Cambridge Journal of Economics*, *37*(6), 1203–1219.

People who have been influential: Ashok Mitra, Prabhat Patnaik, Krishna Bharadwaj, Joan Robinson, Geoff Harcourt

Literature that has been influential:

Michał Kalecki (1976). *Essays on Developing Economies*. Harvester Press.

Prabhat Patnaik (1995). *Whatever happened to imperialism and other essays*. Tulika.

Paul Baran and Paul Sweezy (1966). *Monopoly Capital*. New York: Monthly Review Press.

Ilene Grabel

Ilene Grabel is Distinguished University Professor, University of Denver, and Josef Korbel School of International Studies at the University of Denver, where she is Co-Director of the Graduate Program in Global Finance, Trade, and Economic Integration. Her research and teaching focus on the political economy of international financial policy, institutions, and financial flows; global financial governance; global, regional, and transregional financial architectures; and finance and economic development. Her recent book, *When Things Don't Fall Apart: Global Financial Governance and Developmental Finance in an Age of Productive Incoherence* (MIT Press, 2017), won the 2019 European Association of Evolutionary Political Economy Myrdal Prize, the 2019 International Studies Association International Political Economy Best Book Award, and the 2018 British International Studies Association International Political Economy Book Prize.[1]

Tell us a bit about your background.

I grew up in New York and attended public schools. My father worked on the production side of things in the garment center back when women's clothing was still made in Manhattan. He was a passionate reader. My mother was a secretary at a community college. They were

---

1   Thanks to Suraj Thapa for assistance.

modest people and so it was a vast leap for me to become a professor, an
aspiration I long held because of my love of school and also, I think,
because of my father's passion for reading.

*Why did you choose to study economics and to attend UMass Amherst for
your PhD work?*

When I started my bachelor's degree at Queens College (one of the
colleges in the City University of New York network), I never considered
studying anything but economics. I think there were a few reasons for
this decision (which some might consider a failure of imagination!). I
very much enjoyed the social studies classes I took in high school. In
those days, social studies was a kind of stew involving economics,
personal finance, history, and civics. So an economics major seemed like
an obvious choice.

My decision to study economics was quickly validated during the
first meeting of my first class at Queens College, which was "Introduction
to Macroeconomics," taught by Ray Franklin. Ray was a mesmerizing
teacher and that sealed the deal for me. I ended up working for him as a
research assistant for a few years. I became very close to Kim and Matt
Edel during my time at Queens. (Kim was in the Urban Studies
Department and Matt held joint appointments in Economics and Urban
Studies.) Now that I'm an academic I cannot believe how much time
Kim and Matt let me (and other students) simply hang around in their
offices. They were also great and generous hosts. I spent many an evening at their home enjoying fondue and was always shocked and intimi-
dated when they would say, "Oh, by the way, Andre Gunder Frank (and
any number of other left luminaries) is going to join us for dinner." I
house-sat for them during their annual summer trip to New England
and found their massive library mesmerizing, as well as what seemed an
impossibly exotic array of condiments in their fridge. Bill Tabb and Carl
Riskin were also mentors of mine at Queens College. I worked a great
deal on my graduate applications with the faculty that I've mentioned.
Kim and Matt, as usual, were especially generous readers of my essays
and provided a great deal of guidance on the process.

I was also drawn to study economics because I was very interested in
issues of poverty, development, imperialism, discrimination, and the US
interventions in Central America. Economics seemed to me the best

way to understand these phenomena and to improve the world. I was also involved with activist politics on campus. The left faculty met monthly for a brownbag lunch discussion group. To be among the students who were invited to join this group was a great honor, and these lunches were formative for me.

I received a great deal of encouragement from a very special group of faculty, all of whom made it perfectly clear that I should pursue a PhD in economics and that the only place to do it was at UMass Amherst. And so I did.

What was the overall atmosphere like when you were a UMass grad student? Who were some of the main people that influenced you during your years there?

UMass was a great place to study. Our entering class became extremely close very quickly. We felt that it was important to enact our commitment to collectivism by working together on everything—preparing and sharing study notes, creating shared physical photocopy archives (because we were studying in the pre-pdf, pre-email days—hard to believe now!), studying for exams, and working together in dissertation "support groups." Within the class I became very close to several people—George DeMartino (my study buddy for several years and now my husband of twenty-nine years), Amy Silverstein (now Cramer), and Linda Ewing. There were also deep friendships across classes (many of which are active today), and I found the more advanced students extremely generous in providing support and tips on getting through various hurdles as a graduate student. I'm still surprised when I talk with colleagues who studied at different institutions to hear that their programs were cutthroat and that they received little support from fellow students and faculty. I could not have gotten through UMass without the support I received. And I could not have launched and built a career without the support, networks, and friendships I built at UMass.

The graduate students at UMass were, not surprisingly, very radical in their approach to being students. There was a student organization, the Economics Graduate Student Organization (EGSO), which was very militant. EGSO met at the start of every term and decided who would serve as a teaching assistant and for which professor. EGSO would determine how many discussion sections would be allocated to each student. The organization also allocated some of the research positions, and participated in faculty hiring, some types of faculty meetings, and discussions of curriculum and curriculum changes. I loved being a part of EGSO and I was for one year a co-chair of the organization. My present professor self cannot believe that we had the space (or nerve) to do or say what we did, and I find it impossible to imagine anything like this happening in any other institution.

Not surprisingly, many EGSO members were also very involved in efforts to unionize graduate student employees. I enjoyed being a part of that first drive, which was successful.

Even if the EGSO experience is not easily replicable on other campuses, I'm really heartened to see activism emerging in so many domains on campuses these days. Perhaps things are coming full circle with students at so many institutions becoming very active in many matters, such as university governance and leadership selection, the investment practices of endowments, faculty hiring, matters related to diversity, inclusion, and implicit biases in higher education, and in the #metoo movement.

I found the faculty at UMass to be extremely supportive and I formed very close relationships with several faculty very quickly. Studying macroeconomics with Jim Crotty really changed everything for me. I came to UMass sure that I would focus on Marxian theory, labor, and other subjects that we might think of as traditional parts of the heterodox canon in that period. But one class in macroeconomics got me hooked on Keynes, Minsky, and all matters related to finance, financial instability, and financial crises. These continue to be my central preoccupations. Jim became a very close friend and still is. The times I spent talking with him about my dissertation and the times I spent over dinner at his home with his wonderful wife, Pam Crotty, were extremely important to me. Jim was also very important to me on a personal level because we shared a common class background, as we were both outsiders to academia.

Another faculty member who was and still is very important to me is Jerry Epstein. While Jim turned my attention to finance and macroeconomics, Jerry introduced me to international finance and international financial flows and policy, areas that continue to be central to my work today. I also enjoyed many an evening at Jerry's home with his wife, Fran Deutsch, and still enjoy the chance to stay up late talking with Jerry and Fran whenever I stay at their home during visits to the Amherst area.

I also became quite close to David Kotz, for whom I worked as a research assistant for a couple of years. Though I did not work with David on my dissertation, he was a generous sounding board and mentor. We remain quite close today. I had the privilege of getting to know David's wife, Karen Pfeiffer, both through David and during the year I spent teaching at Smith College in the final year of my dissertation.

In the preface to my recent book, I wrote about the fact that the faculty who mentored me, both as an undergraduate and as a graduate student, remain role models when I interact with my own students. I don't see that I've ever been as generous and inspiring as they were to me. But I continue to try.

Albert Hirschman has clearly been a major influence on your more recent work. What are some of the main perspectives you got out of studying Hirschman?

Albert Hirschman's work has deeply influenced my work, especially the work I've done in the last few years around the global financial crisis and what it has meant for global financial governance and developmental finance. This work culminated in my recent book, *When Things Don't Fall Apart: Global Financial Governance and Developmental Finance in an Age of Productive Incoherence* (MIT Press, 2017). In the book, I use Hirschman's work as the key analytical frame for thinking through the nature of change and structural transformation of the global financial governance architecture—how we understand it, how we know when it is happening, how we assess its significance, and how we think about the issue of scale and the scalability of institutional transformations. I argue that the global financial governance architecture is today marked by "productive incoherence." In my view, productive incoherence can be understood most fully within what I call a "Hirschmanian mindset," by which I mean an understanding of social, institutional, and ideational change informed by Albert Hirschman's key epistemic and theoretical commitments.

Hirschman's work is deeply radical—it challenges us to think differently about social and institutional change; social engineering; the role, power, and rhetoric of economic experts; and the limits to knowledge. The alternative vision of change that I advance in the book, and which reflects key commitments that mark Hirschman's work, recognizes that meaningful change can and should come about through proliferation of partial, limited, and pragmatic responses to challenges and opportunities; and as a consequence of often disconnected, experimental, and inconsistent adjustments in institutions and policies. This vision turns our attention away from epochal ruptures of the sort that occur infrequently in historical terms but that tend to receive disproportionate attention by scholars. Instead, a Hirschmanian approach turns our attention towards more prevalent but prosaic, small-scale, experimental, and evolutionary changes as the wellspring of what can be meaningful transformation.

In the Hirschmanian view, development is to be recognized as a series of transformations, each of which amounts to a social experiment that permits learning by doing and from others. Central to this conception of development as a process of social learning is Hirschman's emphasis on experimentation, particularly parallel experimentation. Critically important as well is the importance of problem-solving in response to previously unforeseen or underestimated challenges. This was Hirschman's conception of the "Hiding Hand." Central to Hirschman's Hiding Hand is his view that uncertainty, ignorance, and error can be the driver of productive action by policy entrepreneurs who develop pragmatic responses to evolving challenges. Think for a moment about the policy groping now underway across the globe in response to Trump. There's no standard playbook here—each country is grasping for viable responses.

Central to Hirschman's understanding of development as a process of social learning and experimentation is his rejection of the tendency that often leads social scientists to prejudge the outcomes of interventions, so that they can declare at the outset that some development represents a "fundamental" or a "superficial" change. An example of such thinking is the epistemic certainty that led some to decide that the global rise of the economies of Brazil, Russia, India, China, and South Africa (the BRICS) is a game changer, while others with similar certainty dismiss the group (especially China) as little more than subimperialists. I'll note also that, in Hirschman's view, even experimental failures can leave in their wake vital linkages, side effects, networks, and knowledge that may be available for and enable subsequent endeavors. This view is also relevant to thinking about possible legacies of the BRICS.

Other aspects of Hirschman's work are pregnant with insights for my own work, including his commitment to what he termed "possibilism" and what he called his "bias for hope." Hirschman's possibilism entails the idea that small-scale, messy, disparate innovations reveal what could be. Hirschman counterposed possibilism with what he called the predominant "futilism" in the social sciences, especially in development economics. Futilism is the view that initiatives that are not entirely consistent with grand theories and social engineering programs are bound to fail. Central to Hirschman's possibilism is his humility and epistemic commitment to fundamental uncertainty. The embrace of uncertainty connects Hirschman quite directly to Keynes, Knight, and Shackle (and therefore also to the contemporary post-Keynesian tradition). Related to his epistemic commitment to uncertainty is Hirschman's recognition (with Hayek and Popper) of the limits of intelligibility in a complex world.

Hirschman's work on "exit, voice, and loyalty" is perhaps his best known. These concepts refer to the circumstances under which actors engage or disengage with institutions that don't serve their needs. This framework is useful in thinking about the threats made by some developing economies to exit the Bretton Woods institutions, some of which culminated in the development of parallel structures. In the spirit of messiness, I note that the development of parallel structures is playing out against simultaneous efforts to use voice to press these institutions to change from within.

Where do you situate Hirschman relative to Marxian and post-Keynesian approaches? What other work do you see as connected to Hirschman's key insights? And where does your work fit relative to the Marxian and post-Keynesian frameworks that are central to leftist research in your areas of macroeconomics and finance?

As I note above, Hirschman's commitment to fundamental uncertainty is a key point of connection between his work and work in the Keynesian tradition. That said, it is essential to understand that Hirschman was deeply suspicious of, and indeed rejected, anything that smacked of an "ism," a grand theory, or social engineering. His impatience with the pursuit of perfection in ambitious utopian projects and other forms of social engineering applied to plans from all corners—socialists, advocates of "big push" and "balanced growth" development models, hydraulic Keynesianism, and neoliberals. The rejection of utopianism had deep roots in Hirschman's personal and professional autobiography—including his practical experiences working on the Marshall Plan and European reconstruction under the auspices of the US Federal Reserve Board; his work as a consultant in Colombia, and deep connections to Latin America more broadly; his two experiences with the World Bank, first as the World Bank's advisor to the Colombian government from 1952 to 1956, and later as a consultant studying project design, management, and appraisal; and his personal history as a refugee from fascism. The latter, in the view of his biographer, Jeremy Adelman, led Hirschman to appreciate the likelihood that grand utopian projects will yield horrific outcomes.

In place of social engineering, Hirschman advocated what he termed "immersion in the particular" and the need to liberate practice from the straightjacket of reductionist models that provided justification for encompassing, homogenous programs. Hirschman's approach instead was one of improvisation in pursuit of multiple development paths, not implementation of a pristine policy blueprint. He favored complexity, messiness, specificity, and contingency in contrast to what he saw as theoretically sanctioned, paradigm-based uniform solutions. In reflecting on his own work, Hirschman said: "with this conclusion I can lay claim to at least one element of continuity in my thought: the refusal to define 'one best way.'"[2] This view was consistent with the work of economic historian Alexander Gerschenkron, whose work illustrated the multiplicity and uniqueness of development trajectories in a variety of national contexts.

In Hirschman's view, attempts by social scientists to domesticate what was fundamentally uncertain, disorderly, contingent, and complex had troubling consequences for developing countries. For Hirschman, as for Hayek (whom he drew upon admiringly), there were "limits to 'intelligibility' of our complex world." Herbert Simon's conception of "bounded rationality" stems from a related recognition that the social world is inherently complex and only partly intelligible. It's striking the degree to which Hirschman anticipates the contemporary turn in economics away from

2   Hirschman, *A Propensity to Self-subversion*, Cambridge, MA: Harvard University Press, 1995, 76.

theorizing the economy as an essentially simple, self-contained system, towards recognition of the economy as an adaptive complex system.

There's an interesting passage in Hirschman where he commends the theorist Louis Althusser, even though he ironically notes that, as a Marxist, Althusser should be what he termed an "inveterate paradigm lover." What Althusser terms "overdetermination" in his account of transformative experiences, such as revolutions, Hirschman notes should more accurately be termed uniqueness, which is obviously something that Hirschman took very seriously.

As far as my own work, I'd say that it's fairly eclectic. In addition to working in the Hirschmanian tradition, I continue to be heavily influenced by Keynes and post-Keynesians, social economics, Marxian-inflected work, feminism, and aspects of poststructuralism. I also draw on work by political scientists in the constructivist tradition in the field of international political economy. I've learned about constructivism because I've spent my career in a school of international studies and I have many political scientists as colleagues.

Much of your work revolves around financial crises and transformations in the global financial architecture. From your perspective, what do you think were the primary causes of the 2007–09 global financial crisis? In what ways does your perspective correspond with or differ from other views out there, including those of both mainstream as well as leftist economists?

The global crisis of course has many roots. Chief among them are the blinders, narrowness, scientific pretensions, and hubris of the neoclassical economic paradigm that was dominant during the long neoliberal era. Many things followed from the dominance of this approach—for example, the use of faulty models of risk assessment that validated decisions made by financial actors; a "this time is different" fantasy that marked the precrisis years; radical programs of financial liberalization, "light touch" financial regulation, and the broader idealization of markets and price signals; securitization of anything that could be securitized; financialization and the financialization of everyday life; shadow banking and the trading of opaque financial assets (such as derivatives); a revolving door between the financial community and financial regulators; and the conflicts of interest that are baked into the way that the credit rating industry operates. The power of the financial community also played a key role in driving behaviors and practices that contributed importantly to the crisis.

I think my perspective on the etiology of the global crisis is in line with that of most heterodox economists. It's been fascinating to see the way in which more mainstream economists have come to articulate narratives about the crisis that resemble those of heterodox economists. Often, they do so in ways that do not acknowledge the prior work of heterodox economists. Nevertheless, I'm heartened by the "rediscovery" of Keynes, Minsky, Marx, Polanyi, and John Kenneth Galbraith by economic journalists, mainstream academic economists, and economists working at policymaking institutions such as the International Monetary Fund. I'm hoping that Hirschman's work also comes to be widely appreciated beyond the work on exit, voice, and loyalty. I think there is evidence that this is happening.

Despite a similar financial crisis origin story, I'd say that my work differs rather markedly from that of most heterodox economists when it comes to making sense of the legacy of the crisis in terms of global financial governance and developmental finance. The failure of the reform agenda after the global financial crisis (and of previous crises as well, namely, the East Asian and Mexican crises of the 1990s, the developing country debt crisis of the 1980s, and the crises of the 1970s) has led many social scientists and other observers to emphasize continuity in financial governance. In my recent book, *When Things Don't Fall Apart*, I call this the "continuity thesis"—it refers to the widely held claim that the opportunity for meaningful reform created by the global crisis has been lost, and that nothing of significance has changed, especially as it concerns developing countries.

I argue in the book that the continuity thesis misses the point. I show that the East Asian and especially the global crisis catalyzed disparate, disconnected innovations across several dimensions of global financial governance. I argue, further, that these discontinuities matter deeply for developing countries. But, to be clear: this is not to say that the global crisis occasioned an abrupt shift from one regime of global financial governance to another. It certainly hasn't. Indeed, I show that continuities in some domains are as salient today as are discontinuities. But I also argue—and this is the key point—that a chief problem with the way that social scientists tend to understand change is as a simple binary in which systemic regime displacement is the only and true test of change. The Bretton Woods era and the neoliberal revolution are the paradigmatic examples of regime displacement. At the other end of this binary thinking is the view that anything less than sharp, unambiguous discontinuity should be dismissed because it is merely trivial, localized, ameliorative, and fleeting. Obviously that flavor of blunt, epistemically certain thinking is not something that resonates for me.

My chief goal in the book is to move beyond these simplistic notions of change and to defend what I call the "productive incoherence thesis." My argument is that the changes we confront today are best understood as ad hoc, fragmented, and evolutionary. It is in this sense that global financial governance, taken as a whole, is today "incoherent." An unruly, muscular pragmatism has broken out in institutional design, governance, and policymaking. The new pragmatic spirit entails learning from experience and learning from others, both successes and failures, adjusting as necessary and in response to new challenges. The result so far has been the emergence of an increasingly dense, "pluri-polar" set of fledgling institutions of financial governance and a diversity of institutional and policy practices that do not cohere around a grand vision. Pluri-polarity, as I use it, refers to increasing diversity, heterogeneity, and inconsistency within the financial governance landscape. And I want to be clear that though I'm encouraged by emergent incoherence in global financial governance, this does not imply that incoherence is without important risks. Indeed, I elaborate on the risks of incoherence in the book as well.

Did you see the 2007–09 crisis coming? If so, what were the main indicators you were observing that provided you with this perspective? If not, what were the things that you did not see coming that you wish you had seen? What do we need to know now in order to give something resembling accurate forecasts as to whether or not another crisis is gathering force?

Many of us had long written about the myriad financial fragilities that were building for more than a decade prior to the crisis. The indicators of fragility included (but were not limited to) high levels of corporate and household debt; the bubble in residential and commercial real estate and stock prices, churning of securitized assets, and the abundance of cheap credit and the ease of getting mortgages; activities in the shadow banking sector; and the presence of regulators who were asleep at the wheel (or worse yet compromised by their prior or hopes of future work on Wall Street). Even the popular culture came to reflect much of this when we consider the popularity of television shows about "fixing and flipping" and getting rich by speculating in real estate.

My Hirschmanian and Keynesian roots mean that I'm not one for forecasting crises. However, keeping one's eyes trained on the kinds of indicators that I've listed above should figure into any discussions of whether another crisis is on the horizon.

From your perspective, do you think we are on course for another major financial crisis in the near future?

Surely other financial crises are on the horizon. We look out at a world that is fraught with a panoply of risks—from Trumpian Twitter-induced shocks; deepening kleptocratic tendencies in the Trump administration, coupled with a commitment to dismantle the financial regulatory architecture and reduce the US role in the Bretton Woods institutions unless they can be bent to the administration's will (to an even greater extent than has been the case over the last many decades); shocks emanating from a range of nationalist and xenophobic governments and political movements; deglobalizing tendencies in many parts of the world (such as those that drove Brexit); the decline of postwar traditions of multilateralism and trade conflicts; unknown parameters of risks associated with cryptocurrency markets and new debt instruments such as collateralized loan obligations; very high leverage rates and debt rollover risks in China and in many other countries to which China is lending; pressure on developing country currencies coming from the capital outflows stimulated by the return to expansionary monetary policy in wealthy countries; possible instability associated with the Chinese government's plan to liberalize its financial system and currency; and the financial risks arising from climate change. Any intensification of these (or other) crisis triggers will test the resilience of the global financial system. It is therefore both prudent and sensible to assume that there will always be new financial crises, and that the most vulnerable nations and economically disadvantaged and politically disenfranchised groups within them will bear the heaviest burdens.

The global financial crisis had the effect of catalyzing a broadening and deepening of global financial safety nets, as I've written about in my recent book. A central question is whether policy-makers are up to the task of responding to the next crisis. We may know that sooner rather than later. Critical in this connection is the fact that central banks are largely out of firepower, the expertise of central banks is under attack in some national contexts (the US most notably), cooperation of the sort that marked the 2007 crisis is not a likely outcome in the next few years, and the legitimacy of the IMF may be compromised if a leader is not chosen through an internationally competitive process (something that has never happened) and, if as seems likely, the governance and quota reform processes at the institution remain stalled.

In your (multiple award–winning) book When Things Don't Fall Apart, *you argue that much has changed in global financial governance since the last crisis. Can you give us some of the key pieces of evidence that you have gathered that support your conclusion?*

I explore the contradictory effects of the East Asian financial crisis of the late 1990s, which I argue laid the groundwork for the uneven, evolutionary changes associated with the global crisis and its aftermath. In the book's four case study chapters, I examine areas of financial governance across which we find continuities, discontinuities, and in some cases, what I term "ambiguities." I'll just highlight now some of the empirical claims that I make in three of the four empirical chapters.

A case that I examine in great depth is the IMF. The global crisis has had complex, uneven effects on that institution. There is a great deal of evidence on the continuity side of the ledger when it comes to the IMF. For instance, the crisis restored the IMF's coffers and central role in crisis management; assistance packages followed a well-rehearsed countercyclical script (as we've even seen very recently in the assistance package to Argentina in 2019); developing countries secured only very modest voting share increases; and the US and Europe exercised disproportionate influence at the institution, for example, by sustaining the postwar "gentleman's agreement" on the leadership of the Bretton Woods institutions, granting systemic risk exemptions to European countries; and the US Congress stalled extremely modest voting share realignments for five years. I'll note that Trump's Treasury team and the acting but still unconfirmed US Executive Director to the IMF displays the administration's signature hostility to multilateral organizations.

The recent appointment of David Malpass to the World Bank is another tick on the side of continuity with leadership selection practices.

The Trump appointees to the Bretton Woods institutions may bring about an important discontinuity, which is reduced US engagement with and influence at these institutions, something that has already begun. This may be the only silver lining of the Trump administration. However, even before the Trump appointees came on the scene, important discontinuities were emerging, especially at the IMF. In terms of discontinuities during the global crisis, IMF leadership, researchers, and staff working with crisis countries normalized the use of capital controls. Developing countries twice took the unprecedented step of lending to rather than borrowing from the IMF (in 2009 and 2012); the institution's client base largely shifted to the European periphery and away from developing countries; and there was evidence of tension between the IMF and Eurozone authorities on debt sustainability in Greece, the decision to grant exceptional access in the larger Eurozone loan packages, the most severe forms of austerity in some crisis countries, and on maintaining the link to the euro in peripheral European economies. In addition, the crisis opened channels for several countries, particularly China, to increase informal influence at the institution. Relatedly, the crisis ushered in a new norm at the IMF in which key positions, including a deputy managing director position, were given to officials from China. In a different vein, but in keeping with the idea of discontinuities at the IMF, in 2015 China achieved a long-sought goal of having the IMF include its currency in the Special Drawing Rights basket.

We also find increasing inconsistency between rhetoric from the institution, research, and its practice with individual countries. I call these gaps between IMF rhetoric, research, and practice "ambiguities," and I explore several key ambiguities at the IMF. An example of one ambiguity concerns the IMF's rhetoric and research on inequality, which has been somewhat progressive, while actual programs in countries like Greece and Argentina have aggravated inequality. The gap between rhetoric, research, and practice reflects not just public relations and organized hypocrisy (in the sense of Kate Weaver's usage, though certainly this is a part of the story), but also increasing contestation and confusion within the IMF.

Productive incoherence is also evidenced by innovations in financial governance architectures in the Global South and East. For institutions whose existence predates the global crisis, we find expansion in the scale of activity, geographic reach, and the introduction of novel mechanisms. These changes are apparent in institutions that provide financial support during crises and development banks that provide long-term loans. Examples of institutions in the Global South and Global East that have expanded their capacity to provide countercyclical crisis support include the Chiang Mai Initiative Multilateralization of the Association of Southeast Asian Nations (ASEAN) plus three countries (Japan, South Korea, and China), the Latin American Reserve Fund, and the Arab Monetary Fund. The Development Bank of Latin America is an example of a development bank that expanded its capacity during the crisis. We also find hybridization of missions within southern and eastern institutions, effectuated by the decision by several regional and national development banks to take on a countercyclical role. Examples of such hybridization are found in Brazil's Bank of Economic and Social Development, the China Development Bank, and the Development Bank of Latin America. We also find southern and eastern institutions that have been created during the crisis, some focusing on countercyclical support, others on development finance, and some doing both. Examples of institutional creation include the Eurasian Fund for Stabilization and Development of the Eurasian Economic Community, the Contingent Reserve Arrangement and the New Development Bank of the BRICS, the Asian Infrastructure Investment Bank, and the other funds that China has created to support the Belt and Road Initiative. Many of the institutions have signed cooperation agreements with one another. And in contrast to its opposition to the Asian Monetary Fund proposal (advanced by the Japanese government at the outset of the East Asian crisis), the IMF has been encouraging the expansion of and connections among these institutions. The IMF is also involved in discussions about "rules of engagement" and is developing an instrument to provide backstop finance to these institutions. In all of this we are observing productive incoherence in the expansion of disparate and overlapping institutions that complement rather than displace the Bretton Woods institutions. Taken together, these developments are increasing the density and diversity of the financial landscape.

Another dimension of productive incoherence concerns capital controls. Most countries used these in the decades after World War II and then dominant Keynesian theory supported their use. Capital

controls fell out of favor in the 1970s and remained so during the long
neoliberal era. Credit rating agencies downgraded countries that dared
to buck the trend by deploying them. Changes in ideas and practices
around capital controls began to emerge unevenly and tentatively in the
1990s, but deepened and became more consistent during the global
crisis. A wide range of developing countries used a variety of capital
controls during the crisis to slow the tide of capital inflows when the US,
the Eurozone, and Britain offered few attractive opportunities to speculators. The change in thinking and practice around capital controls is
dramatic. Capital controls have been rebranded as a legitimate policy
tool, even by the credit rating agencies, the deeply conservative heart of
the economics profession, and by the IMF, which has even prescribed
them to some borrowing and some nonborrowing economies during
the crisis. It's notable that the neoclassical heart of the economics profession has followed the lead of some IMF researchers, who have domesti-
cated the idea of capital controls by now referring to them with the new
neutral technocratic label of "capital flow management" techniques and
listing them as a "legitimate part of the policy toolkit."

Stepping away from the empirics, I'd say that the institutional aperture and innovations that I examine might not persuade those committed to heroic narratives of systemic change. That's unfortunate. From my
perspective, recent crises might be understood as crucial turning points
in a contested, uneven, long-term process of pragmatic adjustment in
financial governance.

*Are you optimistic that what you term our "Age of Productive Incoherence"
in international finance is going to yield a more progressive policy architecture than what has dominated under neoliberalism? What, in your
view, is a post-neoliberal financial architecture likely to look like?*

Notwithstanding the significant risks associated with this age of incoherence, I think it's naïve to think that we should be nostalgic for the
coherent days of the neoliberal era and the monolithic governance
architecture that underpinned it. After all, would it be better for developing countries if the Trump administration had at its disposal a streamlined Bretton Woods architecture through which it could leverage its
power to constrain policy autonomy, frustrate progress on the United
Nation's Sustainable Development Goals, and otherwise wreak havoc

and play out petty grudges? As damaging as Trump's impact has been so far—and the worst may be yet to come—it's at least arguable that he lacks the levers under the evolving global financial architecture to impose his vision on others (at least with the same degree of success enjoyed by the champions of neoliberalism). A Trump in, say, the late 1990s—at the height of neoliberalism's coherence—would arguably have posed a deeper threat to developing countries. Moreover, it is implausible to think that the aspirations of developing countries would be better served by a return to the institutionally sparse, coherent, and centripetal financial and intellectual architecture of the last many decades.

It's best, I think, to consider the present as an interregnum between an era dominated by a dysfunctional Bretton Woods monoculture and a something else, the parameters of which are as of yet unknown and unknowable. Hence the question of whether the architecture is likely to be more progressive in nature or not is not something that we can know right now. However, I think it is safe to assume that the evolving landscape is not likely to meld into a new, coherent global financial architecture that resembles the orderliness of the pre–global crisis world. The array of China-led institutions is complementing, competing, radically reshaping, and above all complicating the Bretton Woods landscape, where the line between advanced economy lending and developing economy borrowing used to be clearly drawn. The vacuum created by the recent US rejection of multilateralism suggests that there will be both greater space and more urgent need for China and others to step into the void. And this of course presents both opportunities and real risks for developing economies, for US power and relevance, and for the shape of multilateralism.

The emerging productive redundancy threatens the streamlined, top-down coherence of the Bretton Woods world, which promised efficiency but in fact generated and socialized extraordinary risks, created vulnerabilities to contagious crises, and deeply underserved developing countries. Redundancy and networks of cooperation among institutions in the Global South and East and between them and the IMF may increase financial resilience by increasing the size and range of crisis support opportunities while also providing new avenues to secure finance for long-term projects. Engineers naturally understand the need for redundancy in safety systems to ensure that the systems do well when placed under intense stress. The increasingly dense and networked global financial architecture is prudent in the very same way, even if it is by no means adequate in its current form to maintain stability during the next big financial crisis—the timing of which, as I mentioned early, is uncertain, though its eventuality is not. Nothing I've said suggests that I think things won't fall apart—indeed they can and always will. But when they do, will a messier, pluri-polar Hirschmanian global financial architecture be better situated to respond to developing countries in a world in which the Trump administration is unlikely to have an appetite to allow the Bretton Woods institutions to perform their traditional roles? Present conditions suggest that we may know the answer to this question sooner rather than later.

Now that you have recently completed a major book, where do you see your research agenda going over the next several years?

I'm intensely interested in the future of multilateralism and pluri-polarity in global financial governance, and I plan to continue to follow these matters closely in the coming years. The thing that's so fascinating about studying finance is that the field changes so quickly and there are always new things that I want to understand. I've been starting some new research on the privatization of development finance, something that has been pushed by the World Bank and a working group appointed by the Group of Twenty. I've also started some new research on the political economy and risks associated with cryptocurrencies. I also may start to work on the financial risks associated with climate change. It's hard now not to think that the spillover effects of climate change are the single most important issue that we face.

Responses on the COVID-19 Pandemic

How would you evaluate the ways different countries or regions have responded to the COVID-19 crisis, both in terms of public health interventions and economic policies?

I remain intensely interested in exploring the spaces where aperture and agency emerge as sites of possibility. As I discuss above, a central theme in my book is that incoherence provides many such spaces, even while it creates serious risks. Indeed, in chapter 8 I discuss the risks associated with incoherence at some length. In work this year I've argued that the diverse policy responses to the COVID-19 crisis provide a window into the operation of the incoherent "order," revealing both its productive *and* its deeply destructive potential.

The failed response to the COVID-19 crisis in the US is a perfect illustration of destructive incoherence. Instead of a federal response to the COVID-19 crisis there was propaganda, denial, and chaos. All manner of destructive incoherence becomes more apparent daily in the US as the COVID-19 crisis unfolds. The same can be said of the process of distributing the vaccine (which is beginning, as of this writing). Balanced budget rules at the state and municipal levels constrain their fiscal capacity and canceled out much of the effects of federal fiscal expansionism associated with the inadequate CARES Act. At the same time the absence of federal leadership in implementing closures and openings of schools and workplaces, and in securing ventilators and personal protection equipment, continue to have horrific consequences in terms of loss of life, mental health, unemployment, poverty, home-lessness, food insecurity, and access to education. Many of these conse-quences will surely ramify across generations.

Absent a federal response to the COVID-19 crisis, US states and municipalities were left to fend for themselves. Some enacted protective policies.[3] We might be tempted to see this as an example of using the space provided by incoherence and aperture. True enough. But I want to be absolutely clear here that desperate intrastate responses are hardly to be celebrated. The absence of federal leadership was nothing short of criminal neglect.

The COVID-19 crisis provided the opportunity for the Trump administration to further its cronyist agenda by bailing out large firms while starving state and local governments and hospitals of much needed funds, while also stirring anti-Asian nativism and exploiting historical racism against Blacks and Black Americans. The Trump administration's decision to halt funding to the World Health

---

3   Similar intrastate dynamics are apparent in commitments to the Paris Climate Accord and living wages made by some US states and cities; Medicare programs in Massachusetts; and policies on immigration, the environment, and private prisons in California.

Organization during the COVID-19 crisis reflects the strength of its anti-globalist impulses and the commitment to punish a multilateral institution for (a real and an exaggerated) tilt towards China.

Destructive incoherence is also on full display in the failure to develop a coordinated global or even a European Union–wide response to the crisis. Nonetheless national governments in many European contexts moved quite far in the direction of expansive, universal social protection. In many European contexts, states supported furloughed workers in ways that were inconceivable in the US. And even Germany moved away from its deficit obsession early in the COVID-19 crisis.

Countries of the Global South and East do not possess the fiscal headroom to respond to the economic, financial, and public health effects of the COVID-19 crisis. This is different from the favorable conditions that many countries enjoyed during the global crisis. Prior to the COVID-19 crisis, economic conditions were already deteriorating. Debt crises have emerged in several contexts and many countries are racing towards this fate. External actors—ranging from the Bretton Woods institutions, private creditors, the Group of Twenty, and donor governments—have said much, but done little to respond to the crises confronting countries in the Global South and East. As of this writing, there is good reason to suggest that these countries will be last in line for the coronavirus vaccine, and that the monopoly system that protects the rents associated with intellectual property will render the vaccine out of reach.

The COVID-19 crisis jeopardizes essential international projects, such as the pursuit of the UN's Sustainable Development Goals and the prospects of new social compacts, while substantially weakening collective responses to challenges in the global commons, such as the refugee, environmental, and COVID-19 crises. The world economy is listing towards another Great Depression as a consequence of the COVID-19 crisis, which is worsening already vast national and cross-national inequalities in human development, while exposing and intensifying the effects of racism and other forms of structural violence. It should also be said that the prospects for global coordination in response to imminent financial crises are, in a word, dim.

Do you draw any general lessons from the COVID crisis about the most viable ways to advance an egalitarian economic project?

The COVID-19 crisis has prompted me to think about what sorts of policy and global governance reforms could provide an *enabling environment* for projects that are progressive, just, egalitarian, feminist, anti-racist, and sustainable. We know that the impacts of all crises are always gendered, racialized, and deeply inscribed by class, power, and position within subnational, national, and global orders. Crises not only magnify inequalities, institutional, and policy deficiencies—they also reveal them. What they do not do is guarantee progressive reform—as Karl Polanyi recognized, they are just as apt to propel fascist movements. With all that in mind, I'll outline some directions for global macroeconomic governance that I see as enabling progressive aims.[4]

It is essential that reconstructed, permissive multilateralisms maximize policy space for experimentation and innovation with strategies that uplift and amplify the conditions of life for disenfranchised communities, promoting economic and social well-being, inclusion, resilience, shared prosperity, sustainability, and recovery from the economic and public health costs of the COVID-19 crisis. I argue for permissive multilateralism*s*—plural, not singular—as an alternative to misplaced nostalgia for a unified, harmonized global governance system (which characterized the post–World War II period).

Permissive multilateralisms may have a chance if (as I hope) the US election marks a renewal of global engagement by the country's leadership. This would be a corrective to the naked self-interested nationalism of the last four years. And it would represent acceptance of what is obviously true—namely, that enduring, deep challenges in the arena of public health, climate, and the economy (including rampant inequality) cannot be addressed without robust, permissive multilateral cooperation supported by well-resourced, legitimate, inclusive institutions of global economic governance. The incoming Biden administration is signaling a cooperative spirit and global outlook. Let's hope that this plays out in practice, but with greater skepticism than previous administrations had about the supposed virtues of liberalized globalization. And let's also hope that the administration's fragile compromise with

---

4 The discussion here draws on Ilene Grabel, "Enabling Global Macroeconomic Governance: Pathways for Reforms That Support a Feminist Plan for Sustainability and Social Justice," policy note prepared for Expert Group Meeting of UN Women, November 19, 2020.

progressive forces within the US helps insulate a Biden administration from capture by the private sector. Speaking pragmatically, permissive multilateralisms may be all that is feasible for a public that has little appetite for grand plans in what I've referred to in a recent paper as our present "ism-less Post-American moment."[5]

Chief on the sovereign debt agenda is the pressing need for a sovereign debt restructuring mechanism (SDRM), something that has been raised and abandoned over several decades. It is a certainty that widespread, lasting debt crises in the Global South and East will be but one lasting legacy of the COVID-19 crisis, promising yet another "lost decade." Many actors, such as UNCTAD and civil society organizations, have developed frameworks and advocated for an SDRM architecture. IMF officials have recently identified the need for an SDRM (as have World Bank officials in the past). Implementing an SDRM is a matter of political will. The private sector must be forced to the table on this matter. This is imperative now that the naïve fantasy of voluntary private-sector compliance with debt restructurings and write-downs has been recognized as such by the Bretton Woods institutions and the G20.

In addition to an SDRM, comprehensive debt relief involving public and private-sector obligations and debt cancellations for the poorest countries are essential. Without it, we consign these countries to austerity. Nothing could be more harmful to a progressive agenda. Debt standstills (such as the G20's Debt Service Suspension Initiative) only kick the can down the road. At the very least, restructuring sovereign debts so that future repayment obligations link debt service to economic growth (or perhaps to other economic, social, and environmental indicators) is an alternative. However, comprehensive debt relief should be a far higher priority.

Capital controls are a tool for expanding policy space for experimentation, especially space for accommodative and expansionary macroeconomic policies. Capital controls can to some degree rebalance political voice by limiting the entrance and exit options available to the

---

5   Ilene Grabel, "Post-American Moments in Contemporary Global Financial Governance," chapter prepared for *Liberalism's End? Populism, Authoritarianism, and the End of the American Order*, edited by Peter J. Katzenstein and Jonathan David Kirshner (under review, Cornell University Press).

holders of capital (see my earlier discussion of Hirschman). As I mentioned earlier, capital controls were quickly re-legitimized during the global crisis. But some ambiguity remains in what is called the IMF's "Institutional View" of capital controls. A more expansive Institutional View should unequivocally involve support for controls on inflows and outflows, should see controls not as a last resort but rather as a permanent and dynamic part of a broader prudential, countercyclical toolkit to be deployed as internal and external conditions warrant, and should reflect the view that controls may need to be blunt, comprehensive, significant, lasting, and discriminatory rather than modest, narrowly targeted, and temporary. Any governance regime that seeks to develop a framework for capital controls should err on the side of generality, flexibility, and permissiveness; should involve and promote cooperation by both capital source and recipient countries; and should embody an evenhanded acknowledgment that monetary policies, like capital controls, have positive and negative global spillover effects that necessitate some type of burden sharing. Capital controls should be understood as part of a broader program to reign in the power of domestic and international finance and rebalance the world economy in ways that move it from its "K-shaped" pattern (in which finance flourishes while the rest of the economy and population stagnates or suffers).

The response of the Bretton Woods institutions to the economic and public health challenges of the COVID crisis has been deeply disappointing. Disbursals have been slow and small relative to vast needs. Emergency financing for immediate relief is overdue. More broadly, and beyond the imperatives of a COVID era response, the BWIs need to be better and more stably resourced. The institutions also need to regain legitimacy and be modernized. Leadership selection processes (which reflect the power and economic dynamics of 1944) should be transparent, merit-based, and inclusive. Steps should be taken to increase the voice and vote of countries of the Global South and East so that the institutions are accountable to their full membership. The institutions also need to become responsive and accountable to a variety of stakeholders (who lack traditional representation within these institutions). The institutions should also be reformed in ways that reflect the global economic role, needs, and lived experience of their full membership and draw on a range of views in decision-making and analysis. And they should develop equitable internal dispute resolution processes.

A more densely populated, messier global financial governance architecture is more likely to be tolerant or supportive of experimentation and a diversity of economic models and approaches. That kind of permissiveness is typically absent under an architectural monoculture that exerts a gravitational pull towards a single idealized model. Speaking practically, this means enhancing the flow of resources to financial institutions in the Global South and East and advancing rules of engagement and backstop financing among these institutions and between them and the BWIs, provided that these connections do not comprise autonomy.

International and domestic public finance and official development assistance (ODA) are essential to the success of any progressive initiatives. And despite the inward political turn that marks sentiment in many countries of the Global North, actors in the global development, feminist, environmental, and social justice communities should continue to articulate a case for the necessity of well-resourced BWIs that play their traditional role in providing public finance and for galvanizing renewed commitments to provide ODA by actors in the foreign aid community.

The challenges of enabling progressive, egalitarian, feminist, green, just, and antiracist COVID-19 recovery plans call for vast, globally inclusive programs of public investment in public health, care economies, and green transformations; and support for universal social protections and universal basic incomes, employment-generating activities, education, and digital access (among other things). As I noted previously, fiscal space for these kinds of initiatives was not available in many countries of the Global South and East prior to COVID-19. Spending on such initiatives was also ruled out by deficit hawks, even in nations that possessed fiscal headroom. It is particularly important for economists and civil society organizations to make a case for accommodative macroeconomic policy frameworks, now and after the coronavirus is controlled, and to challenge the myths peddled by austerity and inflation hawks, as they reassert themselves in the post-COVID-19 environment (as they surely will). It is also important that a wide range of stakeholders be involved in policy design and macroeconomic policy impact analyses.

Addressing tax evasion by domestic and multinational firms and the world's super-wealthy and curbing illicit financial flows are essential to domestic resource mobilization. Many have by now proposed unitary taxation on multinational corporations as a vehicle for curbing corporate tax evasion. In addition, progressive taxation of income and wealth, closing channels for tax evasion, and raising taxes on financial and other firms are key vehicles for mobilizing resources and enhancing fairness.

Does the experience of the COVID crisis shed any light on the way you think about economics as a discipline or, more specifically, the questions you might be pursuing in your own research?

The COVID-19 crisis underscores the importance of scholarship that works across disciplines. And, though it comes as no surprise to those who have long been interested in uncertainty and complexity, I think these matters will become center stage concerns for the discipline as a whole. I also think that it's safe to assume that inequalities, stratification, and resilience will become greater preoccupations for the economics profession in general. For my part, I envision moving some of my research more firmly in the directions I've just mentioned, while also building out the idea of permissive multilateralisms and post-American orders.

The COVID-19 crisis takes me back to the motivations that initially drove me to study economics as an undergraduate and that continue to drive my work. I hope that my work makes the world at least a bit more just.

References

Crotty, James R. "On Keynes and Capital Flight." *Journal of Economic Literature* 21:1 (1983): 59–65.
———. *Keynes Against Capitalism: His Economic Case for Liberal Socialism.* Abingdon, Oxon and New York: Routledge, 2019.
Hirschman, Albert O. *Exit, Voice, and Loyalty: Responses to Decline in Firms, Organizations and States.* Cambridge, MA: Harvard University Press, 1970.
———. *A Bias for Hope: Essays on Development and Latin America.* New Haven, CT: Yale University Press, 1971.
———. "Political Economics and Possibilism." In *The Essential Hirschman*, ed. Jeremy Adelman. Princeton, NJ: Princeton University Press, 2013 [1971], 1–34.
Weaver, Catherine. *Hypocrisy Trap: The Rhetoric, Reality and Reform of the World Bank.* Princeton, NJ: Princeton University Press, 2008.

Representative Publications and Influences

Publications:

Ilene Grabel (2000). The political economy of 'policy credibility': the new-classical macroeconomics and the remaking of emerging economies. *Cambridge Journal of Economics, 24*(1), 1–19.

Ilene Grabel (2015). The rebranding of capital controls in an era of productive incoherence. *Review of International Political Economy, 22*(1), 7–43.

Ilene Grabel (2017). *When Things Don't Fall Apart: Global Financial Governance and Developmental Finance in an Age of Productive Incoherence.* The MIT Press.

People who have been influential: James Crotty, John Maynard Keynes, Hyman Minsky, Jerry Epstein, Albert Hirschman

Literature that has been influential:

James Crotty (1983). On Keynes and Capital Flight. *Journal of Economic Literature, 21*(1), 59–65.

Albert O. Hirschman (2013 [1971]). "Political Economics and Possibilism." In *The Essential Hirschman*, edited by Jeremy Adelman, 1–34. Princeton, NJ: Princeton University Press.

Albert O. Hirschman (1967). The principle of the hiding hand. *The public interest, 6*.

Costas Lapavitsas

Costas Lapavitsas is a Professor of Economics at the School of Oriental and African Studies, University of London. His research and teaching have focused on Marxian and other critical approaches to money and finance and the Eurozone crisis, among other topics. He is the author of many articles and books, including *Profiting without Producing: How Finance Exploits Us All* (2013) and *The Left Case Against the EU* (2018). Lapavitsas founded Research on Money and Finance (RMF), an international network of political economists focusing on money, finance, and the evolution of contemporary capitalism. He has served as a member of the Hellenic Parliament.

What drew you into the study of economics?

I first came across economics in my early teens in Greece, in the mid 1970s, soon after the fall of the colonels' dictatorship. It was a time of profound political change and great release of intellectual energy. Marxism had made a strong return as the Communist Party was legalized after nearly three decades. Everything seemed possible and it looked as if the wheels of history were moving in the direction of socialism. To me, economics was the best way of finding how to actually change the world, not merely wishing to change it.

What were the main intellectual influences that shaped your outlook about politics, the economy, and society?

The determining influence was undoubtedly Marxism. I came across it when I was very young, and its voice made absolute sense to me on politics, economics, and society. I have not changed my mind since those days. On the contrary, I am even more convinced that open and informed Marxism remains the best way to approach these issues. But there are two further influences that I should also mention. The first is historical writing and the second is the classical novel, especially French and Russian. Both of these were a strong part of Greek culture at the time, and I believe that they were equally prominent in many other cultures of the Eastern Mediterranean and the Middle East. I was a voracious reader of history and classical literature from a very young age, and that has placed a definite stamp on my understanding of politics, economics, and society.

Who are the economists you admire the most and why?

My university training in economics was steeped in the British neoclassical tradition. During that time, needless to say, I became thoroughly versed in Anglo-Saxon political economy. A key moment for me, however, was subsequently becoming acquainted with Japanese Marxism and especially the Uno current. I discovered an entire universe of thinkers who approached political economy with deep sophistication.

Still, the bedrock of my understanding of the capitalist economy comes from studying the classical economists. Adam Smith stands out for his extraordinary ability to construct a coherent intellectual system. After reading *The Wealth of Nations*, one has a sense of grasping how the capitalist economy works. David Ricardo, on the other hand, is unsurpassed for his power of pure and concise economic analysis. Arguably, he was the cleverest person who ever did economics. Karl Marx does not have the same analytical power in economics, but his breadth and historical insight is of an entirely different order. He was an ocean, a vast terrain of intellectual connections that put the world in order. He had an unbelievable gift.

Among the monetary theorists, I should mention Thomas Tooke for his incomparable grasp of the institutional and empirical detail of his time, but also for his guidance on how to approach purely monetary issues. Tooke is always one of the thinkers I go back to when confronted with complex questions about money. I find John Maynard Keynes less useful in this respect, but I admire his ability to put the great policy questions of his time in clear and manageable terms, helped by his luminous prose. Last but not least, for me, Rudolf Hilferding is the only Marxist economist of the twentieth century who cuts the mustard with monetary theorists. Without Hilferding there would not really be a Marxist current on money and finance.

Unlike many intellectuals once associated with the left who converted over the years to mainstream economic views, you have not wavered from your early intellectual influences and have kept a highly critical view on capitalism and mainstream economic analyses in general. In this regard, has left political economy kept up, properly speaking, with changes in the capitalist world economy? That is, has political economy developed over the years the proper analytical tools to understand, analyze, and hopefully shift the direction of the contemporary world towards a more rational, humane, and just socio-economic order?

Political economy has developed in a peculiar way during the last four decades. Two features stand out. The first and most notable is the rise of the Anglo-Saxon current, a reflection largely of the dominance of Anglo-Saxon universities across the world. You will find that Marxist political economists across the world have frequently received training in US, English, or Australian universities. The strength of this development is the emphasis on data and empirical elaboration of arguments and analysis. The weakness is the detachment from active politics and the academic nature of the intellectual output. Anglo-Saxon Marxism has historically been the weakest current of Marxism and this, unfortunately, now shows across the world. It is a problem made much worse by the rapid decline of continental European Marxism, especially in France and Italy.

The second feature is the gradual ascendancy of political philosophy and ethical critique within Marxism, at the cost of political economy. This development has occurred as neoliberalism came to dominate mainstream economic thinking. It is a remarkable change from the immediate postwar period, when political economy was still considered the core of the Marxist current, as indeed it was for Marx's own work, or during the period of what we might call classical Marxism, around the First World War. Things became particularly bad during the ascendancy of postmodernism, when there was almost a systematic loss of confidence in the ideas and methods of Marxist political economy. Partly in defense, a rather mechanical Marxist economics also emerged that is obsessed with secondary and often purely technical questions. This still exists and is strangely reminiscent of the conceptual immobility of mainstream economics. One only has to look at some of the putative "Marxist explanations" offered for the Great Crisis of 2007–2009 in terms of the tendency of the rate of profit to fall. However, there are also far more hopeful signs as the retreat of postmodernism has led to a rediscovery of the "material" and the "real" at the heart of capitalism. A sophisticated and fresh political economy, keenly aware of class relations, is making a comeback and forms the core of Marxism for our age.

You have done work on financialization, which many regard as the latest stage in the historical evolution of capitalism. How does contemporary financialization differ from finance capital and the analyses produced by eminent Marxist thinkers at the turn of the twentieth century (for example, Bukharin, Hilferding, and Lenin), and does it represent a new form of imperialism?

Financialization is the most interesting fresh idea to emerge in Marxist political economy, but also more broadly in critical social science, during the last four decades. It seeks to come to terms with the extraordinary rise of the financial system in mature capitalist countries during that period, and the penetration by finance of all nooks and crannies of everyday life. For me, it sums up a period that began in the late 1970s, peaked from the early 1990s to the mid 2000s, and is now in the doldrums. It can be considered as the second period of the rise of finance in the history of advanced capitalism, the first being that of classical imperialism around the turn of the twentieth century analyzed by Hilferding, Lenin, Bukharin, and others among the great Marxists.

The differences between the two periods are of paramount importance, however. The first and most important one is that the concept of finance capital, originally proposed by Hilferding and adopted by Lenin, that is, an amalgam of industrial and banking capital in which the latter has the dominant role, does not hold today. On the contrary, industrial capital has become relatively detached from banking capital, particularly as it holds vast amounts of liquid money capital that is not invested productively. It is wrong to think that banks dominate industrial capital today. Another key difference is that finance has come to penetrate social and individual life in unprecedented ways, including through loans for mortgages and consumption. The rapacious and usurious aspect of finance, which has been characteristic of it since ancient times, has assumed new forms in our time, giving rise to what I call financial expropriation, that is, the extraction of profit directly from personal income and money wealth. Moreover, during the period of financialization the productive structure of the world economy has changed as the center of gravity of manufacturing has moved increasingly to Asia, particularly China. That is where the gains in productivity are to be found, not in the heavily financialized countries of the West.

Financialization corresponds to a new imperialism, to be sure, but there is no territorial redivision of the world, no exclusive trading zones, no incorporation of virgin areas into formal empires. There has also been less military competition among the established powers because the USA has been so dominant. Militarism and imperial aggression during the last three decades have taken the form of intervention that destroys smaller states and creates vast areas of lawlessness, especially in Africa and the Middle East. The main threat to world peace is manifestly Anglo-American militarism. But as the productive structure of the world economy has changed, we will undoubtedly see the rise of political and military power of China and others. Militarism will probably take a far more vicious turn in the coming years.

Since the eruption of the global financial crisis of 2008 and the subsequent euro crisis, you have devoted the bulk of your research and analysis on what might be broadly defined as the political economy of the European Union. Were you always a euroskeptic, or is this more of a recent development linked to the Greek debt crisis and its aftermath?

No, I would not describe myself as euroskeptic even now. I firmly believe in the fundamental solidarity and cultural affinity among European people, especially workers and the poor. The European left has always been internationalist. But the Eurozone crisis and especially its Greek episode cast a harsh light on the EU, its Economic and Monetary Union (EMU) and its common currency, the euro. These are rigid structures that enforce neoliberalism and impose discipline on labor in the interests of capital. There can be no doubt about this any longer. What is also indisputable is that these structures are beyond reform in the interest of labor and the poor. All changes that have taken place in the EMU since the outbreak of the crisis have been inimical to workers.

It is amazing to me that large sections of the European left continue to believe that the EU and the EMU are terrains of struggle that should be defended in the name of internationalism. This is the surest way for the left to detach itself from the workers and the poor of Europe, abandoning them in the arms of the far right. There could be no challenge to capitalism in Europe without a readiness to confront and overturn the institutions of the EU and the EMU. On that I have no doubt at all.

In 2005 you were elected to the Hellenic Parliament as member of Syriza, the party of the Greek radical left. What made you decide to participate in the world of Greek politics as an elected member of a bourgeois parliament?

There is nothing unusual in what I did; on the contrary, it was the natural act of submitting to public judgment the arguments that I had made in the public arena during the previous period. Socialists have always participated in elections and sought to enter parliament to conduct political struggle. Ideas and political beliefs must go through the test of practice, otherwise they remain mostly words.

The experience of participating in elections and parliament was invaluable to me. There is no substitute for doing politics where it matters, that is, with ordinary people, listening to their arguments, being subjected to their questions, and seeking ways of speaking for them while also involving them in activity. The self-emancipation of workers and the poor is far more difficult in practice than it appears in theory, particularly in conditions of cynical financialized capitalism, when the independent organizations of workers have become weaker, and when parliamentary practice has lost even the last vestiges of democracy.

My experience was that parliament has become a hierarchical talking shop which in reality exercises very little monitoring of executive decisions. Just to give you a flavor of that, the third bailout agreement that the Syriza government signed in August 2015 was a huge document exceeding 1,000 pages. The members of Greek Parliament were given less than twenty-four hours to read it before voting. And yet the vast majority of MPs voted in favor because their parties asked them to do so. This truly was a "state of exception" in Schmitt's sense, imposed on Greece by the lenders, and a complete emasculation of parliamentary democracy. I can recall few moments in my life of feeling so alone as during that awful night in the Greek Parliament, when the elected representatives of the nation passed into law an agreement that was destructive of both society and country, without having read it, or even being aware of its main provisions. Parliamentary democracy in our times is a travesty.

When Syriza came to power, there were high expectations that a government of the radical left would not allow Brussels and Berlin to dictate the economic future of the country. What is your assessment of how things have turned out?

The capitulation of Syriza was one of the darkest spots in the history of the European left, a truly shameful moment. To understand it, it is vital to appreciate that the Syriza government came under extreme blackmail from the lenders and the EU, which took the form of withholding liquidity to Greek banks and thus gradually bringing the economy to the point of asphyxiation. Syriza was a broad organization incorporating several currents of thought and argument, but two were dominant. The first centered on Alexis Tsipras, the prime minister, and his narrow circle, also including the finance minister, Yanis Varoufakis. Their view was that electoral victory had given Syriza legitimacy and strength through which they could force the lenders to accept a compromise, thus enabling the Syriza government to adopt different policies. Apparently, they thought that this could be achieved without exiting the EMU and without a decisive rupture with the lenders. The second current effectively argued that this would be impossible and that a rupture, an irreconcilable conflict, would have to take place. For our side to be successful, we argued that it would be necessary to prepare both the people and the party.

Tsipras and his circle won, overturning the expressed wish of the Greek people to refuse a Third Bailout in the referendum of July 2015. His actions were effectively an unconditional surrender to the lenders. The Syriza government subsequently became the most obedient government Greece has had since the start of the crisis, fully implementing the bailout terms. The result has been continuing economic stagnation, rising poverty, and mind-numbing political apathy. Greece has been firmly placed on a trajectory of historical decline and its people feel powerless to change it.

Is this the reason why you walked away from Syriza?

Strictly speaking, we did not walk away from Syriza. About thirty-five of us refused to vote for the Third Bailout, keeping our word to those who had elected us and defending our position. We were right, after all, about the fallacy of Tsipras and his group. It was proven in practice that there was no way that the lenders and the EU would have allowed a Syriza government to pursue a radical path within the institutional framework of the EU. After his surrender, Tsipras forced an election in September 2015 without conducting an internal debate in Syriza. Naturally we had to fight the election under a different banner. Unfortunately, in the conditions of despondency that gradually emerged in Greece after the sellout of Syriza, it became extremely difficult to sustain an independent left presence.

From where you stand, how would you describe the mission, goals, and aims of the European Union, and do you think the current EU can be reformed?

Since the creation of the Single Market in 1986–87, and following the Maastricht Treaty in 1992 and the Lisbon Treaty of 2009, the EU has been on an inexorable path of hardening neoliberalism. There is no surprise in this. The Single Market has its own remorseless logic and it imposes it through the actions of the member states but also through the transnational mechanisms of the EU. The enormous body of European Law, which member states must accept in its totality, and which gives tremendous power to the European Court of Justice, is a guarantor of the neoliberal transformation of the EU. In response to the Eurozone crisis the EU has become even harder in its neoliberalism; indeed, it has institutionalized it through the Fiscal Compact and the Banking Union. The mechanisms of the EU now have the power to police austerity even before member states register deficits that are not allowed by the Fiscal Compact.

There can be no doubt that the EU is a leviathan that impinges upon national and popular sovereignty, while serving the interests of capital against labor. It is imperative for the workers and the peoples of Europe to get rid of the monetary union and to break with the institutions of the EU.

The truly problematic thing in this respect is that much of the European left still has profound illusions about the EU. It believes that the Social Chapter is evidence of a social democratic nucleus within the constitution of the EU, which could be expanded through struggle. From this perspective, it appears that the problem is neoliberal politics and not the very structure of the EU. Presumably, if the left got its act together and left governments were elected in key countries, things could change and reform could become possible.

This view is truly confused and confusing. The experience of Syriza has shown that the machinery of the EU will not tolerate any radical challenges and it will move heaven and earth to defeat them. In this respect, there is no difference between a small country, like Greece, and a large one, like France. A radical French government would very soon realize how hostile and effective the machinery of the EU can be, if confronted by a left-wing challenge. There is no viable way to reform the EU. For radical anticapitalist policies in the direction of socialism it is imperative to confront it directly, reject the common currency, and disobey the directives. If this implies exiting, then so be it. Britain has shown that there is nothing irreversible about joining the EU, nor is it the end of the world to leave it. The real issue is to propose a way of doing so from the left that challenges the power of capital and opens new avenues of collaboration and true solidarity among the peoples of Europe. That was always the mainstay of the European left and it is time that it rediscovered it.

Responses on the COVID-19 Pandemic

How would you evaluate the ways different countries or regions have responded to the COVID-19 crisis, both in terms of public health interventions and economic policies?

The most striking aspect of the pandemic crisis is the way in which it brought the nation-state to the forefront. The state is the real pivot of contemporary globalized and financialized capitalism.

The crisis was caused to a large extent by the state itself, since states imposed the medieval practice of lockdowns and social distancing to confront the disease. A better response would have been mass testing, tracing, and isolating those who were infected, together with strong support at the primary level for the most vulnerable groups. COVID-19 has a class character, hitting harder the poorest and weakest in society, those with long-standing health ailments. But a grassroots strategy would have required substantial resources and, even more important, strategic planning imbued with public spirit. The main neoliberal states in the world were unwilling and unable to deliver it, for instance, in the US and the UK. Lockdowns were the default option, and they have weighed very heavily on workers and the poor.

Lockdowns gave rise to a vast and unprecedented crisis because the world economy never properly recovered from the last great crisis of 2007–09. Most of the important metrics have been below trend for both core and peripheral countries during the last decade. Lockdowns delivered an enormous shock to aggregate demand and supply, which then led to an unprecedented response by nation-states. I don't think that there is anything comparable in the history of capitalism.

Control over fiat money allowed central banks to flood markets with liquidity and drive nominal interest rates to zero. Aggressive fiscal policy effectively nationalized the wage bills and the income statements of private enterprises. Money drafts were made available to families and households. Borrowing by private enterprises increased enormously, often backed by state credit, in a very short period of time. The list goes on and on. The nation-state showed that it might be unwilling and unable to deliver a publicly minded strategy against the disease, but nevertheless that it commands vast power over the economy. We really live in an era of state-based financialized and globalized capitalism.

Quite naturally, then, great differences emerged among countries reflecting the institutions and mechanisms of the state, the varying ideologies that dominate the state machine, and their customs, traditions, and other practices, as well as the structure of national economies. The contest between the US and China took a new impetus. US capitalism continues to control world money, and this is one of its major residual strengths, capable of generating another enormous financial bubble in the midst of an unprecedented recession. But in just about all other respects, it seems to be falling behind Chinese capitalism. Furthermore, the division of the world economy into core and periphery has assumed fresh content. Europe is now firmly divided into core and several peripheries with diverging trajectories. Subordinate financialization in developing countries has continued apace. The period ahead is likely to be one of greater divergence presided over by the nation-state.

Do you draw any general lessons from the COVID crisis about the most viable ways to advance an egalitarian economic project?

It is not difficult to identify the main elements of an egalitarian economic project for the period ahead, a project that would change the social balance in favor of labor and against capital, opening fresh paths towards socialism.

In important respects, there is general agreement among heterodox economists: boost aggregate demand by sustaining household income and increasing public investment to renew decaying infrastructure; protect wages and conditions of employment; ensure full employment through reducing the length of the working week and promoting programs of public works; tackle the obscene inequalities of contemporary capitalism through income and wealth redistribution, including profound tax reform; strengthen the welfare state, especially by promoting a genuine public health service; begin a process of "de-financialization" by intervening in the financial system and creating public banks, both retail and investment; push for "re-localization" of production, a vital step in developing a strategy of development that would protect the environment and create better living conditions.

The list could be easily extended and there would not be much substantive opposition to any of these suggestions. The real problem is not identifying feasible alternative policies. It is, rather, regaining the confidence of the left to challenge capitalism at its core. That is simply gone after the defeats of the last few decades. The problem is also to reconnect the left with the working class, the poor, the dispossessed, and the marginal layers of capitalist society. That is also gone after the defeats of the last few decades. We are confronted with the bizarre spectacle of financialized capitalism becoming ever more dysfunctional, while the left fears to advocate profound reform and working people and the poor look towards right-wing populism for answers. This is the real problem that an egalitarian project has to confront.

Representative Publications and Influences

Publications:

Costas Lapavitsas (2009). Financialised Capitalism: Crisis and Financial Expropriation. *Historical Materialism*, *17*(2), 114–148.

Costas Lapavitsas (2011). Theorizing financialization. *Work, Employment and Society*, *25*(4), 611–626.

Costas Lapavitsas (2013). *Profiting without producing: How finance exploits us all*. Verso.

People who have been influential: Karl Marx, Adam Smith, David Ricardo, Thomas Tooke, Rudolf Hilferding, Kozo Uno, Paul Sweezy

Literature that has been influential:

Rudolph Hilferding (2006 [1910]). *Finance capital: A study of the latest phase of capitalist development* (T. Bottomore, Ed.; M. Watnick & S. Gordon, Trans.; Reprinted). Routledge.

Paul Sweezy (1942). *Theory of capital development*. Monthly Review Press.

Kuzo Uno (1980). *Principles of Political Economy. Theory of a Purely Capitalist Society*, [Keizai Genron, 1964], translated by T. Sekine, Brighton, Atlantic Highlands, New Jersey.

Zhongjin Li

Zhongjin Li is Assistant Professor of Economics at the University of Missouri–Kansas City. She is Co-Director of the Asian Political Economy Program and Assistant Professor of Economics at the Political Economy Research Institute. Li's research focuses on political economy and economic development with a regional focus on East Asia. She has published articles and books including *China on Strike* (co-edited 2019), "A Living Wage, Overtime Work and China's Economic Sustainability" (co-authored 2014) and "Giovanni Arrighi in Beijing: The Historical Transformation of Labor Supply in Rural China of the Reform Era" (co-authored, 2019).

Can you please tell us about your family and educational background?

I grew up in a working-class family in southeast China, roughly sixty miles from Shanghai. The whole region, for centuries, has been known for agricultural advancement and intellectual richness, and in the recent three decades, for growth in the private economy and in the export sector. My grandparents moved from rural to urban areas, due to the Japanese invasion and the civil war, and proudly worked as the first generation of factory workers in the People's Republic. My parents and their siblings all grew up in the city and started to work in factories after graduating from middle school.

When thinking of my family background, three things directly came to my mind: hard work, education, and gender equality. My parents both had long working hours and often attended training sessions or went on business trips in other cities before I turned ten. That was my very first impression of work. It was not easy; they were obviously not lazy, as many scholars later claimed that workers with the "iron rice bowl" were supposed to be. However, they also had a high sense of achievement from their work and developed strong emotional ties with the work units (then state-owned enterprises) they belonged to. This also helps to explain why later they experienced a hard time when their work units were privatized after 2000. The second is the emphasis on education. None of my relatives in my parents' generation went to college, but their children, all my cousins and I, went to college and even graduate school. I was fortunate enough to study in the period when public education received probably the strongest government and community support in China, and my parents always encouraged me to be curious and resilient in my learning process. Last but not least is the idea of gender equality. It is often said that girls born in cities of China's one-child generation have benefited most from this strictly implemented birth-control policy since the late 1970s. But my parents are more serious on gender equality than they would have been, if only due to the pressure from the policy. My family name (Li Zhong) is an explicit combination of both of theirs, with my mother's put before my father's. The arrangement was absolutely unusual then, and not typical even today. All the family decisions were made democratically and as a girl I was never made to doubt what I could possibly do. All these aspects have been influential on my personal and intellectual development.

What led you into the field of economics, and how did you end up at UMass Amherst for your doctorate?

As an undergraduate, I began with international relations as my major subject in Beijing, because I was always curious about the bigger world, and growing up in a small city I initially thought the best way for me to know the bigger world was to aim for a "world" subject. I have to confess that I knew almost nothing when I decided on my major. (In China, students are typically required to declare their majors before entering universities.) However, I have never regretted this decision, because the curriculum design of international relations as a major was broad and nonbinding, allowing me to explore other disciplines. It was truly multidisciplinary, if not interdisciplinary yet. I took courses in economics, psychology, sociology, history, mathematics, computer science, etc. in addition to my main political science ones. It was when I took a political economy course that I started to develop a deep interest in the Marxian approach. Chinese students were required to read and memorize text-book Marxism in high school, so Marxian terminology was not new to me, but I had never been exposed to Marx's original writings before taking that college class. My professor, Fusheng Xie, who encouraged me to apply to UMass Amherst later and remains to this day an intellectual mentor for me, taught me how to read Marx's *Capital* and Harry Braverman's *Labor and Monopoly Capital*, and to rethink China's economic history in the twentieth century. The history course I took introduced me to Maurice Meisner's book *Mao's China and After*, which opened up my mind to think about Chairman Mao. The sociology course I took gave me the opportunity to conduct fieldwork in elementary schools for children of rural migrant workers in Beijing and in sweater factories in my home-town, which were my first political economy explorations of the world around me. At the same time, I was also trained in political science by professors with a wide political and ideological spectrum. However, over time I began to feel as if I knew only the surface of social changes but was still puzzled by the deeper forces beneath them. When I decided to explore further, I was encouraged to apply to UMass to study political economy. At that time, I had already read Professor David Kotz's book on the Soviet Union, *Revolution from Above*, and thought that that type of "interna-tional relations" made more sense to me. I was quite fortunate and remain very grateful to be accepted there, which exposed me to multiple approaches in heterodox economics, and to learn from and work with many professors and fellow graduate students during those years.

Which economists have had a major influence on you? How have they influenced your approach to economics?

I would say Marx and Engels, as well as Marxian economists in general, have had a direct influence on me in terms of their historical materialism and dialectical materialism. The analysis of labor exploitation, class process, and economic crisis has shaped my research interests. Harry Braverman's explicit focus on the labor process, Paul Baran and Paul Sweezy's discussion of development and monopoly capital, Immanuel

Wallerstein's world systems theory, and Erik Olin Wright's reconceptual-ization of class and power are among the ones that strike me the most. Gordon, Reich, and Edwards's 1982 book *Segmented Work, Divided Workers* and other Marxian economists in the Social Structure of Accumulation (SSA) school have also been critical for me to understand capitalist crisis and labor movements from a historical perspective. For analyzing the Chinese economy, I would say William Hinton and Minqi Li are particularly influential on my understanding of the socialist expe-rience and the capitalist transformation. One of my best experiences at UMass was to have a small China study group with my fellow Chinese graduate students in the Economics Department, in which we regularly read books/articles and discussed and debated a variety of economic, political, and social topics directly concerning China's political economy. We worked on a few important projects such as the living wage campaign and the fight against railway privatization. We have kept in touch after graduation and the discussion with them has always been helpful and crucially important for my intellectual development.

Your doctoral research compared the "growth miracles" of three East Asian economies—Japan, South Korea, and China. What, in your view, are the sources of these three "miracles?" In what ways are these three countries' experiences similar and in what ways are they different? In all three cases, is it fair to say that the single most important feature of the model is success with an export-led growth strategy?

The East Asian economies experienced exceptionally rapid growth by historical and international standards. In fact, East Asia stands out as the only region in the capitalist world economy where living standards are catching up to Western countries. I would mention four particular reasons behind the "miracle."

One is the successful accumulation of economic surplus through land reforms and labor mobilization, dismantling the power of land-lords and preparing for industrial development. Japan and South Korea did these under US pressure during the Cold War, while China had a more independent process. But Japan and South Korea later followed a capitalist trajectory of dispossessing the rural peasants and creating a cheap labor supply (proletarianization) for urban industrial capital accumulation, while China had rural collectivization and labor accumulation during the socialist regime and a similar dispossession process and surplus labor utilization in the reform era.

Second is the strong presence of the state and, in particular, the implementation of active industrial policies. The state in Japan and South Korea was able to rely on shifting alliances around particular projects and to implement selective industrial policies and protective trade policies. China was consciously pursuing that course but was also forced to build a self-reliant industrial system before 1978, and has maintained relatively strong state dominance or control in certain industrial sectors and macroeconomic regulation after 1978 (despite that control being weakened in recent decades) .

Third is the limited degree of income and wealth inequality. Japan and South Korea benefited from the land reform, the weakening of the working class and later redistributive policies, while China's rapid growth through market reform benefited from the socialist legacy—not just in industry and infrastructure building, but also in a relatively equal distribution of social resources. This is the social foundation from which the developmental state emerged and became effective.

Fourth is the favorable international situation. The three countries all experienced years of import substitution strategy and then switched to more reliance on exports. The Cold War gave Japan and South Korea a favorable trade environment, which in recent times has become more and more difficult for other developing countries. My research has particularly focused on the first three aspects in terms of the labor regime, power dynamics, and distributive implications.

How does your perspective on the East Asian model differ from those that were developed by some highly influential progressive analysts, such as Alice Amsden, Ha-Joon Chang, and Robert Wade?

The work by Alice Amsden, Ha-Joon Chang, and Robert Wade has played a crucially important role as a response to the conventional wisdom of the market approach, which claims that the success of the East Asian economies was due to "getting the prices right." Their detailed analysis and emphasis on what actually happened in terms of the role of the state is instrumental for us to reconsider what did and should happen to enable economic growth. To some extent, I think the World Bank's 1993 report *The East Asian Miracle* was a reluctant response to their critiques. While the state-led approach is more in line with the actual policies implemented and the important role of state intervention in fostering the rapid development, it is not sufficient to provide a full picture. First and foremost, its theoretical assumption of the developmental autonomy of the state simply rejects the state as a contested terrain for class conflict and reproducing power relations. Its focus appears to be detached from society and fails to explain the reasons why and how the state serves capital accumulation by exercising its power directly against the working class. It also has little to say about why the market would be "governed" in some cases but not in others. Not surprisingly, it fails to explain how, later, the state was reconfigured into a power base of the capitalist class, especially its financial faction in the neoliberal era, and why these forces would unavoidably lead to an economic crisis and recession. It reminds me of what Marx wrote in the *Poverty of Philosophy*, "The economists explain to us the process of production under given conditions; what they do not explain to us, however, is how these conditions themselves are being produced, i.e., the historical movement that brings them into being." Without taking account of the deeper class dynamics and distribution, I think their analysis is incomplete and potentially misleading. Moreover, taking the dichotomy between market and state as an analytical starting point is quite problematic. It reduces the agenda of development into an oversimplified framework about "how much" state intervention is needed, rather than how to build the strong social foundation to ensure more meaningful development. In short, I was inspired by and still admire those progressive scholars' work, but I support approaches that are more radical than the developmental state one.

In what ways, if any, do you think the Chinese, or more generally, the East Asian, model can serve today as a guide for less developed countries throughout the world?

First, I want to mention that development is a knowledge-localized process in which historical context matters. Therefore, we need to be sensitively aware of the material conditions and historical background of the East Asian model. Any simple replication without a careful investigation of local condition tends to fail. Regarding the lessons, I would like to emphasize the Chinese experience in labor accumulation in absorbing and mobilizing surplus labor locally and more localized industrial development to achieve self-sufficiency, as well as equality before the implementation of market reform. The East Asian experience also reflects the importance of active industrial policy, especially in the manufacturing sector, for cumulative productivity increases to catch up to richer countries and to lift the population out of poverty. Also, a relatively equal distribution of income and wealth is crucial for the developmental state to indeed emerge and be effective. This requires the state and the capitalist class to make certain compromises in negotiating with a relatively strong working class and, to some extent, ensure that the benefits of the rapid growth are not entirely exclusive to a small elite or are not immiserating certain laboring groups. With an increasingly unequal distribution, the state would become less willing to promote growth and less effective in doing so. This goes back to my earlier point that we need to understand the state in more concrete and historical contexts, through the lens of the internal conflicts among the state and the emerging classes, and the external constraints that global capitalism has imposed on the economy, rather than taking its "developmental" mandate as given or guaranteed.

Has the Chinese growth experience over the past forty years created better living conditions overall for the people of China—for working people and peasants in particular? You have addressed this issue in some detail with respect to precarious workers, women workers, and migration. What are your general conclusions from this work?

I think judging by the conventional measures, such as GDP and GDP per capita, the Chinese growth experience is phenomenal, and it has significantly changed the landscape of the economy. However, it also has created remarkable inequality in a short period, transforming China from the most egalitarian place in the world by the late 1970s to one of the most unequal economies today. Economic convergence and divergence are both visible within the national boundaries.

My interest in Marxian political economy started from the real-world observation of China's rural migrant workers and the rise of labor precarity as well as from my curiosity about the implications of emerging capitalist development in the Chinese economy. I have paid more attention to the divergence and the left-behind laboring class. For example, my recent work on rural labor supply unpacks the historical process of the transformation of the surplus labor. The work on platform labor reveals the subordination of workers to finance-backed platforms and the precarious labor processes used by the ride-hailing industry. The work on female migrant workers shows that the widely acclaimed flexibility (to stay or to return) of this group is built upon the unequal burden on women workers in the context of rising discrimination in rural land tenure arrangement, urban precarious employment, and weak support for labor reproduction. My general conclusion so far is that the Chinese workers, particularly the 290 million rural migrant workers, are creating the miracles while staying in the shadows; their subordination and deprivation increasingly challenges the sustainability and legitimacy of the current capitalist growth path.

A major issue in the US at present is the influence China is exerting over the US economy through its success in penetrating US markets. This has engendered a trade war between the US and China, led by President Trump. As a progressive Chinese economist living in the US, what is your perspective on these developments?

On the one hand, mounting US imports and huge trade deficits reflect the increasing gain for capital and the steady loss in power of US labor as the current globalization intensifies. It is hard to see offshored manufacturing jobs returning to the US, even if heavy tariffs are imposed on Chinese exports, rather than fleeing to the other cheap-labor and less environmentally regulated countries. On the other hand, the trade war also reflects deep problems fundamental in the Chinese economy, showing how dependent and vulnerable the ruling class and capitalist development are in the global order. Within China, the trade war is portrayed either as a nationalist campaign against US imperialism or a sincere effort to enhance international cooperation, depending on the need for propaganda preparation in different stages of trade negotiations. There is certainly some truth to the development of the Chinese economy encountering US imperialism, but it is, more importantly, a wake-up call for the people on the left to realize the reality of the Chinese economy over the past forty years and not to be confused by the cheering nationalist slogans. China is still a semi-periphery economy in the capitalist world system and relies upon the US to provide it with markets, as well as to maintain the global security for energy and raw material supplies from periphery countries. The key technological sectors in China, for example, the semiconductors and machine tools, still heavily rely on the US and European countries, which was a consequence of abandoning the self-reliant industrial system upon embracing market reform and opening up policies. Therefore, I do not think the trade war shows that China is able to challenge US dominance, as many analysts have argued. Quite the contrary: it reveals how China is not able to, and the Chinese capitalist class does not dare to, challenge US dominance.

Would you say that China has become a capitalist economy, despite the fact that the economy is still being governed by the Chinese Communist Party? Are there elements of communism, as you understand it, which are still important features of the Chinese growth model?

I have no doubt that China has "changed its color" and become a capitalist economy, though there are certain socialist legacies and path dependencies that we need to recognize. For example, the state can still direct large state-owned enterprises and national banks to work on large infrastructural projects. It is a huge advantage for a large country like China, still relatively poor, to gather the national resources to create the key conditions for local development. Also, the state cares more about social stability, which is directly tied to full employment. But do these aspects necessarily indicate socialism or communism? I doubt it. It is clearly not easy for countries under neoliberal capitalism to achieve that goal, since they have to live within a straitjacket of austerity; but it was not impossible for countries like the US in the earlier stage of capitalism. This is part of the reason why, in my research, I emphasize going beyond the state and market to explore the deeper social forces lying behind them. The main contradiction in the Chinese economy, I would say, lies in the rising and unsustainable exploitation of labor and the environment that characterizes the current growth model.

What are the most influential schools of economic thinking in China today? What is the situation with respect to Marxian economics? Are there other schools of nonorthodox economic thought that have attracted interest in China, such as post-Keynesian economics?

Classical liberalism and neo-institutionalist economics have replaced Marxian economics and historical materialism in thinking about Chinese economic issues these days. Steve Cohn's important work showed in depth how the shift in economic research and education is best under-stood as a sociological phenomenon or paradigm shift embedded in China's economic and social transformation. Marxian economics is still officially emphasized, if not more so, but it is actually marginalized in publication and education, not to mention in policy-making circles. However, with sharpening social contradictions, Marxian political economy has been attracting more interest from student-led study groups and worker-activist groups. The Cambridge controversy and works by Joan Robinson, Piero Sraffa, and Luigi Pasinetti in the post-Keynesian economics tradition are also influential in the remaining heterodox economics departments in top Chinese universities. With increasing academic exchanges between China and the rest of the world, more heterodox approaches have been rapidly introduced into China.

One aspect of your research that is highly unusual is that you are equally comfortable using formal quantitative methodologies such as economet-rics as well as qualitative approaches such as field work and interviews. What do you see as the respective strengths and weaknesses of these and other research approaches? What, in your view, are the benefits, if any, of combining these and other research approaches as opposed to focusing on a more limited number of research methodologies?

I choose methodologies according to the requirements of my research questions. While I try to keep myself open to different scientific approaches, I do think methodologies come with certain assumptions that we, as researchers, should be sensitive about. Quantitative approaches assume that the real world is more measurable, while qualitative approaches assume the real world is more dynamic. The former cares more about the discovery of the facts, while the latter focuses more on understanding the "why" question behind the phenomenon. Both, if used appropriately, can give us rich data. I forget who said that interviews are data with stories, but the more interviews I have done, the more I agree with it. Over time, I have become probably more critical of econo-metrics, especially under the influence of the credibility revolution, the statistical versus economic significance as well as the (over) emphasis on randomized controlled trials. But I also believe that econometrics, espe-cially the nonclassical frequentist approach, still has some certain value on inference that should not be entirely rejected. We need to consider more well-grounded alternatives in quantitative approaches, including more epistemologically sound econometrics, while at the same time asking more careful questions about the data measurement and collecting processes. That goes to the qualitative approaches that I have been experimenting with in my more recent projects. As Mao said, "No investigation, no right to speak." Interviews in fieldwork can help get a better picture of research subjects, map social relations, and track dynamics, but we also need to be cautious about any possible tendency of overgeneralization and empiricism. Personally, I prefer a more mixed approach if needed, because both can contribute to the cumulative knowledge process, probably at different stages of research. Paul Baran used to say, "It is better to deal imperfectly with what is important than to attain virtuoso skill in the treatment of what does not matter." That's still true!

What, in your view, are some of the ways in which China's economy is more likely to evolve over the next twenty years? How do you see the role of Marxian economists in China as influencing what the trajectory will be for China?

In 2017, the Chinese Communist Party announced for the first time the goal to basically realize socialist modernization by 2035 and to develop China into a "great modern socialist country" that is "prosperous, strong, democratic, culturally advanced, harmonious, and beautiful" by 2050. In fact, this ambitious goal reflects the mounting challenges the economy has been confronting.

It is very likely that social, economic, and political contradictions will unfold or even become more intensified over the next twenty years. The semi-proletarianization process in China is unlikely to be sustainable, because the second-generation rural migrant workers find it almost impossible to go back when the economy slows down, as the countryside has been already collapsing due to the concentrated government attention on urban and coastal areas for the last thirty years. Migrant workers were largely pushed out of the declining and dispossessed rural areas in the first place. Urban areas have been already experiencing a rise in underemployment and job insecurity, such as low-paid and precarious jobs in the ride-hailing and food delivery industries, etc. At the same time, China's labor force declined for the seventh straight year in 2018, which has pushed up labor costs. With the falling profit rate that resulted from these rising labor costs, the slowdown of private capital accumulation will be more salient, making private capital increasingly flow into financial sectors. What will happen next? We have already witnessed rising housing price inflation and the expansion of shadow banking, leading to further increases in labor costs. In our research on the finance-backed platform economy, my co-author Hao Qi and I have shown that venture capital-supported platforms, indeed, use the financial sector as an alternative outlet for investment and speculation. More social welfare issues and environmental challenges may function as catalysts for social conflicts.

I think Marxian economists have the responsibility to expose the economic contradictions of the current growth model, challenge the dominant development paradigm, and reflect on the historical lessons over the past forty years. It is the time to design bold socialist policies to meet the diverse needs and interests of the popular majority in China.

If asked, what policy recommendations would you make to the Chinese government to improve China's economic future?

In the short run, stop further privatization, adhere to the active industrial policy of green development, and reverse the trend of liberalizing the financial sector. In the medium and long run, more resources should be allocated towards the large, remote rural areas to achieve more balanced development. At the same time, tackle the problem of rising inequality and shift the focus from rapid growth to more social welfare and environmental benefits for the general population.

In what direction do you see your research going in the future?

I will continue my work on applied political economy analysis. I have a book idea on more detailed class dynamics in East Asia and hope to connect to and also reflect on what I wrote in my dissertation. I would like to elaborate more on my argument there that the highly exploitative and economically unstable East Asian model is neither an outlier nor a positive model in capitalist development, but also to discuss more alternatives for the Global South. The second project I am working on is to explore the fundamental link between labor precarity and financial speculation for the platform economy in the economic conditions of the dual surplus in capital and labor after the 2008 crisis. My co-authors and I conducted a few rounds of interviews in different Chinese cities and it has been a fascinating project, even beyond my original expectations. Another project of mine is to focus on urban development as a space for capital accumulation and social contradiction. Being in an urban campus within a highly racially segregated and gentrifying city calls every day for my scholarly attention to turn to the urban topic. Though much of my previous work on urban development and inequality has focused on China, I more and more realize the advantages for me to work on a more general argument with different regional experiences. I have also been learning from my critical interdisciplinary colleagues who work on multiple urban topics. All these new research ideas make me feel so excited and simultaneously anxious that I have so much to explore!

Responses on the COVID-19 Pandemic

How would you evaluate the ways different countries or regions have responded to the COVID-19 crisis, both in terms of public health interventions and economic policies?

It is now the tenth month since the World Health Organization declared COVID-19 a pandemic. Though the entire world is fighting against the virus, countries and regions with more united responses and collective mobilization, both in terms of political/public willingness and mobilization capacity, have witnessed relative success in controlling the spread. In my view we should consider if our COVID-19 responses are truly putting people over profit and self-interest.

As much of my research focus is on China and the rest of East Asia, I mainly follow the measures and results there, while my own living experience is in the American Midwest. In terms of public health interventions, rigorous lockdowns and strict quarantines with national and regional coordination proved effective in controlling the spread as the first response. That was evident in China, though less so in Japan and South Korea. There, free treatment of COVID-patients, confirmed or suspected, along with mass testing as well as contact tracing have gained public confidence. This was stunningly different from the US approach to dealing with the pandemic. Since everyone can be infected, it is extremely important to guarantee free and equal access to public health resources. As most countries experienced shortages in medical equipment, the effectiveness in response also depends on the mobilization of national and regional resources with central and concerted guidance and action. Last but not of least importance, public health interventions require all levels of social engagement and support, from wearing masks to caring for each other. One crucial element in China's response also lies in its community-centered social infrastructure, which has yet to receive much attention from academia. China's community-centered social infrastructure, including community hospitals, neighborhood committees, etc., has proven effective in the COVID-19 pandemic, helping protect people's right to food, health, and livelihood, especially for the poor. The institutions and people working in the community are not mobilized ad hoc only for disaster relief, but rather based on a long-standing social infrastructure that coordinates locally nonexclusive service provision for social reproduction. Instead of individualizing the responsibility and costs of "flattening the curve," state-subsidized and locally supported community services in the age of COVID-19 socializes costs and maximizes effectiveness. What this exemplifies is not just emergency relief—though more of that would have been needed for many countries—but rather a more socialized response and reinvestment in preparedness to deal with imminent public crises that families are intrinsically weak in responding to.

In terms of economic policies, countries prioritizing people's health and safety over reopening of the economy have also achieved more rapid recovery. More targeted fiscal expansion, contingent upon political willingness and economic capacity, is crucial. However, I would also say that, though countries are realizing their dependence on essential workers, many are failing to protect these workers from the increasing precarity that that had begun in the neoliberal era and then intensified during the pandemic. Without addressing job and livelihood precarity, a simple cash subsidy is more likely to benefit only the rentier capitalists. The rising income and wealth gap between the rich and the poor in both Global East and West, North and South, represents the failure of current policies in saving lives and making us a better world.

Do you draw any general lessons from the COVID crisis about the most viable ways to advance an egalitarian economic project?

Actually, the first general lesson I draw concerns the increasing disillusion with the possibility of advancing a sustainable egalitarian economic project within the current capitalist world. Inequality in living conditions and access to life resources, and neglect of environmental sustainability, are the very conditions behind the COVID pandemic, and they have only worsened as the pandemic has hit different parts of the world. If we do not fundamentally address these inequalities, which is not possible without "a revolutionary reconstitution of society at large," the result will be "the common ruin of the contending classes" as Marx and Engels said in *The Communist Manifesto*, since we will most likely be on track to see more frequent epidemics, pandemics, and other challenges, not as random tragedies but as regular disasters. The COVID crisis illustrates how policy responses, in saving the existing capitalist regime, have contributed to, rather than prevented, a further widening of long-standing economic, racial, and gender divides in the world.

The second general lesson is the crucial importance of addressing care inequality on behalf of egalitarianism—an emphasis long argued by feminist political economists. What the market logic follows—either in terms of profiteering in the early stage of PPE shortages or the reallocation of labor in the private sector—fails to achieve a health care system that saves people's lives as well as a care regime that prioritizes decent livelihoods for all. The COVID crisis is a wakeup call for us to strengthen the public sector and build community infrastructure to combat these public challenges. Our care responses should take advantage of the opportunity to shape our collective imagination and efforts to create and maintain social forms and institutions through which we can survive and thrive interdependently.

Does the experience of the COVID crisis shed any light on the way you think about economics as a discipline or, more specifically, the questions you might be pursuing in your own research?

The COVID experience sheds light on the way we engage with nature and with the other parts of human society. It reveals and highlights as never before how we are locked into an interconnected vulnerability in the global capitalist world and why radical changes are needed in all fronts. I think, or I hope, that economics as a discipline would absorb this hard lesson to reflect on how such a narrow focus might reinforce this lock-in effect and contribute to our complacency or blindness. The crisis should also stimulate more reflection and radical thinking on how alternatives should be explored and pursued, to provide healthy and decent livelihoods for all.

I have started an internationally comparative project on community infrastructure building as a key element to protect and improve equal access to social reproduction. Just like we need physical infrastructure to deliver our goods, we need social infrastructure for care to deliver social services, especially the ones with a public goods element such as health. The experience also broadens my previous focus on economic crises. I wish to explore and understand more ecological-epidemiological-economic crises and the social dynamics that can help construct a better alternative.

Representative Publications and Influences

Publications:

Zhongjin Li and Hao Qi (2014). Labor Process and the Social Structure of Accumulation in China. *Review of Radical Political Economics*, 46(4), 481–488.

Ren Hao, Eli Friedman, and Zhongjin Li (Eds.) (2016). *China on strike: Narratives of workers' resistance* (English edition). Haymarket Books.

Hao Qi and Zhongjin Li (2019). Giovanni Arrighi in Beijing: Rethinking the Transformation of the Labor Supply in Rural China During the Reform Era. *Science & Society*, 83(3), 327–354.

People who have been influential: Karl Marx, Friedrich Engels, Harry Braverman, William Hinton, Minqi Li

Literature that has been influential:

Harry Braverman (1974). *Labor and Monopoly Capital: The Degradation of Work in the Twentieth Century*. Monthly Review Press.

David Gordon, Richard Edwards, and Michael Reich (1982). *Segmented Work, Divided Workers: The Historical Transformation of Labor in the United States*. Cambridge University Press.

Minqi Li (2008). *The rise of China and the demise of the capitalist world-economy*. Monthly Review Press.

William Milberg

William Milberg is Dean and Professor of Economics at the New School for Social Research and Co-Director of the Heilbroner Center for Capitalism Studies at The New School. His research focuses on the relation between globalization, income distribution and economic growth, and the history and philosophy of economics. His most recent book (with Deborah Winkler) is *Outsourcing Economics: Global Value Chains in Capitalist Development* (2013). A previous book, *The Crisis of Vision in Modern Economic Thought* (2011), was co-authored with the late Robert Heilbroner.

Can you please give us a sketch about your personal background?

I have lived in the New York City area most of my life. Born and raised in suburban New York in New Jersey and Connecticut, I attended the University of Pennsylvania as an undergraduate and Rutgers University for my graduate work. I am married with three children and live north of New York City—still in the suburbs! My parents were liberal Jews who provided their four sons with a bar mitzvah and a college education. My mother was involved in anti-poverty work in Bridgeport, Connecticut, before she became a grants writer for colleges. She was very involved in local politics and was among a small group of smart and dynamic women who ran the Democratic Party in Westport, Connecticut, for the latter part of the twentieth century. My father was a World War II veteran, a navigator in the US Army Air Corps, who became a management consultant after the war. His business went bankrupt and closed in the 1973 recession. He then got back on his feet as an independent stockbroker. He was, by all accounts, a great navigator, but was never very successful as a stockbroker. My parents both grew up in New Jersey—Newark and Jersey City, to be exact. They were political junkies. They idolized FDR, despised Republicans, and were extremely critical of right-wing governments in Israel. Their idea of a dinner party back in 1974 was to pin a name of one of the many characters from the byzantine Watergate investigation on the back of each of the attendees; they then asked that each person figure out who they were based on the conversations the others at the party had with them (Maurice Stans, anyone?).

What prompted you to study economics at the graduate level?

My interest in economics has many sources and these things are hard to untangle. I was raised to follow the politics of the day, but it was not until my time at Penn that my eyes were opened up to radical thinking. A freshman seminar on Marx and Freud (taught by a graduate student in history) led me to write a long and dense paper on Herbert Marcuse and mass psychology in advanced capitalism. I gobbled up the Marx readings and quickly figured out that at the root of all the politics was . . . economics. I was hooked. I studied Marx in a reading group and majored in economics, although this was a struggle. There were no courses offered on radical economics in my department, so I had to find courses in the history or literature departments. Mostly I was repelled by the textbook economics I was taught, and while I survived it, I did not understand it at the time (this would not happen until I studied the history of economic thought in graduate school with Professor Nina Shapiro). Two economics courses did make an impact at the time, one profoundly. The first was Herb Levine's course on comparative economic systems, where we studied mainly the Soviet economy. Levine was no lover of communism but he was broad-minded and the course at least gave a sense that smart people could think reasonably about alternatives to capitalism and get some perspective on economic systems generally. The other course (there may even have been two) was with Sidney Weintraub, the well-known post-Keynesian macroeconomist and founder of *The Journal of Post*

Keynesian Economics. Weintraub taught intermediate macroeconomics, and while I was not able at the time to grasp the details of what he was presenting, I did get a very clear sense that this line of thinking was critical, progressive-minded (he was promoting a tax-based incomes policy—TIP—at the time), and much more compelling as a way of thinking about capitalism than what I was learning in other classes. Weintraub was a total character. He lectured with the stub of a fat cigar in one hand and would often reminisce about how he would have preferred to have made a living playing professional baseball. I was a mediocre student, but I mustered up the courage to go see him in his office a few times and told him I would like to continue study along the lines of his work. He said, without hesitation, that I should go to Rutgers for my graduate work. His former student Paul Davidson was at Rutgers and was building a strong group of post-Keynesian faculty there.

I should also say that economics was an acceptable major given my socio-economic background from a middle-class Jewish family. My father insisted that I take a course in accounting. I hated it, and barely squeaked by with a C. But an economics major was acceptable, similar to the way it is desired by many kids today who want to go into business. It appears to be practical, although it mainly is not. My father didn't need to know that my real interest was in the philosophical and psychological and historical foundations of economics and in its radical line of inquiry in Marx and anti-imperialism. I was fortunate to spend a year studying in France during my junior year. France in 1982 was experiencing a distinct leftward turn in its politics (Mitterand and Marchais were doing a dance about uniting the Socialist and Communist Parties), the left almost won the elections, and Mitterand would soon be elected president. I read the French papers religiously (my Watergate-era upbringing serving me well) and found myself at numerous rallies, marching and chanting. Today, when I hear arguments about the coincidence of interests among immigrants and the poor, I think of those chants from 1982: *Français/immigrés/une seule classe ouvrière!!* French politics in that era very much broadened my sense of the spectrum of political possibilities. During the summer after the year in France I hitchhiked (yes, we still did that) with a friend to Marseille, took a boat to Algiers and then hitchhiked across the Sahara Desert, through Algeria, Niger, Burkina Faso, and on to our destination in the Ivory Coast. There we did a two-month volunteer stint constructing a medical infirmary in a small village in central Ivory Coast. All of this further radicalized me through contact with underdevelopment. When I returned to Penn for my final year, I studied the history of decolonization in Africa and anti-imperialist theory (Walter Rodney, Frantz Fanon, etc.), and dabbled with the idea of studying African politics rather than economics. One of the other great professors at Penn at the time, Ernie Wilson, talked me out of this idea on the grounds that it was a slog and unlikely to lead to a job. I was happy to reconnect with Ernie in Ann Arbor a decade later. He was, by then, a leading political scientist and I was an assistant professor of economics.

That last year in Philadelphia I also became one of the leaders of the South African divestment movement on campus, which led us to hold numerous rallies on campus and to occupy a meeting of the Board of Trustees to protest the university's endowment investment policy. (Much later in life, I lectured in South Africa for about ten successive winter intensive courses, and I realized that I spent my twenties trying to convince people not to invest in South Africa and my forties trying to convince them to invest in South Africa!) But mostly I spent my undergraduate years being socialized—sex, drugs, and in my case not rock and roll but enormous amounts of jazz. I dabbled in the trumpet (my brothers are all musicians), and I spent many weekends in college in the basement Foxhole Café on the Penn campus, stoned and rocking to the music of Sun Ra, Sonny Rollins, Rahsan Roland Kirk, McCoy Tyner, Dewey Redman, Dee Dee Bridgewater, and many, many others who played at the Foxhole at that time. Philly had an extremely lively jazz scene, and we were completely on top of it. Did this prompt me to study economics at the graduate level? I will just say that living in West Philadelphia opened my eyes to American poverty and inequality in a way that one does not see as a suburban kid who went to the Big City on weekends. The jazz scene was part of the West Philly experience, and since I knew very early on that I would not make it as a jazz trumpeter, I would have to find something else that had meaning in this unequal and clearly unjust time of Carter's stagflation and the doldrums of the late 1970s that would bring the Reagan revolution in the 1980s. I will simply add that unlike most economists today, I did not read Heilbroner's *Worldly Philosophers* as a high school or college student. West Philadelphia and the African American jazz scene were much greater influences on me in pursuing the study of radical economics.

You went to Rutgers University for your graduate studies and studied with Alfred Eichner. What attracted you the most about Eichner's work?

Alfred Eichner became my mentor at Rutgers, but in fact I never took a class with him and it was only in my last year or two at Rutgers that he had a great influence on my thinking. He died of a heart attack at age fifty-one in 1988, the year after I graduated from Rutgers, and, in some ways, it was after his death that I came to realize the power that his thinking had on me beyond simply his great skills as a mentor. This was in part due to the fact that Rutgers was a battleground then between the neoclassicals and the post-Keynesians. The post-Keynesians were allied with other heterodox types, such as the Marxists Lourdes Beneria and Michelle Naples, and the institutionalist James Street. The post-Keynesian group of faculty members had been built up by Paul Davidson and included Jan Kregel, Nina Shapiro, and Al Eichner. Paul was the ringleader. He had been at Rutgers longer than the others, had more status in the profession than the others, and had been responsible for hiring them. The post-Keynesian faculty members were outnumbered by the neoclassical faculty, who numbered more than twenty, but both sides were committed to beating out the other—to what end I am still not sure. It was a battle of ideas, which also became a battle of egos, as it so often does in academe. Eichner was not allowed to teach any of the graduate core courses. When Radhika Balakrishnan (who started in the PhD program the same year I did) and I proposed to take Nina Shapiro's history of economic thought courses before taking the required econometrics courses, we had to engage in a long dispute with the graduate director (we prevailed). I studied with Davidson and Shapiro (Kregel left soon after I arrived) and was heavily influenced by both of them and have great respect for both of them as thinkers. Nina in particular remained a close friend and eventually became a co-author. She passed away at age seventy-one this year. I was also very influenced by H. Peter Gray, a Keynesian international economist who had broad interests in trade and finance and who understood the importance of institutions and organizations in driving economic performance and outcomes. He and I also co-authored a paper on profits in transnational corporations.

Eichner had developed a theory of oligopoly markup pricing which I found very compelling because it was rooted in a theory of the firm that was more realistic than the neoclassical one, and, in particular, because it provided a strong connection between microeconomics (firm and consumer behavior) and the macroeconomy (investments, saving, and income determination). The work had been done in the 1970s, before I got to Rutgers, and it gave Eichner some renown in parts of the profession. By the time I got to Rutgers, Al was onto another project of building a massive multi-equation Keynesian macro model, operational for econometric estimation. The project was enormously ambitious and the book manuscript—which was not complete when he died—was over 800 pages. Eichner was inspired by Keynesian growth theory but also by Luigi Pasinetti's multisectoral model. My dissertation was an empirical test of Pasinetti's model in the area of international trade. It was very classical, with a labor theory of value, in which technological change (assumed exogenous) drove relative labor values (and thus price movements) and as a result, was expected to lead to changes in the pattern of international trade. My work was a massive input–output study of US-Canadian technological change and trade. Eichner was deeply supportive and gave me lots of encouragement. But over the years I have realized that his earlier work on the firm and pricing in fact influenced me more. My *Outsourcing Economics* book leans much more on Eichner's markup pricing, profits, and investment theory than it does on Pasinetti's multisectoral approach. I so wish Al had been around to help me work through the issues in the book—I likely would have finished the book years earlier.

You joined the Economics Department at the New School for Social Research in 1991, and have been there ever since. Since 2013, you have also served as dean at the New School. The New School Economics program is renowned globally for its commitment to advancing "heterodox" approaches in economics. What exactly does it mean to be heterodox in economics? What are the primary ways in which the New School program, as a whole, pursues these questions?

I have worked at the New School for Social Research since 1992, beginning as an assistant professor and working my way to full professor and then dean. It has been a remarkably fertile environment for thinking and learning and teaching and I am (almost) never bored here. I have from the beginning been a strong believer in the distinctive mission of the Economics Department at the New School for Social Research. And as dean I have come to learn that each department at the New School for Social Research has its sense of intellectual distinctiveness and it has been honestly an honor to be able to provide leadership here, first as department chair and for the past six years as dean. Since I believe in the mission of the place, I have not found fundraising, for example, to be the burden it normally is because I am raising funds for students who want to pursue research on big social and political questions in a very courageous and admirable way.

At the New School, you worked very closely with Robert Heilbroner until his passing in 2005. What were some of the ways in which you and Heilbroner connected, both professionally and personally? What were some of the most important things you learned by working with him?

I was going through some old files recently and found a typed letter from Bob Heilbroner to an economist in Europe where he described me as his "alter ego." I feel very lucky to have crossed paths with Bob. We had a very similar sensibility towards capitalism, economics, and scholarship. We talked not just economics, but politics and family. And we listened carefully to each other, whether it was in the classroom co-teaching, or in the cafeteria over coffee.

I mentioned the *Worldly Philosophers* in jest above. After college, I did eventually read it. I also kept up with Heilbroner's popular writings, in the *The New York Review of Books* or *The New Yorker*. While I was working at the New York Fed after college, I would take courses at the New School and one semester I took Bob's course in the history of economic thought. (The Fed had a generous benefit of paying tuition for courses in one's field. Using this benefit, I took classes at the New School in economic development with Andre Gunder Frank and Teresa Turner as well as Heilbroner's history of thought course. I also took Fritz Machlup's course at New York University in international finance and he would teach in full tuxedo with tails! This distracted from my learning about balance-of-payments adjustment mechanisms, but I do remember him saying that the word "inflation" is improperly used in economics. One should always specify "price inflation," since anything can get "inflated" and thus one should not presume the word referred to the price level.)

Bob's course in the history of economic thought was mesmerizing, and I recall approaching him after class one night and asking if he really believed, as he had stated in the lecture that night, that Samuelson's text was deeply ideological. I don't recall his answer in detail, but it further impressed me that this famous and refined scholar could so calmly articulate such a heretical point of view. I never imagined that I would eventually teach this course with him, much less co-author two books with him and inherit this course from him when he would leave the New School.

Soon after I arrived at the New School as an assistant professor, Bob came into my office and plunked himself down and asked if I would like to teach the history of thought course with him. In retrospect, I think that he was getting tired and needed someone with new energy and even some new ideas. Of course, I said yes right away. Quickly we became very close friends. I knew I would never be the writer or thinker he was, and I continued to do empirical and slightly technical theoretical work that he respected but that never fully caught his interest. But I also was able to learn an enormous amount from him—while also becoming his close friend. Bob had an extremely open and probing mind and his interests ran across the history of economic thought and into psychoanalysis, anthropology, history (of course), politics, art, and music. He read in enormous quantities and I cherish the books he handed down to me (when he was losing his sight at the end of his life he offered me many wonderful texts on the history of economic thought) that have margins full of his careful handwritten comments on the text—from Mill and Meek to Quesnay and Keynes, these hardback volumes are filled with his red magic marker reactions to the text.

Heilbroner was a deep thinker and a great writer, and the two traits were connected. Bob's thinking emerged in his writing. Writing was his lifeblood and when he couldn't write he felt completely stymied. When we were writing a short book that became *The Crisis of Vision in Modern Economic Thought*, the division of labor was that I would write the first draft and he would rework it into Heilbronerian form. I promised to get him a draft of one of the chapters one Friday during the summer. I didn't get it done, and he phoned me from his vacation house on the beach that afternoon and when he learned that he would not be getting the envelope in the mail from me that day, he was not happy and he reacted by saying, "You will ruin my fucking weekend if you don't get me that chapter." That was when I understood how important working and writing was for him—much more pleasurable than a relaxing weekend at the

beach. I learned a lot of economics from Bob, since we co-taught graduate courses in the history of economic thought and the methodology of
economics. He had, as you can imagine, very well-prepared notes and
he would give a brilliant set of lectures on Smith, on Marx, on Marshall.
Those are the ones I remember most. He largely disliked Ricardo because
Ricardo made such an effort to purge the work of history and culture.
And his lectures on Keynes were inspiring, but not particularly in touch
with the latest developments in post-Keynesian thought. But, in addition to learning economics from Bob, I learned that one has a responsibility as a writer to make things clear without sacrificing sophistication
or nuance. I would write a long, multipart sentence and Bob would cut
two-thirds of the sentence, move the last part to the front of the sentence,
and the result would be a much clearer and more powerful sentence
without any loss of meaning. And remember, he didn't use word process-
ing software for this. He used a pen, Wite-Out, scissors, and a stapler.
And he used all those tools without hesitation. He did the same careful
editing with his own work. The end result—those many beautiful
books—looks so effortless and simple, as if the words rolled smoothly
off his pen. They did not. Every sentence was crafted with care and with
a brutal desire to find meaning and beauty.

*Two of the foundations of heterodox economics are the works of John
Maynard Keynes and Karl Marx. Various schools of Keynesian, post-
Keynesian, Marxian, neo-Marxian, and post-Marxian thought have
emerged in the past several decades. How have you incorporated the
perspectives of Keynes and Marx into your own work? Do you characterize your work as fitting cleanly into any of the various schools of thought?*

My training is very much in the post Keynesian tradition, beginning
with Weintraub, and then with Paul Davidson, Al Eichner, and Nina
Shapiro. My thinking follows that of the monopoly capital school of
classical economics and is strongly influenced by the tradition of
post Keynesian microeconomics. The premise of my work on international trade is that power asymmetries are at the heart of production and exchange relations. The asymmetries reside in both oligopoly product markets and oligopsony factor markets. It is the
coincidental strengthening of these two asymmetries in the late
twentieth and early twenty-first centuries that has been behind the

slow growth with historic levels of inequality that characterizes many industrialized countries and which create significant obstacles for developing countries. My approach to the theory of international trade has been closer to the classical than the neoclassical approach, as I have focused on profits and profitability and its consequences for investment, innovation, and aggregate demand. This is more Ricardo than Marx, but it is distinctly anti-neoclassical, both in the sense that it avoids the static theory of the determination of the international division of labor as in the Heckscher-Ohlin view, and in the sense that the notion of upgrading in global value chains is based on an effort to defy comparative advantage (to use Ha-Joon Chang's phrase) in order to raise productivity rather than accept a given low-wage equilibrium.

I should add that, by proposing an amalgam of Marxist and post-Keynesian thought, my writing has probably not had the impact it might have had if I had been strictly in one camp. Moreover, I have focused on the firm and on gender dynamics in labor markets and these are not typical strengths of post-Keynesian (or Keynesian) thought, and so my "fit" in that group has been uncomfortable. I was very influenced by Alfred Eichner and Nina Shapiro, both of whom I am sad to say, passed away relatively early in life. Eichner, Harcourt, Kenyon and others proposed a markup pricing model that connected micro behavior to the macroeconomy through investment. But it also had implications for the macroeconomy through the monetary system, since they argued that firm profitability expanded savings and thus the money supply. While this is an endogenous theory of money, it was an uncomfortable fit for most post-Keynesian monetary theorists. I have always been more interested in the production side of the economy, and have understood financialization to be both a cause and effect of the Baran/Sweezy/Eichner power asymmetries I described above. Shapiro's influence was enormous, as her critique of neoclassicism and combination of Marx and Keynes and Schumpeter brings a sensibility to understanding capitalism that has influenced me deeply. When Radhika Balakrishnan and I were writing a recent review essay on Shapiro, we spoke with David Levine, who said that the work of Baran and Sweezy had an important influence on both him and Nina because it introduced demand into a framework focused on exploitation and monopoly power, and thus liberated them from a strict belief in the labor theory of value and allowed for a radical Keynesianism.[1] When I learned this, I realized that a similar sensibility had infused my own thinking. Nina explores this in an important paper from the late 1970s called "The Revolutionary Character of Post Keynesian Economics."

Among other things, Heilbroner was a great historian of economic thought. How important do you think it is for economists to be seriously grounded in the history of economic thought?

Economists should avoid studying the history of economic thought. If you are formulating an advance in dynamic stochastic general equilibrium (DSGE) modeling, you should not think about the Walrasian formulation of equilibrium, in which there is an artificial auctioneer who establishes prices that will clear the market and only then do transactions take place. If you are a trade theorist, you should not be burdened with the notion that Ricardo's theory of trade (one of the original formulations of the theory of comparative advantage) was aimed at understanding the consequences of trade for capital accumulation and economic growth, specifically the possibility that free trade could reduce the real wage, raise the profit rate and total profits, leading to an increase in investment and economic growth. If you are a public finance microeconomist, you should not read Smith's *Wealth of Nations* carefully, in which he lays out fourteen reasons why the state should play an active role. And you should certainly not read the *Theory of Moral Sentiments*, which lays out in elaborate detail (and in 1759!) why psychological dimensions of economic behavior are social, that is how individuals are impacted by socialization, the views of others (the impartial spectator), and thus how endogenous "preferences" are in reality. And, by all means, no one doing equilibrium modeling should read the work of Keynes or Steindl or else you would find yourself questioning why equilibrium conditions play such a central role in economic thought when they are only relevant to equilibrium, not to social life in any way. In general, I find that reading original writings of pathbreaking economic thinkers reveals many of the difficulties encountered in the creative process, the nuances in thinking that get left out in subsequent textbook renderings,

---

1   R. Balakrishnan and W. Milberg, "Firm Innovation and Capitalist Dialectics: The Economics of Nina Shapiro," *Employment and Labour Relations Review* (October 2019).

the importance of the very particular debates and problems of the moment. It is all very distracting. So I would recommend that economists absolutely should avoid studying the history of economic thought.

Your 2013 book with Debra Winkler, Outsourcing Economics: Global Value Chains in Capitalist Development, *is a major contribution to our understanding of the contemporary epoch of globalization. Can you please summarize what you consider to have been the main themes and conclusions that you advanced in this book?*

Outsourcing Economics was the result of years of research on international trade and global value chains.[2] The premise of the book is that the liberal era of the late twentieth century was one in which the international division of labor and the industrial organization that molded it took on a new form. Capital was able to capture new profit opportunities by fragmenting the production process and locating different parts of the process in different countries. Business, rather than the state (and certainly much more than labor) had the clear upper hand in making these determinations about the location of production. So, the global value chain (GVC) is the industrial organizational form that capital takes when it is freed from restriction on the movement of goods and money. The particular form is oligopsony power of lead firms as they establish supplier markets. The book explores the extent of this phenomenon on the particular way that globalization took place and its implications. One of the important implications is for countries' choice of development strategy: countries have largely accepted the new production structure and have sought ways to enter into global value chains and to industrialize from that position by "upgrading." We try to show empirically: (1) that industrial upgrading is very difficult and uncommon; (2) that industrial upgrading is not associated necessarily with rising employment or wages, what we refer to as "social upgrading"; (3) that the process is highly gendered, that it has involved (until recently) disproportionally bringing female labor into the international production networks; (4) that the process has supported the financialization of nonfinancial corporations. Underpinning these largely empirical

---

2   William Milberg and Deborah Winkler, *Outsourcing Economics; Global Value Chains in Capitalist Development* (New York: Cambridge University Press, 2013).

findings is the argument made in the early part of the book that the emergence of global value chains as the organizational structure for much of international trade requires a rethinking of the theory of international trade. The notion of upgrading is by definition at odds with the classical and neoclassical theories of trade in which social optima require following given relative efficiency advantages. The global value chain approach thus appealed to my long-standing critique of the theory of international trade. GVCs emerged in sociology first, and this was a positive and a negative. The positive is the rich treatment of the organizational nature of the firm and its internal (labor-management) and external (interfirm) relations. In a sense, this put meat on the bones of the input–output approach, on which I had spent years working. The negative was that the sociologists tended to avoid the economics of market structure, pricing, investment, and profits that economics provides. In the book, we tried to bring together the best of the sociological approach with the best of the economics.

What are the main ways in which the reality of global value chains becomes a defining constraint on economic policymaking in various country settings? For example, do global value chains mean that developed high-wage economies cannot expect to sustain a strong manufacturing sector?

This is a fascinating question because the interest in global value chains has spanned across the spectrum of political economy, from the very neoliberal World Trade Organization (WTO) and World Bank, to the progressive developmentalist scholars in sociology and development studies, to some Marxist scholars in political science and economics. Since the publication of *Outsourcing Economics*, I have been invited to review scores of articles from a radical perspective seeking to come to terms with GVCs, and I have been invited to lecture at the WTO and publish my work with the World Bank. GVCs have captured imaginations across the political spectrum. Pascal Lamy, former head of the WTO, has claimed that the GVC framework offered the possibility of imagining a new era of trade liberalization. And my co-author Cédric Durand has, with his students at University of Paris, published a series of articles on how GVCs are the new source of underdevelopment and financialization. In the middle are researchers like Gary Gereffi and Tim Sturgeon, who see GVCs as a reality requiring a new and tricky role for the state that seeks to promote industrialization. All this is to say that scholars and policy-makers of all stripes see the need to identify the constraints on government policy that result from the expansion of GVCs. My own view is that there is a schizophrenia of sorts in all this. GVCs are premised on liberal trade, the increased mobility of capital, and the power of large, lead firms. In this context, industrial development is a clear challenge and the policy constraints are, a priori, significant. This challenge has been the focus of most GVC research. My criticism of this literature is that it is largely based on case studies, which is great, but that there has been a tendency to select cases based on success. And even that success tends to be defined over a short time span. Industrialization is a long-term process that relates not only to productivity and wages, but also to skills and social protection and fiscal capacity. These are established only over time, so a snapshot of a particular industry at a particular time can be misleading. This leads to a more general point that GVC policy work tends to assume the presence of high levels of aggregate demand and thus tends to assume that if an industry can offer world-class quality, it will not have any demand constraints. There are at least three problems with this. The first is that the backdrop to economic history over the past forty-five years of GVC expansion has been the sustained presence of excess capacity. This has contributed to the possibility that GVCs, as lead firms, have taken advantage of excess and cheap labor and enhanced the ability of powerful firms to encourage competition among supplier firms—what Winkler and I call the endogenous asymmetry of market power in GVCs. The second problem is that even advanced economies are subject to cyclical declines in demand. When the Great Recession hit in 2007, the future of export-oriented development strategies was thrown into doubt, and there were hopes that China might pick up the slack in world demand, and calls from many corners for a more inward-oriented, domestically generated demand growth strategy. The third problem is that of lead firm maturity and the associated financialization of these firms, which has been associated with declines in investment out of lead firm profits and a stagnationist (to use Steindl's phrase) tendency that has again emerged in the current moment as we go into the next economic downturn.

Following up on the previous question, does the reality of global value chains mean that high wages are unsustainable in advanced economies?

Does it correspondingly mean that the institutions that developed under capitalism to support the well-being of the working class—unions, first and foremost—are fighting against overwhelming odds?

An additional appeal of the GVC concept that I failed to mention above is how power struggles, institutions, and market structures in advanced countries are of direct consequence for social and economic outcomes in developing countries—that corporate governance structures in the largest companies in the US, for example, have clear consequences for wages and working conditions in developing countries such as Bangladesh. Similarly, the ability to severely regulate labor in, say, China, has enormous consequences for production, employment, and profitability in the US economy (consider Foxconn's role in Apple's profitability and domestic employment). This implies that policies that are seemingly unrelated to trade policy should be the focus of trade policy rather than tariffs and quotas. Antitrust regulations, corporate taxes, financial regulation, labor market protections, active labor market policies: those interested in a just globalization would be well advised to consider these policy issues before worrying about trade protection.

I would add that the current debates over Trump's trade policy have raised some of the issues related to the constraints that global value chains pose for labor. Leftist policy advocates have largely supported Trump's protectionism. But there are a few prolabor arguments against tariffs. First is the fact that they raise prices and thus lower real wages. Second is that retaliation will lead to a vicious downward spiral of reduced world trade and economic activity and that employment will be negatively affected. The third argument is the GVC one, in which tariffs affect the price of intermediate products and thus disrupt efficient supply chain networks. But this third argument is really about profits, and thus the labor impact is conditional on the relation of profits to investment, what I have called "the dynamic gains from trade" à la Ricardo. The problem with this third argument, as I have elaborated in a number of papers, is that financialization, and in particular share buybacks and dividends payments, have been a leakage from the channel of dynamic gains. In this spirit, I would argue that financial regulation is more important than trade protection in a proworker global economy.

The East Asian economies have achieved rapid and sustained rates of economic growth through developing export-led economies. China is, of course, now the most spectacular success story in terms of growth, but the earlier experiences of South Korea, Taiwan, Singapore, and earlier still, Japan, are also significant. How would you characterize this export-led growth model within the analytic framework you developed in Outsourcing Economics? *More generally, what would you see as both the favorable and unfavorable features of this growth model?*

Export-led growth served some East Asian countries very well, but it must be acknowledged that this was not simply due to the opening up of export markets but to an entire developmental strategy which has been carefully studied and described by Amsden, Wade, Chang, and others. It certainly constitutes an early form of value chain development strategy, but I have argued that the prominence of global value chains has made the traditional export-oriented industrialization strategy in need of revision. For one, the production and sale of intermediates requires close collaboration with buyers of intermediates. This goes beyond the sale of microwave ovens to Kmart (an important step in Korea's industrial strategy). But this dynamic raises the problem of the oligopsony nature of lead firm–supplier firm relations. This must be combated in any development plan in the era of GVCs.

The neofascist populist right has gained tremendous momentum throughout the world in the past decade. One of the major drivers of this development seems to be resentment against the forces of neoliberal globalization. Can you envision a globalization project that is anti-neoliberal, in the specific sense of also supporting egalitarian institutions such as a strong social welfare state, full-employment policies, and effective labor unions?

Indeed, the "golden age of capitalism" after World War II and up until the early 1970s was such a period, in which trade was somewhat liberalized, capital flows regulated, and in which even in the US the social protections that emerged in the New Deal era were solidified. There were serious problems in this era as well, as, for example, Katznelson shows in his book about the New Deal and its aftermath regarding racial inequality and access.[3] But the era showed that global capitalism could be regulated, social protections expanded, and economic growth rates could be robust. In fact, the comparison along these lines for the pre- and post-1975 eras (as Andrew Glyn did so rigorously) would indicate that the more regulated capitalism is better for economic growth. Of course, the proverbial genie cannot be put back in the bottle, and so any notions of returning to that era while eliminating its problems are, I think, misplaced. Part of the reason for this is the change in the structure of production, both in terms of value chains and in terms of inequalities in compensation and in the outsized role of finance. So, a new capitalist era of regulation and social protection may be possible, but would look different from the golden age structure of accumulation. It would require considerably more regulation of corporate behavior and freedom for labor union organizing and bargaining, and a strong emphasis on corporate profits taxes that cannot be avoided through the use of tax havens.

What do you see as the most important projects that heterodox economists should be pursuing over the coming decade?

I am involved in a project with my colleague Teresa Ghilarducci, funded by the Hewlett Foundation, on the barriers to the success of heterodox economics in the US. We have written a long report that I hope will be published soon. We argue for an expansion of the intellectual project of explaining capitalism through deeper and more serious engagement with other disciplines. Heterodox economics today is a diverse set of theories built on insights from Marx, Keynes, and Kalecki to contemporary thought in feminism, post-Keynesianism, stratification, institutionalism, and neo-Marxism. Expanding this ongoing intellectual project would demand deeper connection to other social sciences, history, and law, as well as interdisciplinary fields like gender studies, Black studies, environmental studies, social innovation, and urban studies. An important motivation for elevating heterodox economics is to gain insights from these fields and build a narrative of capitalist dynamics that is useful across disciplines and to a more diverse population. The focus might be on concepts of power, inequalities, institutions (business

3   Ira Katznelson, *Fear Itself: The New Deal and the Origins of Our Time*, New York: Norton, 2013.

enterprise, the family, and the state) and generally on the creation and distribution of value. Heterodox economics can also be much bolder in framing and supporting policies. For instance, Kaleckian structuralist macroeconomics can underpin efforts to resist wage suppression. Feminist economics has shaped policies to pay for care work and redefine GDP measurement. Institutionalists have long identified policies to correct inequalities by changing governance structures at the firm level and antitrust activity of the state to balance power. Even the Polanyi tradition of the "double movement" can support notions of the need to legitimate markets with a strong role for the state.

Second, we argue that heterodox economists should continue to work on creating, with the support of philanthropy and publishers, a coherent set of materials for all teaching levels on the heterodox approach to understanding capitalism, including accessible syllabi, teaching materials, and curated interactive discussions among scholars about new approaches and needs. A new, high-quality "textbook" (perhaps free) for case study analysis and problem-solving is needed. An element of this effort could focus on policy analysis, to build practical skills for putting heterodox ideas into practice.

Third, we need to diversify the entire economics profession, orthodox and heterodox. The American Economic Association sponsors the National Education Association (NEA) and the Committee on the Status of Women in the Economics Profession (CSWEP), but economics has not made significant progress in diversifying faculty. Curriculum and training sessions are included in affirmative action steps needed at all levels of instruction. A proposal from UMass Amherst for a summer institute providing heterodox economics training to people from underrepresented groups in the profession may serve as a model.

And, fourth, we need to engage more with the mainstream of the profession. Heterodox economists have not engaged sufficiently with the mainstream, even though there are many active heterodox organizations. There needs to be more self-conscious coordination, communication, and presence among these organizations, through workshops, shared funding, coordinated panels at meetings, listing of employment opportunities, and sharing of curriculum and pedagogy. This engagement will require new resources. One issue for consideration is dropping the term "heterodox." A common theme emerged in our interviews: many economists do not like to self-marginalize by calling themselves "heterodox" economists.

What are some of the projects that you yourself are planning to work on in the coming years?

I have two book projects planned and someday when I am not dean I will happily get back to them. The first is a popular book on global value chains. It will be the story of global capitalism told through a series of case studies about the technology, production, corporate strategy, marketing and sales of . . . balls—the baseball, the tennis ball, the golf ball, the soccer ball, and the basketball. The inspiration is Marx's notion of commodity fetishism and the idea is to show the social "life" of things through a popular commodity related to sports. When you cut the baseball down the middle, you see its component parts and you cannot help but explore the trade secrets involved in the leather treatment that are carefully guarded by American corporations so that a Chinese firm does not get it, the labor practices associated with sewing balls together (it's never been mechanized and yet Haitian production was too low in quality so it was moved to Costa Rica), and the relation between the wages and work conditions of ball sewers and those at the top end of the value chain, the players and owners. When you cut the golf ball in half you discover the rubber technology first developed by two MIT graduates whose work led them first to garner the major contract with the US Army in World War I for the production of gas masks. One of these guys was a golfer and hypothesized that the reason his ball was always veering left or right was that the core was not perfectly spherical. He (literally in this case) cut the ball open and found out he was right. He then went to work on creating a perfectly spherical core. This project became the Titleist corporation, and the firm still has an R&D factory in Massachusetts. The working title is "Keep Your Eye on the Ball: Globalization and Professional Sports."

The second project is a historical treatment of Jewish economists. The idea for it came from a contentious book by John Murray Cuddihy on Marx, Freud, and Lévi-Strauss that takes their Jewishness—and in particular their sense of "other-ness" and even "dirty-ness"—as a driving force in their thinking.[4] My book will begin with Ricardo and Marx, and then will have a chapter on the exile economists who came to the New School in the 1930s, focused on Colm, Lederer, Lowe, and a few

---

4   J.M. Cuddihy, *The Ordeal of Civility: Freud, Marx, Levi-Strauss and the Jewish Struggle with Modernity*, New York: Delta, 1981.

others (perhaps ending with Heilbroner). Then there will be a chapter on general equilibrium analysis, using the work of Arrow, Samuelson, Solow, Debreu, and others to argue that general equilibrium (GE) theory played a psychological role for these economists as the ideal of ethnic assimilation. Finally, there will be a chapter on Jewish economists today—Paul Krugman, Joe Stiglitz, Larry Summers, Jeff Sachs, and Alan Blinder—who are fully assimilated, highly successful members of the academy who have each largely abandoned the project of economic theorizing and taken on a public role as journalist or policy advocate. The trick will be to avoid the essentialism of saying that their "Jewishness" accounts entirely for their economics, but at the same time to make the case that economic thought at its most creative is deeply embedded in the culture and politics of the moment, not in any universal claims on humanity.

A friend once told me that "research is me-search," and I suppose I am no exception in this regard.

Responses on the COVID-19 Pandemic

Do you draw any general lessons from the COVID crisis about the most viable ways to advance an egalitarian economic project?

Some very important political economy lessons for understanding the US economy have been thrust to the forefront in the past year as a result of the pandemic. These have to do with some of the most basic institutional formations of advanced capitalist economies: the role of the state in social and intellectual property protection, the democratic governance of the corporation, and the legacy of racism and its place in driving a severely unequal distribution of wealth. None of these features are new, and need little elaboration. But the pandemic has revealed with a newfound rawness the challenges that they pose for American capitalism. For example, with respect to the state, it has become very evident in the pandemic that the decoupling of social protection, especially health insurance and retirement security, from employment, can be doubly disastrous for well-being. Most European welfare systems have from their origins, disconnected an individual's attainment of these protections from the individual's employment status, with the result that the

negative impact of the pandemic has been much reduced. The disproportionate incidence of the virus on African Americans has been a stark
reminder of the vulnerability of certain occupations to the risk of disease
and has made clear the devastating insecurity that comes with the
poverty of private wealth suffered by Black Americans. The US model of
corporate governance has also come into question as the spike in unemployment resulting from the pandemic was exacerbated by the longer-
term trend of disempowerment of US workers through the decline of
unions and the increased strength of corporate governance favoring
short-term shareholder value. And even the development and distribution of the vaccine has shown the cruelty that comes with the rigid
guarding of intellectual property in the hands of a few corporations. The
research that led to the rapid development of the vaccine was largely
underwritten by public funds. The private capture of profits from the
innovation limits the social return, and the rigidity of the intellectual
property regime means that a good that would have major benefits globally will be available only slowly and in a limited way beyond the rich
countries.

As I said, these challenges are widely debated in the contemporary
political moment, and I do not claim any expertise in any of it. I am a
consumer of the superb analysis of many radical and some nonradical
economists who write on these issues. But I take it as the responsibility
of all academic economists—even the nonexperts—to take these issues
on in their teaching. If we cannot provide the millions of economics
students in undergraduate economics classes a chance to grapple with
these fundamental issues and teach them ways to analyze them, we will
not have done our job.

*Does the experience of the COVID crisis shed any light on the way you
think about economics as a discipline or, more specifically, the questions
you might be pursuing in your own research?*

I will give a narrow and a broad answer to this question. The narrow
issue concerns the resilience of global value chains, the subject of my
current research with Stephen Gelb. Shortages in many countries of
medical consumables such as personal protective equipment and phar-
maceuticals during the COVID-19 pandemic have led to many calls for
"re-shoring" and "shorter" value chains in order to increase supply

resilience and national security through self-sufficiency. I would argue that the current crisis does not mean the end of the GVC era. Although some GVCs will change in structure and geography, re-shoring will be limited. The persistence of significant international gaps in wages and of the deep relations between lead and supplier firms will likely lead to a recovery of GVC trade as the world economy recovers post-pandemic. The costs of switching out of well-developed supplier and distribution networks and full-package outsourcing arrangements are too high for many lead firms. Moreover, the global macroeconomic environment and specifically the possibility of a slow post-COVID recovery will increase competitive pressures facing lead firms, affecting their willingness and ability to incur substantial restructuring costs. Gelb and I argue that this is not necessarily a bad outcome for "resilience," especially because new crises—financial, climate, technological—may create new categories of "essential" goods, and as domestic regional supply disruptions may be as consequential as international chain breakdowns.

The broader answer concerns the continuing need to expand the way economics is taught and used in policy formulation. As much as ever in the history of capitalism, ideas from heterodox economics are relevant and crucial to both understanding and improving economic outcomes. The role of academic programs that train undergraduate and graduate students to think clearly about power, history, inequality, and economic democracy—in addition to supply and demand—could not be more important than they are today in the wake of the pandemic.

Representative Publications and Influences

Publications:

William Milberg and Deborah Winkler (2013). *Outsourcing Economics: Global Value Chains in Capitalist Development*. Cambridge University Press.

Robert Heilbroner and William Milberg (1996). *The Crisis of Vision in Modern Economic Thought*. Cambridge University Press.

William Milberg and Peter Spiegler (2013). *Methodenstreit* 2013? Historical Perspective on the Contemporary Debate Over How to Reform Economics. *Forum for Social Economics*, 42(4), 311–345.

People who have been influential: Alfred Eichner, Nina Shapiro, H. Peter Gray, Robert Heilbroner

Literature that has been influential:

Alfred Eichner (1976). *The megacorp and oligopoly: Micro foundations of macro dynamics*. Cambridge University Press.

Alfred Eichner (1991). *The macrodynamics of advanced market economies* (1991 ed). M.E. Sharpe.

Alfred Eichner (2008). *The megacorp and oligopoly: Micro foundations of macro dynamics*. Cambridge University Press.

Léonce Ndikumana

Léonce Ndikumana is Distinguished University Professor and Professor of Economics at the University of Massachusetts Amherst. He is also Director of the African Development Policy Program at the Political Economy Research Institute. His research focuses primarily on African economic development, macroeconomic policy, global tax issues, and capital flows. Ndikumana has served as Director of Operational Policies and Director of Research at the African Development Bank, and Chief of Macroeconomic Analysis at the United Nations Economic Commission for Africa (UNECA). His most recent work examines the extent, causes, and effects of capital flight from African countries. He is the author or co-author of more than sixty articles and reports and several books, including *Africa's Odious Debts: How Foreign Loans and Capital Flight Bled a Continent* (co-authored with James K. Boyce 2011), based on an award-winning article in the *Journal of Development Studies* (co-authored with James K. Boyce), and *Capital Flight from Africa: Causes, Effects and Policy Issues* (co-edited with S.I. Ajayi 2015).

Your background, coming from a poor rural community in Burundi, is hardly typical among US academics, in economics or otherwise. Can you please give us a sense of how you got from rural Burundi to being a US economics professor?

I was born and grew up on a farm in the south of Burundi. My parents were farmers and raised cattle—cows, goats, and sheep. In my childhood, I actively participated in the work on the farm, growing a variety of crops and herding cattle. We were fortunate to have a fertile land that provided for most of our food needs, while also generating the cash income needed to buy products that were not grown on the farm as well as school supplies. Moreover, my father was quite entrepreneurial, always looking for ways to generate additional cash income from trading crops and nonfarm products.

I attended elementary and high school in Catholic schools. While the majority of children of my age were able to attend elementary school, few were fortunate to continue to high school. This was not because they were not intellectually capable, but simply because there were not enough seats in the few boarding high schools to accommodate more candidates. I was indeed one of the few lucky ones to attend high school.

I was also fortunate to attend a high school that was well funded by the government and a congregation of Catholic Brothers from Quebec, Canada—Les Frères de l'Instruction Chrétienne. The excellent all-around education I received at the Ecole Normale de Rutovu (a teacher training high school) provided me with the adequate background to be admitted and succeed in college. Admission at the Ecole Normale de Rutovu was quite competitive. The school typically recruited the top kids in Catholic elementary schools. I graduated from high school in 1980 and was recruited to teach in junior high school at the same school, which I did for two years. Due to the shortage of teachers with university degrees, it was typical at that time for high schools to recruit top graduates to teach in junior high school.

I attended the University of Burundi and majored in economics, one of the coveted majors along with medicine, law, and engineering. I graduated in 1986, and was hired as a junior lecturer (*professeur assistant*) in the Economics Department in 1987. In 1989, I was appointed as chief of finance of the university and promoted to director of administration and finance shortly thereafter, a function I occupied until I left for graduate school in August 1990.

Under the sponsorship of the USAID through the African Graduate Fellows program (AFGRAD), I was admitted in the PhD program at Washington University in St. Louis, Missouri. I spent the fall 1990 semester at Southern Illinois University in Carbondale (SIUC) in the English as a Second Language program, learning and perfecting my

English in preparation for graduate school. I started at Washington in January 1991.

My six years in St. Louis remain among my best years in the US; I learned a lot, but I also enjoyed my social life, especially when my family (my wife Gaudence and our two older kids, Chris and Alice—Olivier was born in the US in 1998) joined me in August 1993. I still have fond memories of my time in St. Louis, including good times with my class-mates as well as the long-lasting bonds my family and I developed with my host family—the Thompson family (Ken and Alice and their daugh-ters—my sisters—Laura and Julie).

When I applied for graduate school, my interest was to specialize in the area of public economics because I was intrigued by the functioning of the public sector in developing countries. However, I eventually developed interest in macroeconomics, thanks primarily to Professor Steve Fazzari, and in economic development with inspiration from Professor Douglass North (recipient of the 1993 Nobel Memorial Prize in Economic Sciences). Professor Fazzari would eventually become my dissertation advisor as well as my volley ball teammate. The latter rela-tionship was as important as the former! (Our team won the intramural competition one year, beating the men's volley ball club!)

Upon graduation, I was hired as assistant professor at the University of Massachusetts Amherst in September 1996. I am currently serving as a distinguished university professor and department chair since the fall of 2017.

How, if at all, was your life affected by the genocide in Rwanda and Burundi in the late 1980s and early 1990s?

Burundi and Rwanda have experienced episodes of ethnic conflict, some minor, others major. The first major ethnic conflict I witnessed in Burundi occurred in 1972 while I was in sixth grade. My father along with many relatives, including all my maternal uncles, died that year. In August 1988, another ethnic conflict erupted in the north of the coun-try. I then joined a group of twenty-six other Hutu intellectuals in sign-ing an open letter to the president, urging him to take the appropriate measures to prevent a full-blown crisis. The letter brought to the atten-tion of the president that the country was facing a grave risk of descend-ing into a crisis similar to that of 1972, and urged him and his government to undertake the appropriate measures to prevent violence in the country side, stop arbitrary arrests and killings of Hutu intellectuals by the security services, and to engage in an open dialogue about institutionalized ethnic divisions and exclusion in order to begin a process of political opening in the country. This exercise in democratic expression earned me and some of my colleagues five months in the maximum-security prison of Mpimba. Those were painful months not only for me, especially since I was convinced that we did not break any law but rather were contributing to a valuable cause in peace and institution building, but most importantly for my family, who were very concerned about my fate in light of the dark history of execution or "disappearance" of political prisoners that is associated with the prison of Mpimba. I was freed with my colleagues in February 1989 following pressure from the international community and the regional leaders on the president of Burundi. I will eternally be grateful to my wife for her incredible courage, wisdom, and perseverance during those hard days, as well as my extended family, friends, and the international community for their support. Following my release from prison, I was reinstated in my position at the University of Burundi and appointed shortly thereafter as chief of finance in the administration, and was later promoted to the position of director of administration and finance.

What have been the major intellectual influences on your life and thinking?

It is difficult for me to identify a single major intellectual influence on my life and thinking. I have been strongly influenced by people around me from my early childhood, to my high school, college, graduate school, and until today. My parents have made the most important mark on my life and my thinking. They instilled in me the sense of hard work and determination, but also a deep sense of family and community. My family is my motivation and it is my ultimate objective. I have also been influenced by some of my teachers in high school, college, and graduate school. My high school teachers pushed me to always be, not the best, but the best of myself—seeking to reach higher and higher all the time. In graduate school, Professor Douglass North cemented in me the love for economic development and the appreciation for the role of institutions in understanding the behavior of agents and the performance of national economies. Professor Steve Fazzari gave me an appreciation for non-market-clearing approaches to macroeconomics and the importance of careful policy analysis. These two have been critical in my development as a researcher and an educator and I am eternally grateful for their guidance. Being part of the UMass Economics Department has helped me to consolidate my appreciation for pluralistic approaches to economic analysis, and the value of intellectual openness in understanding real economic and social issues. My experience in the "policy world" at the African Development Bank and the United Nations provided me with an opportunity to appreciate the complexity of economic policymaking and the limitation of economic theory in explaining real economic outcomes. This further strengthened my conviction that economic research is best approached with an open mind and with humility, given the complexity and changing nature of the economic and social phenomena that, as economists, we seek to explore in our careers. If I had to do it again, I probably would follow the same trajectory in my education and professional career.

How did you end up teaching at UMass Amherst? How do you like being part of a program that has the reputation as a leading leftist economics program in the world?

UMass Amherst was highly appealing for me coming out of graduate school. With my work grounded in the Keynesian tradition, precisely New Keynesian macroeconomics, I found UMass Economics both welcoming and enriching. I considered the tradition of embracing pluralistic approaches to economics to be especially conducive to professional growth for a young scholar willing to understand how real economies work. My view then and still now is that no single theoretical perspective is adequately suited to explaining the complex phenomena that we as economists seek to understand, such as economic development, unemployment, poverty, inequality, growth and stagnation, and the role of government policy in addressing these economic phenomena.

Your main specializations are macroeconomics and African economic development. Can you describe your approaches in these areas relative to alternative schools of thought in academic economics?

My approach to economics is primarily empirical and institutional, guided by the interest of discovering the complex drivers of the behavior of agents and the factors behind national level phenomena both at the domestic and global level. My work does not belong to a particular "school of thought." Instead, I tend to draw from all approaches of economic analysis to anchor my ideas, guide my empirical exploration, and shape the interpretation of my findings. What is clear in my work is the belief that institutions matter, that government policy plays a critical role for real economic outcomes, and that markets need a strong helping hand to produce desirable outcomes from a societal perspective. Partly due to my upbringing and partly due to my training and research, I take the issues of economic and political equity and inclusion very seriously. An economy besieged by inequality and exclusion will always underachieve; and a nation plagued by inequality and exclusion has no chance of political and social stability. Indeed, equity and inclusion are the pillars of economic prosperity and peace.

In the past, many African leaders, including Kwame Nkrumah and Sékou Touré, firmly believed that Africa's level of development was a condition created by outside intervention and domination. Is this view still prevalent among today's African leaders? What is your own view on this perspective?

The early African leaders evolved in a global environment characterized by domination and subordination, with the West controlling both the economies and the political systems in Africa. It was true then that the continent was used as a source of human and material resources that fueled the economies of the colonizing powers. It was therefore natural to conclude that African development problems were to a large extent the outcome of domination and subordination by the West.

African leaders of today are also aware of the unequal distribution of power in the world in favor of advanced economies. They live in a world where global governance is dominated by countries with large economies and elite clubs of rich countries (for example, the G7 and the G20), where developing countries have at the most an "observer seat," while at the same time being held to the rules deliberated and decided upon by those clubs. So African domination and marginalization has not changed; it has only taken various forms over time.

My own view is that economic prosperity will continue to be the basis for global decision-making. It is all about economics. And Africa's chance to secure its fair share in global governance is predicated on its success in launching and sustaining strong and inclusive development.

Many East Asian economies have experienced strong growth over twenty to thirty years or more. This has basically not happened to date in sub-Saharan Africa. In your view, what have been the major factors holding back strong growth in Africa? How does foreign aid fit into the picture? A help or a burden?

Compared to East Asian economies, African economies have especially lacked on three major fronts: innovation-led productivity increases; economic transformation; and growth-friendly institutions. This has been a result of many factors, some of which cut across the continent, while others are country-specific. Some of the factors are domestic; others are external and global. At independence, African countries inherited extractive and extrovert economies that had been structured to serve the interests of the colonial powers and the global economy. The government-led development model launched by the new nations eventually became unsustainable due to the heavy burden on the government budget and weak technical capacity. The funding of government development programs by external borrowing exposed the young economies to debt distress that eventually put them at the mercy of the international financial institutions in the 1980s, which imposed structural adjustment programs as a condition for further funding. These primary sector–dominated economies became vulnerable to deterioration in the terms of trade that further compromised African economies' external position.

In addition, the continent has experienced a disproportionate share of conflicts and political instability that have compounded the negative effects of the macroeconomic and structural woes that have compromised their development prospects.

Has foreign aid helped or hindered development in Africa? While there is no consensus in the empirical literature on the impact of aid on development in general and in the case of African countries in particular, the emerging evidence from sectoral and micro-level analysis indicates that targeted aid does produce the intended positive outcomes.

Thus, for example, positive results have been documented in the case of aid to the health sector that targets particular goals such as malaria prevention through provision of treated mosquito nets, prevention of diarrhea through investment in clean water and sanitation, as well as aid to the education sector, such as improvement in school attendance and completion through provision of school lunch programs. What is emerging is that aid does work, but it needs to be effectively managed and tightly monitored with an efficient collaboration between donors and recipient countries. What is also clear is that the volume of aid currently distributed to African countries is way below the amounts required to fill the large and widening financing gaps faced by these countries. If aid is to make a decisive impact in helping to propel African economies onto a sustainable development path, it is indispensable to increase both its volume and its effectiveness. That will help increase the benefits from aid while also positioning African countries to eventually graduate from aid. Good aid must eventually do itself out of a job.

How successful have sub-Saharan African economies been in reducing poverty over the past thirty years? What have been the real achievements, as well as the major failures, to date?

The story of poverty reduction in Africa is a mixed bag. On the one hand, many countries have recorded substantial declines in various measures of poverty, whether measured in terms of lack of resources to meet basic needs (lack of decent income) or to hedge against shocks (lack of assets), or in terms of lack of capabilities (skills, knowledge, technology, social capital, etc.), or in terms of various measures of well-being (health outcomes, access to services, nutrition, etc.). Certainly today, more African babies survive than thirty years ago, and life expectancy is much longer; universal elementary education is nearly achieved in the majority of African countries; health services are more accessible than three decades ago. On the other hand, these gains in social development pale in comparison with those in other regions, and relative to the continent's resource capacity. In short, African countries have underperformed relative to their peers in other regions and relative to their own capacity. The reasons for the poor performance are linked to the same causes of slow growth I described above. But we must add an important factor, which is inequality. Even when African countries have been able to achieve meaningful levels of growth, this has not translated into proportional declines in poverty, partly due to high levels of inequality in the distribution of gains from growth. In many cases, growth has been led by capital-intensive sectors such as oil and minerals that create few jobs and produce inadequate positive spillover effects on other sectors. Moreover, African governments have not been successful in designing and implementing effective redistributive mechanisms to support segments of the populations that are "left behind"; the growth tide has not lifted all the boats. The failure to reduce poverty fast enough in Africa is both a story of failure to sustain high growth and failure to redistribute the gains from growth.

Your research shows that capital flight is a severe problem for most sub-Saharan African countries. Can you describe your main research findings and what you see as their major implications? What, in your view, would constitute a realistic program for dramatically reducing capital flight out of the region?

Capital flight refers to the outflow of capital that is not recorded in the country's official statistics as consolidated in the balance of payments. It consists of funds that have been recorded as entering the country but whose use cannot be traced in the official statistics. These involve both government funds that are embezzled by the political elite as well as private wealth that is transferred illegally abroad to evade taxation or scrutiny on the legitimacy of its origin.

Our research shows that capital flight is a serious drain on financial resources from Africa, a capital-starved continent. Our recent estimates show that between 1970 and 2015, a sample of thirty countries (those with adequate data) lost the staggering amount of $1.4 trillion through capital flight. We also find that the phenomenon has gotten worse since the turn of the century. This is puzzling because this period witnessed growth acceleration and an improved policy environment in the continent, which should encourage domestic investment and discourage capital flight. These figures instead confirm our long-standing finding that capital flight from Africa is not driven or motivated by the search for higher returns to capital abroad. Instead, this suggests that wealth holders are seeking protection from legal scrutiny thanks to the anonymity that offshore financial centers provide.

Capital flight is induced and facilitated by economic and institutional factors pertaining to the local conditions in Africa as well as the helping hand of institutions and agents in foreign markets where the flight wealth is concealed. It follows that the fight to curtail capital flight from Africa must be waged on two fronts. On the domestic front, efforts must be centered around increasing transparency and accountability in the management of national resources including borrowed funds, as well as establishing effective regulatory mechanisms for recording, tracking, and monitoring cross-border financial and trade flows. Indeed, a substantial part of flight capital occurs through misinvoicing and smuggling of trade across borders. On the global front, Africa's development and trading partners must commit to genuinely enforcing the rules of transparency and accountability in banking to break the veil of anonymity on the ownership of private wealth in banking centers. They also must commit to systematic and accurate reporting of imports and exports from and to Africa, as well as fighting base erosion by their multinational enterprises, especially those operating in the natural resource sector in Africa. An important element of the strategy is automatic and systematic country-by-country reporting of profits and tax payments by multinational corporations operating in Africa. For these global strategies to have a chance of success, African countries must be given a seat at the table in all global bodies involved with policies related to combatting illicit financial flows and corporate tax evasion—not as observers, but as legitimate and equal voting members. In a sense, the strategy requires that global governance becomes more inclusive and participatory to raise Africa's voice and representation in global decision-making.

Your research has also focused on the issue of foreign loans and their direct link to capital flight, which ends up producing "odious debts." What makes these debts "odious"?

Our empirical research demonstrates a tight relationship between funds that enter African countries as public loans and flows that leak out of the continent as capital flight. We conclude that rather than financing development, a substantial part of borrowed funds instead finances private capital accumulation for the African political and economic elite. That is why we talk of "odious debts." Public debt is odious when three conditions are present: (1) the loan was contracted without the consent of the people—for example, by an autocratic oppressive regime; (2) the loan was not used to the benefit of the population; that is, it did not actually finance development activities; (3) the lenders were aware or should have been aware of the first two facts. In this case, the loans are illegitimate and the population can challenge the obligation to repay them. In other words, the population can invoke its right to repudiate the debt by putting the burden of proof on the lenders to demonstrate that the borrowed funds were used for their intended legitimate purposes. If they cannot prove that, then the population of the debtor country is under no obligation to incur the costs of repaying the loans.

You have worked for the African Development Bank in the capacity of director of operational policies and director of research. What in your view are the major contributions that can be made by the African Development Bank and other development banks to promoting equitable growth, expanding job opportunities, and reducing poverty in Africa? How does microfinance fit alongside development banking?

My experience at the African Development Bank helped me appreciate the critical role that public development financing institutions play in supporting economic development in Africa and in other regions. The mission of regional development banks is on three fronts: financing for development; policy advice; technical assistance. This is accomplished through mobilization and allocation of development finance as well as through knowledge generation and policy dialogue. Because of limited resources, regional banks are most effective when they strategically focus their investments based on their capacity as well as the specific needs of the region. While I was at the African Development Bank, its focus was primarily on financing for infrastructure and private sector development, two pillars of economic development in Africa.

In general, development banks are critical in filling the gaps in financing in areas that are not served by commercial banks. These are often strategic areas, including agriculture, as they are regarded as "risky" by commercial banks. In this context another type of financing institution that serves a critical niche in African economies is microfinance. These institutions cater to the needs of individual operators, micro, small, and medium enterprises that are deemed not creditworthy by commercial banks. Yet it has been demonstrated that microfinance institutions can be effective at alleviating poverty and creating employment through the financing of these forgotten segments of the economy. In my view, the development of microfinance institutions is key to achieving the goal of access to finance for all and for stimulating a private sector–led development in Africa.

In recent years, the African Development Bank has been trying to promote "green growth" for Africa. How do you envision a green growth path for Africa? Is it realistic, or even fair, to ask African countries to contribute to a global climate stabilization project when, clearly, Africa has not been a significant contributor to climate change?

The African Development Bank has been at the forefront of the movement for environment preservation, the fight against climate change and supporting the transition to clean energy and promoting "green growth." Green growth in Africa is not only desirable but it is in fact the only way forward in the medium and long term. It is well known that while Africa contributes very little to global climate change and pollution, it suffers a disproportionate burden from environmental degradation that originates from industrialized economies. But African countries also suffer the consequences of production and consumption systems that do not incorporate climate protection and environment restoration. The African Development Bank has been championing the mainstreaming of environmental protection in all its operations. It can also play a major role in promoting knowledge on climate change adaptation and green growth through its research and policy dialogue.

Is it realistic and fair to expect African economies to contribute to the global project of climate stabilization when they have little responsibility for global environmental degradation and have limited resources to finance climate preservation and climate change adaptation? The answer is yes! First of all, African economies rely heavily on environmental resources that need to be protected and utilized judiciously—notably land, water, and forests. It is therefore important that the continent's development strategy be centered on optimizing the use of resources while minimizing negative impacts on the environment. Second, it is important to understand that these objectives cannot be achieved overnight. What is needed is for Africa to position itself on a path that enables a steady transition from conventional production systems to more environmentally efficient systems, especially in the areas of power generation. The program of climate stabilization is naturally expensive. African economies will need strong and reliable support from the global community to achieve this goal, through equitable allocation of global funds for climate preservation and climate change adaptation.

How do you see your own research projects developing over the next several years?

Over the next several years, I plan to continue research that contributes to our understanding of the challenges and potential faced by African countries in achieving their development goals in the context of a challenging global environment. My work will involve further detailed institutional analysis of capital flight, analysis of the impact of foreign aid, development of macroeconomic policies for promoting inclusive and sustainable growth, and exploration of the strategies for Africa's successful integration into the global economy.

Responses on the COVID-19 Pandemic

How would you evaluate the ways different countries or regions have responded to the COVID-19 crisis, both in terms of public health interventions and economic policies?

The world has experienced an unprecedented pandemic with a heavy toll both in terms of loss of human lives and destruction of livelihoods across the world. By and large most countries, or I should say, most governments have undertaken a range of measures to minimize the impact of the pandemic on their populations and their economies. But what is most distinctive has been the disparity in the capacity to respond to the crisis. In particular, developing countries have faced major challenges in mobilizing the financial resources and human technical capabilities to respond to the crisis, due to chronic financing gaps and prolonged underfunding of the health sector. The lack of social safety nets in these countries makes it impossible to implement preventive measures such as lockdowns or remote working. With governments in the Global South facing chronic financing shortages, they are not equipped to fund the necessary interventions to support workers who lose their jobs and firms that face collapse in demand.

Thus far, the incidence of COVID infections and the number of deaths in the Global South have been much lower than in the advanced economies. But this may be temporary, due to the closure of international travel. Looking at the damage that the pandemic has done in the United States and Europe, it is clear that a spread of the virus in the Global South would wreak havoc, given the lack of capacity of the health systems and the precarious nature of living conditions for the majority of the population. Therefore, the only viable strategy is prevention.

Do you draw any general lessons from the COVID crisis about the most viable ways to advance an egalitarian economic project?

The emerging evidence demonstrates that the impact of the COVID crisis has been uneven, and the effects have fallen mostly on the populations that were already at the bottom of the economic distribution. Low-wage workers, households in low-income areas, and people of color have been much more affected by the pandemic both in terms of human losses and economic deprivation. One of the lessons learned from this crisis is that economic livelihood and health are intricately linked. For the poor, the pandemic has often forced them to make the impossible choice between their lives and their livelihoods: if they do not go to work, they cannot feed themselves and their families. But by going to work in unsafe environments, they expose themselves and their families to the risk of dying from the coronavirus.

Building societies that are resilient to pandemics and other forms of crisis requires addressing the structural issue of inequality, not only along income lines but also in terms of access to basic services, including health care and sanitation. Achieving this objective requires building the necessary institutions and capabilities that facilitate access to decent employment for everyone, and giving a chance to every citizen to build basic wealth—such as home ownership—which is critical for absorbing shocks to income.

Does the experience of the COVID crisis shed any light on the way you think about economics as a discipline or, more specifically, the questions you might be pursuing in your own research?

The COVID crisis has indeed reemphasized a number of ways I think about economics as a discipline, which informs the way I do my own research. I will illustrate with two examples. First, at the national level, the crisis has brought to light why the economics profession must take inequality seriously. On the one hand, the negative effects of the pandemic are unequally distributed, with the populations at the bottom of the ladder shouldering most of the damage. On the other hand, and partly as a result of this first effect, policies to support the poor during the crisis find little support in the dominant segments of the populations, because they do not suffer the consequences of the crisis as severely as the poor. In fact, the rich segments of the population have done very well during the crisis, as illustrated by the massive increase in financial wealth and profitability of large corporations, especially in the digital sector, since the onset of the pandemic. So there is little incentive within the centers of power to change the system. The economics profession, especially on the progressive side, has a responsibility to produce and disseminate evidence on the detrimental effects of inequality on society, so as to guide the debate on possible solutions to address the structural problems of inequity and exclusion in modern societies.

Second, on the global side, the pandemic has demonstrated the critical importance of globalization in terms of both its advantages and its disadvantages. Globalization implies that crises and their consequences cannot be confined within national borders. Regardless of where they originate, pandemics and economic crises have consequences that affect all populations around the world. This was also evidenced during the 2008 global financial crisis. Globalization also implies that resolving pandemics requires a global partnership, and that no country can do it on its own. In particular, it is critically important for the international community to devise effective mechanisms and mobilize adequate resources to support efforts of governments in the Global South to minimize the impact of the crisis and position their economies for a speedy postcrisis recovery. Therefore, now more than ever, it is important to strengthen international participatory institutions such as the United Nations and its specialized agencies, to provide a framework for mobilizing collective crisis-response programs and resources, and to deliver the necessary assistance to all populations in need around the world. And once again, solving global crises as well as structural problems of poverty and deprivation requires addressing the problem of unequal distribution of resources and capabilities at the national and global level. The world has sufficient resources to feed every human being; the existing deprivation around the world is due only to the fact that some countries and segments of the population have more than they need while others do not even have enough to survive. The problem of international development is not a problem of lack of resources, it is a problem of inequitable distribution.

Representative Publications and Influences

Publications:

James K. Boyce and Leonce Ndikumana (2001). "Is Africa a Net Creditor? New Estimates of Capital Flight from Severely Indebted Sub-Saharan African Countries," 1970–96. *Journal of Development Studies*, 38(2), 27–56.

Leonce Ndikumana and James K. Boyce (2011). *Africa's odious debts: how foreign loans and capital flight bled a continent*. Zed Books Ltd.

Linda Pickbourn and Leonce Ndikumana (2019). "Does Health Aid Reduce Infant and Child Mortality from Diarrhoea in Sub-Saharan Africa?" *The Journal of Development Studies*, 55(10), 2212–2231.

People who have been influential: Douglass North, Steve Fazzari

Literature that has been influential:

Steven Fazzari and Hyman Minsky (1984). "Domestic monetary policy: If not monetarism, what?" *Journal of Economic Issues*, 18(1), 101–116.

Steven Fazzari, Glenn Hubbard, and Bruce C. Petersen (1987). "Financing constraints and corporate investment," *Brookings Paper on Economic Activity*, 1, 141–195.

North, D. C. (1990). *Institutions, Institutional Change and Economic Performance*. Cambridge University Press.

Özlem Onaran

Özlem Onaran is Professor of Economics at the University of Greenwich, Director of the Greenwich Political Economy Research Centre, and Co-Director of the Institute of Political Economy, Governance, Finance and Accountability. Her research focuses on issues of inequality, wage-led growth, employment, globalization, gender, and crises. She is a member of the Scientific Committee of the Foundation of European Progressive Studies, Scientific Advisory Board of Hans Böckler Foundation, and the Policy Advisory Group of the Women's Budget Group. She has published more than seventy articles in books and peer reviewed journals such as *Cambridge Journal of Economics*, *World Development*, *Structural Change and Economic Dynamics*, *Eastern European Economics*, and *Review of Political Economy*.

You were born, raised, and educated in Turkey. Tell me about your educational background and the economic theories that dominated teaching and research at Istanbul Technical University, where you attained your doctorate degree.

I wanted to study medicine, but then a scholarship made me decide to change my choice to study industrial engineering in 1988. As an irony of history, while studying engineering, I got familiar with Marxist economics, in particular with Ernest Mandel's long waves of capitalism and David Harvey's work. I wanted to do research on the labor process and technological change. I wanted to "not just understand the world, but also to change it," as Marx put it, so I decided to do a master's degree in economics at Bilkent University in Ankara. This experience was very disappointing, because there was no element of political economy, and it was dominated by neoclassical economics teaching without any real-world relevance. Even the econometrics course was far from stimulating our curiosity and equipping students with basic skills to do research on the urgent issues of our time. The only exceptions were Erinç Yeldan and Erol Balkan, from whom I learned about alternative economics and got the inspiration to do research that matters for peoples' lives. The end of my master's coincided with a major economic crisis in Turkey in 1994, so my efforts to find a research assistance job to fund my PhD at a place where I could research alternative economic theories proved to be futile. Eventually, I ended up getting a job at a large private bank in Istanbul as an economist at the research department, led by Hasan Ersel, who was a former academic, and who had to leave the university after the military coup in 1980. This turned out to be a big opportunity for me as he had a deep understanding of real-world macroeconomics, not just the main-stream but also alternative Keynesian, Marxist, and institutionalist theories. He created a research environment where we could get train-ing in macroeconometric modeling at the bank as well as starting a PhD. Both learning from the life experience of Hasan Ersel and sharing an exceptional work environment with other junior researchers, who are now important economists in Turkey (such as Yelda Yücel and Ahmet Çimenoğlu) was very educational for me. Nevertheless, I kept looking for an academic job and took the first opportunity in 1998 to get back to the university, this time to Istanbul Technical University (ITU), as a research assistant for a salary that was one-seventh of my salary at the bank. This is the place where I could get back to my original research idea about the labor process and technological change, and where Nurhan Yentürk, my supervisor, Hacer Ansal, and Lerzan Yentürk had made substantial contributions in heterodox economics. Gradually my research evolved from Marxist labor process to an analysis of the labor markets from a structuralist perspective.

How would you characterize your own approach as an economist, relative to the various schools of thought? Among economists, who has influenced your thinking the most?

I define myself as someone who has learned from Marxist, Keynesian, and feminist economics, and I try to synthesize these schools of thought in my research. Michał Kalecki and Amit Bhaduri, in his work with Stephen Marglin, on the impact of wages on growth and employment, have been particularly important for me because they develop a "general theory" of wage-led versus profit-led demand regimes that makes Marxist, Keynesian, or even neoclassical hypotheses special cases. This post-Kaleckian strand within post-Keynesian economics has shaped most of my analytical work and my joint research with Engelbert Stockhammer. In particular, the applied research by Bob Pollin, Jerry Epstein, and Philip Arestis, bringing the contest between orthodox and heterodox theories onto empirical terrain, gave me the inspiration to become an economist who addresses the most burning socially relevant questions of our time. Recently, feminist economists—Diane Elson and Sue Himmelweit from the Women's Budget Group and İpek İlkkaracan, Elissa Braunstein, and Stephanie Seguino—helped me embark on feminist macroeconomic modeling to develop a feminist post-Kaleckian research agenda. Finally, I am learning from ecological economists, and their thinking on policies to bring together equality, full employment, and ecological sustainability.

How did you end up teaching at the Vienna University of Economics and Business, and later on at universities in the UK?

I moved to Vienna for personal reasons, and the precariousness as well as the small size of the academic job market in Austria meant that, sooner or later, I had to look for academic jobs in other countries or take a nonacademic research job in Austria. Because I was very convinced of the importance of freedom of thought that comes with a university job, I opted for the former. Britain offered itself with a very large academic market, where heterodox economists are able to form a critical mass at some institutions. Eventually, following in the footsteps of Philip Arestis, I started at the University of Greenwich in 2012. Philip had edited the *Thames Papers in Political Economy* from 1974 to 1988 at the Thames Polytechnic, which then became the University of Greenwich. Building on this heritage, I revitalized the political economy tradition, founded the Greenwich Political Economy Research Centre (which is now the Institute of Political Economy, Governance, Finance and Accountability), and started the *Greenwich Papers in Political Economy*. Together with a young team of lecturers, we have been one of the very few universities in the world to launch a full-blown pluralist economics curriculum at both undergraduate and postgraduate levels, one that has been acknowledged by student leaders of the Rethinking Economics movement. We have a large body of PhD students, whom we supervise to embark on careers in research and policy. We have a strong engagement with the community outside academia, too. And, recently, we have launched a free series titled "Economics for Campaigners." The change in the policy stance of the Labour Party under the leadership of Jeremy Corbyn also increased the space for me to interact with politicians—in particular, with the team of the Shadow Chancellor John McDonnell. So after working in five countries and at nine universities, I do not plan to leave Britain any time soon.

The impact of structural adjustment programs on wages and the labor market in Turkey was among the early research topics that you focused on as a young academic. How did you get involved in this area of work?

I grew up during the years of structural adjustment, austerity, and neoliberalism in Turkey; my father had to retire early, taking a voluntary redundancy as an employee at a public bank. I experienced what austerity did to families. I have seen my mother cooking everything with homemade ingredients and recycling the upholstery of our sofa and chairs to sew a coat for me and two jackets for herself and my brother. This is austerity live, not an abstract theory of liberalization of an "Alice in Wonderland" type. When I became a feminist and socialist political activist and chose to do a PhD in economics, I wanted my work to be useful to show that structural adjustment had real costs for the livelihoods of working people.

What have been your main findings within this area of work, in particular, on the issue of how "flexible" labor markets impact wages? What do you make of the claim that flexible labor markets are critical for advancing productivity?

Labor market flexibility has been the polite word for attacking the rights of organized workers and trade unions. All these policies have "achieved" is a dramatic fall in the share of labor income in national income. These low-road labor market policies and resulting low wages have been detrimental for demand and growth in both advanced and emerging economies, and have created disincentives for business investment and innovation as well. In the absence of a healthy increase in investment in physical machinery and equipment, productivity has also stagnated. Secular stagnation is not a puzzle; it is an outcome of neoliberal labor market policies and rising inequality as well as cuts in public spending and the spread of financialization.

Gender economics has grown in influence in recent years. In what ways are gender issues critical for understanding the operations of capitalist economies?

Despite decades of improvements in legal rights and education, gender gaps in income and wealth remain at very high levels across the world. For example, the recent gender pay gap reports by the large companies in Britain show that men earn, on average, almost 20 percent more than women, despite decades of improvements in legal rights and education. One explanation is women's concentration in occupations with lower hourly pay and/or part-time work. Another is the existence of "glass ceilings" the further up we look in organizational hierarchies. These relate to some fundamental features of our societies: women tend to spend more time taking care of the children or the elderly within the household than men. Also, care services in the market are undersupplied or unaffordable. These features have gendered economic outcomes. Gender inequality has a crucial impact on key economic and social issues in the world, including stagnation in productivity and demographic and care crises.

There is evidence that more income in the hands of women increases household spending on children's education and health and thereby affects long-run productivity.

Acknowledging the role of care or reproductive labor in an economy has important implications for public policy. The need for social infrastructure is not sufficiently met under the present circumstances with inadequately low public spending in this field; currently private providers fill in the gap by supplying these services, which are provided either at very low wages and low quality (to ensure an adequate profit) or as luxury services for the rich. This leaves a large unmet demand for social services, and a large part of the remaining care deficit is currently being covered by invisible unpaid female labor within the gendered division of labor in the private sphere at home. A substantial rise in spending in social infrastructure by the state or by nonprofit/community organizations is required to cover this care deficit. Crucially, a strong investment in public services in social infrastructure improves gender equality and reverses one of the most persistent dimensions of inequality in our societies, because it provides care services that are otherwise provided by the unpaid invisible domestic labor of women. Public provision of these services offers women a genuine choice to participate in social and economic life more equally, if they wish to do so. This in turn further increases productivity by unleashing the full potential of women. Moreover, in the current gendered, occupationally segregated labor markets, these sectors employ predominantly women, and more social public spending leads to closing the gender gap in employment. This is why they are labeled as "purple" public investment by feminist economists.

However, these jobs need to be made attractive to both men and women by improving pay, working conditions, and job satisfaction, as well as training and education requirements in these industries. A new orientation of policies towards creating high-skilled, decent jobs in the social infrastructure sector should be promoted instead of the current reliance on low-pay service jobs and weak labor unions in this sector. Such policies would put gender equality in pay and employment at the heart of an equality-led development strategy. However, if women are concentrated in the types of paid work where the prospect of higher wages does not exist, these policies may still be insufficient to significantly improve women's incomes and equality. Wage policies should reflect the added value of social infrastructure for society, and should gradually target the problem of occupational segregation. The public sector can contribute to making sure that we value adequately what matters for our society. This is a clear break from current policies of low pay in the care sector as well as the pay freezes for public-sector workers, who are predominantly women.

While it is crucial to recognize the vast amount and importance of time women spend on unpaid care in the household, which is not accounted for in the standard national accounts and measures such as GDP, this policy aims to publicly provide the necessary social services, that is, to socialize these activities and radically decrease the amount of unpaid private care. For example, universal free childcare and nurseries open for sufficiently long hours benefit mothers and fathers by giving them an equal chance to balance work, social, cultural and political life. Needless to say, there will always be the need and desire for care provided by family members for children or the elderly in the domestic private sphere, and regulations such as sufficiently long paid parental leave equally available for both mothers and fathers, and working time arrangements that facilitate combining care and work for both men and women, to ensure that time for caring can be equally shared between men and women. Diane Elson calls for a reorientation of economic policy with an aim to "recognize, reduce, and redistribute" unpaid care work.

There is also an important potential alliance between those supporting the agendas for Green development and gender equality. A larger proportion of a society's time spent caring for each other is also a greener alternative, whether that is in paid or unpaid time, as these activities are much lower in terms of their carbon intensity. Furthermore, social infrastructure services are very labor-intensive and therefore public investment in this area is a vehicle for generating more employment for a given rate of growth in national output—a target more consistent with low carbon emissions.

You've done considerable work on economic globalization. What do you consider to be the main forces associated with globalization in the contemporary world economy? What are the main ways that globalization has impacted Turkey and other middle-income economies?

Most importantly, globalization in the late twentieth century took place as part of a massive shift in economic policy towards neoliberalism, combined with austerity, privatization, welfare state retrenchment, financialization, deregulation in the labor markets, and decline in trade union power and collective bargaining. Capital came out as the winner of this process of globalization in both the developed and developing/emerging economies, and large segments of the working people lost. There has been a dramatic race to the bottom in the share of labor income in national income globally, while the share of profits has increased since the 1980s. In our research project for the Institute of New Economic Thinking together with my former PhD student Alexander Guschanski, we find that the impact of the rise of global value chains on both advanced and emerging economies is particularly interesting. On both ends of the global value chain—the offshoring of production away from advanced economies and the relocation towards emerging economies—there is a negative impact on the labor share. Integration into global value chains in the form of increased exports of intermediate goods from the emerging economies to the advanced economies, and increased imports of intermediate inputs by the advanced economies from the emerging economies, as well as financial globalization, has led to a substantial decline in the wage share in both parts of the world. This implies that globalization affected labor adversely worldwide through an increase in the bargaining power of capital.

In what ways has globalization affected social structures and culture throughout Europe?

Rising inequality has been a strong concern for people throughout Europe. Indeed, this was a core concern among the deprived working-class people who voted for Brexit in the EU Referendum in Britain in 2016. Most of the "Leave" voters believe that their loss of income, lack of decent jobs or lack of access to health services, schools, or housing, is due to increased migration—in particular from Eastern Europe after the EU enlargement in 2004. Interestingly, our research shows that migration has not been a cause of rising inequality in Britain or Europe, and it does not have a negative impact on either the share of wages on total income or real wages even in the service sectors predominantly hiring low-skilled labor, which also employ a large share of migrants.

On the contrary, inequality increased because of the increased fallback options of capital related to increased imports, in particular import of intermediate inputs: offshoring, capital mobility in the form of outward foreign direct investment (FDI) and financialization, along with declining fallback options of labor related to the decline in collective bargaining power of trade unions, deregulation of the labor market, zero-hours contracts and false self-employment contracts, austerity, the housing crisis, and rising household debt. This is not a new phenomenon but a process that gained momentum since the 1980s. The quick conclusions related to the impact of immigration on inequality, without adequately decomposing the impact of all other factors, misses the point that correlation is not causation. The simultaneous rise in immigration and inequality does not mean that the former causes the latter. Mostly the debate about migration is taking place without any reference to a progressive approach to foreign trade and capital mobility. We, migrants, are visible to people.

Imports or firms that relocate also cause job losses—but this process is less visible than migrants. The problem is not labor mobility but uncontrolled capital mobility, the asymmetry between the options and power of labor and capital, exploitative employers, unorganized migrants as well as unorganized local workers, and lack of public spending in infrastructure to mitigate the impact of rising population. Indeed, migrant workers are the much-needed care workers in an aging society, making a positive contribution to productivity and paying more in taxes to the government budget than they use in terms of benefits. However, the neoliberal government does not channel these tax revenues to public spending, and, as a result, people feel the brunt of high rents and crowded hospitals. We understand peoples' grievances, but the real solution to these concerns requires tackling the real causes of inequality and disempowerment. If the balance of power were to shift in favor of labor and unions were to have a strong voice when migrants come to work, it would be possible to set the terms and conditions under which they work. Conversely, if migrants will not be allowed to come, firms will go to where cheap labor is, given the current situation with free capital mobility. It is a lot harder to set the conditions of work abroad to avoid a global race to the bottom in wages than organizing both local and migrant workers at home.

A lot of your recent research has been on analyzing the differences between "wage-led" and "profit-led" capitalist economies. Can you explain the main issues at play here?

Neoliberal economic policies have seen wages as costs to businesses. The mainstream assumption is that, when the wage share falls and the profit share increases, growth will increase; investment by firms picks up; and exports become more competitive thanks to lower labor costs. This thinking guides policies across the world, which promotes wage moderation. The main point of these policies is to treat wages as only a cost item. However, wages play a dual role in the economy: rising wages are both a cost to employers and a potential source for new sales. The post-Keynesian/post-Kaleckian models we work with bring the demand-side effect of wages into the analysis and allow this dual role.

In a research project we have done for the United Nations International Labour Office in 2012, I and Giorgos Galanis present a global macroeconomic analysis building on this post-Keynesian/post-Kaleckian theory to estimate the effect of income distribution on aggregate demand in the G20. Because the majority of middle- and low-income people depend on wages, a decrease in the wage share implies a redistribution of income from middle- and low-income households to high-income households, who spend a lower share of their income than people at the bottom. Therefore, a decrease in the wage share leads to a decrease in household consumption, and that in turn leads to a decline in demand and ultimately affects firms' investment. However, at the same time, higher profitability is expected to stimulate investment for a given level of aggregate demand. Finally, exports and imports depend on relative prices, which in turn depend on nominal unit labor costs, which are closely related to the wage share. The total effect of the decrease in the wage share on aggregate demand depends on the relative size of the reactions of consumption, investment, and net exports. Whether the negative effect of a lower wage share on consumption or the positive effect on investment and net exports is larger is an empirical question that depends on the structure of an economy—such as the difference in the propensity to consume out of wage and profit income, the sensitivity of investment to sales versus profitability, the impact of labor costs on prices, labor intensity of production, sensitivity of exports and imports to domestic prices relative to foreign prices, and the importance of foreign markets relative to the size of the economy. If the total effect is negative, the demand regime in the economy is wage-led; otherwise, the regime is profit-led. Neoliberal economic policy assumes that econo-mies are always profit-led, whereas in post-Keynesian models the rela-tionship between the wage share and demand is an empirical matter and depends on the structural characteristics of the economy.

Based on our global model we calculate the effects of a simultaneous decline in the wage share in the G20—that is, the global race to the bottom in the labor share. Three important findings emerge. First, domestic private demand (the sum of consumption and investment) is wage-led in all G20 countries, because consumption is much more sensitive to an increase in the profit share than is investment. Second, foreign trade forms only a small part of aggregate demand in large coun-tries, and therefore the positive effects of a decline in the wage share on net exports do not suffice to offset the negative effects on domestic demand. Finally, even if there are some countries which are profit-led, Planet Earth as a whole is wage-led. A simultaneous wage cut in a highly integrated global economy leaves most countries with only the negative domestic demand effects, and the global economy contracts. Furthermore, some profit-led countries contract when they decrease their wage share, if a similar strategy is implemented also by their trading partners. Beggar-thy-neighbor policies cancel out the competitiveness advantages in each country and are counterproductive. As long as we do not trade with Mars, this will remain the case. I read a lot of science fiction and I trust one day we will interact with other intelligent life forms across galaxies, but not just yet!

A global wage-led growth regime is economically feasible. We also present an alternative scenario, where both wage-led and profit-led countries can grow along with an improvement in the wage share, and the global GDP would increase by 3.05 percent.

The microeconomic rationale of pro-capital changes in income distribution conflicts with the macroeconomic rationale. First, at the national level in a wage-led economy, a higher profit share leads to lower demand and growth. Thus, even though a higher profit share at the firm level seems to be beneficial to individual employers, at the macroeconomic level a generalized fall in the wage share generates the problem of realization of profits due to deficient demand. Second, even if increasing profit share seems to be promoting growth at the national level in the profit-led countries, at the global level a simultaneous fall in the wage share leads to global demand deficiency and lower growth.

At the national level, if a country is wage-led, such as in Europe, the US, South Korea or Turkey, low-road labor market policies that lead to a fall in the wage share are detrimental to growth. There is room for policies to decrease income inequality without hurting the growth potential of the economies.

In economic areas with a high intra-regional trade and low extra-regional trade, macroeconomic and wage policy coordination can improve growth and employment. Europe is a good example of this, where the wage moderation policy of the European Commission has not been conducive to growth.

Debt-led consumption, enabled by financial deregulation and housing bubbles, seemed to offer a short-term solution to aggregate demand deficiency caused by falling wage share in countries like the US, UK, Spain, Ireland, Turkey, and South Africa until the Great Recession. The current account deficits and debt in these countries are matched by an export-led model and the current account surpluses of countries like Germany, Japan, and China, where exports had to compensate for the deficiency in domestic demand due to the fall in labor's share. However, this model is also unsustainable, since it can only coexist with imbalances and debt accumulation in the other countries in the world.

By definition, wage-led economies will be more egalitarian than profit-led economies. What are the ways that economies can transition successfully from being profit-led to being wage-led? What are the main barriers to transitioning from being profit-led to wage-led? Are the barriers mainly political—as in opposition from capitalists, as the profit-receiving class— or are there significant economic barriers as well?

First of all, the positive effects of higher wages on demand are encouraging in the sense that equality is not an impediment to growth. However, the magnitude of the positive effects is economically small, particularly if implemented in only one country. Hence, equality-led growth is not the silver bullet to achieve high levels of employment and development. The impact of policies for equality-led development would be substantially amplified if they are combined with policies to stimulate investment, in particular via targeted public investment in physical and social infrastructure. Second, in a profit-led economy, the transition to a more equal and wage-led regime would require structural change—for example, relying less on low-road, low-wage policies for productivity and export competition but more on high-road, high-wage, high-productivity policies. This transition would be substantially facilitated by public investment and industrial policy. Increasing public investment in the short term would stimulate growth and in the medium term would lead to a rebalancing of these economies, making them less reliant on export demand, and changing the structure of their exports towards less labor-intensive goods as well as goods with a lower price elasticity of demand in the medium term. This would help develop a more diversified economic structure, and thereby potential for higher increases in living standards in the future.

International coordination is also crucial to make these policies more effective. In 2014, I presented a simulation of the effects of a coordinated mix of policies in the G20 targeted to increase the share of wages in GDP over the next five years by 1 to 5 percentage points and to raise public investment in social and physical infrastructure by 1 percent of GDP in each country. This policy mix could lead to 3.9–5.8 percent higher GDP in the G20. The effects of both wage and fiscal policies are stronger if policies are implemented simultaneously in a large bloc due to strong positive spillover effects on demand. The International Trade Union Confederation, and the Trade Union Advisory Committee of the OECD, who lead the L20, which brings together trade unions from the G20 countries, used this research for policy advocacy at the G20 meetings in 2014.

In 2017, with my colleague Maria Nikolaidi and former PhD student Thomas Obst, we did research for the Foundation for European Progressive Studies on the impact of a coordinated policy mix of a simultaneous increase in public investment along with more progressive taxation and increase in the wage share in the EU15. The result is 6.72 percent higher GDP in the EU with positive effects in each country. Private investment increases as well—overall public spending does not crowd out but rather "crowds in" private investment despite a rise in tax rates on profits. Despite the rise in public spending, the budget balance in Europe as a whole improves because of the beneficial fiscal effects of higher economic growth and higher tax rates. Growth, private investment, and budget balance improve both in the periphery and core countries of Europe. Hence, expansionary fiscal policy is sustainable when wage and public spending policies are combined with progressive tax policy; the impact is stronger when these policies are implemented in a coordinated fashion. Such a coordinated policy mix, along with a properly designed industrial policy, can ensure genuine regional convergence and social cohesion and open up space for equality-led development in the global economy overall.

One important lesson is that labor market policies to increase equality are more effective if they are embedded in macroeconomic policies geared towards ensuring full employment in order to rebalance both power relations and the structure of the economy. Increasing the social wage via higher public spending in public services and social security, restoring and strengthening the welfare state, supporting job creation, and restructuring with a large public investment program centered on physical investments and social infrastructure are key aspects of an equality-led macroeconomic strategy.

Rebalancing growth via increasing equality and domestic demand in the emerging economies would also be helpful in addressing global imbalances. However, this rebalancing can take place only in an international environment where the advanced countries not only leave space for developmentalist policies and support technology transfer, but also create an expansionary global environment.

Given the profit-led structures in many small open developing countries, an equality-led development strategy can more easily be triggered by a step forward by some large economies in terms of radically reversing their low-road labor market policies. While a coordinated global boost to wages might appear as wishful thinking, in fact the exact opposite has been happening in the last four decades of "converging divergence" between labor and capital globally, largely following coordinated policies by international institutions such as the IMF, World Bank, and European Commission. Our results clearly highlight the limits of strategies of international competitiveness based on wage competition in a highly integrated global economy. It is now on the advanced countries to reverse this trend.

Global policy coordination for equality-led development can create space for domestic demand-led egalitarian growth rather than a narrow export orientation based on low wages in the developing countries. If the developed countries fail to make such a move, South–South cooperation can be an option to thrive in a large bloc and avoid wage competition.

Last but not least, without moderating the process of financialization the impact of policies as well as policy space for global development would be limited, as our research with my former PhD student Daniele Tori shows. Implementing appropriately designed taxation and corporate governance that create incentives to decrease dividend payments and share buybacks—such as higher taxation of dividend payments and capital gains—and decoupling executives' remuneration from share prices are key policy tools for creating a level playing field. At the global level, taming financial globalization via adequate capital controls and a coordinated financial transaction tax would contribute to rebalancing the bargaining power of capital and labor.

Is this politically feasible? Well, Kalecki has famously written in his important piece on the "Political Aspects of Full Employment" that capitalists will never agree to policies that foster full employment, because they do not want to lose the threat of the sack and give up class discipline in the factories. As we learned from Marx, a capitalist economy will always be unstable. But this does not mean that there is no room for policies to extend the area of maneuver of the labor movement.

In what direction is your research agenda shaping up for the years ahead?

Currently, I am very engaged with political and trade union movements in Britain, Europe, and elsewhere to campaign for and implement these policies. The office of the new progressive South Korean President Moon issued the policy paper "Economic Paradigm Shift," which includes "income-led growth" as one of four policy pillars. This builds heavily on the concept of "wage-led growth." I and Engelbert Stockhammer were invited to speak at the Karl Polanyi Institute Asia Conference and the Korea Development Institute in October 2017 to economists working for the ministries. We had a one-page interview in a major Korean daily newspaper, *Hankyoreh*, with the headlines "Distribution is not the result of the growth, but the source of the growth" and "when wage is raised, productivity will also be raised." In June 2018 Robert Blecker and I spoke at a panel assessing the first year of the Moon administration's policies.

In terms of research, an important new project is about gendering macroeconomics. We have just started a new project on "the effects of income, gender and wealth inequality and economic policies on macroeconomic performance in the UK," funded by the Rebuilding Macroeconomics Network/Economic and Social Research Council, with Cem Oyvat and my former PhD student Eurydice Fotopolou. The aim of our project is to investigate the effects of gender, income, and wealth inequalities on macroeconomic outcomes. We talk about "inequalities" in the plural. Persistent gender inequality in pay and employment likely interacts with other dimensions of inequality, in particular the fall in the labor share and the increase in wealth concentration in the last four decades. Most macroeconomists have worked with genderless models, and gender studies have not dealt with macroeconomic modeling, with some notable exceptions, such as the Women's Budget Group-UK, Stephanie Seguino, Elissa Braunstein, and İpek İkkaracan. In our project we aim to develop an interdisciplinary, gendered macroeconomic analysis. We will bring together structuralist, post-Keynesian and feminist economics, gender studies, and sociology. This will integrate realistic features of gendered behavior and social norms, such as reciprocity, caring, and nonselfish motives. We will use the model to analyze the effects of changes in inequalities, different types of public spending in social versus physical infrastructure, and redistributive tax policies. We will focus on the effects on productivity, growth, employment of men and women, public and private debt, and private investment. We aim to examine if and how a policy mix may affect different social groups. What would the effect of closing gender pay gaps via upward convergence in female and male wages have on employment of women and men? What difference might public spending in physical versus social infrastructure (childcare, education, health and social care) have on women and men?

We aim to broaden policy impact analysis beyond considerations of GDP, by focusing on employment and inequalities. The results could inform policy-makers on an appropriate mix of labor market and fiscal policies. This may help with tackling multiple dimensions of inequalities and achieve both a stable macroeconomic environment and social cohesion. This also crucially requires gendering macroeconomic analysis and gender mainstreaming in policy-making.

Last but not least, with my PhD students Ben Tippet and Stephanie Manea, and colleagues Tomas Rotta and Raphael Wildauer, we are researching on the causes and consequences of wealth concentration in terms of ecological, macroeconomic, and financial instability.

Responses on the COVID-19 Pandemic

How would you evaluate the ways different countries or regions have responded to the COVID-19 crisis, both in terms of public health interventions and economic policies?

Looking at the situation from Britain, years of public-sector cuts, deregulated labor markets with zero-hours contracts and dodgy self-employment practices, low wages, and high household debt have made the effects of the pandemic much worse and reduced the effectiveness of emergency policies. There has been a dramatic rise in poverty and reliance on community-organized food banks even by people in work. The furlough scheme has not been designed well enough to prevent a substantial increase in unemployment and poverty. There is also a visible deficiency in state capacity to plan and coordinate basic processes like test, trace, and isolate compared to countries like Germany, South Korea, China, and New Zealand. Finally, COVID laid bare a massive deficit in the social care infrastructure.

Do you draw any general lessons from the COVID crisis about the most viable ways to advance an egalitarian economic project?

There are two important lessons from the pandemic: first, the crisis and class, race, and gender inequalities exacerbate each other. All crises leave distributional scars. Racial and gendered profiling of occupations and labor market segmentation and discrimination mean that workers, people of color, and women workers are concentrated in sectors such as retail and hospitality that are most adversely effected with the lockdowns and restrictions, and were more likely to work under precarious, part-time, or zero-hours contracts. This increased their income loss and insecurity. Similarly, frontline workers, such as those in care homes or supermarkets, with a large share of women and people of color, have been exposed to high health risks without adequate protection. Renter or indebted households face a future with looming debt or even eviction, while high-income households or workers who could continue to work from home increased their savings during the lockdowns. These teach us a lesson: to tackle both the public health crisis and the economic fallout in the aftermath of the pandemic, we have to tackle inequalities.

The second lesson is to recognize the importance of the reproductive sector and acknowledge the deficit in care infrastructure. With nursery and school closures and home schooling, the burden of increased unpaid domestic care time fell disproportionately on women. This has substantially increased the time poverty of women and reversed former gains made towards gender equality. This makes it more urgent than ever, to recognize, redistribute, and reduce unpaid care work, to put it in Diane Elson's words. This, in turn, invites the need for adequate public provision of care and recognizing it as social infrastructure investment and not simply current spending. Policy should value what matters. It is not enough to call care workers "key workers" or "heroes"; we need decent care jobs with decent wages and working conditions and adequate career prospects for care workers. This is not just a matter of good social policy; our research shows that public spending in health and social care, childcare, and education has a substantial positive effect on productivity in the rest of the economy.

Does the experience of the COVID crisis shed any light on the way you think about economics as a discipline or, more specifically, the questions you might be pursuing in your own research?

The COVID crisis opens space to rethink the role of public investment as well as public ownership in key sectors of social and physical infrastructure. This is a chance for progressive economists and activists to link short-term emergency policy responses to long-term rebuilding of our societies in the aftermath of the COVID crisis. While better designed short-term responses such as flexible short working time arrangements, job guarantee schemes, supported by education grants and retraining schemes, and paid on-the-job training are very important, there has never been a better moment to make the case for permanent public-sector job creation with decent wages to provide much-needed high-quality universal free basic services in social care, health, childcare, education from early childhood to university, and Green public investment in renewable energy, public transport, and housing. This is what I call a Purple/Green/Red New Deal. In our recent research, synthesizing post-Kaleckian and feminist economics, we explore a policy mix of increasing public social and physical infrastructure investment, labor market policies to increase real wages of both men and women with an upward convergence in wages closing gender gap, and more progressive taxation of both income and wealth. The bottom line is that building a caring and sustainable society in the aftermath of the crisis is possible, and while public spending is partly self-financing, taxation of wealth helps not only to scale up the public sector to a substantially different level to respond to the multiple crises of climate change and care, but also to tackle inequalities as well as financialization. Bringing wealth concentration and the need for progressive taxation of wealth into the picture will become more important as fiscal conservatism makes a come-back following the drastic increase in public borrowing during the pandemic.

Finally, the disastrous and chaotic management of the crisis by governments relying on outsourced private services and/or bureaucratic civil service machines opens space to emphasize the need for a radical structural change, including in decision-making and ownership in key sectors, towards national coordination in combination with collective, municipal, and cooperative ownership and democratic participatory decision-making. Health and social care, education, energy, water, and transport are among these key sectors where private for-profit provision proved to lead to high prices, low quality, and inadequate level of supply. And in the next phase of the economic crisis, when the rise in the debt of low-income households and small and medium enterprises triggers a new credit crunch and banking crisis, it will be time to remind people to add banking to that list—a lesson that was missed after the financial crisis in 2008.

Representative Publications and Influences

Publications:

Özlem Onaran and Giorgos Galanis (2014). Income distribution and aggregate demand: National and global effects. *Environment and Planning A*, *46*(10), 2489–513.

Özlem Onaran, Cem Oyvat, and Eurydice Fotopoulou (2021). A macroeconomic analysis of the effects of gender inequality, wages, and public social infrastructure: the case of the UK, *Feminist Economics*, forthcoming.

Alexander Guschanski and Özlem Onaran (2021). The decline in the wage share: falling bargaining power of labour or technological progress? Industry level evidence from the OECD, *Socio-Economic Review*, forthcoming.

People who have been influential: Amit Bhaduri, Michał Kalecki, Stephen Margin, Diane Elson, Sue Himmelweit, Engelbert Stockhammer

Literature that has been influential:

Michał Kalecki (1943). "Political Aspects of Full Employment." *Political Quarterly*.

Amit Bhaduri and Stephen Marglin (1990). "Unemployment and the real wage: The economic basis for contesting political ideologies," *Cambridge Journal of Economics*, *14*(4), 375–393.

Diane Elson (2016). Gender budgeting and macroeconomic policy. *Feminist economics and public policy: Reflections on the work and impact of Ailsa McKay*, 27–37.

Robert Pollin

Robert Pollin is Distinguished University Professor of Economics and Co-Director of the Political Economy Research Institute at the University of Massachusetts Amherst. His books include *The Living Wage: Building a Fair Economy* (co-authored 1998), *Contours of Descent: US Economic Fractures and the Landscape of Global Austerity* (2003), *An Employment-Targeted Economic Program for South Africa* (co-authored 2007), *Greening the Global Economy* (2015), *Economic Analysis of Medicare for All* (co-authored 2018), and *Climate Crisis and the Global Green New Deal* (co-authored 2020). He has worked as a consultant for the US Department of Energy, the International Labour Organisation, the United Nations Industrial Development Organization, and numerous nongovernmental organizations in several countries and in US states and municipalities on various aspects of building high-employment green economies. He has also worked with many US nongovernmental organizations on creating living-wage statutes on both the statewide and municipal levels, on financial regulatory policies, and on the economics of single-payer health care in the United States. He was selected by *Foreign Policy* magazine as one of the "100 Leading Global Thinkers for 2013."

Tell me about your background.

I come from an affluent Jewish family, growing up in the Maryland suburbs of Washington, DC. But this actually says very little about my background. All four of my grandparents were immigrants from the Ukrainian region of the Jewish Pale of Settlement. They came to the US just before World War I. They were all poor people from shtetls and had little, if any, formal education. To the end of their lives, their spoken English was heavily inflected and accented with Yiddish—they spoke "Yinglish." My maternal grandparents were politically communists, though I am not sure if they were small—or big—"C" communists. My maternal grandfather worked as a milkman during the 1930s Depression, living in St. Louis. He and my grandmother later opened up a small grocery store in an African American neighborhood outside St. Louis. They eventually moved to Washington, DC, and opened a liquor store. There were sixteen siblings total on the side of my paternal grandparents. Many of my great uncles and aunts had been factory workers, then began driving trucks to sell cakes, then moved into operating small-time grocery stores, check-cashing businesses, and real estate businesses. Several were also communists, a few being quite vociferous about their beliefs at family gatherings.

My paternal grandfather, Morris Pollin, was not as openly political as many of his siblings, though he followed current events avidly. But he was the one in his family who ended up becoming quite successful in business, as a plumber, then as a plumbing contractor, in Washington, DC. This was during the 1930s Depression. My grandfather moved to Washington because he saw that the federal government was expanding rapidly under the New Deal. There was lots of work in construction. He effectively rode that wave, becoming the largest plumbing contractor in the city. This was despite the fact that he never went to school one day in his life, as he regularly, and regretfully, reminded me. With respect to my grandmother, Jennie Pollin, it never seemed to have fully registered with her that she was no longer a poor girl from the shtetl. Most of the time, she still dressed in the same *shmatas* (rough translation: "old rags") that she might have worn in her early days.

My father, Abe Pollin, initially went into the real estate business with my grandfather and his two brothers, then ventured off on his own when he was in his mid thirties and I was around eight. My mother was at home with my siblings and me—the typical 1950s US suburban arrangement. My father started to become a well-known figure in the Washington area when I was a teenager, when he bought what was originally the Baltimore Bullets NBA professional basketball team in 1964.

He bought the team only because he was a flat-out sports fanatic; there was no financial calculation involved in his decision. He subsequently moved the team to Washington and later changed their nickname from the Bullets to the Wizards, as a modest form of protest against gun violence. He continued to own the team for forty-six years, until he died in 2009. He was also active in other areas of professional sports, including being the founding owner of the Washington Capitals hockey team and building two sports arenas in the DC area. Besides being a professional sports entrepreneur, my father was primarily known in the DC area for being a very active philanthropist, supporting lots of humanitarian and liberal political causes. For example, he worked quite actively and passionately around fighting hunger, both globally with the United Nations and in the DC area. He was also outspoken and militant in supporting a living wage initiative in Montgomery County, Maryland, in 2003, and openly denounced some local rabbis who waffled in their position on this measure. More generally, the list of such things my father worked on actively was quite long. He did it not as a person with sophisticated political lines, but as someone who was sincerely compassionate and trying his best.

Growing up in this milieu, it was not surprising that I should become engaged politically growing up in the 1960s in the Washington, DC area, even though I was living in Bethesda, Maryland, a boring, affluent white suburb. I had become well aware of the civil rights movement by the time I was in junior high school, with the anti–Vietnam War movement following soon thereafter. I became somewhat involved in these things with some friends as early as tenth grade. But one thing I hadn't connected in high school was that doing intellectual labor—as in reading and writing books—had any particular connection with being a political activist. In short, I was a passionate and pretty active—though completely unschooled—political lefty well before I started down the path of being an intellectual worker.

Were you politically active during your student days?

I went to college at the University of Wisconsin-Madison in the fall of 1968. I first got interested in Wisconsin only because a friend of mine who played bass guitar in my high school rock band had moved to Madison when his father became dean of students there in 1967. But I soon got the vibe that Wisconsin was a left political hotbed. That sounded great to me. I was not the least bit disappointed. Before I went to my first class at Wisconsin—like literally within three days of showing up in Madison—I had gotten involved in the campus movement to eliminate a mandatory class with the Reserve Officers Training Corps (ROTC). We actually succeeded in getting the requirement abolished— a very early, heady victory as a campus antiwar activist. I remained active politically throughout my four years as an undergraduate at Wisconsin. But, again, it was not difficult to do so. The antiwar movement was deeply ingrained in the campus and community culture, as was, more generally, the 1960s ethos.

What made you switch from history to economics, and why did you choose The New School for graduate studies, an institution with quite a distinct progressive reputation?

Becoming a history major at Wisconsin was, yet again, an easy and obvious choice. I had no idea about this when I first showed up in Madison, but Wisconsin at the time had the most renowned leftist history department in the US and probably the world. The best-known figure there was William Appleman Williams, the historian of US imperialism. But unfortunately, Williams left Wisconsin just around the time I started taking school seriously. Still, there were other outstanding faculty members there who influenced me enormously—people in history and other fields as well. The main influences for me in history were four outstanding left historians: Tom McCormick, who followed Williams in doing diplomatic history; Maurice Meisner, the outstanding left historian of contemporary China; Georges Haupt, a major historian of European socialism; and finally, the great figure at Wisconsin in that era, Harvey Goldberg. Goldberg was a phenomenon at Wisconsin. I have never encountered a lecturer anywhere close to Goldberg in terms of his ability to combine rigor, depth, and passion. He gave lectures twice a week and 500 to 700 students showed up. He lectured on the European left, the history of socialism, political movements in the Third World, Rosa Luxemburg and Lenin, Vietnam, the Chinese Cultural Revolution— basically any burning issue of the day, as well as random but brilliant expositions on topics such as the architectonic structure of an egg. In my senior year of college, I was lucky enough to take a small seminar with him. For my term paper, following Goldberg's suggestion, I did an oral history of the shutdown of a major manufacturing plant in Madison, the Gisholt Machine Company. I had never heard of oral history or Gisholt until Goldberg told me about both topics. With this project, I ended up interviewing lots of former Gisholt workers at their homes. They told me what the shutdown meant to their lives and the life of their community. This was an early instance of deindustrialization that has now proceeded for fifty years under neoliberalism.

When I finished college, I definitely felt deeply engaged both politically and now intellectually as well. However, I had no idea how to pursue these commitments into adult life. At the time, I was adamant that I did not want to become an academic. I saw the academic life as excessively privileged—roughly the equivalent to a country club for people who liked to read books more than play golf. So I worked briefly in construction, as a gofer for a roofing company. This was a fun job that also paid well for somebody my age. This was before wage stagnation became the norm for US working-class jobs. I then traveled to South America with a close friend from college. Our goal was to make it to Chile, but not before we had acquired a reasonable facility with Spanish on the way. Chile was the goal since we wanted to observe developments in a country led by the first democratically elected Marxist head of state, President Salvador Allende. I left Chile in mid-July 1973, only two months before the fascist coup that overthrew Allende.

Within days of the overthrow of Allende and the installation of fascism under General Augusto Pinochet, I began reading about how the Pinochet government was putting together his economic policy team led by "los Chicago boys." These were right-wing PhD economists who had studied at the then bastion of right-wing economics, the University of Chicago, led by the venerated Professor Milton Friedman. It was in reading about the Chicago boys that I first started thinking about studying economics seriously. I knew instinctively that I vehemently opposed what the Chicago boys were offering in Chile, but I also knew that I couldn't explain my opposition in a way that would matter one whit to anyone. Over time, I reached the conclusion that studying economics systematically made sense if I wanted to have a more coherent opposition to right-wing Chicago economics and its allies, and more positively, if I wanted to think seriously about egalitarian political programs such as Allende had tried to implement in Chile.

Once I figured that out, it was an easy choice to go to the New School. At that time, as now, the New School was one of the only programs in the US that enabled you to study political economy from a variety of left perspectives. In addition, for me it was a major attraction that the New School was right in New York City. This was more consistent with my view that I didn't want to just be going to a country club for people who liked reading books (that's to say, a typical university campus), but would rather be right in the heart of a big, boisterous, multi-ethnic city. This was before huge swaths of the city had been converted into playgrounds for global billionaires.

I understand that one of the individuals who made a huge imprint on you and may have actually influenced your decision to pursue an academic career was Noam Chomsky. Why Chomsky?

I first started reading Noam Chomsky's writings when I was a sophomore in college in 1969. At the time, he was publishing a series of articles in the *New York Review of Books* denouncing the Vietnam War. I had just come across the *New York Review*, including Chomsky's articles, in a local Madison bookstore. At the time, I had no idea who Chomsky was, nor had I previously heard of the *New York Review*. Chomsky by then had already emerged as a great figure in linguistics. But I could have barely offered one or two sentences then describing what linguistics was, much less having any familiarity with the cutting-edge thinkers in the field. Also, Chomsky had not yet become CHOMSKY, the person widely recognized as the most respected and influential public intellectual in the world. The sole attraction for me to Chomsky was that his writings on politics for the general reader were, over and over again, like a gale force. Even as an eighteen-year-old college sophomore, I was blown away by their combination of relentless intellectual rigor and equally relentless moral passion, while still, somehow, also being easily accessible to somebody like me, at my eighteen-year-old, literally sophomoric level of understanding. As I kept up with Chomsky's writings from that point onward, I was not the least bit surprised to observe how his reputation rapidly grew to become the great global voice for reason and social justice that he has been for the past five decades.

With that as background, it is also true that Chomsky was directly responsible for my deciding to go into academia, even though at that point I had never met him and had corresponded with him by mail only one time. After returning from South America, I got a job at what was then the second largest mainstream newspaper in Washington, DC, the *Washington Star*. My specific job was as a "dictationist." This was 1973–74—just before computers and the internet had become pervasive. My job as a dictationist was to sit at a huge table along with other dictationists and take phone calls from reporters who were away from the newsroom. The reporters would dictate their stories over the phone to us, and we dictationists would type them up and give our typed pages to the papers' editors.

Anyway, I was on the late shift one night at 3 a.m., with one other dictationist, Barbara Palmer, who was also a friend. Barbara was nice enough to listen to me moan over the fact that I couldn't figure out what to do with my life, having already gone through a job as a roofer, and at that time, seeing firsthand the severe limitations of working in mainstream journalism. But I had also told Barbara my reasons for never wanting to go into academia, that it just seemed all too cushy for somebody with serious left political commitments. It was at that point that Barbara just blurted out, "How can you be so totally against academia, when your hero, Noam Chomsky, is an academic?" What Barbara said was obviously true; and I obviously could have figured that out on my own. It was also true that many of the people I held in extremely high esteem, such as my history professors at Wisconsin, were also academics. I had never thought of them as people who were just looking for cushy lives in an intellectual country club. Nevertheless, when Barbara stated the obvious truth to me about Noam Chomsky being an academic at 3 a.m. in the *Washington Star* newsroom, it was a Eureka! moment in my life. It was at exactly that moment that I began thinking about trying to do intellectual labor as an academic in the way that Chomsky had done his work. I wasn't going to follow the specifics of Chomsky's path, as in pursuing linguistics as my area of specialization, nor did I ever delude myself for a second into thinking I could come close to reaching Chomsky's level of accomplishment. And yet, there was no question that my complete turnaround from being militantly anti-academic to ending up spending my entire adult life as an economics graduate student and then as a professor began with Chomsky as my role model.

What intellectual influences shaped your views on economics?

I clearly entered into economics with a strong ideological commitment—or what Joseph Schumpeter more judiciously termed a "pre-
analytic vision." My pre-analytic vision was as a committed leftist. But
what that meant more specifically was, and remains, an open question.
When I began graduate school in 1975, one-third of the earth's population lived under some version of socialism or communism. But US
imperialism was hell-bent on violently destroying a communist project
in Vietnam and had just destroyed a democratic socialist project in
Chile. At the same time, the advanced capitalist economies mainly operated within broadly social democratic/Keynesian variants of capitalism.
So the overarching question as a leftist economist was to understand the
alternative pathways to most effectively build truly egalitarian democratic societies, putting all labels aside, and being willing, as Marx
himself had said, to "ruthlessly criticize" all that exists, including all
prevailing models of communism/socialism, and, for that matter all
authors, including Marx himself. Indeed, my favorite quote from Marx
is "I am not a Marxist."

   That said, my major intellectual influences in economics must start
with Marx. The second giant is equally obvious, John Maynard Keynes.
Michał Kalecki is a major force for having brought together two of the
most critical insights from Marx and Keynes: from Marx, the idea that
capitalism requires a reserve army of labor—mass unemployment—in
order to be able to exploit workers and extract profits from the production process; and from Keynes, the idea that, at least technically, full
employment is achievable under capitalism through policy interventions that sustain a high level of overall demand in the economy. Kalecki
brilliantly reconciled these two contradictory ideas from Marx and
Keynes by arguing that, technically, Keynes is right, we can operate a
full-employment version of capitalism through active demand management; but that Marx was right in insisting that capitalists will not accept
full employment capitalism in the long run since it will give workers too
much bargaining power and thus eat away at capitalist profits. What we
do with Kalecki's insight here remains a profound open question—a
political as well as technical question. In fact, the prevailing answer for
the last forty years has been to affirm Marx. That is, neoliberalism was
the   answer   to   social   democratic/Keynesian   capitalism,   since

neoliberalism, fundamentally, is a much more aggressively pro-capitalist version of how capitalism operates. Neoliberalism has successfully stripped away bargaining power from workers throughout the advanced capitalist societies.

So, beyond the obvious figures of Marx, Keynes, and Kalecki, two more surprising significant influences were the right-wing economists, Joseph Schumpeter and Milton Friedman. Schumpeter shows how one can be serious methodologically in ways similar to Marx—to be seriously grounded in history and the history of economic thought, to care about institutional analysis, and to still end up being committed to capitalism as a system most capable of advancing technical innovation that eventually will produce higher living standards. As a leftist, one needs to grapple with this perspective, and to check one's own predispositions against that.

In terms of Milton Friedman—I probably spent more time in graduate school reading Friedman, on my own, than any other economist other than Marx and Keynes. This all began with my observations about the installation of "los Chicago Boys" in Chile after the fascist coup. My position was that if I wanted to be against Friedman and his school, I needed to understand what they were up to. That was one of the main things that led me into doing financial macroeconomics for my doctoral dissertation. Friedman was the leading exponent of monetarism—one variant of financial macroeconomics. If I thought that this was totally wrong—which I did—I needed to make sure I understood exactly why it was wrong.

Beyond these major figures, I was also greatly influenced in graduate school by many of my professors, especially Paul Sweezy, Bob Heilbroner, Anwar Shaikh, and David Gordon. These are all major figures in left political economy, but they all made distinct contributions, both generally and in terms of how I connected with them. I first studied Marx seriously with Sweezy, who, at the time, was the most accomplished Marxist economist in the world. Sweezy and Harry Magdoff were also then co-editors of the periodical *Monthly Review*. As early as the late 1960s, Sweezy and Magdoff began writing regularly in *Monthly Review* about what we can now call financialization. They were documenting how financial markets and institutions were becoming increasingly dominant in capitalism. This was engendering excessive levels of financial speculation as well as increased power for financial capitalists—that is, Wall Street—over even nonfinancial capital.

Bob Heilbroner was a great influence in terms of the sweep of his perspective and his capacity to ask big questions and give deeply insightful answers to these questions. The titles of some of his books are themselves evocative of his approach: *Marxism: For and Against*; *Inquiry into the Human Prospect*; and *Between Capitalism and Socialism*. Anwar Shaikh was, and is, a great theorist. He took a lot from Marx, but then pushed out from there, never allowing himself or his students to take anything for granted. What do we really mean by competition? What is the logic behind comparative advantage? How effectively does the welfare state really redistribute income from capitalists to workers? David Gordon was the person who inspired me to become committed to working as effectively as possible with the full toolkit of contemporary statistics and econometrics. He was the one who insisted that we leftists should use all available techniques to advance our own perspectives and not cede this huge methodological field to orthodox economists. David was also fearless in taking on any and all questions that seemed important to real-world left political economy. It didn't matter whether he was an expert on a particular question. He dove in head-first and learned.

Beyond my own faculty mentors at the New School, the major influence on me during graduate school was somebody I never met until after I had finished my PhD. That was Hyman Minsky. In graduate school, I started reading Minsky's work on what he termed the Wall Street paradigm, explaining the root causes of systemic instability of capitalism within this Wall Street paradigm. Minsky's work thus had clear connections to what Sweezy and Magdoff were writing about financialization. Minsky also was extending Keynes in original ways. For my doctoral dissertation, and for several years after I finished my dissertation, my research focus was on developing empirical analyses that synthesized Sweezy/Magdoff, Minsky, and more broadly, Marxist and Keynesian perspectives on financial macroeconomics. This was also the foundation for my critical perspective on Milton Friedman and monetarism.

After leaving graduate school in 1982, I was also deeply fortunate to work with many outstanding colleagues at both University of California, Riverside, and UMass Amherst. Initially, my close comrades were Howard Sherman and Victor Lippit. Some years later, we were joined by Keith Griffin and Aziz Khan, as well as Dave Fairris and Gary Dymski. Keith Griffin was an outstanding egalitarian development economist. I was, and am, inspired by his commitment to solving real-world practical problems as opposed to engaging in strictly academic jousting on behalf of one or another school of thought. Aziz Khan was an equally outstanding development economist. He was the most creative empirical economist I have ever encountered. His work was focused on developing economies, especially conditions for poor people in these economies. He would almost always face serious data limitations with his projects. Nevertheless, he was a master at figuring out how to produce rigorous and meaningful findings no matter what the data limitations he faced in any given situation.

At UMass Amherst, I have been blessed with a great group of inspiring and creative co-workers. I would especially acknowledge Jerry Epstein, Jim Boyce, Nancy Folbre, Jim Crotty, Michael Ash, and Léonce Ndikumana. What I have learned from each of them is almost entirely distinct from the others.

I can easily keep going with this listing but will exercise now a bit of restraint. I will just mention a few other names. One is Rudolph Meidner, the great economist of the Swedish Trade Union Confederation for roughly thirty years starting in the mid-1950s. Meidner was one of the main architects of the Swedish social democratic model. This model tried to answer the profound question posed by Kalecki: how could you operate a version of capitalism that maintained a sustained commitment to full employment and an egalitarian social welfare state? The Nordic social democratic model developed by Meidner and others has been the most successful at pushing the institutions of liberal capitalism to their limit in allowing democratic politics and egalitarian goals to gain ascendancy over acquisitiveness. There is much we can learn both from their successes and their failures.

I need also to mention that my work has been strongly influenced by the work of political activists. These are people on the front line fighting for social justice. Some of them have, on occasion, asked me to help with the work they are doing. This has always been a great challenge. I have tried my best to support their efforts as much as possible.

You taught for many years as a professor at the University of California, Riverside. What brought you to UMass Amherst?

I began teaching at UC Riverside in the fall of 1982, right after having received my PhD at the New School. I spent sixteen years at UC

Riverside. It was an excellent place to do work in political economy, despite the fact that we also faced relentless opposition from orthodox economists through most of my years there. I moved to UMass Amherst in 1998, in part for personal reasons—to be closer to my family in the Washington, DC area and also my wife's mother in Rhode Island. But I also saw UMass as the opportunity of a lifetime for someone like me, who worked in political economy. I thought of UMass as having the strongest political economy program in the world. Why wouldn't I want to be part of it, if given the opportunity?

Tell me about the vision and mission of the Political Economy Research Institute, which you co-direct along with Gerald Epstein?

The idea to start PERI at UMass Amherst was Jerry Epstein's, who was then already a senior faculty member at UMass. Jerry both thought of the idea and then did a huge amount of time-consuming, thoroughly unglamorous, but critical bureaucratic work over two years to make it a reality. The vision of PERI today remains basically what it was at its outset in 1998: to develop a body of rigorous economic research that can, first, evaluate the operations of capitalism in our contemporary historical era; and second, help shed light on how to create more democratic, egalitarian, and ecologically sane societies—whether these societies call themselves "socialist" or something else. I think the ethos of PERI is captured beautifully in an observation made by my late professor, Bob Heilbroner, when he wrote: "Too often a vehicle for mystification, economics can best become an instrument for enlightenment if we see it as the means by which we strive to make a workable science out of morality."

Is economics for you a science or more of a policy guide?

If one is practicing economics as I think it should be practiced, it is, in equal parts, science and policy guide. That is why the field was long referred to as a "moral science." Let's consider one straightforward case in point, the consideration of minimum wage and "living wage" laws, one area in which I have worked. As a matter of morality, it is easy to make the case that all people who show up at work and do their job should be entitled to a living wage—a wage high enough to support themselves and their family members at a minimally decent level. That is a straightforward ethical judgment. But then some messy analytic questions emerge, starting with this one: What if, by raising the minimum wage to a living wage standard, you then discourage employers from hiring low-wage employees, since the employers believe that these low-wage employees aren't worth the extra wages the law requires them to pay? That is, the employer judges that the workers are worth bringing on the payroll at, say, $8 an hour but not $15 an hour. If this is the case, then establishing a living wage standard ends up hurting these very low-wage workers that the measure is trying to help, by increasing the likelihood that they will be unemployed.

This is often treated as a classic case of the so-called "law of unintended consequences" in economic policy—doing harm while trying to do good. However, until we conduct analytic work on the question, we don't really know whether the unintended consequence will actually result, or, even if the unintended consequence does result, whether its effects are significant or insignificant. A lot of my own work on establishing living wage statutes at the level of cities has been about trying to gauge the relative magnitudes of the "intended effects" of living wage laws—helping to raise living standards for low-wage workers and their families—versus the unintended effect of increasing unemployment among the low-wage workers. The answer I found consistently was that the intended consequences dominated the unintended consequences— that workers do experience at least modestly improved living standards through living wage measures, while the negative employment effects turn out to be mostly negligible or nonexistent. My findings were in line with the broader research literature on the impact of minimum wage laws since the mid-1990s, which was well summarized by the Harvard economist Richard Freeman: "The debate is over whether modest minimum wage increases have 'no' employment effect, modest positive effects, or small negative effects. It is not about whether or not there are large negative effects." But to get to this point in the consideration of living wage laws requires economists to deal with the issue in terms of both the moral questions at hand and the objective analysis of impacts— that is, the intended versus the unintended consequences.

For many years now, you have been developing what we might label the vision of a Green Economy and have, in fact, recently produced commissioned studies on Green economics for the States of Washington, New York, Colorado, and elsewhere. Can you talk a little bit about the Green Economy and its importance in the Anthropocene epoch?

To date, my focus within the broad rubric of Green economics has been fairly narrow, on defining a viable global path to stabilizing the climate. I haven't devoted serious research attention to related ecological issues around planetary boundaries, such as biodiversity loss as well as air and water pollution. I have been concentrating on the climate crisis for the simple reason that it is the matter of greatest urgency.

In terms of climate change and Green economics, my basic concern is as follows. The Intergovernmental Panel on Climate Change (IPCC) estimates that to achieve the 1.5 degrees maximum global mean temperature increase target as of 2100, global net carbon dioxide (CO_2) emissions will have to fall by about 45 percent as of 2030 and reach net zero emissions by 2050. As such, by my definition, the core of what has become known as a Green New Deal is to advance a global project to hit these IPCC targets, and to accomplish this in a way that also expands decent job opportunities and raises mass living standards for working people and the poor throughout the world. It is that simple.

In fact, purely as an analytic proposition and policy challenge—independent of the myriad of political and economic forces arrayed around these matters—it is entirely realistic to allow that global CO_2 emissions can be driven to net zero by 2050. By my higher-end estimate, it will require an average level of investment spending throughout the global economy of about 2.5 percent of global GDP per year, focused in two areas: (1) dramatically improving energy efficiency standards in the stock of buildings, automobiles and public transportation systems, and industrial production processes; and (2) equally dramatically expanding the supply of clean renewable energy sources—primarily solar and wind power—available at competitive prices relative to fossil fuels and nuclear power to all sectors and in all regions of the globe. These investments will also need to be complemented in other areas, the most important of which is to stop deforestation and support afforestation. This means, first of all, supporting the communities that live and work in and around the rainforests, so that they can earn good livings through undertaking the critical work of protecting the forests from land-clearance "developers." Meanwhile, the entire global fossil fuel industry will have to be put out of business over the next thirty years, in order for us to have a chance of hitting the emissions reduction targets.

A major area of my research on this project has been about its impact on employment opportunities and communities. The idea that building a green economy should be a source of job creation should be intuitive, even though it is frequently portrayed as exactly the opposite—as a job killer. This is because building the green economy necessarily entails building—it means large-scale new investments to dramatically raise energy efficiency standards and equally dramatically expand the renewable energy supply. Spending money on virtually anything will create jobs. The only relevant question should then be how many jobs get created through building a green economy, and correspondingly, how many jobs will be lost through the contraction and eventual dissolution of the fossil fuel infrastructure. In fact, my research with co-authors finds that countries at all levels of development will experience significant gains in job creation through clean energy investments relative to maintaining their existing fossil fuel infrastructure. Research that we have conducted has found that this relationship holds in all of the eleven countries we have considered, including the US, China, India, Indonesia, Germany, Brazil, South Africa, South Korea, Spain, Greece, and Puerto Rico. It is also true at the level of individual states within the US.

At the same time, workers and communities throughout the world whose livelihoods depend on people consuming oil, coal, and natural gas will lose out in the clean energy transition. So another area of my research focuses on how to ensure a just transition for these workers and communities that will be negatively impacted by the demise of the fossil fuel industry. It is only a modest exaggeration to say that the fate of the planet depends on whether we can put in place just transition policies for these workers and communities. Without such adjustment assistance programs operating at a major scale, the workers and communities facing retrenchment from the clean energy investment project will, predictably and understandably, fight to defend their communities and livelihoods. This in turn will create unacceptable delays in proceeding with effective climate stabilization policies.

One final major part of my research on the Green economy/Green New Deal is on the costs of mounting this project. As I note above, it will cost upwards of 2.5 percent of global GDP per year every year for thirty years to hit the IPCC emissions reduction target of zero net emissions by 2050. At

the same time, it is important to emphasize that this clean energy investment project, the centerpiece of the Green New Deal, will, over time, pay for
itself in full. This is true even under strictly conventional, narrowly focused
cost calculations, which put aside, among other things, the rather significant benefit of contributing towards staving off an ecological catastrophe.

A global clean energy investment project will save money over time
because it will deliver lower energy costs for energy consumers in all
regions of the world. This results because raising energy efficiency standards means that, by definition, consumers will spend less for a given
amount of energy services, such as being able to travel 100 miles on a
gallon of gasoline with a high-efficiency hybrid plug-in vehicle as opposed
to 25 miles per gallon with the average car on US roads today. Moreover,
the costs of supplying energy through solar and wind power, as well as
geothermal and hydro, are now, on average, roughly equal to or lower than
those for fossil fuels and nuclear energy. As such, the initial upfront investment outlays can be repaid over time through the cost savings that will be
forthcoming. This means that perhaps the most critical policy issues for
mounting a successful global Green New Deal are around financing.

*An alternative to the proposed Green New Deal scheme for rescuing the
planet from the catastrophic effects of global warming is the transition to a
new economy beyond waste and continuous growth. This line of thinking
has coalesced as a "degrowth" movement. In your view, is degrowth realistic or even desirable?*

My short answer is no. But, before explaining why, I want to first make
clear that I have lots of respect for most of the researchers and activists
who advocate degrowth. I share virtually all their values and concerns.
To be more specific, I agree that uncontrolled economic growth produces
serious environmental damage along with increases in the supply of
goods and services that households, businesses, and governments
consume. I also agree that a significant share of what is produced and
consumed in the current global capitalist economy is wasteful, especially much, if not most, of what high-income people throughout the
world consume. It is also obvious that growth per se as an economic
category makes no reference to the distribution of the costs and benefits
of an expanding economy. As for gross domestic product as a statistical
construct aiming to measure economic growth, there is no disputing

that it fails to account for the production of environmental "bads" as well as consumer goods. GDP also does not account for unpaid labor, most of which is performed by women. GDP per capita also tells us nothing about the distribution of income or wealth.

Recognizing all of these areas of agreement, it is still the case, in my view, that on the specific issue of climate change, degrowth does not provide anything resembling a viable stabilization framework. Consider some very simple arithmetic. Following the IPCC, we know that global CO_2 emissions need to fall from its current level of 33 billion tons to zero within thirty years. Now assume that, following a degrowth agenda as an emissions reduction program, global GDP contracts by 10 percent over the next thirty years. That would entail a reduction of global GDP four times larger than what we experienced over the 2007–09 financial crisis and Great Recession. In terms of CO_2 emissions, the net effect of this 10 percent GDP contraction, considered on its own, would be to push emissions down by precisely 10 percent—that is, from 33 billion to 30 billion tons. The global economy would still have not come close to bringing emissions down to zero, despite having manufactured the equivalent of a Great Depression in the effort to achieve this. Moreover, any global GDP contraction would result in huge job losses and declines in living standards for working people and the poor. Global unemployment rose by over 30 million during the Great Recession. I have not seen any degrowth advocate present a convincing argument as to how we could avoid a severe rise in mass unemployment if GDP were to fall twice as much as during 2007–09.

Clearly then, even under a degrowth scenario, the overwhelming factor pushing emissions down will not be a contraction of overall GDP but massive growth in energy efficiency and clean renewable energy investments (which, for accounting purposes, will contribute towards increasing GDP) along with similarly dramatic cuts in oil, coal, and natural gas production and consumption (which will register as reducing GDP). In other words, the global fossil industry will have to "degrow" to zero by 2050 while the clean energy industry massively expands.

Are you optimistic about our ability to tackle global warming before civilized life as we know it comes to an end?

Here, I revert to Gramsci's great aphorism: "Pessimism of the mind; optimism of the will."

*Another issue which you have tackled extensively from a policy standpoint
is that of introducing a universal health care program for the only advanced
Western country in the world without one. How did you get involved in
such a project, and how likely is it that the United States will adopt a
universal health care program in our lifetime?*

My work around the economics of single-payer health care systems in
the United States is one case of me having been recruited into the work
by political activists. This was in 2017, and the activists doing the recruit-
ing were RoseAnn DeMoro and Michael Lighty, at the time, the executive director and policy director of the California Nurses Association/
National Nurses United. The California Nurses Association/National
Nurses United at the time, under the leadership of RoseAnn, was the
most creative and militant labor organization in the US. So when they
asked me to take on this project, I had no option other than to say yes.
That said, until RoseAnn and Michael contacted me about doing a study
for a single-payer bill they were sponsoring in California, I had never
considered the topic in any serious way. Once my co-authors and I did
this study for California in May 2017, we were then recruited, again by
RoseAnn and Michael, but now also by Bernie Sanders, into studying
the 2017 Sanders proposal for a national Medicare for All health care
system. We finished that study in November 2018. I continue to do work
in this area, most recently at the request of Congresswoman Pramila
Jayapal, who introduced a bill into the US House of Representatives in
2019.

Our studies have basically amounted to a review and synthesis of the
existing body of research on a range of specific topics. One such topic is:
how much will demand for health care services likely go up if we eliminate all direct cost-sharing burdens for individuals—no premiums,
deductibles, or copayments? Another is: how large would be the savings
resulting from the dramatic simplification of all the administrative functions of health care delivery as well as the elimination of profits from
private health insurers? A third is: why is it that US health care consumers spend roughly twice as much for a range of the most common
prescription drugs relative to people in all other high-income economies? And the big question that hangs over all these previous ones: how
is it that, under the present US health care system, we spend roughly
twice as much per person as is spent in other high-income countries,

but that these other countries—all of which guarantee universal coverage—produce superior health outcomes on average?

It is well-established that the most basic cause of this poor US performance is inadequate access to good-quality care. As of 2018, roughly 9 percent of the US population, 28 million people, are uninsured. Another 26 percent, 86 million people, are underinsured—that is, they have insurance but are unable to access medical care because their deductibles or copays are prohibitively high. A large share of the remaining 65 percent of the population who are adequately insured still face high costs as well as anxiety over whether they could manage financially when they face any serious health issue.

Facing this reality about the present US health care system, the case for a single-payer system pretty much writes itself. What our research has concluded, most fundamentally, is that a single-payer system for the US, roughly comparable to the system in, say, Canada or France, is capable of delivering good-quality care for all US residents while still saving roughly 10 percent in overall costs relative to our existing system. Our findings are broadly consistent with a range of other recent studies, as shown in a 2020 meta-analysis of twenty-one such research projects, conducted by Jim Kahn of the University of California, San Francisco, and his co-authors.[1]

How likely is it that universal health care will become a reality in the US anytime soon? That is hard to say. If you asked me that question in, say, 2000, when RoseAnn DeMoro was in the early stages of leading the campaign for single-payer health care from her position with National Nurses United, one would have to conclude that it was an outlandish pipedream. The issue barely registered in any mainstream political circles. But due to the efforts of the nurses' union and many other progressive groups, as well as Bernie Sanders' principled and effective advocacy of the measure during his two presidential campaigns in 2016 and 2020, Medicare for All is now a serious topic of discussion in mainstream US circles. For example, in the 2020 Democratic Party primary season, all the candidates had to somehow grapple with Medicare for All. It was a primary focus of the entire Democratic Party debate, even

1   James G. Kahn et al., "Projected Costs of Single-Payer Healthcare Financing in the United States: A Systematic Review of Economic Analyses," *PLOS Medicine*, January 15, 2020.

while several of the candidates were committed to obfuscating the truth, taking their talking points directly from the propagandists employed by the private health insurance and pharmaceutical companies.

Which brings up an obvious but fundamental point: Of course, we still have the private health insurance companies and pharmaceutical companies to contend with. They have hundreds of billions of dollars in profits to lose through the transition to a single-payer system. It is highly cost-effective for them to keep most of the Washington political class in their pockets and to spew out propaganda about the evils of a single-payer system. How will that dynamic all play out in the coming years? That is anybody's guess. Again, it is useful to revert to Gramsci: "Pessimism of the mind; optimism of the will."

Do you have a vision of your future research agenda?

If I had to choose one big topic on which I hope to make some advances in the coming years, that would be on the economics of the Green New Deal. If we believe climate science, as represented by the Intergovernmental Panel on Climate Change, we then are facing a truly existential crisis with climate change. We have maybe thirty years to fundamentally change the trajectory of economic activity on a global scale to bring greenhouse gas emissions to zero. Accomplishing this task entails an enormous range of analytic and policy-related challenges. This is so, even if, as I said above, in my view, the basics of a global Green New Deal are simple—that is, invest about 2.5 percent of global GDP per year in dramatically improving energy efficiency and expanding renewable energy capacity, while also putting the global fossil fuel industry out of business. But within that simple framework are lurking hundreds of more detailed questions that need to be answered as carefully as possible. The economic questions involve, among other areas, macroeconomics, industrial policy, finance, and labor market issues at their core, all areas in which I have worked for many years. A critical factor for me is to be able to demonstrate unambiguously how climate stabilization is fully consistent with expanding decent work opportunities, raising mass living standards, and fighting poverty in all regions of the world. Considered in this way, the Green New Deal can serve equally as a viable macroeconomic framework for fighting austerity and supplanting neoliberalism. If my future research succeeds in making some contributions along these lines, I will have considered those efforts as time well spent.

Responses on the COVID-19 Pandemic

How would you evaluate the ways different countries or regions have responded to the COVID-19 crisis, both in terms of public health interventions and economic policies?

I will focus first on the US, my own country, in comparison with some other countries. The response of the late and thoroughly unlamented Trump administration to the COVID-19 pandemic was nothing short of disastrous. Let's begin with figures on lives that were needlessly lost in the US due to Trump's toxic combination of incompetence, indifference, hostility to science, and racism. As of the end of December 2020, US deaths from COVID had reached 332,000, nearly six times more than the total US death toll from fighting in Vietnam, and approaching the 407,000 total deaths fighting World War II. We will certainly exceed the World War II death toll before the virus has been brought under control through vaccinating the population.

This level of US deaths from COVID amounts to 1,012 per 1 million people. By comparison, Canada's death rate as of the same end of December date was well less than half that of the US, at 402 deaths per million, even while Canada itself was also a relatively poor performer. Germany's death rate, at 372 per million, was below Canada's and 63 percent lower than the US, but Germany was also a relatively poor performer. Among the strong performers, the death rates at the end of December 2020 were 36 per million in Australia, 25 per million in Japan, 17 per million in South Korea, and 3 per million in China, even though the virus first emerged in China. If the US had managed the COVID pandemic at the level of, say, Australia, fewer than 12,000 people would have died as of the end of December 2020—as opposed to 332,000.

Vietnam was the most extraordinary case during the COVID pandemic. At the end of December 2020, it had experienced a total of 35 deaths in a country of 95 million people, which amounts to a death rate of 0.4 per million. This is for a country in which the average per capita income is about 3 percent of that in the US. It is also a country, of course, that US imperialists tried to destroy fifty years ago. If the US had handled COVID at Vietnam's level of competence just between March and December 2020, then just 131 people would have died in the US rather than 332,000.

Within the US, it is not surprising that the impact of COVID varied hugely based on race and class. Thus, the death rate for African Americans was 68 percent higher than that for whites, and the death rate for Hispanics was 30 percent higher than the rate for whites. Infection rates were similarly skewed according to race. By income measures, again not surprisingly, roughly half of all lower-income people experienced trouble paying bills and 35 percent were forced to rely on food banks to avoid going hungry during the pandemic. These figures were still high for middle-income people, with 12 percent of even middle-income families relying on food banks to keep themselves going. These figures correspond with the fact that, during the peak of the pandemic, only 7 percent of full-time workers in the lowest 25 percent of earners were able to work remotely in their main job, while 56 percent of those in the highest 25 percent of earners were able to work from home. Since the intersection between low-income workers and Black, Hispanic, and other people of color is high, the pandemic put these communities at much greater risk.

In terms of managing the pandemic-induced economic collapse, the massive $2 trillion stimulus program—10 percent of US GDP—that Congress passed and Trump signed in March 2020, the Coronavirus Aid, Relief, and Economic Security (CARES) Act did provide substantial support for unemployed workers. Roughly 73 million people—44 percent of the entire US labor force—filed initial unemployment claims between mid-March and mid-December. Most of them received $600 per week in supplemental support through the end of July, until Trump and the Senate Republicans chose to kill off this program. While it was available, it more than doubled the support most unemployed workers would have otherwise received to get through the crisis.

The CARES Act did also deliver huge bailouts for big corporations and Wall Street. Adding everything up, it was clear even at the time of passage that the CARES Act was not close to meeting the magnitude of the oncoming crisis. Among other features, it provided only minimal support for hospitals on the front lines fighting the pandemic, and even less support for state and local governments. In May 2020, the excellent

Upjohn Institute economist Timothy Bartik estimated that state and local governments were staring at upwards of $900 billion in budget shortfalls through the end of 2021, equal to an average of about 20 percent of their entire budgets.

As of this writing at the end of December 2020, a second, much more modest $900 billion recovery program (4.4 percent of GDP) has just passed and was reluctantly signed into law by the lame duck President Trump. But the only way that the Republicans would accept even this deal was if state and local governments would receive zero support through the measure. In its current ideological concoction combining neoliberalism and neofascism, the Republican party has no interest in supporting publicly financed health care and education. As a result, unless things change immediately under the incoming Biden administration, we will soon see in 2021 mass layoffs of nurses, teachers, firefighters, school custodians, along with office support and service workers at schools and hospitals. These budget cuts will increase the difficulties we face in digging out of the COVID slump in 2021, and even this assumes that the population vaccination program ends up being far more effective under Biden than it has been initially under Trump.

The policy failures by the US federal government—mainly here, again, the Republican-controlled Senate along with the Trump White House—do not end here. Consider, for example, the fate of the Paycheck Guarantee Act, which had been proposed in April 2020 by Congresswoman Pramila Jayapal of Washington, the leader of the House Progressive Caucus. Under Jayapal's proposal, the federal government would have provided grants to all private- and public-sector employers of all sizes to enable them to maintain their operations and keep all of their workers on payroll, despite the falloff in revenues they were about to experience from the pandemic and lockdown. Through this program, the US would not have experienced significant spikes in the unemployment rate in 2020. Workers would also not have lost their employer-based health care coverage. This plan was similar in design and scope to policies that were in place in several European economies, including Germany, the UK, Denmark, and France.

The impact of the failure of the US to pass the Jayapal proposal quickly became evident. Considering the available data by country through November 2020, US unemployment averaged 9.9 percent, while the rates for countries that had Jayapal-type programs in place included the UK at 4.0 percent, Germany at 4.4 percent, Denmark at 5.8 percent, and France with the highest rate, at 7.0 percent.[2] For the US economy, the difference between having an unemployment rate of 9.9 percent versus, for example, the 5.8 percent rate in Denmark translates into 6.5 million more people without work—more people than the entire populations of Los Angeles and Chicago combined. In addition, a minimum of 15 million people—including unemployed workers and their family members—lost their employer-sponsored health insurance as US unemployment rose.

Certainly, on average, Europe has handled the unemployment crisis resulting from the COVID pandemic much better than the US. But we also need to resist making sweeping endorsements of recent policies and actions in Europe. In terms of managing the COVID crisis, the UK, France, Italy, Spain, and even Sweden have death rates comparable to that in the US. Between April and October 2020, unemployment averaged 16.1 percent in Spain under a Socialist government, and 8.7 percent under the Social Democrats in Sweden.

In fact, European policy-makers have been undermining their welfare state policies for forty years now, since the ascendance of neoliberalism, beginning with the election of Margaret Thatcher in the UK in 1979. It is a valuable exercise for us to envision what my late, great professor Robert Heilbroner used to call "slightly imaginary Sweden." But in doing so, we need to recognize that egalitarian policies in Sweden today bear only a weak resemblance to the robust welfare state that operated forty years ago.

In terms of broader implications and lessons, it is clear that the countries that performed poorly in controlling COVID need to start learning some basics of public health policy from Australia, Japan, South Korea, China, and—in a great historic irony—maybe especially Vietnam. For the US, step one would be to establish Medicare for All, so that every US resident has access to good-quality health care without having to fear financial ruin should they get sick with COVID or anything else.

Creating something resembling a minimally effective public health system through Medicare for All would, in turn, enable us in the US to

---

2 Unemployment figures are from the OECD: data.oecd.org/unemp/unemploy-ment-rate.htm, accessed 12/30/20.

advance a sustainable long-term recovery on the foundation of a Green New Deal. It is important to also recognize here some critical ways in which the climate crisis and the COVID pandemic intersect. First, a prime underlying cause of the COVID outbreak, as well as other recent epidemics, including Ebola, West Nile, and HIV, has been the destruction of animal habitats through deforestation and related human encroachments, as well as the disruption of the remaining habitats through the increasing frequency and severity of heat waves, droughts, and floods. It is also likely that people who are exposed to dangerous levels of air pollution will face significantly more severe health consequences than those who have been breathing cleaner air. A study done on SARS, a virus closely related to COVID, found that people who breathed dirtier air were about twice as likely to die from infection.[3]

To conclude then, both the public health and economic consequences of the COVID-19 pandemic only reinforces the point at which I ended the pre-COVID parts of this discussion: that is, by emphasizing the centrality of advancing a Green New Deal as the core project for building a global economy on foundations of equality, democracy, rising mass living standards, and ecological sanity. These issues will certainly remain a focus of my own work moving forward.

Representative Publications and Influences

Publications:

Robert Pollin (1997). "Financial Intermediation and the Variability of the Saving Constraint," in R. Pollin ed., *The Macroeconomics of Saving, Finance and Investment*, University of Michigan Press, 309 – 365.

Robert Pollin (2003). *Contours of Descent: U.S. Economic Fractures and the Landscape of Global Austerity*, Verso.

Robert Pollin, Jeannette Wicks-Lim, Mark Brenner, and Stephanie Luce (2008). *A Measure of Fairness: The Economics of Living Wages and Minimum Wages in the United States*, Cornell University Press.

Noam Chomsky and Robert Pollin (2020). *Climate Crisis and the Global Green New Deal: The Political Economy of Saving the Planet*, Verso.

---

3   Full references on these points are in Noam Chomsky and Robert Pollin, *Climate Crisis and the Global Green New Deal*, London and New York: Verso, 2020, 141–4.

People who have been influential: Paul Sweezy, Harry Magdoff, Robert Heilbroner, David Gordon, Anwar Shaikh, Noam Chomsky, Hyman Minsky, Keith Griffin, Aziz Khan, Milton Friedman, Joseph Schumpeter, Jerry Epstein

Literature that has been influential:

Robert Heilbroner (1980). *Marxism: For And Against,* Norton.

Harry Magdoff and Paul Sweezy (1987). *Stagnation and the Financial Explosion.* Monthly Review Press.

Hyman Minsky (1982). *Can "It" Happen Again? Essays on Instability and Finance.* M.E. Sharpe.

Keith Griffin and Jeffrey James (1981). *Transition to Egalitarian Development,* Palgrave Macmillan.

David Card and Alan Krueger (1995). *Myth and Measurement: The New Economics of the Minimum Wage,* Princeton University Press.

Malcolm Sawyer

Malcolm Sawyer is Emeritus Professor of Economics, University of Leeds, UK. He has been the Principal Investigator of the very large five-year EU-funded project Financialisation, Economy, Society and Sustainable Development (FESSUD), and was Managing Editor of the *International Review of Applied Economics*. Sawyer has written dozens of articles and many books on issues of monetary and fiscal policy and financial markets, including *Finance and the Macroeconomics of Environmental Policies* (with P. Arestis, 2015), *Economic and Monetary Union Macroeconomic Policies* (with P. Arestis, 2013), and *The Euro Crisis* (2012).

You studied mathematics at Oxford but went on to pursue a graduate degree in economics at the London School of Economics (LSE). Was this a natural transition for you, from mathematics to economics, or did your interest in economics develop as a result of other factors, including perhaps your political interests or commitments at the time?

I would not describe it as a "natural transition," though it was a relatively easy one to make in that there was a push at the time to up the mathematical training of economists. It was at a time when student grants to pursue university education in the UK were relatively (at least in hindsight) well-funded, including postgraduate study, with financial support from a government funding agency available for mathematics graduates to transfer into economics. I did not at the time envisage the study of economics as being a "natural progression" from mathematics, and did not see economics as an academic discipline where my mathematics background would give me some form of comparative advantage (though my graduate studies at the LSE were much more straightforward for me than for my nonmathematical colleagues). I was (and continue to be) focused on the key ideas, and continue to think that mathematics can sometimes enable some of the implications of an idea and analysis to be worked through, but it does not itself provide the original ideas and insights. I find it hard to think of any area of enquiry within economics where mathematics has changed the ways in which the economy is analyzed.

My interests in economics and politics had developed well before I went to university, though growing up in a small town there was no opportunity to study economics or politics at school. Indeed, looking back, I find it surprising that in a small, inward-looking, and socially conservative town I developed such interests! When I had secured a place to read mathematics at Oxford, I lacked the confidence and knowledge to move from mathematics to PPE (philosophy, politics, and economics). Fortunately, being a student at Oxford provided many opportunities to develop economic and political interests.

Much of economics in the twentieth century could be framed in terms of a clash between the foundational ideas of Keynes versus Hayek. Whose influence dominated the intellectual climate at LSE when you were there as a student?

I was a student at the LSE from October 1966 to July 1968. This was the time of the student protest movements, which at the LSE started in January 1967 with protests against the appointment of Walter Adams as the director, based on his role as principal of University College of Rhodesia and Nyasaland, and collaboration with the white Smith regime, which had made its unilateral declaration of independence (UDI) from the UK in 1965. It culminated in sit-ins and lockouts. The more general climate was one of rebellion among students—linked with issues of student power and involvement, alongside opposition to the Vietnam War and anti-apartheid. There was little if any "spill-over" into serious questioning of the economics or other courses within the student body.

The intellectual climate with regard to the teaching of economics was rather close to the "neoclassical synthesis" based on a Keynesian (IS/LM) macroeconomics and neoclassical microeconomics. There was a general flavor of "positive economics" (as reflected in the title of the then most widely-used introductory text in the UK, Lipsey's *Introduction to Positive Economics,* which had been developed from Lipsey's first year lectures at the LSE) with econometric hypothesis testing. There were dashes of dissent and some opportunity, for example, to take lectures in Marxian economics, but that was very limited and did not form any part of the degree program.

The general political environment was much more interventionist than would now be contemplated. In the UK, the Labour government elected in October 1964 had introduced an indicative National Plan (which did not last long), with thoughts of mimicking French success; prices and incomes policy to address the emerging problem of inflation were the order of the day—under both a Conservative government in the early 1960s and then a Labour government from 1964 to 1970. There were the beginnings of the neoliberal "revival": the influence of the Mont Pelerin Society was beginning to assert itself—coming through the publications of the Institute of Economic Affairs in the UK, and the beginnings of monetarism. However, Hayek and more generally Austrian economists, did not feature at all, as has continued to be the case in most economics programs. The microeconomics was the static equilibrium optimization of neoclassical economics, and not the Austrian entrepreneurial discovery approach under fundamental uncertainty. The representatives of the "free marketers" would be much more Chicago than Austrian, and Friedman and Stigler (*The Theory of Price*) featured heavily on the reading list. I suspect that I would have found a Hayekian analysis rather more interesting than the sterility of the Chicago one!

Your own work has been clearly influenced by Keynesian tenets. Why was Keynes appealing to you, and not Hayek?

The trite answer could be that I was not exposed to Hayek and other Austrian economists, for example, von Mises. Austrian economic analysis has generally received very little attention in economics programs, and that was the case during my own studies. Prior to my formal study of economics, much of my reading had been in relatively popular books such as those by Jan Pen (*Modern Economics*), and later Galbraith (*New Industrial State*), and Baran and Sweezy (*Monopoly Capitalism*). Initially, those written from a broadly Keynesian perspective had an appeal—they made sense to me, and they chimed with my naïve feelings for positive government action to ensure something approaching full employment and to enhance growth (slow economic growth being perceived as a major UK failing at the time).

How, if at all, did Marx exert influence on you in the early stages of your career as an academic economist? How would you describe ways in which Marx may still be a significant influence on your thinking and research work?

The influence of Marx on my work would be a rather indirect one, coming more from reading works by writers in the Marxian tradition than a detailed study of Marx. An early and notable example would be Baran and Sweezy's *Monopoly Capital*. A more immediate influence came from working with Sam Aaronovitch (leading to our book, *Big Business*, published in 1975), which focused on the rising levels of industrial concentration, the processes of concentration, and centralization with high levels of mergers and acquisitions.

What do you consider to be the main contributions of Michał Kalecki? What are the significant ways in which Kalecki's ideas have influenced your own work?

At one level, Kalecki's contributions as far as capitalist economies are concerned come from his macroeconomic analysis with the principle of effective demand, emphasis on the cyclical and unemployment-prone nature of capitalism, the significance of investment, and the general concept of degree of monopoly. Examples are his writings on the potential use of fiscal policy to secure full employment, alongside his warnings on the political and social obstacles to the implementation of such policies. These and other ideas resonate with me, and form the underlying basis of much that I write on fiscal policy, austerity, and more generally macroeconomics. The immediate way in which Kalecki's work strongly influences my own relates to fiscal policy and its potential—it is difficult to improve on the insights in his writings in 1943–44 on the potential for fiscal policy, and on the political and social constraints on the achievement of full employment through such policies. Other ways in which there is a strong influence come through ideas such as differential propensities to spend and to save—in Kalecki out of wages and profits, and now extended to other income categorizations, and the inherently cyclical nature of capitalism. Setting out the sectoral balance sheet (as between private sector, government, and foreign sector, for example) has influenced many post-Keynesians and is invaluable for thinking about surpluses and deficits. A full evaluation of Kalecki's contributions would also have to include his writings on socialist planning and on developing economies. At another level I am attracted by what I would see as his interplay between empirical observations and analysis, and the avoidance of the type of theorizing that dominates mainstream economics.

You have left an indelible mark on the evolution of scientific journals and scholarly publications in economics, having founded the International Review of Applied Economics *and serving as series editor of* New Directions in Modern Economics, *and co-editor of the annual publications of* International Papers in Political Economy. *Can you talk about this experience? How, in your view, have these venues exerted an impact on the field of economics and perhaps also on policy-making?*

I would like to regard each of the publications that you mentioned as providing platforms for a wide range of predominantly heterodox economists to develop and promote their ideas. But also platforms where there could be engagement with mainstream economists in areas of common interests (though not common mode of analysis). As most, if not all, heterodox economists have found, however good and solid their work is, there is a lack of interest and willingness on the part of mainstream economists to engage with them on their work.

Another major institutional commitment of yours has been to direct the European Commission project, FESSUD—Financialisation, Economy, Society and Sustainable Development. FESSUD was supported by the European Commission in the aftermath of the 2007–09 global financial crisis and Great Recession. In designing the FESSUD project, what did you and your collaborators see as the major failings of orthodox thinking on the operations of financial markets and institutions? What do you see as the major contributions of FESSUD in creating a more viable literature on macro finance issues? In what ways can the major findings from the FESSUD project be used to prevent a recurrence of the financial crisis? What do you see as the critical areas of research that need much more attention in this area in the wake of FESSUD?

The FESSUD project brought together researchers from fifteen partner institutions (one of which was an NGO), largely European. Although centered in economics, it was overtly interdisciplinary and pluralistic, and political scientists, sociologists, and human geographers were centrally involved.

The FESSUD project in its construction and design drew heavily on existing relatively informal networks in which my colleagues at Leeds and myself had been involved in—networks which could be broadly described as post-Keynesian, Kaleckian, and Marxian, and whose members interacted at a regular series of international conferences and workshops. We did not explicitly discuss or set out the faults with orthodox thinking, and no doubt colleagues in the FESSUD project would bring a range of critiques. Indeed, it was necessary (through pressures from funders and others) to show that we were taking mainstream economics seriously, through a series of papers within the FESSUD project that served to expose many of the weaknesses of the mainstream approaches, particularly in the areas of finance and macroeconomics.

Personally, I would highlight three avenues of critique of mainstream economics and finance. The first would be the construction of a macroeconomics (such as the "new consensus macroeconomics") that does not incorporate money and its endogenous creation by banks; there is the general neglect of finance and credit, thereby limiting or even excluding any understanding of the roles of the banks and financial sector in the generation of financial crises. The second would be its foundations in methodological individualism with utility optimization under circumstances of risk, thereby ignoring fundamental uncertainty and positing the centrality of equilibrium analysis. This is a major blockage to understanding and explaining financial crisis. The third is the underlying efficiency assumptions, notably in the areas of finance, so that expansion of the financial sector enhances efficiency and growth, and that the rewards to the financial sector are a reflection of productivity rather than rent.

The contributions of FESSUD cannot be easily summarized and there is no single headline advance. I would, though, highlight the breadth of coverage, reflected in the title, which includes economy, society and sustainable development, and reflecting the ideas of the pervasiveness of finance and financialization. Amongst its contributions I would point to:

- The mapping of the processes of financialization in the period since circa 1980
- Adding to our understanding and explanations of the global financial crises of 2007–09
- The alternative ways to regulate the financial sector
- Exploring what may be termed "financialization of the everyday," particularly in terms of household debt, financial inclusion and exclusion through to expansion of finance into pension provision, etc.
- Consequences of financialization for the environment and sustainability
- The development of macroeconomic policies particularly with regard to the euro area

You wrote several papers during the outbreak of the economic crisis, criticizing both the architecture of the single currency union as well as the actual policies of the EU authorities in addressing the crisis. In what ways do you think that the euro as a currency union contributed to the financial crisis? Do you think that the euro can play a constructive role in promoting an egalitarian full-employment agenda in Europe? What would you consider as possible ways to restructure the currency union? If you think it should be abandoned altogether, what would you propose as a better alternative?

In general, I would not view the existence of the euro currency union as a direct cause of the financial crisis, though its construction may well have limited any policy responses in the buildup to the financial crisis and constrained policy reactions to the crisis itself. Although most attention on the generation of the financial crisis has been given to the American subprime crisis and its contagion effects, there were banking crises in some member states of the euro area (Ireland and then later Spain) and in the UK (and also Iceland). The Irish and Spanish banking crises had been preceded by unsustainable credit and property price booms. It could be argued that the construction of the euro area and the role of the European Central Bank, with its sole policy objective of price stability, precluded any interventions to address those credit booms and its inability to gear its policies to the needs of individual countries. Further, the reliance on the policy instrument of interest rates applicable across the currency area precluded a differentiated policy approach directed at countries where credit and property prices were booming. However, previous experience and also the concurrent experience of the UK and its property price boom does not suggest that policy responses to dampen down the credit boom would have been taken even if it had been possible to do so.

There were signs of difficulties within the euro area that had emerged and had, to some degree, been recognized before the financial crises—notably the widening current account imbalances with deficits in a number of countries (notably Greece and Portugal) having reached well over 10 percent of GDP. The current account deficits involved these countries' borrowing from abroad on an increasing scale, and as members of the Eurozone in effect borrowing in a foreign currency. Issues of the sustainability of such deficits and their tendency to grow were already rising. The financial crises and the onset of recession brought some of those issues to the fore—notably the implications of the borrowing that had been undertaken. The ways in which banks and financial institutions in countries such as Germany and France had lent to those in the Mediterranean countries—whether to individuals and corporations or to government (through purchase of government bonds)—played a considerable role in the "bailout" policies.

Do you think that the euro can play a constructive role in promoting an egalitarian full employment agenda in Europe?

At the present time and for the foreseeable future, the construction and promotion of anything close to an egalitarian full-employment agenda would come at the national level rather than the European level. The bulk of policies that could be thought relevant to such an agenda are in the hands of national governments—whether education, wage policies, employment, structure and level of tax, etc. Membership in the EU places limitations on the pursuit of such policies, whether directly through the policy agreements or indirectly—in the areas of tax, there is a requirement for a value-added tax, and the free movement of capital may serve to limit the rate of corporation tax (though that hasn't prevented countries engaging in a race-to-the-bottom mentality). The construction of the euro, including the Stability and Growth Pact, the Fiscal Compact, and the role of the European Central Bank, etc., have put in place policies that run counter to any egalitarian and full-employment program. The legal framework, embedding the policy agenda in European institutions, and the need for unanimity among nations to significantly change that agenda, all mitigate against significant change. The present arrangements for the euro area with the Fiscal Compact and attempts to secure a "balanced structural budget" position impose an austerity agenda. As I have argued elsewhere, the achievement of a balanced structural budget may often be impossible and pursuit of a balanced budget builds in an austerity agenda.

There are, of course, many political barriers to the development and adoption of an egalitarian full-employment agenda. Having a single currency poses economic issues but does not per se prevent the adoption of a full employment agenda—in the same manner that having a single currency within the US or China does not prevent such an agenda (though in those cases it is accompanied by a large role for central government and significant fiscal transfers between the constituent regions/states). The euro does, though, bring its own barriers—limits on fiscal policy, constraints on public investment, etc.

In sum, I find it difficult to view the euro as playing a constructive role in the promotion of an egalitarian full-employment agenda, and its present construction and policy arrangements play more of a destructive role. What could, though, be said is that the reconstruction of the euro project could be undertaken in ways that would not only foster a full-employment agenda, but would also aid the functioning of the euro area. But the possibilities of such a reconstruction are in my view close to zero.

What would you consider as possible ways to restructure the currency union? If you think it should be abandoned altogether, what would you propose as a better alternative?

The restructuring of the currency union requires (at a minimum) the redesign of fiscal and monetary policies. Countries must have the freedom to adopt fiscal policies that serve the interests of their citizens rather than having to worship at the altar of balanced budgets. It would require the reform of the mandate of the ECB (to include high levels of employment and financial stability in its objectives). It would require the development of significant fiscal transfers between the member countries.

For the relationships between countries within the EU, there are alternatives—including flexible exchange rates between (re-introduced) national currencies and "currency blocs" within a clearing union. The adoption of a more flexible exchange rate between member countries of the EU would avoid some of the difficulties of the currency union, including having to ensure a common inflation rate, and most notably not requiring a single central bank setting a single interest rate for the whole of the Eurozone. While a national central bank would be constrained in the degree to which it would be able to set an interest rate that diverged significantly from its neighbors, it would (if policy instruments developed) enable it to focus on financial stability in its own country.

There are feasible alternative exchange rate regimes that could offer some improvement over the single currency through their impact on policy regimes with regard to fiscal and monetary policies. The issue is not the availability of alternatives but whether there are the political forces and the opportunities to be able to do so. It may be a lack of imagination on my part, but the political and practical obstacles to the return to a set of interlinked national currencies seem so large as to rule out such a set of arrangements.

What is your overall assessment of the prospects for left political economy moving forward, in both Europe and the US, as well as globally? In what ways do you think left political economists have succeeded? In what ways would you like to see this community do better?

In Europe in general, I am rather pessimistic on the prospects for heterodox political economy. The general trend over, say, the last four decades has been, in my view, in the direction of decline in those prospects. This has not, of course, been a uniform trend and there have been occasions when prospects appear to be improving.

There has been a sharp decline in the number of economics departments where heterodox economists would have much chance of being appointed and where there is any serious teaching of heterodox economics—at most an optional course in post-Keynesian and/or Marxian economics may be offered. The training of the next generation of heterodox economists is severely restricted, and education in most economics departments barely mentions heterodox economics and economists. There is a general squeeze on pursuit of a heterodox research agenda—within economics, research is often judged in terms of whether it is published in "top" journals, which are predominantly mainstream journals with very limited access accorded to heterodox papers.

There have been the successes of building a community (or set of overlapping communities) of heterodox political economists, establishing journals, organizing conferences, and generally surviving in a hostile environment. In some areas coherent research agendas have been developed; two examples spring to mind—the analysis of endogenous money and credit creation, and the wage-led/profit-led framework, which are thoroughly analyzed, have important implications for the development of economic policies, and which receive empirical support. Yet these agendas have had minimal impact on economic policy or any recognition from mainstream economics.

If you were able to start your career all over again, what would you do differently, if anything?

Looking back, my "path" was mainly (entirely?) set by chance rather than calculation: the political atmosphere of the late 1960s, a number of times when job and other opportunities arose, meeting those who became close collaborators (notably, Sam Aaronovitch and Philip Arestis), and the directions in which my research took as a result, etc. In one sense, I would not act differently in that I would take opportunities as they arose, even if some of those that I took were later regretted, and of course not to know what the consequences would have been of those I declined. In another sense, I would have wished to have spent less time studying and teaching neoclassical economics, and less time puzzling over its weaknesses. I would have wished to spend more time developing heterodox economics and more time engaging with other social science disciplines.

Responses on the COVID-19 Pandemic

How would you evaluate the ways different countries or regions have responded to the COVID-19 crisis, both in terms of public health interventions and economic policies?

My answers focus heavily on the experiences of the pandemic in the UK. I write this in December 2020 when the second wave of infection, illness, and deaths is well underway and we are experiencing returns to forms of lockdown, limitations on who we meet with, etc., though with policies varying by region and nation and changing on a frequent, and often confusing, basis. Alongside these changing limitations on social and economic activities, there have been shifting fiscal policies providing financial support to some but not to others.

The UK government has at times been slow to acknowledge the seriousness of the pandemic and then to implement lockdown policies even after having received advice from its top level advisors in SAGE (the Scientific Advisory Group for Emergencies) and others, first during March and then again in October. There has been a strong tendency to resort to British exceptionalism, such as "we'll develop a world-beating track-and-trace system," only to find that the system developed was a failure.

The macroeconomic policy responses have often been characterized in terms of "do whatever is necessary" to provide financial support to families and businesses and to resource the health service. Thoughts of balanced budgets and debt reduction went out the window, at least temporarily, though at the time of writing there appear to be thoughts in government of future austerity in a drive to reduce the public debt. The large budget deficit has not involved any significant financing issues (since the Bank of England provided finance as required) nor any funding issues, and much of that can be ascribed to the large rise in private-sector household savings. The rise in household savings is not surprising during times when many retail outlets, services, hospitality, and entertainment were limited (and often closed).

The pandemic came at the end of a decade of austerity policies where expenditures on the health service, education, and other areas were driven by the agenda of reducing budget deficits rather than by an agenda of building up public services. Effects of the decade of austerity had left the National Health Service (NHS) with a lack of any spare capacity to cope with the pandemic.

In terms of dealing with the pandemic, a health service is on the front line, and in the UK case that's the National Health Service, which is (largely) free at the point of use, and where the vast majority of hospitals are publicly owned and operated. Many members of the present Conservative government have been long-standing advocates of privatization of parts of the health service, and the effects of a possible UK–USA trade deal following the UK's exit from the EU on private finance and provision in the health service is of major concern.

The combination of test and trace being largely contracted out to private companies has strong elements of developing a neoliberal agenda of privatization. There are two areas of supply related to the health service that have caused substantial problems and have related to the role of the private sector and the relationship between public and private. These are the provision of personal protective equipment (PPE) and the "track and test" system. The events in these two areas have highlighted many of the problems of the neoliberal market approach.

Throughout the first months of the coronavirus crisis, there was a great shortage of personal protective equipment. This was a major cause of concern, particularly in care homes. The shortages reflected the lack of preparedness for a pandemic. The particular areas of concern relate to poor contract arrangements, difficulties in monitoring, lack of relevant experience, and the close links of many of the companies to the Conservative Party, through which the contracts were awarded.

The privatized and often centralized test-and-trace operations, which often involved layers of subcontracting, undermined the established system for contact tracing run by local public health protection teams in the public sector. The failures of the privatized operations have led local authorities in many cases to revive public health contact testing. The test-and-trace systems have been a major source of difficulties in counteracting the coronavirus. The key difficulties can be identified as arising from chaotic and expensive privatization instead of relying on properly funded local expertise.

There was often the (false) dichotomy posed between health and the economy (treating the economy as some machine separate from human beings), though this was often posed by free marketers and those on the right of politics. The effects on economic activity were generally overstated by the focus on market output and GDP. There was a neglect of the health and social effects of the lockdown—the effects on mental health of prolonged isolation, lost schooling, etc.

Do you draw any general lessons from the COVID crisis about the most viable ways to advance an egalitarian economic project, focusing on this question in any way that you wish?

The inequalities and disparities from COVID-19 have reflected and reinforced many pre-existing inequalities between households, between ethnic groups, and between regions.

There have been significant disparities in illness and death rates. Areas of high deprivation suffered the highest death rates from COVID-19. The death rate has been higher for those in Black, Asian, and Minority Ethnic (BAME) groups than in white ethnic groups. Those who were able to work from home suffered little by way of income loss, and they tended to be in nonmanual, higher-paying jobs. In contrast, those in the lower parts of the earnings distribution (with the exception of key workers in health and social care) were likely to be in sectors shut down, though their earnings were to a considerable extent supported by the extensive furlough scheme.

There have undoubtedly been harmful effects on children's education, which will have long-term effects. These have fallen particularly on children in low-income households who are unlikely to have access to computers and to the internet (there was some half-hearted attempt to provide computers) and to receive home schooling (easier to provide by parents working from home).

The shortcomings of the welfare "safety net" were exposed, though these shortcomings had long been well-known: for example, low level of sickness benefit and delays in payment of universal credit. There were some modifications, though time limited; and it remains to be seen whether there will be any future improvements: my guess would be that there will not as an austerity mentality returns.

Does the experience of the COVID crisis shed any light on the way you think about economics as a discipline or, more specifically, the questions you might be pursuing in your own research?

It has not fundamentally changed the ways in which I think about economic analysis—the tools that I deployed precrisis I have applied in analyzing the crisis itself and in thinking about the world post-COVID.

The COVID crisis and responses to it have raised issues of what may be termed decision-making under fundamental uncertainty, and ways in which government and others may prepare. It can be readily recognized that dealing with COVID-19 was an exercise involving many dimensions of fundamental uncertainty ranging from the nature of the virus, rates and ways of infection, effects on health, etc., through to the ways in which individual behavior would respond. The UK government had prepared a 2019 National Security Risk Assessment, which was said to be a comprehensive planning document that sets out the risks facing the UK and what was needed to prepare for them. Yet despite an "influenza-type pandemic" being at the top of the list of concerns, there was a general lack of preparedness in areas such as availability of personal protective equipment and fiscal measures to support incomes and employment in face of shutdowns.

It will be relevant to further examine the fiscal responses of government to the pandemic and their effectiveness. The initial responses of (rightly) abandoning any attempt to maintain their own fiscal rules have continued, though with signs of reversion to "where's the money coming from?" and more worryingly the scale of the public debt (over 100 per cent relative to GDP) and the threats of austerity in an illusory search for budget surpluses to reduce the outstanding debt. The macroeconomic responses revealed a willingness to support the level of disposable income. There will be a need to examine the fiscal policy and monetary policy responses, which were not novel in themselves but novel in their scale and speed. It will be necessary to examine the specific financial support packages for their design and effectiveness. It will also be necessary to examine the usefulness of fiscal policy rules that are not sufficiently adept at responding to large shocks to economic activity.

Representative Publications and Influences

Publications:

Malcolm Sawyer (1985). *The economics of Michał Kalecki*. London: Macmillan.

Malcolm Sawyer (2018). "Approaching budget deficits, debts and money in a socially responsible manner" in P. Arestis and M. Sawyer (eds.), *Frontiers of Heterodox Macroeconomics*, Palgrave Macmillan. pp. 45–87.

Malcolm Sawyer (2022), *The Power of Finance: Financialization and the Real Economy*. Agenda Publishing.

People who have been influential: Michał Kalecki

Literature that has been influential:

Collected Works of Michał Kalecki, volumes I to VII (edited by Jerzy Osiatyński, published by Clarendon Press, Oxford 1990 to 1997).

Michał Kalecki (1938). The determinants of distribution of the national income. *Econometrica: Journal of the Econometric Society*, 97–112.

Michał Kalecki (1944). 'Three ways to full employment' in Oxford University Institute of Statistics, *The economics of full employment*, Oxford: Blackwell, reproduced in Collected Works of Michał Kalecki vol. I pp. 357–376.

Juliet Schor

Juliet Schor is Professor of Sociology at Boston College. Her research focuses on consumption, time use, and environmental sustainability. Schor is the author of many papers and widely read books, including *The Overworked American: The Unexpected Decline of Leisure* (1992), *The Overspent American: Why We Want What We Don't Need* (1998), *Born to Buy: The Commercialized Child and the New Consumer Culture* (2004), and *True Wealth: How and Why Millions of Americans Are Creating a Time-Rich, Ecologically Light, Small-Scale, High-Satisfaction Economy* (2011). She is a cofounder of the Center for a New American Dream (newdream.org), a national sustainability organization where she served on the board for more than fifteen years. Schor has received the American Sociological Association's award for Public Understanding of Sociology (2014), the 2011 Herman Daly Award from the US Society for Ecological Economics, and the Leontief Prize from the Global Development and Economics Institute at Tufts University (2016).

Can you tell me about your background and how you ended up going to the University of Massachusetts Amherst to pursue a PhD in economics?

I grew up in southwestern Pennsylvania, in a small town in the midst of coal mines and steel mills. My parents, New York Jews, were blacklisted in the 1950s and came to Pennsylvania to start a clinic for the Mineworkers' Union. So I was a "red diaper baby," but one who didn't know about their past until I was an adolescent. Nevertheless, I began reading Marx when I was young and got involved in political activity. In college, I studied economics and philosophy (what else would a young leftist study, after all!). There was no left-wing economics in my university. I reached out to the economists at UMass to come and speak, which got me very interested in their program. I left college early to start graduate school. However, I didn't see a PhD as necessarily a career decision at that point. Naively, I just felt I needed to learn more and felt the need to move on from undergraduate education. I wanted to go straight to UMass, but got heavy pressure from family and mentors to go to a conventional program. I started at the London School of Economics, but was dissatisfied. A year later, I matriculated at UMass.

What appealed to you most about left political economy?

Perhaps because I grew up in a working-class town (with a tiny professional and small business community) I have always been drawn to class analysis. I was also politically radical, and left political economy dovetails well with that kind of politics. I also tend to have an analytic orientation, which fits both economics and political economy. In marketing there's a concept called "FLAG—Fits Like a Glove." That describes my relationship to political economy . . . it felt intuitively right to me. Perhaps whatever I unconsciously absorbed from my parents was also at play.

Some years ago you wrote a best-selling book titled The Overworked American: The Unexpected Decline of Leisure. *What are the main arguments of the book? Moreover, to what extent has there been any change at all in US society since the publication of the book with regard to work and leisure?*

The main argument of *The Overworked American* is that there is a bias in capitalist economies towards taking productivity growth in the form of more output rather than more leisure. This was an argument that Marxists and the monopoly capital school often made, but without a good analytic basis. I developed a micro-foundation of the output bias, rooted in labor discipline. (Longer-hours workers are easier to control because their cost of job loss is higher, other things being equal.) I also identified the role of salaried work and per person fringe benefits as key to employers' preference for "long-hours workers." The book documented the rise of paid working hours from 1969 to 1989 in the US. This was a departure from an earlier trend of declining hours (pre–World War II) as well as from Western European countries, with whom we had been on a common downward trajectory of hours until the war. There was also a story about a growing bimodal distribution of hours. An increasing minority of people had too few hours, and their underemployment was growing. A declining majority had too many, and their hours were rising. I also identified what I called the "work and spend" cycle, in which workers preferred (ex ante) to trade off future wage increases for more free time, but weren't offered that option. They got the wage increases, spent the money, and their preferences (ex post) adjusted to their new time/wage trade-off. It was a story of endogenous preferences, a concept that would subsequently gain currency in the discipline.

Since the book was published, there have been a number of changes. In the 1990s and into the mid-2000s, paid working hours continued to rise on average. However, there were important divergences. Higher educated workers' hours rose more. Structural under- and unemployment increased. With the financial crisis of 2007, hours declined dramatically and only gradually began to increase. Labor force participation plummeted and remains low. The upward trend of hours stalled out.

What role, if any, does unpaid labor in the household play in your assessment of overwork? With women having moved increasingly into the paid labor force, to what extent have we seen a shift from unpaid to paid labor— such as household labor to, say, office jobs—as opposed to a shift from leisure to labor?

I included estimates of trends in household labor, and I devoted a chapter to exploring why labor-saving technologies in the household usually don't save labor, and developed a model to show how women's household work changes as their paid labor increases. The big picture was that as women added paid work their household labor declined, but only by about half. So as women increased their hours in the labor force, their total work burden increased a lot. This was key to the time squeeze in the household that sociologists, notably Arlie Hochschild, identified. One reason is that men didn't increase their household labor by much, and that asymmetry generally remains. (That's partly explained by gender intransigence and partly because men's hours of paid work did not fall as women increased their paid work.) On the technology front, I argued that standards rose as technology improved, so that women just kept doing more—clothes and houses were cleaner, cooking expectations ratcheted up, etc. The work expanded to fill the available time.

You followed up The Overworked American *with* The Overspent American, *focusing on commercialism and consumerism in the US. What's wrong with consumerism? Isn't this what capitalism is supposed to be all about as the standard of living increases?*

The biggest issue is that an economic system devoted to delivering continuous increases in material goods and services is leading to planetary catastrophe, via the accumulation of greenhouse gases in the atmosphere, mass species extinction, looming water shortages, and ecosystem collapse. It's simply not possible to safely deliver the aspirational consumer lifestyle to even the populations of the Global North, much less those of the Global South. I don't see this as a consumer-driven process—my analysis in *The Overworked American* identifies labor market dynamics as the driving force of the output bias. However, the consumer dimension of it is central to political legitimacy and ideological support for the economic system. So yes, to a certain extent the consumer lifestyle is a key argument for capitalism.

The book argued that consumption, contrary to the way mainstream economics treats it, is a deeply social process and that people consume according to their social environments. I argued that reference group comparisons drive spending, that consumption is the basis of social esteem (à la Veblen and Bourdieu), and that rather than see consumption as a primarily functional activity, we need to understand its social and symbolic dimensions. This is much more accepted now in mainstream economics. This opens the door to considering prisoner's dilemmas in consumption—more consumption doesn't necessarily make people better off but instead raises norms. My approach tied into the emergent literature on happiness and income and the idea that after a certain level of income, increases yield far less additional well-being. The other dimension, of course, was that consumption upscaling increasingly required more labor effort as wages stagnated. That dynamic undermined well-being. This was also a period of growing inequality. In the first chapter of my book, I argued that one consequence was that consumer aspirations were increasingly being set by lifestyles among the top 20 percent of the population, the group that (at that time) was getting a larger share of income. Later, of course, it would be the 1 percent, whose consumer patterns are much farther out of reach. A key point was that aspirations were rising far faster than incomes, which led to an "aspirational gap" and consumer frustration and dissatisfaction. The aspirational gap was also implicated in rising consumer debt.

How are the decline of leisure and the rise of consumerism connected to each other?

In some sense, they are two sides of the same coin. Had we taken productivity growth in the form of leisure, incomes would have stabilized, thereby avoiding the ratcheting up of consumer lifestyles. Hours of leisure would be less "commodity intensive" because stable incomes would be spread over more hours of leisure. Instead of Disneyland, people would camp more. DIY would have flourished even more than it has. We would have a more participatory and less spectator-driven culture. Another impact is that time-stressed people use goods as rewards, compensation, and substitutes for loss of a reasonable pace of life, meaning, and strong social relationships.

To what extent can we trace the rise of overworking and decline of leisure to the long-term trend of wage stagnation? That is, people have less leisure because it has become increasingly difficult to make ends meet.

There is no doubt that wage stagnation is important, especially lower down in the income distribution. Households added earners and hours as wages flattened. However, there are other factors at work as well. Employers, especially of salaried workers, became more demanding with respect to hours of work. People complied as good jobs became scarcer. Growing inequality, not just stagnation, also resulted in longer hours, as a number of studies have shown. But the other aspect is that consumption norms continued to rise, so that a stable income became a problem because it resulted in falling behind socially driven needs. This was particularly true among higher-income groups, for whom consumer norms escalated rapidly, since they are more tied to the spending patterns of the very wealthy. The upper middle class took on considerable debt in a vain effort to keep up. I haven't seen a study that parsed out all these factors, so I can't be more specific. But I do think it varies across the income distribution.

Would you say that consumerism remains a trait associated primarily with American culture? Do we see similar patterns in other high-income economies? What about lower- and middle-income economies?

Consumerism is an ideology that puts goods and services at the core of social meaning and aspirations. There are certainly consumerist trends in many countries. In Western Europe, there has been some Americanization of their consumer culture; however, the fact that they continue to have much more equal distributions of income and wealth has insulated them to some degree. Most of the Western European countries also have not gone down the maximal output path but have continued to reduce hours of work. In the Global South we see consumerist trends among the emergent middle classes, who are eager for goods such as washing machines, scooters and cars, and electronics. Who can blame them?

Continuous economic growth has been regarded as essential for a successful economy and the improvement in the standard of living. Can we have a viable economy without continuous economic growth? If so, what would it look like?

The only kind of viable economy we can have at this point is one that rejects continuous growth. We are already beyond planetary boundaries on key indicators, and need to urgently reduce the human footprint on the planet, especially with respect to carbon and other greenhouse gases. Economists were sanguine that growth could dematerialize, hence their view that the rules of physics don't apply. But decades after the profession's confident rejection of the "limits to growth" school, we have made almost no progress on dematerialization in total. We are dematerializing relative to GDP, but not "absolutely." (This is also called decoupling.) So we have to find a different way. In my view the key for the wealthy countries is to reduce hours of work rather than expand output. I've done a number of papers showing that countries and states that have shorter hours of work have lower carbon emissions, other things being equal. Hours reductions represent a pathway to reduce eco-impact that doesn't destabilize the labor market (because it gradually pulls out supply). It should also be compatible with rising well-being, due to the prisoner's dilemma effects noted above. Leisure time isn't subject to that dynamic, but income is. Trading income for time should therefore be welfare enhancing. The key to a high-satisfaction, low eco-impact economy is to maintain productivity growth and reduce work effort. People will regain control over their time in a context where consumption norms are not rising. They can meet consumption needs in more social, lower-cost ways. Of course, we'll also need to do more to provide public goods and economic security. Right now, people need to amass wealth to avoid catastrophic outcomes. But if public goods were high quality and universally available, shorter hours would be more viable.

In your most recent book Plenitude: The New Economics of Wealth, *you made the case for alternative energy, recycling, and moving away in general from the consumerist lifestyle associated with contemporary America. Do you feel that American society is ready for such an environmental, economic, and personal transformation?*

Yes and no. There's plenty of social critique of consumerism, even among highly consumerist people. So, in one sense, there's an opening. Polling data show great openness to a less consumerist path. People also want to address climate change and protect the natural environment. But this will be a huge change for this country. We have been following the post–World War II consumer model for seventy years now. I see changes among young people, who are much more open to these alternative ways of living. The key will be whether the public goods are there to allow them to reject the "work and spend" lifestyle. Will they be confident they can get health care, pensions, childcare, and education for their kids if they don't accept the highest-paying jobs they can find? It'll also require a big expansion in democratic ownership forms—cooperatives, trusts, and the like—that offer more security.

To make it work, we need to address extreme inequality, oligarchic rule, and inadequate social capital. I think we should start at the municipal level to revive democracy, provide public goods, and build common security. And that is happening to some extent.

But I suspect that this change won't occur until circumstances force it. There's a good deal of inertia in consumer practices. We saw a flowering of many alternative practices in the wake of the financial crash and

Great Recession. Climate and financial destabilization are likely to make this way forward more compelling and appealing. That's a painful way to do it, but we seem stuck.

In your view, how much can a slow- or no-growth economic model be an effective framework for supporting climate stabilization, in the US and elsewhere?

"An effective framework" suggests two issues. First, is it a viable path? I think it's necessary and viable because I don't think we can achieve the kinds of emissions reductions that we need to achieve if we expand the economy rapidly. The scientists tell us that Global North countries such as ours must achieve 8 to 10 percent reductions annually. We've never gotten anywhere close to that. In 2007, total carbon dioxide emissions in the US were 6,130 metric tons. By 2016, after a combination of recession, switching from coal to gas, and expansion of renewables, they had fallen only 13 percent, or a mere 1.4 percent annually.[1] In 2017, overall carbon emissions fell only 0.66 percent, with all the reduction in the power sector. Emissions from transport, buildings, and industry rose.[2] (Growth in aviation emissions alone erased one-third of the decline from the power sector.) The 2017 numbers are considerably below even the United States' inadequate Paris pledge. (In addition, these are only territorial emissions and exclude embodied emissions from trade, which are substantial for the US.)

The outlook for the future is not promising without major policy change. The large gains from getting off coal will begin to taper off and then disappear. Transportation is already the largest sectoral contributor to emissions in the US and other countries. A radical shift off beef and dairy would help a lot, but that seems even more unlikely than a deliberate slowdown in growth. The few countries that have had success with absolute emissions decoupling (like Germany) have coupled slow growth/reduced hours with an energy transition. Add the dietary shift, a massive shift to renewables, and a hefty carbon tax, and that's a recipe for a serious climate response.

1   See www3.epa.gov/climatechange/ghgemissions/inventoryexplorer/index.html#allsectors/allgas/gas/all.
2   See rhg.com/research/final-us-emissions-numbers-for-2017/.

Recently, your research has been exploring the so-called "sharing economy." What's that all about, and why is the "sharing economy" important in the campaign on behalf of a sustainable economy and lifestyle changes?

I got interested in the "sharing economy" in 2008 when I was writing *Plenitude*. That book put forward a model for households to live differently. The principle was to reduce hours of paid work in conventional employment, develop multiple income streams to weather employment instability, and meet consumption needs with less cash. The sharing economy seemed like an opportunity for households following this model. On the one hand, it offered cheaper goods and services, non-cash access to durable goods through loaning or gift platforms, and a range of other options for meeting needs without spending much money. These included time banks, repair collectives (to fix broken items), food swaps, and the like. At the same time, the monetized platforms such as Airbnb, TaskRabbit, and Uber/Lyft offered opportunities for people to earn additional cash.

The sharing economy has evolved since the early days in which the for-profit platforms were new and small and had an alternative vibe. (Uber excepted. Uber has never considered itself part of the sharing economy, and has always had a faux "free market" orientation and a conservative bent.) At its inception, the for-profits and not-for-profits shared a common good discourse and at least put forward claims of creating something different than business-as-usual capitalism. In the ensuing years, the for-profits accepted a lot of venture capital and have in many ways been converging to business as usual. The nonprofits have not been able to scale in the way Airbnb or the ride-hailing platforms have. But they do provide some of the benefits I originally saw for "plenitude" households—they offer cheaper options and ways to make money. In the research my team and I have done since 2011, we have found people who are attempting to carve out alternatives to conventional paid employment using these platforms. We find that they work well as a supplement to other sources of income. And for people with a valuable asset like an apartment or home to rent on Airbnb, there are considerable sums to be made. However, it is hard for people to earn more than poverty level incomes if they try to earn all their income on a labor platform like Uber or TaskRabbit, either because wages are too low (such as for driving or delivery work) or if wages are higher (as on a platform like TaskRabbit), there's not enough work to be found.

For sustainability, the claims of the for-profit platforms haven't been borne out. That was predictable from a standard economic point of view. These platforms make the services cheaper and thereby increase demand. We find that Airbnb induces travel. Uber and Lyft reduce the demand for public transportation and they also substitute for walking, cycling, and non-mobility (that is, staying put). So the sustainability claims are unlikely to be right. Airbnb touts reduced hotel construction and lower energy use in private homes, but it seems very likely that these potential savings are dwarfed by the carbon associated with additional plane flights that cheap accommodation makes possible. However, this is a topic we don't yet have much research on. On the other hand, there is a growing body of research on ride-hailing that suggests that it leads to increased congestion and emissions, and to higher-carbon travel. Finally, the platforms that tried to get people to share household items like tools, lawn mowers, or camera equipment have almost all failed. It seems that there's just not enough demand for that kind of practice in the US yet.

My sense is that sustainability will only be served in the "sharing sector" if true "sharing" relationships develop. I'm thinking about sharing food waste (a major contribution to greenhouse gases), durable goods, housing, and other high-impact items. In transport, we need large investments in public options, rather than more private cars (whoever owns them). This kind of solidaristic, community sharing is making more headway in Europe than in the US. I suspect that's because there's more social capital and history of collective action there to build on. But I haven't given up on local initiatives in this country. We just don't have a compelling model yet for many of these services.

Where do you see your work going over the next five years?

I am increasingly feeling the need to work on climate change. I have already refocused my activism in that direction. And I've been collaborating on a series of papers on the "drivers" of carbon emissions since about 2010. I'm interested in the culture of climate-in-action, as well as thinking more about how to address the climate crisis via changes in economic and consumption practices. If the policy environment changes, I'd like to study policies that could help reduce hours of work. Right now, there doesn't seem to be an audience for that kind of direction.

I'm also interested in the intersection of climate and inequality. One of the series of papers I've done shows that higher domestic inequality in income and wealth (measured as the top of the distribution concentration, not Gini coefficients) is highly correlated with carbon emissions. My co-authors and I have shown this across countries, across the OECD specifically, and across the US states. I'm interested in exploring exactly why that relationship shows up and how we might address inequality and climate simultaneously. I'll likely continue a combination of qualitative and quantitative research, as I've been doing for about a decade.

Responses on the COVID-19 Pandemic

How would you evaluate the ways different countries or regions have responded to the COVID-19 crisis, both in terms of public health interventions and economic policies?

Of course, there have been vast differences in how countries have responded to the virus in terms of the public health dimensions—contract tracing, testing, quarantine requirements, etc. New Zealand was exemplary, and was able to quickly protect its population. Sub-Saharan Africa, despite being so poor, has also had an enviable response, showing that financial resources are not the main factor in protection against a pandemic. The US, of course, has been an utter disaster. As I write these words, we've just reached more than 3,000 deaths in one day—the equivalent of a 9/11 loss. It's hard to believe our government basically abdicated its responsibility to respond. But in addition to the public health dimensions, the difference that really stands out to me is the economic. In Europe, governments in France, Spain, Italy, the UK, and other countries quickly decided to support employment by paying 80 percent of the salaries of employees even as their employers furloughed them. Originally intended as a short-term measure, these programs have been extended this fall. The Germans have even committed to these funds through the end of 2021. This humane, albeit expensive, response has allowed populations in these countries to avoid the pain that the virus could have inflicted on their economic well-being. By contrast, in the US we see lines at foodbanks stretching for miles, more than 10 million Americans unemployed, many facing an eviction cliff, and widespread economic distress. A report today revealed that shoplifting is up here as millions are going hungry, and that the items being stolen are bread, pasta, and baby formula. In the early days of the pandemic, there was good community spirit and a pulling together; now it's Hobbesian cruelty with Black and brown Americans bearing the brunt of the pain.

Do you draw any general lessons from the COVID crisis about the most viable ways to advance an egalitarian economic project?

In the early days of the epidemic, many of my colleagues in the climate world were optimistic that the experience of lockdown, with minimal purchasing of nonessential items, reduced travel and commuting, more time with family, and an emphasis on solidarity and public health, would lead to a permanent change in people's priorities. They hoped that the cleaner air we were experiencing would make people demand an end to uncontrolled air and carbon pollution. It seems clear that that shift didn't occur. One reason is that they were focusing on a privileged section of the population—the wealthy and middle-class people whose jobs went virtual, whose incomes continued, and who were able to protect themselves from the virus. Their lived conditions were so different from those of frontline workers, Black and brown households, and others who were bearing the brunt of the virus. In addition, the cynical use of the virus by right-wingers to pull the pandemic into the culture wars splintered the early solidarity and forced us to fight the death cult that the GOP has become. So how do we construct an egalitarian pathway out of this mess? The first cleavage to focus on should be the middle class/working class divide. We need to advocate for policies that bring these two groups together. A one-time wealth tax, like the one now under consideration in the UK, would bring the focus to the rapid wealth accumulation of billionaires during the pandemic. We also need robust measures to ensure security, but that benefit people in highly precarious positions and the broader middle class. Examples include a basic income for households earning below $150,000, eviction protection, an expansion of food benefits (in terms of eligibility and monthly amounts), and a revamped PPP program that excludes big businesses and chains. While most of this should be deficit-funded, the wealth tax and a hefty carbon tax are two sources of revenue that we should pursue. The former will make a small dent in extreme inequality, while the latter is imperative for planetary survival.

Does the experience of the COVID crisis shed any light on the way you think about economics as a discipline or, more specifically, the questions you might be pursuing in your own research?

I've been impressed at how rapidly economists pivoted to COVID research. One insight is that atomistic models are even less useful in an era of pandemics and ecological breakdown. The economics of networks, a growing field, should become even more important. In terms of my own research, the COVID crisis upended a new research project on gig work, but we were able to adjust our recruitment strategy and the gig platforms we are looking at. For gig workers, the pandemic has intensified pre-existing inequalities, but it has also introduced new cleavages. Another area of research for me is the relation between working hours and carbon emissions. The pandemic has expanded the conversation about reducing worktime, especially in Europe. I think it's a crucial component of decarbonization, and in addressing extreme inequality and economic recovery. I'm excited to do more work on that issue going forward.

Representative Publications and Influences

Publications:

Juliet Schor (1991). *The Overworked American: The Unexpected Decline of Leisure*. Basic Books.

Juliet Schor (2011). *True Wealth: How and Why Millions of Americans Are Creating a Time-Rich, Ecologically Light, Small Scale, High-Satisfaction Economy*. Penguin Random House.

Juliet Schor (2020). *After the Gig: How the Sharing Economy Got Hijacked and How to Win it Back*. University of California Press.

People who have been influential: Pierre Bourdieu

Literature that has been influential:

Pierre Bourdieu (1977). *Outline of a Theory of Practice*. Cambridge University Press.

Pierre Bourdieu (1984). *Distinction: A Social Critique of the Judgment of Taste*. Harvard University Press.

Pierre Bourdieu (1993). *The Field of Cultural Production*. Columbia University Press.

Anwar Shaikh

Anwar Shaikh is Professor of Economics in the Graduate Faculty of Political and Social Science at the New School for Social Research. He is one of the world's foremost scholars of classical political economy. Within that broad tradition, he has written on many topics including macroeconomics, international trade, finance theory, political economy, US macroeconomic policy, national and global inequality, and past and current global economic crises. His most recent book is *Capitalism: Competition, Conflict, Crises* (2016). His other books include *Globalization and the Myths of Free Trade* (2007) and *Measuring the Wealth of Nations: The Political Economy of National Accounts* (with E. Ahmet Tonak 1996). In 2014, he was awarded the NordSud International Prize for Literature and Science from Italy's Fondazione Pescarabruzzo.

Can we start by telling me how you got into economics?

As with many things in life, it was an accident. I was an engineering undergraduate at Princeton, and after that I went to live with my parents in Kuwait, where my father was posted (he was in the Pakistani Foreign Service). I worked in the desert as an engineer, and got "desert blindness" (severe conjunctivitis due to heat and humidity). While I was recovering, I was offered a job at the Kuwait American School to replace a teacher who had been let go. There I taught physics, math, and social science for a year and discovered that I really liked teaching.

At Princeton, I had attended talks by Martin Luther King and Malcolm X, and was impressed by their critiques of racism (not hard to grasp given my own experiences). In Karachi, Lagos, and Kuala Lumpur, I had seen abysmal poverty and great wealth side by side. In Kuwait, for once there seemed to be no problem about money. Nonetheless, there was considerable poverty. I was working in the desert myself, alongside workers from all over the Middle East and India and Pakistan, who labored in brutal searing heat yet were minimally paid. It seemed to me that things could be done differently.

Once again, by chance I happened to speak to someone who suggested that I might consider graduate education in economics in order to address my concerns. I applied to graduate school at Texas and Columbia, and ended up at choosing the latter. However, it soon became clear to me that neoclassical economics, which was already the dominant school by then, was a fundamentally inadequate foundation.

Looking back, and in connection with the evolution of your own thought and research, which economists have most influenced you and why?

If one rejects the neoclassical framework, where does one go? Marx's work convinced me that real competition was a dominant force in capitalism. Geoff Harcourt's brilliant article on the Cambridge capital controversy was extremely influential because it introduced me to a vibrant analytical tradition I had not known before. Kalecki seemed to sketch out a different path for macroeconomics. Robert Heilbroner's fabulous introduction to the history of economic thought (which I had encountered in a course at the Columbia Business School!) had a lasting effect on my thinking. Ronald Meek's essays on the labor theory of value were important. Joan Robinson's fearless critique of neoclassical economic analysis was wonderful. Later, I took a course with Luigi Pasinetti when he taught at Columbia one year, and he introduced me to Piero Sraffa's slim and elliptical book. I also met Ernest Mandel, who combined political activism with historical and analytical depth. I studied anthropology, Soviet industrialization, and Chinese development. And throughout, there was Marx!

In 1968, I joined the occupation at Columbia, was active in the antiwar movement, and was a founding member of URPE. I lived and taught in Harlem, teaching math and social science to young people considered unteachable by New York City public school educators. All of these events shaped my concrete understanding of US society.

By the time I was writing my PhD dissertation in the early 1970s, I was firmly opposed to standard economics and committed to looking for a coherent theoretical and empirical framework. But if one rejects the neoclassical framework, where does one go? I believed that real competition was a dominant force in capitalism, whereas perfect competition was the foundation of neoclassical analysis. Perfect competition was also the reference point for the monopoly and imperfect competition schools, since it was used to justify their claim that capitalism was "no longer" competitive—as if that fictitious construction was ever operant! Imperfect competition had become the foundation of most left macroeconomics, as in Kalecki and post-Keynesian economics, which created another hole to be filled.

It became increasingly evident to me that Smith, Ricardo, and Marx *had* provided a coherent and systematic alternative, and that this had been lost to subsequent discourse. I also found that Keynes explicitly insisted that competition was the foundation of his macroeconomics, and that he explicitly rejected imperfect competition. These "Four Greats" derived their theoretical understanding from keen observation of actual capitalist history and dynamics. They understood that the conflict of capitalist competition went hand-in-hand with conflict between capital and labor. It became my goal to reconstruct these foundations, to build upon them, and to demonstrate their theoretical reach and empirical efficacy in the modern world. This project put me outside neoclassical, Marxian, and radical orthodoxies.

My publications indicate that, from 1973 to 1986, I focused on theoretical issues: value and distribution, the neoclassical production function, the falling rate of profit, the theory of international trade, and crisis theories in various schools of thought.[1] From 1987 to 1994, my empirical work began to appear (often after many years of prior effort): the role of profitability in postwar growth and crises, the social wage in the postwar welfare state (with Ahmet Tonak), profits and capitalist long waves, the empirics of international trade and exchange rates, and Tonak/Shaikh empirical mapping between Marxian categories and national income accounts. At the same time, my theoretical work extended to the

---

1   Listed at anwarshaikhecon.org.

nonlinear dynamics of effective demand and growth. From 1994 to 2000 I worked on theoretical and empirical explanations of inflation, the stock market, and relative prices. From 2000 to 2006 empirical macro-modeling became an important area of investigation, in my work with Wynne Godley and subsequently as a member of the Levy Institute Macromodeling Group. After 2007, macro and international economic policy became increasingly important, and in the second decade of the 2000s I extended the analysis to the theoretical and empirical determinants of income inequality.

All the while, I was consciously excavating, repairing, and extending the logical structure of a proposed synthesis of classical and Keynesian economics in which all propositions derived from the same basic foundations, after allowance for concrete factors. In 1998, I began to put it all together in the book that appeared eighteen years later as *Capitalism: Competition, Conflict, Crises* (Oxford University Press, 2016). It was a long haul.

Have your views on the power of Marxism to explain the operations of capitalist economies changed over time?

My work is an attempt to construct a new economic framework from the economic analyses of Smith, Ricardo, Marx, *and* Keynes. Many Marxian economists rejected my arguments as too focused on competition; most Keynesian and post-Keynesians rejected them as being too classical; and most neo-Ricardians rejected them as being too Marxian. But a small number of people, including former students, sustained me in my belief that the project was worthwhile.

Marx and Marxism are two different things. What passes for the *economic* analysis of Marxism comes from Hilferding, Lenin, Magdoff, Sweezy, and Baran. Monopoly plays a central role here, and I have criticized this in various articles and certainly in my book (chapters 7 and 8). Marx relies on competition in his detailed analysis of the operations of capitalism: surplus value as the main basis of profit (but not *his* only basis, as I note in chapter 6, section II), the struggle over the length and intensity of the working day, the determinants of relative prices, the dynamics of the reserve army of labor, the mobility of capital and labor across regions and nations, the driving forces behind technical change, the theories of differential and absolute rent, etc.

At the same time, the grievously unfinished nature of Marx's work (he wrote only volume I for publication, volumes II and III being put together by Engels from a mass of unfinished manuscripts and fragments) leaves us in the dark about credit and cycles, international trade, exchange rates, financial markets, the stock exchange, the world market, the concrete movements of wages and labor markets, the recurrence of crises, the role of effective demand, and many other crucial issues. Marx studied all of these in detail, and we know that he intended to write about them. Yet he did not, and what he left behind was highly incomplete. What I have tried to show is that one can construct a coherent framework to address these questions from the works of the four great economists.

The rate of profit is central to your analysis of the laws of motion of capitalism. Why is that so?

I argue in my book that the profit rate depends on the relation of the real wage to productivity and to the capital intensity of production. This is Ricardo, Marx, Sraffa, etc. Real competition involves price-setting firms seeking to undercut their competitors by offering lower prices. The survival advantage in price-cutting goes to firms with lower costs: hence the relentless drive to cut costs, to pursue lower wages, and to develop new, lower-cost technologies. The struggles between capital and labor over the length, intensity, and remuneration of the working day, the mobility of capital to lower-cost regions, and never-ending technical change are all grounded here.

Real competition provides a theoretical and empirical explanation of relative prices, stock and bond prices, interest rates, and exchange rates. At the microeconomic level, firms continue to invest only if their expected return on investment exceeds the safe yield afforded by the interest rate: that is, only if the expected net rate of return on investment is positive. This same net rate motivates the flow of capital across industries, more rapid where profit rates are high and less rapid where they are low. The end result is a turbulent equalization of industry profit rates on investment around an economy-wide average rate, with the corresponding regulation of actual market prices by theoretical prices (prices of production) reflecting this economy-wide average rate. The same process can be shown to operate on the interest rate, the stock market, and exchange rates. Real exchange rates are international relative prices regulated by the relative real costs of export and import goods. Hence higher-cost nations will tend to have persistent trade deficits covered by international debt—just as we find in practice. The notion that free trade leads to balanced trade, that is, that it makes all nations equally competitive, is one of the great fallacies of conventional economics. It is unfortunately taken as the point of departure for most heterodox arguments, which then have to rely on monopoly power to explain the facts. I show in chapter 11 of my book that real competition can explain the observed patterns of international trade.

This approach also provides a natural foundation for the theory of effective demand. In the same manner as individual investments, *aggregate* investment is driven by the difference between its aggregate expected rate of return (Keynes' marginal efficiency of capital) and the interest rate. Only now the interest rate is regulated by the profit rate and the expectation of profitability is linked to actual profitability in the reflexive manner proposed by Soros. The loop between micro and macro is then closed on the basis of real competition. It should be noted that Keynes insisted that his theory was grounded in "atomistic competition," not imperfect competition, and that Kalecki's original formulation of his own theory of effective demand was based on the notion of "free competition." My book seeks to return the theory of effective demand to its proper ground.

When we speak of aggregate supply and demand, we mean *aggregated* supply and demand, aggregations of the outcomes of millions of decisions taken by individual agents whose actions are themselves regulated by profitability. Individual firms engage in production (supply) on the basis of near-term expected profitability of operations, and in the process they pay for materials, labor costs, dividends, rents, and interest payments. Payments for materials constitute demand for intermediate inputs, while the other payments become the foundation for personal income from which consumption demand emerges. At the same time, firms generate investment demand for new plant and equipment on the basis of their long-term expected net profitability. Hence short-term profitability regulates all of capitalist supply as well as consumption demand, while long-term net profitability regulates private investment demand. *Real macroeconomics is neither supply-side nor demand-side: it is profit-side.* Of course, aggregated supply and aggregated demand never match directly, but instead fluctuate ceaselessly around each other. This is turbulent equalization once again, now at the aggregated level, expressed in business cycles and waves of various durations.

In Capitalism: Competition, Conflict, Crises, *you show that the story of capitalist development is a mixture of wealth and poverty, development and underdevelopment, conflict and cooperation. Is this path unique to capitalism, in your view? Don't we see similar patterns throughout history, regardless of the economic system in place?*

Yes, of course, we can find similar patterns if we abstract from the elements that are different. Yet feudal peasants, slaves, and caste members are not the same as capitalist workers. Nor are their lords capitalists, merely because they live off a surplus. That is the whole point in Smith and Marx: capitalism is a new form of social organization with its own logic and laws of motion. The "cooperation" of peasants and slaves is brought about in a different manner than that of workers. Workers can change jobs, peasants and slaves cannot. Capitalist growth is fueled by the incessant growth of profits, which is itself dependent on incessant technical change discussed in the previous section. Capitalists joust with each other with prices, not with lances and spears.

Capitalist economies are structured differently and perform differently. We can think of differences between East Asian countries and the US, or even between northern and southern Europe. We can also think of differences in terms of policy regimes, in particular between neoliberal variants and social democratic variants of capitalism. Given such differences in the operations of capitalist economies, is it effective as a first approximation to think of capitalism as basically one economic system with a universal set of laws? Alternatively, would it be more reasonable to think of distinct variants of capitalism, with significantly distinct laws of motion?

Despite the concrete differences among capitalist economics, they share the fundamental quality that capitalism is driven by profitability at the *cellular* level. As I argued in a preceding answer, this drive gives rise to specific patterns within which workers struggle over the length and intensity of the working day and over real wages in relation to productivity, while capitalists struggle over markets, resources, and the globe.

These are the sources of the common patterns, and will remain as such as long as profit-making is the dominant mechanism. The depredation of the Earth comes from the intrinsic drive of capitalism: capital assesses whether or not outcomes are profitable, not whether they are socially desirable or undesirable. It is within this frame that we can locate the concrete factors that distinguish capitalist nations from each other. Yes, Japanese food is different from US food, but now there are McDonald's and sushi houses in both countries, and skyscrapers everywhere. In order to assess the effects of differences, we have to have an understanding of the underlying commonalities. Yes, birds come in a wide variety of sizes and colors, but they are fundamentally alike in the biological sense.

In my analysis of international trade, I show that the *same* set of forces can explain the *central* movements of both US and Japanese real exchange rates, even though concrete factors account for some of the fluctuations. Early Korean growth was fueled by its rapid industrialization aided by policy decisions. In order to assess the effects of such policies, we must have an understanding of growth, international trade, and the effects and limits of state intervention. All economic theories proceed in this manner, even though they differ in some fundamental ways.

You have been quoted as saying that "nations don't trade, businesses do." Can you elaborate a bit on this? Why is it important for understanding global trading patterns?

Actually, Adam Smith said that. Domestic exporters succeed in foreign markets because they can provide cheaper commodities than the producers in those countries. Similarly, domestic importers bring in commodities from abroad because they are cheaper that way. It follows that countries with many lower-cost goods will tend to enjoy trade surpluses and those with many high-cost goods will tend to suffer trade deficits. This is the foundation for Smith's theory of absolute advantage, which I show is both logically and empirically superior to the Ricardian/neoclassical theory of comparative advantage (chapter 11 of my book). I also show that this approach can explain the empirical movements of real exchange rates. American accusations that China, and in earlier times Germany, Japan, and South Korea, achieved their trade surpluses by manipulating their exchange rates are based directly on the belief that unfettered markets will lead to balanced trade in each country. Unfortunately, many heterodox economists turn to neoclassical theory in discussing such issues.

John Maynard Keynes, and, to a considerable extent, a large share of post-Keynesian economists, believe that, with proper policies, full employment can be attained and sustained under capitalism. Moreover, they also think that, under full employment capitalism, poverty can be eliminated and a reasonably equitable society can be sustained. Do you think these assessments have merit?

Capitalism can certainly reduce poverty and improve the distribution of income. But the market plays a fundamental role in generating a *characteristic* pretax income distribution, as I show empirically in chapter 17 of the book. Changing the post-tax distribution by redistributing from the rich to the poor has long been on the agenda of the welfare state. Yet the state always operates within the limits of the resistance of the rich. Changing the pretax distribution would be even harder, because it would require changing profits themselves. If the wage share was raised by fiat, the profit share and profit rate would be lowered accordingly. Not only would the resistance be even fiercer, but there would also be negative consequences for growth and employment. Post-Keynesian economics glosses over this feedback by assuming that monopoly power fixes the profit share—which as Kalecki recognized, implies that monopoly power also fixes the wage share (the ratio of the real wage to the productivity of labor). Under given length and intensity of the working day, the productivity of labor is also determined by firms through their choice of technologies. Then workers and hence the state would have *no* influence on labor's standard of living. This is patently false in light of the history of working-class struggles. At the end of his life, Kalecki tried to fudge this issue by positing that sufficient labor militancy might scare capitalists into lowering their monopoly markups. I have argued that post-Keynesian economics gets itself into this quandary because it has no theory of the rate of profit.

As for full employment, I disagree that it is sustainable unless key mechanisms of the market are suspended. High demand tends to raise prices and interest rates, while high levels of employment tend to raise the real wage, which in turn reduces the profit rate and encourages the import of labor and the displacement of workers through mechanization. During World War II, massive deficits brought the economy to full employment precisely because prices, interest rates, and wages were frozen in the service of the war effort. In the 1970s, modest stimulus policies aimed at raising employment led to inflation and stagflation, because wages, prices, and interest rates were free to move. In a recent publication, I have applied this understanding to explain the initial success and subsequent problems of the Lula/Dilma policies in Brazil.

You recently completed your magnum opus, Capitalism. *Are there any major issues beyond those that you cover in this book that you are planning to explore in future work?*

I have been working on the empirical determinants of the distribution of incomes, including by race and gender. Chapter 17, section II.4, introduces the empirical evidence and the theory. Several papers on my homepage, www.anwarshaikhecon.org/, develop and extend this argument.[2] At the same time, I have been working on the policy implications for macroeconomics and for development (for example, the Lula/ Dilma years in Brazil).[3]

Responses on the COVID-19 Pandemic

How would you evaluate the ways different countries or regions have responded to the COVID-19 crisis, both in terms of public health interventions and economic policies?

The current pandemic is fueled by the age-old interaction between viruses and animals, including humans. Most of these interactions are benign, but mutations constantly arise, and sometimes these worsen

---

2   Anwar Shaikh, "Income Distribution, Econophysics and Piketty," anwarshaikhecon.org/; Anwar Shaikh, Nikolaos Papanikolaou, and Noe Wiener, "Race, Gender and Econophysics of Income Distribution in the USA," anwarshaikhecon.org.

3   Anwar Shaikh, "Successful Macroeconomic Stimulus," Progressive Economics Group Policy Brief 11 (September 2017), anwarshaikhecon.org; Anwar Shaikh, "Paths to Development," *FIDE* (December 2018), anwarshaikhecon.org.

existing viral diseases such as influenza and even generate terrible new diseases such as AIDS, Ebola, and COVID-19.

Their rapid mutability makes viruses particularly powerful. It takes about twenty years for humans to replicate, but it takes only about a day for a virus. Mutations arise from errors in DNA replication that are not corrected by DNA repair mechanisms. Only a small fraction of such errors confer an advantage in any given environment, which is itself also mutable.

Capitalism is itself a supremely mutable social organism. It is constantly inventing new activities and new markets, driven by its incessant need for profit. And here, the key point is that capitalism's mutability derives from its constant trial-and-error processes. Individual firms produce particular items for an imagined profit derived from expected sales to potential customers. In order to produce, firms buy raw material and machinery and hire workers. They also pay out dividends to stockholders and interest to bond holders and banks. Thus, the planned production of each firm directly generates some input demand, some consumption demand based on disbursements of wage and property incomes, and some investment demand based on their planned changes in scale. The demands emanating from each firm confront the supplies produced by other firms, and vice versa.

Marx and Hayek both emphasized that these millions of individual plans, each based on imagined outcomes, do not, indeed cannot, immediately mesh. Even in the best of times, almost 50 percent of new businesses fail in the first five years. It is the collision of plans and expectations, expressed through individual markets, that provides feedback to individual firms. And on this basis, they change their actions and their products. *They mutate.* Yet they retain a key bit of genetic code, which is the drive for profit. This is the secret behind the dynamic character of capitalism.

Marx views capitalism as a wasteful and destructive system that will someday be surpassed by a better social form. Hayek views capitalism as the most dynamic, and therefore the best of all possible, human social forms. Both vehemently reject the fantasy world of perfect competition, rational expectations, and optimal outcomes.

Representative Publications and Influences

Publications:

Anwar Shaikh (1979). Foreign Trade and the Law of Value: Part I. *Science & Society*, 43(3), 281–302. JSTOR.

Anwar Shaikh and E. Ahmet Tonak (1996). *Measuring the Wealth of Nations: The Political Economy of National Accounts*. Cambridge University Press.

Anwar Shaikh (2016). *Capitalism: Competition, Conflict, Crises*. Oxford University Press.

People who have been influential: Karl Marx, Arghiri Emmanuel, Geoffrey Harcourt, Luigi Pasinetti, Joan Robinson, Ronald Meek

Literature that has been influential:

Arghiri Emmanuel (1972). *Unequal Exchange: A Study in the Imperialism of Trade*, New York, *Monthly Review Press*.

G.C. Harcourt (1969). "Some Cambridge Controversies in the Theory of Capital." *Journal of Economic Literature, 7*(2), 369–405.

Luigi Pasinetti (1977). *Lectures on the Theory of Production*. New York, Columbia University Press.

William Spriggs

William Spriggs is a Professor and Former Chair of the Department of Economics at Howard University. He currently also serves as Chief Economist for the American Federation of Labor and Congress of Industrial Organizations (AFL-CIO). He is the author of dozens of articles in academic journals, mainly on issues of labor markets, labor market discrimination, and educational opportunity. From 2009 to 2012, he was the Assistant Secretary for the Office of Policy at the United States Department of Labor. He has also held many positions on the boards of nonprofit organizations, many of them associated with the trade union movement. He is a former president of the National Economics Association, the organization of America's professional Black economists. Spriggs was the 2016 recipient of the National Academy of Social Insurance's Robert M. Ball Award for Outstanding Achievements in Social Insurance, and the 2014 NAACP Benjamin L. Hooks' Keeper of the Flame Award.

Can you please describe your personal background a bit?

I grew up in a house of educators. My father finished his PhD in particle physics while I was reaching kindergarten. My mother was an elementary school teacher. Both my parents were veterans of World War II. My father volunteered before the war started and was initially assigned to the "Buffalo Soldiers," before being transferred to US Army Air Corps where he graduated as a fighter pilot with the famed Tuskegee Airmen.

My mother was a WAC and served the sergeant of the motor pool. Despite these responsibilities, neither of them knew how to drive a car, since their families didn't own one when they entered the service. So I had the upbringing one would expect given such parents, who were very academically accomplished and extremely personally disciplined, and who lived very purposeful lives.

How did you get interested in studying economics? What made you decide to pursue a career as a PhD economist?

I grew up idolizing civil rights attorneys. My father's first academic job was teaching at Howard University. My neighbor was the chair of the Math Department at Howard, and his wife was a law professor there. The law faculty at Howard were my heroes. When I was growing up, almost every month Howard's Law School faculty, students, or alumni were winning some case to end segregation in some area of life; and the Black newspapers were filled with news of the first Black person to get some job, or move into some neighborhood, or attend some school because of those efforts. However, my family friend thought most of the victories had been won and what was now needed were people trained in economics who understood where the barriers lay that were not the result of the things lawsuits could win. Essentially, they insisted I end my law school ambitions and find out what it would take to go far in economics.

Which economists would you cite as having influenced you to a significant extent? How did these people shape your thinking?

I was greatly influenced by Arthur Goldberger, who taught the entry-level graduate econometrics course when I started at the University of Wisconsin–Madison. He had a very strong personal sense of justice. He showed how to use econometrics to debunk many theories that were racist, like some work on genetics and intelligence. And, that he was such a high-ranking person in his field, but taught the introductory course to graduate students said a lot about his attitude as a teacher. In my dissertation, I used the work of David Swinton, who had an early theory of what is now treated as "stratification economics." I found his work with the Black Economic Research Center (BERC), an effort funded by the Ford Foundation as a mirror to the NBER, to show a practical way to pursue economics in asking questions important to the Black community. I also found the work of his colleague Robert Browne, and the BERC founder, to be very important, because Brown's work on the loss of Black land wealth after 1921 inspired my dissertation topic. I was also helped greatly in graduate school by Jeffrey Williamson, who took extreme interest in my work and very carefully read my work and took it seriously. I try to be as focused with my own graduate students.

A major focus of your research, starting with your 1984 PhD dissertation, has been on the income, wealth, and living standards of African Americans. From your research, what would you say have been the major trends in economic outcomes for African Americans over the past fifty years? Have conditions been generally improving or worsening?

There has been little major change in the relative position of African Americans' economic position in the US over the last fifty years. Rapid gains were made in the late 1950s and 1960s as many of the obvious barriers to advancement were erased. Those barriers included being fully incorporated into the protections of the Fair Labor Standards Act, easing of discrimination in employment in the public sector, advances into the industrial base of America's heartland on the basis of the Fair Employment Practices Commission work during World War II, which increased Black union membership in the automobile, tire, rubber, aircraft, and steel industries in the 1950s, and the ending of overt hiring discrimination. The Black poverty rate plummeted during the 1960s from those gains.

Things changed in the 1970s. Global competition from Japan in the late 1970s decimated the highly unionized industrial base of the upper Midwest, the region of the country that pulled up Black income gains. The loss of union jobs in the upper Midwest was devastating to the gains of the 1960s, because industrial unions are one of the best interrupters of white privilege. Oddly, the period after 1970 allowed for the greatest gains in educational attainment by African Americans, and the most significant closing of those gaps where Black agency could influence the outcome, including educational attainment and the dramatic decline in Black teen pregnancy and the birth rate to single Black women.

But those gains have done nothing to improve the earnings of African Americans relative to whites, mainly because since the 1980s, disparities in employment and earnings between African Americans and whites have not closed within educational attainment categories. The difficult hurdle the Supreme Court placed in designing of race-conscious affirm-ative action policies makes it too difficult to address the systemic economic barriers faced because of race. In essence, our system has been allowed to reinvent Jim Crow. It was therefore not surprising to see in the data of Raj Chetty and his colleagues in studying children born in the late 1980s that there is no convergence in Black–white intergenera-tional mobility; this lack of convergence is deeply rooted in the greater downward mobility of African American children from their parents' income gains.[1]

To what extent would you attribute the general conditions for African Americans in the US to being the result of racism? What are the specific ways in which racism impacts economic well-being for African Americans? Have there been any effective policy measures to counteract racism in the US in terms of economic outcomes, and if so, what have they been?

I think the Chetty data make clear that there are sweeping effects tied to race.[2] His data show that there is no significant closing of racial gaps as African American incomes rise. This is repeated in other data sets, whether it is persistence in intergenerational education attainment, or in wealth accumulation. And there is no convincing data to show that there is a class component to these racial gaps. Racism permeates America's economic order. Wealth disparities and residential segrega-tion reinforce those patterns. That makes it hard to design race-neutral programs, since, because so many things are correlated with race, that one screen alone will miss the racial disparities within that screen. For example, a desire to use a class-based affirmative action admissions process over a race-conscious approach ignores how test scores are highly correlated with race, so that within classes, whites would still be advantaged. Or, take the fact that even low-income white families have

1   Raj Chetty et al., "Income Segregation and Intergenerational Mobility across Colleges in the United States," NBER Working Paper 23618 (July 2017), in *Quarterly Journal of Economics*, forthcoming.

2   Raj Chetty et al., "Race and Economic Opportunity in the United States: An Intergenerational Perspective," NBER Working Paper 24441 (December 2019), in *Quarterly Journal of Economics*, forthcoming.

significantly more wealth than high-income Black families, which means that scholarship aid would still be needed even by high-income Black families compared to low-income white families.

Unions are a powerful antidote to wage gaps that result from discrimination. Unions disrupt the assertion of white privilege by limiting discretionary actions where race can be a main factor. Similarly, public-sector workers benefit from work environments with less supervisory discretion. African Americans are more likely to work in larger organizations, where to address the agency issue of lower-level managers discretionary authority is also limited relative to smaller employers, who are less likely to use structured employment relations. Meaningful enforcement of affirmative action and antidiscrimination in hiring is a proven tool. And is underfunded given the benefits it could achieve.

High-pressure labor markets reduce discretion as well. The 1990s are a clear testament to running the economy near full employment coupled with an aggressive Office of Federal Contract Compliance Programs, as occurred under President Clinton. The combination achieved record low unemployment, low poverty, and high incomes in the Black community.

Do you observe major differences in economic outcomes over time within the African American community? That is, do we see increasing inequality within the African American community that mirrors the general rise of inequality in the US? What do you think are the major causes of the patterns of inequality that you observe within the African American community?

Inequality is higher within the African American community than overall inequality. But, the Chetty data clearly show that intergenerational inequality is significantly lower in the Black community because high-income Black families have little means to replicate their status with their children.

What do you think of the argument that, along with racism, the fundamental economic problem facing the African American community is the fact that the US economy is capitalist; and that, to be more specific, capitalism breeds inequality and thrives on racism?

Racism is its own force. It is used within capitalist and socialist states to buffer against the perennial economic dilemma of scarcity. Within the

US, racism has been used effectively, particularly in the South, to perpetuate its perverse form of oligarchy within a capitalist structure. But the South is unique because such a large share of the Southern state populations were African American, and democracy presents a different threat to oligarchs in such a setting unless the oligarchs can redefine social terms. In many states outside the South, capitalism didn't revert to such overt racism. Except in major northern cities, public schools were not de facto segregated until the 1960s. I think given the racial history of post-Castro Cuba, and the experience of African descendants in various Latin American countries during their turns to socialism, none of those nation-states was without issues of racism.

Have you experienced any significant surprises in your research work relative to what your prior views were coming into it?

Yes, I was very surprised that except for the major northern cities, African Americans did not experience more education segregation than they did. And I am amazed by how little attention has been paid to that issue. For instance, in the 1936 Olympic Games, the US track team, spearheaded by African American athletes, won the 100–, 200–, 400–, and 800–meter gold medals and helped secure the win in the 4x100–meter relay and medaled in the 110–meter hurdles. All those athletes attended integrated high schools outside the South.

In addition to your work as an academic economist and researcher, you have extensive experience in the world of economic policy-making institutions, including the US Joint Economic Committee and the US Department of Labor, as well as with several think-tanks, including the Economic Policy Institute and the Urban League. How would you describe your work in the policy-making world as distinct from your academic work? Does academic research, by you and others, exert a significant influence on policy debates? Can you give some examples where academic research, by yourself or others, has exerted a positive influence on policy-making, as well as some examples where policy-making has proceeded by ignoring research?

The key area in which policy-making ignores academic research is in pushing for better enforcement strategies and funding to fight discrimination in the labor market. Policy makers are overly focused on human capital as the explanation of racial income gaps, rather than discrimination.

Academic research is very important in the policy-making arena, especially if it is not directed at solving racial inequality. The policy world ignores publication bias, insisting on using published findings to be a fair arbiter of sound policy decisions. It is unfortunate, since publication bias greatly affects who gets to have input, and on which questions there is a sense of what policy can achieve; and perhaps more importantly, on what it *cannot* achieve, since a major source of publication bias is the failure to publish studies that show no results.

I think my role in policy-making has been to use my ability to independently assess the validity of economic research and not rely solely on the issue of published research; and especially when published findings can be contradictory—as, for instance, in the case of the minimum wage.

I greatly relied on academic research and thinkers in my work at the US Department of Commerce in devising benchmarks to defend the US minority procurement programs in the *Adarand v. Peña* case. The end result was a new and novel approach that won the case.

At present, you now combine both your academic and policy-making roles, working both as an economics faculty member at Howard University and as chief economist for the AFL-CIO. How do these two worlds interact in your work?

My credibility as an academic helps me as a voice when I talk to other academics on behalf of the AFL-CIO. And I think my record in the areas where I have done research helps me frame research questions to other academics in pursuing research that can be helpful to the AFL-CIO and American workers broadly speaking. My prior policy connections have been immensely helpful in the relationship between the AFL-CIO and the Federal Reserve Bank, since many Fed bank governors had interacted with me either in the Clinton or the Obama administrations. The platform of the AFL-CIO also helps me in thinking up research for my graduate students to pursue. And it has helped open doors for them in getting data or opportunities to present their work. The AFL-CIO's standing within the National Bureau of Economic Research has given me a voice in trying to make economics more open to different viewpoints.

US labor unions have been in long-term decline. This, in turn, is frequently cited as a major factor contributing to the long-term rise of inequality in the US. In your view, what have been the major factors contributing to the weakening of the US labor movement? What do you think can be done to reverse this pattern?

The US labor movement relied greatly on an American policy consensus that dominated in the postwar era of proving that capitalism was superior to socialism in providing broadly shared prosperity to the world. The policy consensus is gone, and the government signaled it no longer viewed the broad policy objectives in those terms when Ronald Reagan summarily dismissed the striking federal air traffic controllers. Strike activity in the US abruptly declined when the government clearly signaled that the rarely used weapon of permanently replacing striking workers was not going to be interfered with. Strikes are the only credible bargaining tool in the US system of collective bargaining. Strikes are necessary to conduct effective organizing campaigns.

The major path of the decline in union density has been the inability of unions to organize large numbers of nonunion workers, not so much the loss of existing union members. In fact, union membership is roughly flat over the last ten years.

Declining union density also leads to political imbalances at the state and local level. The quick increase of the number of states with single-digit union density has meant more states have lacked the political balance to maintain strong democracies. States with low union density have laws that are decidedly to the disadvantage of workers on all levels of their lives. Those states invest less in K–12 public education, have weaker worker safety nets including lower access to unemployment benefits, lower replacement rates of unemployment benefits, lower benefits to poor single mothers, worse worker compensation protection, and higher incarceration rates. Those states are also more likely to pass laws limiting the right to vote, with specific measures that hurt lower-income families. Under those conditions, it is harder to organize workers.

Since we have returned to prewar conditions of union power it is necessary to return to the prewar condition of the original Wagner Act.

That means repealing the Taft-Hartley amendments added in 1946. Currently under consideration in the House of Representatives is a bill to do just that. The Protecting the Right to Organize Act will update our labor code to reflect the more contentious relationship between management and labor and provide more tools to the labor movement that will allow for more effective organizing and leveling the playing field. It is also necessary to amend our trade agreements to prevent arbitrage of labor standards. The abdication of protecting US law through regulatory arbitrage in trade agreements is to the detriment of American standards. Ultimately, this regulatory arbitrage will also mean the inability to enforce the needed steps to reduce greenhouse gases.

A major challenge facing the US working class—both inside and outside of the labor movement—has been globalization, specifically in the form of trade and immigration policy. What would be an equitable approach to trade and immigration policies in the US—"equitable" in the sense that it would support the well-being of US working people while also taking care to recognize the life circumstances and challenges of workers and the poor in other parts of the world?

Trade pacts do not help workers in low-income countries by simply providing low-wage jobs. Trade under those conditions does not provide a path to ever-higher wages. Trade agreements can only lead to rising living standards when they cut off global competition on the basis of low labor standards. Agreements based on low standards make for an assured race to the bottom and lead too many nations to base growth on exports. Clearly, not all nations can run export trade surpluses. It also does not help when nations see migration and overseas remittances back home as a major form of hard currency. It robs nations of their most important growth factor, which is labor. None of these policies so far has helped in truly enabling sustained growth.

What current trade has demonstrated is that the old beliefs that some countries could not industrialize because of skill gaps is false. Now, it is up to the world to understand that sustainable development means rising living standards based on the high wages that industrialization alone can provide. Immigration questions will quickly change when global living standards are pushed to rise.

*Why was the North American Free Trade Agreement bad for US workers,
if, indeed, you think it was? Can you envision a trade agreement between
the US, Mexico, and Canada that would fairly support the interests of
working people in all three countries? If so, what might such an agreement
entail?*

NAFTA was bad because it failed to deliver any raises in the wages of
Mexican workers resulting from their increased integration into North
American manufacturing. Shifting the jobs, but not the wages, to Mexico
has resulted in low growth for too many Mexicans and a strengthening
of the Mexican oligarchs. Similarly, in the US, the loss of jobs and wages
has only exacerbated US inequality. The failure of Mexico to transform
its industrial work force into part of the North American middle class
has put more pressure on Mexico and Latin America, with slow growth,
to stem deteriorating living standards. Those pressures are evident in
the continued desire to emigrate to the US to take low-wage service
sector jobs over industrial jobs at home. Or to create the basis for a
strong domestic market that could spur further growth and stability.
Hopefully, recent changes in Mexican labor law will allow for an authen-
tic voice of Mexican workers to demand and win the wages they deserve
that can spur North American growth and slow the push to emigrate
from Mexico. Such an agreement must have meaningful labor law
enforcement and seek to push up labor standards in Mexico.

*How do you see your work evolving over the next several years, both in the
area of academic research and in your policy engagements?*

I hope to continue to do work on inequality. It is the greatest threat the
US faces. It is greater than global warming, because it is drastically slowing America's potential growth and is exacerbating America's fragile
experiment in a multicultural democracy. The US now faces a huge existential threat, not too different from the moment before the Civil War
when it had to decide which path to follow: its truer path towards
democracy or towards oligarchy and racial division. Both were always
present in the US—American history is neither all one or the other.
And, at various moments, America has had to choose when the question was called. But the market-based system that dominated the postwar era was only possible by successfully addressing inequality under

the New Deal. America need not reinvent itself to follow the progression of policies from the New Deal through 1980 to get back on a sustainable path of shared prosperity and democracy. We can only hope to ensure that the 1980–2020 period is viewed as the aberration. If, on the other hand, we come to view the period of 1946 to 1980 as an aberration, then the US experiment is doomed. We should not underestimate the global implications of a regressive America on a planet where inequality is tearing at the seams of nation-states.

I hope to continue to be a voice in policy-making. I think having a practical eye for policies that succeed is key—and I hope I can contribute to those policies.

Responses on the COVID-19 Pandemic

How would you evaluate the ways different countries or regions have responded to the COVID-19 crisis, both in terms of public health interventions and economic policies?

Among OECD member countries, the US stands out for two glaring omissions: first and most important was a failure to put in place novel coronavirus safety regulations and protocols for workers who could not safely distance at work, whether frontline health or emergency response workers or workers who could not telework; and second, the haphazard way in which the US tried to keep workers and employers tied together. The failure on the first count led to a failure to contain the virus through lockdown efforts, since so many workers were needed to go outside their home bubble. As a consequence, social cohesion was breeched and solidarity fell. This was exacerbated by a national leadership that gave every appearance that because the workers who were put at risk were disproportionately Black, it would be better for the US to chase "herd immunity" as a policy rather than aggressively fight the virus. The fracturing of the worker–employer tie has led to more permanent layoffs now, and a rising share of long-term unemployed that will be difficult to connect back to jobs. With a vaccine in hand and a clear timetable of when we might expect the virus to be under sufficient control to allow greater mobility, Europe will be far ahead of the US in reconnecting their workforce and resuming work at a rapid pace. If there is pent-up demand for services like travel, hotels, and restaurants, Europe will face fewer challenges and less inflationary pressures. New Zealand gets the gold medal for aggressively attacking the virus and having leadership to maintain national unity and social cohesion.

Do you draw any general lessons from the COVID crisis about the most viable ways to advance an egalitarian economic project?

Going forward we will encounter more episodes like the COVID pandemic, on different scales. We do not have the patience to take on such problems without better, more empathetic leadership that can rouse national purpose and national unity. We are at great risk because the issue of national unity has become a partisan issue, and economic failures from natural causes turn into partisan blame. The next disaster could be a massive flooding of the Mississippi Valley, or greater damage from Western fires or the next great hurricane. Responses to these possible disasters are all vulnerable to partisan division in the current political climate. We mostly lack the stomach to provide the proper support for those most vulnerable when a region's economy collapses in the face of disaster.

Does the experience of the COVID crisis shed any light on the way you think about economics as a discipline or, more specifically, the questions you might be pursuing in your own research?

Each new disaster will present novel challenges. They all entail problems of restricted demand or supply functions. Economists' knee-jerk response of looking at all phenomena as market driven is dangerous when the issue requires imagination to see how to counterbalance the market failures resulting from restricted demand or supply. That requires believing in planned solutions, as opposed to market-based solutions. Economists' reflex is to let the disaster breed inequality through accepting the disparate effects of restricted demand/supply as market-driven effects that should not be tampered with. Economists, for instance, were quick to interpret the dominance of Amazon as a result of market forces and ignored any issues of equity from requiring brick-and-mortar stores to stop operating during the pandemic; or to see McDonald's dominance in take-out food over eat-in, sit-down restaurants as a market force rather than an equity issue to be addressed because of orders to stop people eating at indoor restaurants. We have already seen such attitudes towards New Orleans in the aftermath of Hurricane Katrina. Further, economists have handcuffed themselves to advocating large-scale policies only if they are "proven." Since we don't have big data for the bulk of US history, we cannot have "proven" policies for handling similar disasters of the past, like the Mississippi flood of 1927. As a result, economists lose the power of imagination to propose useful solutions for lack of "identification."

Representative Publications and Influences

Publications:

William M. Rodgers III and William E. Spriggs (1996). "What does the AFQT really measure: Race, wages, schooling and the AFQT score," *The Review of Black Political Economy*, 24(4), 13–46.

William E. Spriggs and Rhonda M. Williams (1996). "A Logit Decomposition Analysis of Occupational Segregation: Results for the 1970s and 1980s," *The Review of Economics and Statistics*, 78(2), 348–355.

William E. Spriggs and Rhonda M. Williams (2000). "What Do We Need to Explain About African American Unemployment?" *Prosperity for All? The Economic Boom and African Americans*, 188.

People who have been influential: Arthur Goldberger, David Swinton, Robert Browne

Literature that has been influential:

David H. Swinton (1977). A labor force competition theory of discrimination in the labor market. *The American Economic Review*, 67(1), 400–404.

David H. Swinton (1988). Economic status of Blacks 1987. *The State of Black America*, 130, 132.

Robert S. Browne (1973). *Only Six Million Acres: The Decline of Black Owned Land in the Rural South*. Black Economic Research Center.

Fiona Tregenna

Fiona Tregenna holds the South African Research Chair in Industrial Development and is a Professor of Economics at the University of Johannesburg. Her primary research interest is in issues of structural change, deindustrialization, and industrial development. She is the recipient of many awards and grants for her research. She serves on a number of high-level boards and advisory panels and councils including the Presidential Economic Advisory Council advising South African President Cyril Ramaphosa on economic policy. In the past she has worked for, among others, the National Labour and Economic Development Institute, the Congress of South African Trade Unions, several universities, and as a consultant to various research institutes and international organizations such as UNCTAD, UNIDO, and the ILO.

Were you involved in politics as a young student in South Africa? If so, can you describe how you got involved, and your main areas of activism?

Yes, I became politically active as a teenager. This was during the dying years of apartheid: the country was still ruled by the apartheid regime with Black South Africans not even having the vote, Mandela and most other long-term political prisoners had been recently released, and the country was moving towards a transition to democracy. Yet, despite the negotiations underway, it was by no means clear how the transition would unfold—whether the apartheid regime or some faction thereof

would attempt to halt the steps towards change and block democratization, whether the violence would escalate, or whether it would be a
peaceful transition. The area of the country where I was studying—
Pietermaritzburg in the Natal Midlands—was undergoing low-intensity
civil war between the liberation forces and the Inkatha Freedom Party
backed by the apartheid security forces. I personally was insulated from
this as a middle-class white university student, but thousands of people
in the area were killed during this period.

During my university days I was active in the African National
Congress–aligned student movement the South African Students' Congress
(SASCO), the African National Congress Youth League (ANCYL), and the
South African Communist Party (SACP). By the time I left high school I
had already independently formed strong political views, and knew that I
would become politically involved as soon as I had the chance.

I would say that my political views formed primarily as a response to
apartheid, and in rejection of the system in which I had grown up and
through which I had gained privileged opportunities. In my younger
teenage years, this came through more as a strongly felt sense of injustice at the "unfairness" of racial discrimination, at the extreme poverty
in which most Black South Africans lived, at people being imprisoned
for their beliefs, and so on. Over time, I guess I understood more about
the structural nature of apartheid as a system of oppression, the underlying economic structure, and so on. Secondarily, I had an intellectual
attraction to left-wing ideas that developed during my high school years,
albeit in a rudimentary way. These came together during my intellectual
and political journey. By the time I was around fifteen or sixteen years
old, I considered myself a communist, despite not personally knowing
anyone on the left, and still being quite naïve in many ways.

Being politically active in South Africa during that period was a
formative and transformative experience for me, one that fundamentally influenced the path that my life has since taken.

*How did you come to study economics? Was it directly linked to your
engagement with politics?*

Right, it came directly from my political involvement. I actually initially
studied science in my first year at university, as I'd done some novel scientific research while at school and had travelled to the then-Czechoslovakia

and to the UK for that. But at university, I wasn't engaged with the sciences and wanted to do something closer to the politics that was by then fully occupying me. When I switched to the social sciences, I originally took undergraduate economics courses as fillers. Undergraduate economics is generally excruciatingly boring and divorced from understanding any real economic issues. My undergrad economics was no different. Looking back now, I am amazed that I stuck it out. I think that many students drop economics at that stage because it doesn't engage them, and they don't get to the stage when it can potentially get interesting and relevant (although many graduate economics programs are of course just as irrelevant). I could not really see any connections between my undergraduate economics courses and the economic issues that were engaging me, in South Africa and internationally. The material was dry and dull, the assumptions were farcical, and it was completely detached from the economic problems of the day. During my undergraduate years, I was more interested in political science and law. At that time, the early 1990s, negotiations towards a new South African constitution were a central arena in which the "action" was happening, with lawyers playing key roles in that terrain, so that seemed exciting.

It was only at Honors level—in South Africa the Honors degree is a separate degree equivalent to the fourth year in the US or UK systems—that economics began to get interesting. For the first time, I had a lecturer—Simon Roberts—who was progressive, and made economics relevant. Simon had recently arrived in South Africa from the UK via Botswana, and I took a course with him on South African economic policy issues that actually applied economics to real-world issues and to the economic policy debates happening in the country at the time. Simon is now a close friend and a colleague at the University of Johannesburg. We work closely together in research on industrial development, I was the respondent at his professorial inaugural lecture, and we recently co-edited a book on structural transformation in South Africa (with Antonio Andreoni and Pamela Mondliwa).

Alongside my economics courses gradually getting more interesting, it was becoming increasingly clear that progressive economics skills were sorely needed at that time. With South Africa's new constitution agreed upon, debates around policies for a democratic South Africa were taking center stage, with economic policy debates at the fore. Even with the ANC elected in 1994, there was initially considerable fluidity and uncertainty as to what sort of policies would be implemented. Much of this contestation was within the ANC and Tripartite Alliance (comprising the ANC, SACP, and trade union federation COSATU), with different ideological groupings pushing very different policy agendas. Even within the ANC itself, some factions were advocating neoliberal structural adjustment policies, while others were supporting the ANC's historical stance on nationalization of the means of production. There was intense contestation. The ANC had always been a "broad church" ideologically, and these debates reflected that, but during that period there was definitely a shift to the right in dominant economic thinking within the ANC.

At that time, I was also getting closer to the trade union movement, as well as already being heavily involved in the SACP, ANC (especially the ANCYL), and student movement. The need for "hard" economics skills was becoming very apparent. Not many people in the movement had formal economics training, and debates tended to be dominated by a relatively small number of people who could throw around concepts and who spun a line about "realities," mostly in support of conservative policy stances. Outside the movement, the loudest voices in economic debates were those of bank economists. I was strongly "pushed" (or deployed) in the direction of focusing on economics and to study that further.

I guess it was inevitable that I would be drawn to heterodox economics. My frustration with the conventional economics that I had been taught at university, my leftist political views, my desire to make sense of the economic problems surrounding me and to find solutions to them, meant that neoclassical economics was never going to work for me.

Who were important teachers or sources of inspiration during your initial years of work in economics?

Looking back, there are so many people, both economists and non-economists, who have encouraged, motivated, influenced, taught, and inspired me, and to whom I am grateful. These include the leading communists who recruited me into a Marxist study group when I was just an eager seventeen-year-old, trade unionists from whom I learned about economic policy engagement and popular economics, and so many others.

I spoke earlier about Simon Roberts, who was the first progressive economics lecturer I had. I also began to read more widely about various approaches beyond mainstream economics. During this period, the mid and late 1990s, Ben Fine and some other SOAS economists were helping develop economic policy alternatives for COSATU, and it was exciting to see what economics could be used for—that was definitely an influence and inspiration. Ben has produced an incredible body of work spanning Marxist theory, South African political economy, and much else.

In my first job, as a researcher at the National Labour and Economic Development Institute (NALEDI, the research institute of COSATU), I met James Heintz, who is now a distinguished economics professor at UMass Amherst. At that time, he was working on his PhD dissertation at UMass under the supervision of Sam Bowles, who was quite actively involved in economic policy debates in South Africa at that time. James came for what was initially supposed to be a year, I think, but ended up staying for a couple of years. At that time there was very little economics expertise in the labor movement, and James really helped in filling that gap, with his combination of technical skills, macroeconomic expertise in particular, progressive commitment and "political economic" under-standing of what was happening in South Africa. James and I have kept in touch ever since then and I always follow his work with interest; I was delighted that he recently contributed a chapter (co-authored with Karmen Naidoo) to a book I co-edited (with Arkebe Oqubay and Imraan Valodia). I first learned about UMass Amherst from James and ended up going there for graduate study.

At UMass, I learned a lot more economics and was exposed to a healthy range of heterodox perspectives, which helped me to clarify my own views. I took many graduate courses and deepened my knowledge and technical skills in a range of fields within economics. The dynamic community of graduate students is one of the great things about UMass.

I then did my PhD at Cambridge. This was a very different Cambridge from the earlier heyday of Cambridge economics: the few remaining heterodox economists were pretty much marginalized by the time I got there, and there was a strong focus on quantitative modelling. I was fortu-nate to be supervised by Gabriel Palma, who is the one who got me started on manufacturing, structural change, and deindustrialization. I learned so much from him about this, and also from his deep and original think-ing about Latin America, inequality, and much else. At Cambridge I also benefited from many conversations, guidance and feedback from Ha-Joon Chang, Geoff Harcourt, Bob Rowthorn, and the late Ajit Singh.

While previously employed by the trade union movement in South Africa, I had worked on industrial policy and developed COSATU proposals in this area. At UMass this was not at all an area of focus, in common with most other US economics departments, including heterodox ones. Yet a lot of the seminal work in this field (on structural change, industrialization, the role of manufacturing, deindustrialization, industrial policy, etc.) has been done at Cambridge, and I got into it there. This goes back to the earlier work at Cambridge of greats such as Nicholas Kaldor, Luigi Pasinetti, Joan Robinson, Michał Kalecki, and others on issues including the sectoral structure of the economy; and more recently the work of Bob Rowthorn, Ajit Singh, and Gabriel Palma on deindustrialization and of Ha-Joon Chang on industrial policy. My own work in this field draws on and engages with (including challenging some aspects of) this "Cambridge" intellectual lineage.

One of your main areas of research is on the manufacturing sector as an engine of growth. Why is manufacturing important in terms of advancing growth?

In Kaldorian and structuralist approaches, manufacturing is considered innately superior to other sectors as an engine of development and growth. This is a strongly sector-based perspective, with a belief that sectors are distinguished by nontrivial common characteristics, lending growth a sector-specific character. A unit of value added or a job in manufacturing "counts more" for growth and development than does a unit of value added or a job elsewhere in the economy. So the manufacturing sector is seen as having a special role in the growth process, as an engine of growth. Manufacturing is thought to have superior scope for learning-by-doing; increasing returns to scale and overall for cumulative productivity increases; strong growth-pulling linkages with the rest of a domestic economy; technological progressivity; and other characteristics that accord it a special role in the growth process. Beyond growth, manufacturing also matters because industrialization can be transformative of social relations and can be a modernizing, progressive influence on society. I have recently been developing a concept of "transformative industrialization" and what this might mean today, in particular for African countries.

From this perspective, industrialization is the key route for developing economies to catch up with developed economies. In the policy sphere, this was reflected in developing countries' drives to modernize and "catch up" through industrialization, especially during the 1950s through the 1970s. This view suggests that deindustrialization would negatively affect economic growth.

My own views draw heavily on these perspectives. However, I place a stronger emphasis on the heterogeneity of activities within sectors. There are certainly important common denominators within sectors that are relevant for growth, manufacturing has a special role to play, and industrialization remains an important path for growth and development. But I think it's also important to recognize the degree of heterogeneity within sectors and that growth is both sector- and activity-specific. This points to the importance of drilling down below the level of the broad sectors to look at the characteristics of subsectors and of activities within them, and is also suggestive of a greater contingency and conditionality in outcomes.

An issue that has gained increasing attention in recent years is "premature deindustrialization." Can you give us your understanding of that term? How, if at all, does this phenomenon connect with issues around North–South trade?

I have suggested defining premature deindustrialization as cases where the share of manufacturing in a country's employment and GDP is lower than would be expected based on their level of income per capita, as well as the country having income per capita below that of the international turning point of deindustrialisation, and where the country's manufacturing share is falling further. This can be conceptualized in terms of the classic inverted U curve, identified by Bob Rowthorn and developed further by Gabriel Palma, among others. The share of manufacturing in total employment or GDP is regressed on income per capita and its square, plotted with the log of income per capita on the horizontal axis and manufacturing share of employment or GDP on the vertical axis. This typically shows the manufacturing share rising up to a turning point, then declining as deindustrialization sets in. In my conceptualization, we can think of premature deindustrializers as those countries falling below the curve and to the left of the turning point, and where their manufacturing share is in decline.

Premature deindustrialization is typically brought about by shifts in policy, rather than just with the incremental maturation of advanced economies. Trade liberalization, liberalization of product markets, austere monetary policy, and financial liberalization are all likely to bring on premature deindustrialization.

Where deindustrialization is premature, it will typically have especially negative effects. A prematurely deindustrializing country will have garnered less of the benefits of manufacturing for growth by the time deindustrialization begins. Furthermore, it is less able to develop a dynamic, high-productivity services sector that could potentially act (at least to some extent) as an alternative engine of growth.

The negative effects of premature deindustrialization will tend to be most pronounced when it occurs in low-income countries that have not yet really industrialized, as appears to be the case in a number of sub-Saharan African countries. I have termed this "pre-industrial deindustrialization"—the phenomenon, particularly evident in sub-Saharan Africa, where deindustrialization begins at extremely low levels of industrialization. Not only are these turning points far lower than the turning points of earlier episodes of deindustrialization in advanced economies, but even after decades of deindustrialization those advanced economies still have far higher shares of manufacturing than the "peaks" at which some sub-Saharan African countries began deindustrializing. I have no doubt that the failure to meaningfully industrialize is among the reasons for Africa's poor growth and development over at least the past half-century.

Coming back to the last part of your question, North–South trade has certainly been one of the sources of deindustrialization in advanced economies. Import penetration from lower-unit-cost producers has been a long-standing source of deindustrialization in the Global North. In the case of premature deindustrialization, South–South trade can also be a key contributing factor. The emergence of China as a manufacturing behemoth, with the combination of relatively low-unit costs and advanced technological capabilities for its level of income per capita, and with the benefits of great economies of scale, has squeezed manufacturing in many middle-income countries, as well as making it more difficult for low-income countries to gain a foothold on the industrialization ladder. At the same time, the rapid industrialization and growth not only in China but also in other Asian economies could also serve to demonstrate possibilities to other developing countries. Finding a viable industrialization path is certainly more challenging now than it was in the 1960s, but it remains possible.

To get to the specific case that you know best, can you describe the role of manufacturing as a growth engine in the case of South Africa? Is South Africa experiencing a case of premature deindustrialization in your view?

I do believe that South Africa has prematurely deindustrialized over a long period of time. While my analysis of intersectoral outsourcing suggests that deindustrialization appears to have been worse than it actually has been—the reallocation of employment from manufacturing to services due to domestic outsourcing makes the scale of deindustrialization appear larger than it really is—the fact remains that South Africa has been on a path of deindustrialization since around the early 1980s.

Of course, there are a host of valid political and economic explanations for South Africa's pathetic growth performance, but I see deindustrialization as one of the relevant explanations. We have lost out on some of the potential growth and employment benefits that we could have obtained, had we had a manufacturing sector growing in size, diversity, and sophistication. I don't see the services sector in South Africa as capable of acting independently as an alternative engine of growth. This relates also to the financialization of the economy over this period. Within capital, it is largely the interests and voices of the financial sector that have dominated in policy debates. Government has lacked the political will to take decisive steps to reverse the deindustrialization that began during apartheid.

After democratization, it was about fifteen years before the country started implementing industrial policy in any meaningful sense, during which time there was further deindustrialization. While we do now have serious industrial policy, I don't see this as being anywhere near the scale required to effectively support industrial development and structural transformation, and it is completely undermined by conservative macroeconomic policy and by deficiencies in other areas.

South Africa has a highly developed financial sector. What role do you see the financial sector playing in South Africa's growth trajectory?

South Africa does have a large and sophisticated financial sector, and in the standard global rankings South Africa scores highly in this respect. But has it served us well—what has the economy gained from this "advanced" financial sector? To put it simply, the financial sector should ultimately be serving the rest of the economy, making it work better and grow faster. The resources that are absorbed by the financial sector can be a drain on the rest of the economy if the financial sector is not appropriately articulated with the "real economy" and is not facilitating growth. If the financial sector grows increasingly out of proportion to the rest of the economy, absorbing much-needed capital and skills yet not facilitating growth of the productive sector, I don't believe that this is anything to celebrate.

In South Africa, the financial sector has also facilitated massive capital flight and other forms of capital outflows, both legal and illegal. The financial fraction of capital has also had an outsized influence on policy debates, with business voices from the banks often dominating those from the manufacturing sector. This has manifested in policy outcomes— for example, in macroeconomic policy, favoring the financial sector yet not supporting (or actually harming) domestic manufacturing.

I think that the financial sector has an absolutely crucial role to play in any country's growth and development, and South Africa's sophisticated financial sector could potentially play a much more positive role, but it needs to be transformed in various ways and to be much more tightly regulated and disciplined.

Twenty-five years after the end of apartheid, poverty and inequality remain deep structural problems for South Africa. In fact, according to World Bank 2018 data, South Africa is the most unequal country in the world. What is your assessment of these figures?

That poverty, inequality, and unemployment remain as high as they do, twenty-five years after democratization, is a devastating indictment of the record in power of our democratic government. In 1994, we would not have expected that this would be the outcome twenty-five years later. Yet this outcome derives in large part from policy choices that were made. It did not have to be like this. Nobody can honestly say that we have done enough. In some areas, policy choices have made things worse. Inequality, poverty, and unemployment are not only terribly high, but also remain racialized in character.

Some advances have been made in reducing poverty, in particular through social grants. A large proportion of the South African population receives these grants, with the Child Support Grant and Old Age Pension in particular having a huge impact. Without these, poverty would be far, far higher. Yet it is of course far from ideal to depend on social grants to lift people out of poverty—what we really need is a structural transformation towards a more inclusive economy, in which the majority of people are involved in and gain incomes from the productive economy.

Inequality and unemployment are intrinsically linked in South Africa. It's not coincidental that we have the highest or one of the very highest rates worldwide in both unemployment and inequality. I don't believe that we will bring down the extremely high level of inequality without dealing decisively with the crisis of unemployment. Of course, this is not easy to do. But if we carry on with current policies, or with merely incremental changes in those policies, neither inequality nor unemployment will be dealt with. The current situation is neither sustainable nor acceptable in any sense.

You are a member of the Central Committee of the South African Communist Party. What, in your view, is the relevance of Marxism today?

I'm actually no longer a member of the Central Committee or any other SACP structures, but I did serve there for several years, as well as previously having sat on branch, district, and provincial structures from 1992 onwards.

I believe that Marxism has continuing relevance, both analytically and politically. Analytically, it provides us with powerful tools for understanding and critiquing capitalism. In my own research, for example, I have used Marxist tools of analysis to better understand sector specificity, structural change, and deindustrialization. It is obvious that some of Marx's analysis, written about a century and a half ago, will be outdated or less applicable today, with all the political, economic, technological, environmental, and social changes that have happened. For instance, Marx was writing during the time of the First Industrial Revolution and the early stages of the Second Industrial Revolution, which provided the animating context and subject matter of much of his work. Yet we are now in the Fourth Industrial Revolution, with changes that we could scarcely have imagined a few decades ago, let alone them being conceivable in the nineteenth century. Marx's analysis shouldn't be treated as a biblical canon, to be mechanically applied and defended. In my view, it ought to be a living body of thought, developing over time, not just in interpretation, but in the theory and substantive analysis itself, and we should be comfortable with diverse Marxist perspectives. As well as synthesizing elements of Marxist thought with elements of, for instance, structuralist thought.

Politically, this also remains relevant to an emancipatory project. It goes without saying that Marxism doesn't provide a blueprint or plan of struggle or program for any country. Each country has its own characteristics at any point in time, and I don't think that there can be any ideological framework that provides a universally applicable set of truths and strategies that can be practically applied either in gaining or in using political power. For instance, I generally don't believe that an insurrectionary road to power is either feasible or desirable at this point in time. And a "green" approach that emphasizes environmental sustainability needs to be a far greater priority than it has traditionally been in most Marxist thought (and broader left perspectives). The relevance and value of a Marxist approach needs to be specific to time and place, and needs to go along with democracy and freedom. For all the dynamism of capitalism, and the material and technological progress it has engendered, it has also brought great unevenness in outcomes across countries and peoples, inequality, conflict, ecological damage—many people still do not even have their basic needs met even in the richest countries of the world, and exploitation will always be at the heart of the capitalist accumulation process.

Where do you anticipate your work in political economy going over the next several years?

I think that most of my coming work will be applied in nature. There is still a book I have in mind theorizing sectoral structure and change, but I don't know when I'll find time for that. I'm currently leading a major research project on innovation and inclusive industrialization; I am working much more than previously on innovation and technological change, which I see as crucial aspects of the microfoundations of structural transformation and of "catching up." I'm also expanding my work on industrialization and deindustrialization with a focus on sub-Saharan Africa. I want to engage more with why this region has over a long period industrialized less than the rest of the world, how this has affected growth and development outcomes, what sort of industrialization is feasible in low- and middle-income African countries today, the prospects for what a country like Ethiopia is currently doing, and so on. And lots of other things . . . I have many ideas and not enough time to do even a fraction of them!

Where do you see global politics going? Do you see left political economy, and leftist political programs, experiencing a period of growing strength over time?

Left political economy within the academy remains pretty weak, I think, outside of quite isolated pockets of teaching and research. The economics discipline remains largely untouched by the most recent global financial crisis, increasingly obsessed with quantitative methods for their own sake, restricted and misled by unrealistic assumptions, and disengaged from real economic issues. The growing student-led challenges to the state of academic economics and curricula is exciting. Here in South Africa, in recent years we have held the Rethinking Economics for Africa (REFA) festival, which my center is a partner in. These are fantastic gatherings of mainly students, not only critiquing but also imagining alternatives.

In terms of global politics, it's uneven but I certainly don't see any wholesale shift to the left. If anything, on balance there currently seems to be a shift to the right. At the same time, the ways in which production and distribution are currently organized, as well as the ways in which political power is accessed and wielded even in modern democratic states, have led to outcomes that are neither moral nor sustainable—not sustainable politically, socially, ecologically, or economically. It's a challenge to us as the left, to capture people's imaginations, come up with alternatives that are creative and viable, and in cases where we are entrusted with political power, to really use it boldly to change things structurally and to change people's lives for the better.

Responses on the COVID-19 Pandemic

In your view, how would you evaluate the ways different countries or regions have responded to the COVID-19 crisis, both in terms of public health interventions and economic policies?

A wide range of factors have mediated the public health and economic outcomes from COVID-19 across countries. I am absolutely not surprised that countries such as South Korea and Vietnam have handled things so well, compared with disastrous health and economic outcomes in many countries—both developed and developing countries. Amongst the multiple factors that matter, I am especially interested in the importance of state capabilities. Here I am talking about the broad set of capabilities, not just state capacity. These capabilities include both technical and political economy dimensions. These include the ability to design and actually implement appropriate policies, the nature of the articulation between the state and market(s), the degrees of horizontal and vertical coordination in public policy and between public institutions, and the agility and dynamism of the state in adroitly adapting institutions and policies to changing conditions. These relate more to the nature of the state than its direct size, although of course a "hollowed out" state would be unable to perform effectively. Where state capabilities have been eroded over time, this naturally undermines the ability to manage the public health and economic dimensions of a crisis such as COVID-19. State capabilities take time to build up, it is just not feasible to develop them overnight in a crisis situation. And the outsourcing of fundamental roles to the private sector does not work in situations such as this. Needless to say, the issue here is not only about state capabilities as such, but about the political will to use them, in this case in managing the public health and economic aspects of the crisis.

Given my own research focus, I have been particularly closely engaged with the impact of the crisis on manufacturing, the role of countries' manufacturing sectors in responding to the crisis, and the implications for industrial policy going forward. I see a strong relationship between the types of state capabilities that have proved important in managing both the public health and economic aspects of the crisis, and the sorts of state capabilities that are important in industrial policy. This is not just a coincidental overlap: the sorts of capabilities that are not just required for the successful implementation of industrial policy, but which are in fact built up through the actual practice of industrial policy, have also been relevant in managing both the public health and economic aspects of COVID-19, and are also likely to position states well to deal with other emergencies in the future.

COVID-19 has drawn attention to the importance of productive capacity and capabilities in manufacturing, with part of this being productive systems that can be adapted to urgent needs. Looking ahead, industrial policy also needs to take account of the changing international organization of production (including through global value chains), of technological change, and of the need to move towards more environmentally sustainable production.

Do you draw any general lessons from the COVID crisis about the most viable ways to advance an egalitarian economic project, focusing on this question in any way that you wish?

We need to recognize the "crisis [or crises] before the crisis" and what fundamental changes are called for to address that. Pre-COVID, there were crises of climate change; of poverty, unemployment and inequality within countries; and of many developing countries being left behind rather than catching up. COVID has both exposed and deepened these fault lines, within and between nations.

COVID-19 has also demonstrated how interconnected the world is, with this being clearer than ever both in terms of public health and economically. This underscores the importance of strengthening multi-lateralism and global solutions. For instance, in the vaccination drive, national or nationalist approaches are not viable because the emergence of COVID variants in countries with less access to vaccines also directly threatens those countries that have moved ahead alone.

Similarly within countries, the experience of this pandemic has laid bare how interconnected people are, the costs of unequal access to resources, and that it is impossible for elites to fully insulate themselves from the rest of society. Even with "gated communities", private security, private education, private healthcare, and so on, everyone is vulnerable to infection. Of course, the wealthy are far better able to protect themselves, and have far superior healthcare in the event of illness, but people have been struck down across the income spectrum. Living in a society with vastly unequal access to sanitation and other infrastructure and services, in which a large section of the population live in congested living conditions, in which there is underinvestment in the public health service and general running down of the state, means higher infection rates and risks for everyone. This is just one way in which extreme income inequality is unsustainable (let alone being fundamentally wrong in other ways).

Yet it is by no means obvious that a post-COVID world would be more egalitarian than in the past. Elites are typically best placed to protect and advance their interests in periods of crisis and change. It is not only progressive forces who are dreaming of a different world. There will be intense ongoing contestation over post-COVID economic policies. In this, the links between scholarship and both the policy domain and wider popular struggles are important for progressive scholars.

Representative Publications and Influences

Publications:

Fiona Tregenna (2009). Characterising deindustrialisation: An analysis of changes in manufacturing employment and output internationally. *Cambridge Journal of Economics*, 33(3), 433–466.

Fiona Tregenna (2014). A new theoretical analysis of deindustrialisation. *Cambridge Journal of Economics*, 38(6), 1373–1390.

Bilge Erten, Jessica Leight. and Fiona Tregenna (2019). Trade liberalization and local labor market adjustment in South Africa. *Journal of International Economics*, 118, 448–467.

People who have been influential:

Historical: Karl Marx, Joan Robinson, Piero Sraffa, Raúl Prebisch, Albert Hirschman, Nicholas Kaldor, Michał Kalecki, Celso Furtado, Hollis Chenery

Recent/contemporary: Alice Amsden, Ben Fine, Gabriel Palma, Ha-Joon Chang, Geoff Harcourt, Bob Rowthorn, Ajit Singh, James Heintz

Literature that has been influential:

Celso Furtado (1964). *Development and underdevelopment: A structural view of the problems of developed and underdeveloped countries*, University of California Press, Berkeley.

Albert Hirschman (1958). *The strategy of economic development*, Yale University Press, New Haven.

Nicholas Kaldor (1978). *Further essays on economic theory*, Duckworth, London.

Thomas Weisskopf

Thomas Weisskopf is Professor Emeritus of Economics at the University of Michigan. His early research focused on issues of Third World development and underdevelopment, with particular attention to India. In the late 1970s, his research interests shifted to the macroeconomic problems of advanced capitalist economies; among other things, he undertook studies of trends in productivity growth and profitability from a neo-Marxian political economic perspective. In the 1990s, he worked primarily on problems of economic transition and institutional development in the formerly socialist economies of the East, concentrating especially on the interaction between political and economic change in Russia. More recently he has worked on discrimination and affirmative action in the comparative context of the United States and India, and on the growth of economic inequality in each of these two countries. Weisskopf has co-authored nine books, including (with Samuel Bowles and David M. Gordon) *After the Waste Land: A Democratic Economics for the Year 2000* (1991). His most recent book is *Affirmative Action in the United States and India: A Comparative Perspective* (2004). He has also published more than 100 articles in a wide range of journals in the fields of economic development, macroeconomics, comparative economic systems, political economy, and public policy.

Can you tell us a bit about your background and how you ended up pursuing economics as your major field of study?

No doubt influenced by my physicist father, I was initially interested in mathematics and physics as possible fields in which to major in college. But well before entering college I had also developed a strong interest in political and social issues, stimulated by frequent trips to Western Europe—including two full years abroad—made possible by my European-born parents. By the time I committed to a major at the end of my sophomore year at Harvard, I had decided that economics would offer a desirable combination of analytical rigor and attention to real-world politics and society. An excellent teacher of introductory economics—Richard Gill—had clinched the deal for me.

Your father was the eminent nuclear physicist Victor Weisskopf. He had been an important contributor to the Los Alamos project to create nuclear weapons, but then became an important figure fighting for nuclear disarmament. To what extent did your father's political commitments and activism influence you?

My father's interest in and involvement with political issues certainly encouraged me to take a strong interest in such matters and to develop a liberal social-democratic outlook much like his. His activism actually started when he joined a Viennese socialist youth organization in the 1920s. Nuclear disarmament was only one of many issues that he discussed with me well before I reached college. When I was becoming politically aware, he was no longer as much of an activist as he had been in his earlier years. I think my own increasing activism, starting in the early 1960s, had more to do with the influence and example of friends that I made as an undergraduate at Harvard, who connected me to student groups led by activists such as Todd Gitlin (whose leadership of the anti-nuclear organization "Tocsin" I remember well).

In the early stages of your career in the 1960s you were interested in applying quantitative economic methods to problems facing Third World economies, and in fact you spent much of the 1960s working at the Indian Statistical Institute in New Delhi. What were your main interests while working in India? What were some of the main things you learned from your years there?

My four years at the ISI had a formative impact on my thinking about economic issues. My first year in India, working as an economics instructor just after graduation from Harvard, I was mainly interested in learning as much as I could about a country vastly different than any I had ever spent time in. I was especially attracted by the commitment of Indian leaders—including the director of the ISI, P.C. Mahalanobis, who had been Prime Minister Nehru's chief economic advisor—to find a "third way" socialist path to development, drawing on the best of the capitalist West and the communist East. After two years of graduate economics at MIT, I returned to the ISI to conduct research for my PhD thesis on a development planning model for India. At the time, I felt that such quantitative methods could have a significant salutary effect on the economic future of the country, and I looked forward to a future role as an expert economic advisor. After finishing up the thesis in a final year at MIT, I returned to the ISI for two years as a visiting junior professor to teach economics and to participate in economic policy research at the institute. During these years, I became increasingly disillusioned with the role of a technical economic expert and—thanks to lengthy discussions with Indian friends and colleagues—I became much more aware of the political constraints that affect economic policy-making and that had been undermining India's apparent commitment to a desirable socialist development strategy. I also began to read widely in the Marxist and post-Marxist literature on economic history and analysis. Rejecting the idea of becoming a development policy advisor, I accepted the offer of an assistant professorship at Harvard, with a view to working on a more radical political economic understanding of the issues I was most interested in. When I returned to the US in 1968, I found that the trend of my own thinking was completely consonant with that of my American friends (some old, many new) who were active in the growing radical political economic community.

When you returned to the United States in the late 1960s, the Vietnam War was still raging on and the ideology of the New Left had spread throughout college campuses and become something like a full-fledged political movement. How influential was the experience of the Vietnam War and the emergence of the New Left in converting you to radical political economy?

The experience of the Vietnam War was—in an unusual way—critical to my progression from a liberal to a New Left perspective. As I was finishing my PhD thesis at MIT in 1965–66, I was planning to serve for two years as an assistant to the chief economist at the USAID mission in India. However, the acceleration of the US war effort in Vietnam during that year led me ultimately to turn down that job, because I felt strongly that I could not in good conscience represent the US at a time when its foreign policy was so shameful. To my great good fortune, my friends at the ISI provided me with a much more acceptable and rewarding opportunity to return to India for those two years. The Indian intellectual environment that I was able to enter inspired me to reorient my thinking about political and economic issues in a considerably more leftward direction than would have been possible had I been working at the USAID.

In 1968, you joined a small group of like-minded economists in founding the Union for Radical Political Economics (URPE), which, surprisingly, is still around after all these years. Tell us about the initial aims of URPE from your perspective as one of its founders. Why do you think URPE has survived for fifty years while so many New Left organizations from that period ended up rather quickly in the dustbin of history?

There are many early URPE documents that set out the aims of the organization, and different members of URPE will probably have somewhat different recollections about what we were trying to accomplish. To my mind the initial aims of URPE included most importantly: (1) the development of radical political economic analyses of economic issues that would be much better than those provided by mainstream economics, because they would be based on a much broader and deeper understanding of the social, political, and historical factors influencing economic outcomes; and (2) the development of analyses of economic issues that would contribute to the capability of organizations seeking to bring about a much more just and humane economic system in the US and elsewhere in the world. (The point, according to Marx, was not just to understand the world, but to change it for the better.) A good URPEr would do both good intellectual work (radical research and teaching) and good political work (participating actively in, and providing useful economic input for, progressive social and political movements). Unfortunately, radical political economists have had much less success with respect to the second objective than the first. Although many of us have worked actively over the years to support progressive movements and policies, our side has not been very successful in stemming the reactionary trend that has prevailed in much of the world in recent decades.

I think that there are several reasons that URPE has survived for so much longer than most other New Left academic organizations. For one thing, economics differs from other social sciences in that it has a very strong analytical orthodoxy—based on, but not limited to, neoclassical microeconomics. Radical political economists critical of this orthodoxy thus tend to be seen—and to see themselves—as distinctly different from, and in many ways in opposition to, mainstream economists. In all the other social sciences, there is much less of a dominant orthodoxy, and hence much more room for different currents—even radical ones—to be accepted as part of the already somewhat heterogeneous mainstream discipline. Radical political economists therefore have a much greater need for the kind of intellectual community offered by a dissident academic organization. Second, economics is distinctive in the degree to which it is linked to, and tends to serve, the world of business. This imparts a conservative, pro-capitalist outlook to the practice of economics and the politics of most economists, very different from the atmosphere in which most other social scientists work—and it heightens the need for radical political economists to establish a supportive dissident community like URPE. URPE members from the beginning have been very successful in building and maintaining a vibrant intellectual and activist community, through myriad collective activities such as the editing of the journal *Review of Radical Political Economics*, the holding of annual informal summer conferences, and a variety of forms of outreach to progressive activists. URPE has played an especially important role in providing support for the teaching and research of radical political economists, who often lack such support in their own institutions.

What was it about the Marxian political economy approach, in particular, that you found appealing in the effort to understand development and underdevelopment and, indeed, the global capitalist economy? How did your understanding of the concept of imperialism develop out of this framework?

I found the basic Marxian notions about the interaction of the forces and the relations of production, and the relationship between base and superstructure, to be extremely helpful to an understanding of the long-run dynamics of different types of societies—capitalist or otherwise. Equally helpful is the central Marxian focus on power, wielded by dominant classes against subordinate classes, which is indispensable in explaining political and economic events. To understand development and underdevelopment, it is particularly important to delve into long-run historical trends and to examine the way in which the power relations of the class structure affect economic policies and outcomes. Marxian political economy—from Karl Marx to Paul Baran—seemed to me well suited to address what was happening to the economies of India and other developing nations. For subordinate nations, not only their internal class structure but also their relationship to (the powerful classes of) the dominant nations is also critical to their development—hence the importance of imperialism. I don't think that my understanding of the concept of imperialism is unique in any way, but my approach to imperialism was strongly influenced by the writings of well-known social scientists from the developing world.

Your 1979 paper in the Cambridge Journal of Economics, *"Marxian Crisis Theory and the Rate of Profit in the Postwar US Economy," was an early, and highly influential, project developing rigorous quantitative approaches to analyzing a Marxian understanding of macroeconomic instability and crisis. How would you characterize the main findings of this paper? How do you think the results of the paper continue to shed light on our contemporary macroeconomic conditions?*

I think that the main contribution of this paper was to show that different Marxian theories of capitalist economic crisis—each of which provides an explanation for a significant decline in the overall capitalist rate of profit, which is seen to trigger a crisis—can be made amenable to empirical testing with readily available macroeconomic data. I sought to test the three most prominent Marxian theories of a falling rate of (before-tax) profit in the context of the US nonfinancial corporate sector over the long-run period from 1949 to 1975, as well as over shorter-run periods from one business cycle to the next, and within business cycles, during the same twenty-six-year period. The main findings of this research were that falling rates of profit—during most of the shorter-run periods as well as over the twenty-six-year long run—were attributable primarily to a rise in the strength of labor vis-à-vis capital, which in turn was linked to declines in the size of the reserve army of labor (measured by the unemployment rate). Also contributing to profit decline in the nonfinancial sector over the long run was a decline in the rate of US productivity growth and weakening US hegemony within the world capitalist system.

I would not claim that the empirical results of my paper continue to shed light on macroeconomic conditions in the contemporary era, because so much has changed over the last fifty years. The US economy during the time period covered by the paper was characterized by "regulated capitalism," in the terminology of the methodological approach known as social structure of accumulation (SSA) analysis. Since the early 1980s, however, the US economy can best be characterized by a successor SSA labeled "neoliberal capitalism," which arose out of the crisis linked to the falling rate of profit in the latter part of the preceding SSA. An entirely new empirical analysis of trends in the profit rate in the neoliberal era would be necessary to draw any concrete conclusions about the sources of those trends. However, my work on this paper did lead directly to my interest in joining Bowles and Gordon in our analysis of the long-wave booms and crises of the US economy and, in particular, the crisis of the "regulated capitalist" SSA.

Following from your Cambridge Journal *article, you began a collaboration with Samuel Bowles and David Gordon to advance Gordon's social structure of accumulation theory and apply it in particular to the US economy of the 1980s. This led to the publication of both* Beyond the Waste Land *in 1984 and* After the Waste Land *in 1991. How would you characterize the main approaches and findings of these books and the related multiple research papers you produced with Bowles and Gordon over this period?*

My work with Bowles and Gordon on the macroeconomic problems of the US economy, over a decade and a half, was exciting and rewarding— a great example of collegial collaboration that I feel lucky to have been able to take part in. The underlying approach of our work was that of SSA analysis, carried out by means of rigorous quantitative assessment of relevant statistical data. SSA analysis, in the hands of many radical political economists, has proved to be very useful to an understanding of the long-run evolution of the US economy. Our basic finding was that the US economy by the 1970s and into the early 1980s was performing well below its potential. Productivity growth was slowing down, profit rates were falling, and the economy was failing to meet the needs of far too many people (hence the use of the word "waste" in both titles). We found much evidence that this failure was attributable to the exhaustion of the post–World War II American "regulated capitalist" SSA.

Our (very ambitious!) aim in writing these books for the general public was to provide support for a political movement that would be able to build a much more prosperous and much fairer new SSA, in the wake of the crisis of the old one. In both books, we sought to outline the kind of fundamental changes in the US economy that would usher in a significantly improved model. Our proposals were social democratic, not revolutionary, in nature, because we felt that this offered a politically realistic way forward. In a variety of articles published in economics journals, we reported in detail on the research that underlay many of the arguments raised in the books. Alas, as it turned out, a new SSA did indeed arise from the ashes of the old one, but it proved to be a harshly neoliberal SSA that has generated far more inequality, injustice, and instability than the previous one.

How would you say that the social structures of accumulation approach works within a Marxian framework of analysis? What would you identify as other major influences?

The SSA framework is completely compatible with a Marxian framework of analysis. Indeed, it derives from the Marxian analysis of successive modes of production, in which a growing contradiction between the dynamic forces of production and the static relations of production (characterizing an existing mode of production) generates a growing crisis that can ultimately be resolved only by the defeat or collapse of the currently dominant class and its replacement by a new dominant class associated with a new and more vibrant mode of production. SSA analysis applies this logic to the dynamics of a capitalist economy, in which the analysis of successive capitalist regimes—or social structures of production—proceeds along the same lines as the Marxian analysis of successive modes of production. A focus on class, and on the power that dominant classes exercise over subordinate classes, characterizes both the original Marxian and the contemporary SSA forms of analysis.

The main other influence on the SSA approach has been the French "regulation" school, whose members were also inspired by Marxism. Michel Aglietta's foundational book, *A Theory of Capitalist Regulation: The US Experience*, was published in English in 1976—just as David Gordon and others in the US were developing SSA analysis. Robert Boyer and other left-leaning Parisian economists developed and disseminated the ideas of the regulation school at the same time, and they were widely read by anglophone radical political economists. The regulation theorists' notion of a "Fordist regime of accumulation," used to describe advanced capitalist economies in the post–World War II era, has much in common with the "regulated capitalist" regime of SSA analysis.

Following from your work on US macroeconomic questions, your research then shifted its focus to understanding late developments of "actually existing socialism" in Eastern Europe and the former Soviet Union. You also began researching the theory and practice of market socialism. How would you characterize market socialism? Do you think that some version of market socialism may have been a viable option for the former Soviet Union and Eastern Europe? Why do you think market socialism never successfully took hold in this region?

Market socialism is a form of socialist economy, in which (1) the means of production are largely owned not by private corporate or individual proprietors, but either by public entities or worker-controlled organs; and (2) the output of producing units are distributed to customers through markets rather than according to government plan. The state plays a major role in taxing, spending, and regulating economic affairs, and it may own some key elements of economic infrastructure, but it does not undertake comprehensive economic planning nor organize producers and consumers into collective nonmarket decision-makers.

When the governments of the former Soviet Union and its satellite nations collapsed in the late 1980s and early 1990s, I was hopeful that the circumstances in at least some of the successor states would be propitious for the development of a kind of market socialism in a democratic framework. At the time of the regime changes in these countries, the absence of an entrenched capitalist class, combined with a widespread desire to supplant top-down bureaucratic planning with a decentralized market-oriented system, seemed to open up the possibility of introducing a new "mixed" market-and-socialist alternative. There were indeed strong supporters of such a system to be found in Russia and quite a few Eastern European countries.

I believe there are several reasons that nothing like a market socialist system actually arose in any of these countries. First, people were so fed up with the kind of bureaucratic socialism they had experienced for decades, and so impressed by the much greater economic progress achieved in the advanced capitalist countries, that they lacked confidence in any form of socialism and saw great promise in a capitalist alternative. Second, it turned out that there were many opportunists among the powerful and/or well-placed people in the old regimes—and even among their opponents—who recognized that they could take advantage of the instability and uncertainty of the transitional period to use capitalist rules of the game to their own advantage. The constituency for constructing a fairer and more egalitarian market-socialist system simply did not have the political power to overcome those who saw in a form of "wild" capitalism great opportunities for personal and familial gain. Third, pro-capitalist forces from the West—government officials, financial institutions, economic advisors—flooded into the former "Second World" to offer funding, advice, and technical assistance geared to establishing economic institutions and practices characteristic of their own capitalist economies. In retrospect, the outcome—in most of these countries, a dubiously democratic crony-capitalist system—seems to have been overdetermined.

We hear the term "neoliberalism" a lot. What would you consider to be its main tenets? And why, in your view, has neoliberalism become the dominant economic paradigm globally for the past forty years?

I would describe neoliberalism as corporate-dominated capitalism expanded from a national to an international scale. Its main tenets are ostensible allegiance to laissez-faire, or the primacy of the (so-called) free market, which in fact involves an economic system structured by powers-that-be with property rights favoring big business, as well as rules and regulations constraining efforts by governments to meet ordinary people's needs. Neoliberalism entails support for policies of privatization, liberalization, deregulation, and not infrequently programs of fiscal austerity that reduce spending on behalf of the general public. We have seen all this before, in the pre–World War II era, but just not on a global scale.

I think the rise to dominance of neoliberalism since the late 1970s has everything to do with the travails of the prior regulated capitalist SSA in most of the advanced capitalist world, and the concomitant ability of right-wing political forces to accumulate power—first in the UK with the election of Margaret Thatcher and the Conservatives, then in the US with the election of Ronald Reagan and the Republicans, and later on in almost every other advanced capitalist nation. The 1970s saw significant declines in the profitability of corporate capital due to the rising strength of popular forces around the world as well as to various economic shocks. The SSA of regulated capitalism was deteriorating, and some kind of major structural change was clearly needed for economic—if not social—progress to continue. Right-wing political forces proved more adept and ultimately much more powerful in taking command of the structural change. Once having gained the political power to restructure the economy, these political forces and their allies in private business were able to establish institutions and organizations that would enable them to remain in power—or at least remain highly influential—in succeeding decades. To this end, the ideology of neoliberalism, drawing on nineteenth-century liberalism, could and would play a strong supporting role—an economic paradigm perfectly suited to the powers that were in command.

For the structure of the world economy—and its supporting ideology—to change in a fundamental way, there will have to be nothing less than a major crisis of the current neoliberal SSA. Because of the extent to which the powerful global class of neoliberal corporate and government leaders have succeeded in maintaining and expanding their power in recent decades, a crisis sufficient to bring down the neoliberal SSA will have to be exceptionally deep—at least as deep as the one that in the 1930s brought down the liberal SSA of the first three decades of the last century, and surely deeper than the crisis that befell the intervening regulated capitalist SSA. It appeared to some that the financial crisis of 2008 might usher in a sufficiently profound crisis, but the powers-that-be managed to avoid such an outcome—at least in the short run. Political and economic developments around the world have become increasingly chaotic over the last two years, so perhaps we are indeed witnessing the beginning of the next true capitalist crisis.

What are you mostly concerned about with regard to the current phase in the evolution of both capitalism (and socialism)?

There is much to be concerned about in the evolution of both capitalism and socialism. In the case of capitalism, the dominant neoliberal SSA in the advanced capitalist world has proven detrimental to the majority of people in those countries—especially the working class and those dependent on public support—as wages have stagnated and social programs have been curtailed. It is true that a significant fraction of the populations of such rapidly developing countries as China and India have enjoyed significant economic gains in recent decades. But every human being, regardless of their economic status, has much to fear in the failure of the world's powers-that-be to slow the warming of the planet, which threatens all of us with an increasingly harsh environment.

As for the socialist world, it hardly exists any more. Putatively social-ist countries such as China, Vietnam, North Korea, and Cuba are either essentially crony capitalist (China and Vietnam) or controlled by lead-ers with no serious claim to the vision of a democratic socialism that has inspired true socialists for centuries. The closest that the world has come to such a socialism can be found in the social democratic countries of Scandinavia, but these nations represent not true socialism, but a form of socially regulated capitalism. This may be the best that one can hope for in most parts of the world, given the nature of contemporary politics, even if and when the current neoliberal SSA collapses.

What do you see as some positive recent developments, both politically and in the terrain of economics research and policy advising?

It is really hard to discern positive developments politically in the United States, since Donald Trump squeaked into the presidency and launched a whole series of dangerous and extreme right-wing measures—with the acquiescence or (more often) the enthusiasm of a Republican Party that has veered well towards the extreme right over the past few decades. And it is hard to be more sanguine when considering the rest of the world, where for the most part the same right-wing, authoritarian, and nativist tendencies are all too widespread.

Returning to the US political scene, I do nonetheless see some basis for hope that positive developments will begin to assert themselves in the future. (The critical question is whether this can happen before it is too late to avoid irreversible damage.) The depredations of the Trump administration and its congressional supporters have exposed a lot that is rotten in American society; in reaction, more and more people may well demand fundamental change. Progressives are gaining influence in the Democratic Party, and the Democratic nominee for president in 2020 may well come from the progressive wing of the party—and have an excellent chance of replacing Trump (or a Republican successor). If the current neoliberal SSA does enter into a profound economic crisis, that will accelerate the demand for fundamental change—indeed, it would probably be an indispensable prerequisite for such change. Of course, the change would not necessarily be for the better. However, the fact that young Americans in ever greater numbers are saying that they would prefer socialism to capitalism is a sign that the possibility of significant leftward movement in American society and its governance is expanding.

As for the terrain of economics research and policy advising, URPE members have long provided useful economic assistance to progressive groups such as labor unions and grassroots citizens' organizations, as well as progressive political candidates (such as Bernie Sanders). There is every reason to expect that, in the undoubtedly turbulent years ahead of us, there will be many opportunities for left economists to work towards long-needed policy changes. Whether or not such positive changes will actually be realized will of course depend on the evolution of the political environment.

What are some of the major current research questions that you think need to be answered by left economists, including yourself?

At this point in my life, approaching eighty years, I don't consider myself still a productive economic researcher, and I hesitate to suggest to other left economists what kind of research questions they might most usefully address. Everyone should decide that for themselves. If I were younger, however, I would concentrate my own studies and research on the political economy of climate disruption. No threat to the future of humankind is greater than the warming of the planet Earth. Global warming leading to climate disruption is already wreaking havoc in many parts of the world, and this can only get much worse if present trends continue.

Climate disruption is not only a uniquely threatening phenomenon, but one that is uniquely difficult to deal with. The danger is clear, but it is slow to manifest itself, it requires costly action that will pay off only in the long run, and it requires unprecedented collective action on a global scale. Understanding how to make progress in restoring and maintaining the health and the diversity of our natural environment requires the kind of multidisciplinary political economic approach that radical political economists have advocated ever since the founding of URPE.

Representative Publications and Influences

Publications:

Thomas E. Weisskopf (1979). "Marxian crisis theory and the rate of profit in the postwar US economy," *Cambridge Journal of Economics*, 3(4), 341–378.

Samuel Bowles, David M. Gordon, and Thomas E. Weisskopf (1986). "Power and profits: The social structure of accumulation and the profitability of the postwar US economy," *Review of Radical Political Economics*, 18(1–2), 132–167.

Samuel Bowles, David M. Gordon, and Thomas E. Weisskopf (1990). *After the waste land: A democratic economics for the year 2000*. ME Sharpe.

People who have been influential: Samuel Bowles, Arthur MacEwan, Andrew Glyn

Literature that has been influential:

Karl Polanyi (1944). *The great transformation: The political and economic origins of our time*. Farrar & Rinehart.

Maurice Dobb (1946). *Studies in the Development of Capitalism*. London: George Routledge and Sons, Ltd.

Paul A. Baran (1968). *The Political Economy of Growth*. Monthly Review Press.

Index